Praise for *The Voyage of the 'Discovery'*

"A splendidly written book by one of the most gifted of all polar explorers." —**Charles Neider,** author of *Edge of the World: Ross Island, Antartica,* and *The Grotto Berg: Two Novellas*

"The photography has caught, in the most vivid and admirable way, the wild grandeur and beauty of these valleys, mountains, and ice basins. No finer or more unique views ever enhanced an explorer's book. . . . [This work] will have a conspicuous place among the annals of polar effort, and it is worthy of it." —*New York Times*

"Enthralling. . . . Scott has written a most admirable narrative, a faithful record of toil, isolation, and daring adventure. It is difficult to lay the book aside until the very end of the story—dramatic to its close—has been reached. . . . *The Voyage of the 'Discovery'* will always hold a high place in the library of travel, and will be read with fresh delight long after its achievements have been outdone. . . . A splendid piece of work." —*Spectator*

THE VOYAGE

OF

THE *DISCOVERY*

VOLUME II

Maull & Fox Photo

Emery Walker Ph. Sc.

London: Published by Smith, Elder & Co 15 Waterloo Place.

THE
VOYAGE OF
THE *DISCOVERY*

CAPTAIN ROBERT F. SCOTT

Foreword by Fridtjof Nansen

New Introduction by Ross MacPhee

*WITH 270 FULL-PAGE AND SMALLER ILLUSTRATIONS BY
DR. E. A. WILSON AND OTHER MEMBERS OF THE
EXPEDITION, PHOTOGRAVURE FRONTISPIECES, TWELVE
PLATES IN FACSIMILE FROM DR. WILSON'S SKETCHES,
PANORAMAS, AND MAPS*

IN TWO VOLUMES

VOLUME II

Cooper Square Press

First Cooper Square Press edition 2001

This Cooper Square Press hardcover edition of *The Voyage of the* Discovery, *Volume II* is an unabridged republication of the deluxe edition first published in New York in 1905 with the exception of the following alterations and additions: the deletion of one large fold-out map; the reproduction in black and white of twelve plates (originally colored by hand); the gathering together of the photos (originally scattered throughout the text) into three inserts to reduce the number of blank pages; and the addition of a preface by Robert F. Scott from Volume I, a foreword by Fridtjof Nansen (from the 1929 one-volume "cheap" edition), and a new introduction by Ross MacPhee.

Published by Cooper Square Press
An Imprint of the Rowman & Littlefield Publishing Group
150 Fifth Avenue, Suite 817
New York, New York 10011

Distributed by National Book Network

Library of Congress Cataloging-in-Publication Data
Scott, Robert Falcon, 1868–1912.
    The Voyage of the 'Discovery' : Scott's first Antartic expedition / Robert F. Scott
        p. cm.
    Originally published: New York : C. Scribner's Sons, 1905.
    Includes bibliographical references (p.).
    ISBN 0-8154-1079-4 (v. 1 : cloth : alk. paper)—ISBN 0-8154-1151-0 (v. 2 : cloth : alk. paper)
        1. Discovery (Ship) 2. Antartica—Discovery and exploration. 3. British National Antartic Expedition (1901–1904) 4. Scott, Robert Falcon, 1868–1912—Journeys—Antartica. I. Title.
    G850 1901 .D68 S36 2001
    919.8'904—dc21   2001037176

∞ ™ The paper used in this publication meets the minimum requirements of American National Standard for Information Sciences—Permanence of Paper for Printed Library Materials, ANSI/NISO Z39.48–1992. Manufactured in the United States of America.

CONTENTS

OF

THE SECOND VOLUME

CHAPTER XV

WHAT HAD HAPPENED DURING OUR ABSENCE IN THE SOUTH

CHAPTER XVI

OUR SECOND WINTER

CHAPTER XVII

COMMENCEMENT OF OUR SECOND SLEDGING SEASON

CHAPTER XVIII

RETURN FROM THE WEST

ILLUSTRATIONS

IN

THE SECOND VOLUME

MAPS

INTRODUCTION TO THE COOPER SQUARE PRESS EDITION

KNOCKING FATE

Let us imagine it was the butler who answered the insistent knock on the door of Sir Clements Markham's home on Eccleston Square, Belgravia. There, late in the afternoon of June 5, 1899, stood a caller in the uniform of a Royal Navy lieutenant: a man of medium height, in his early thirties, with broad shoulders, narrow waist, and piercing eyes of an unusual purple hue. Against the etiquette of the time, he had not sent over his card earlier in the day. But the lieutenant was not unknown to Sir Clements, for they had met on a half-dozen occasions over the past twelve years, some official, some curiously accidental, none lengthy.

Sir Clements already had half an idea as to why the caller had come. An enthusiastic, jingoistic supporter of the Royal Navy and of the empire that it maintained, Markham took a great interest in young officers who showed promise—promise, that is, for Sir Clements' projects. The man before him that day was such a person, but it would be difficult to ascertain from his service record that he possessed the qualifications and capacities that Markham was then seeking. In fact, his visitor's specialization was torpedoes and what we would now call "systems," a rather technical area of undoubted significance for naval warfare but of no obvious relationship to what the caller was now proposing. He had just heard, he said, that the Royal Geographical Society (RGS) and the Royal Society had announced the organization of an Antarctic expedition. He hoped that Sir Clements, as RGS president and as a leading member of the expedition's organizing committee, would consider him for the post of expedition commander.

So BEGAN the journey of Robert Falcon Scott (1868–1912) to prominence and tragedy, a trek that would end little more than a dozen years later, in a tent and in death, on the Ross Ice Shelf of Antarctica. Like Columbus and Magellan, Scott is one of the few explorers whose name and principal accomplishments seem to be universally known. This in itself is remarkable: Columbus and Magellan are famous for their firsts, but Scott is chiefly known for having come in second— and, of course, dying in circumstances that might make gods weep.

Scott conducted two expeditions to Antarctica: the 'Discovery' expedition of 1901–1904, and the 'Terra Nova' expedition of 1911–1913. These are more formally, but less frequently, referred to as the National Antarctic Expedition (NAE) and the British Antarctic Expedition (BAE). The first produced little in the way of long-lasting results, either scientifically or geographically. Neither did the second, but this is almost beside the point. Scott's expeditions are tributes to human endurance and cooperation under some of the most trying and dangerous conditions that this planet has to offer. They are also indictments: of Scott himself; of a cultural milieu that championed risk while perverting responsibility; of brass rings that had to be grasped, whatever the cost in human suffering.

Life at the edge is powerfully attractive; thus it is not surprising that Scott's expeditions are massively documented. Indeed, no Antarctic expeditions mounted before or since have been so thoroughly—one might say obsessively— examined and dissected. However, in this large literature there is only one book that Scott himself wrote for public consumption—*The Voyage of the 'Discovery'*, made available again in this facsimile of the rare deluxe edition (only 1,500 copies were ever printed). And what a work it is! Within these pages Scott emerges as one of the most literate participants in the so-called "heroic age" of polar exploration. Indeed, in this regard he is perhaps equaled only by Fridtjof Nansen, the famous Norwegian explorer who once dreamed of exploring Antarctica himself aboard his beloved 'Fram.'

Although other hands edited Scott's diaries after his death, we shall never know what kind of book Scott would have written had he lived through the terrible events of early 1912. Thus, *The Voyage of the 'Discovery'* remains the one text that reveals to us how he wanted his works and days to be perceived by his contemporaries and by history.

Antarctic heroes—a very special class of over-achievers—have to be rediscovered by each new generation. And what is rediscovered may be quite different from those aspects that previous generations considered important. Ponder the rise and fall of the respective fortunes of Scott and Ernest Shackleton, of 'Nimrod' and 'Endurance' fame. For most of the twentieth century, Scott was the better—if not always the more favorably—remembered. After all, it was Scott who enjoyed a hero's death. All Shackleton accomplished in his 1914–1916 expedition was the rescue of his entire command, first by keeping them going—mentally and physically—after losing their ship 'Endurance' to the ice, then by sailing 800 miles to South Georgia in a twenty-two-foot dinghy through the roughest seas in the world. Everyone survived, but as Shackleton and his men conducted no exploring or ring-grasping, the expedition was judged a failure. Roland Huntford, author of the masterworks *Scott and Amundsen* and *Shackleton*, could thus reasonably say of Shackleton in 1984 that he was "half forgotten today." But by 2000 the *Zeitgeist* had altered: getting everyone through was considered a more worthwhile accomplishment than getting them heroically dead. This time, it has been Shackleton and the 'Endurance'—not Scott and the 'Terra Nova'—that have provoked new museum exhibits, documentaries, and books. The Boss Who Cared is now a more compelling moral fable than The Owner Who Didn't, or who cared differently. One expects the wheel will turn yet again.

IMAGINING ANTARCTICA

Antarctic landscapes are so far outside common experience that they might as well be from another planet. Dimensionality is often difficult to evaluate under Antarctic skies because there is no familiar context in which to judge distance, height, or depth. When looking at the magnificent early photographs reproduced in this volume, notice that your eye is drawn almost magnetically to any human figures present. Is this because the presence of people makes this terrible place accessible, reassuring us that, yes, this is part of Earth and it is possible to live there? *Live?* Well, no, not exactly; for us it seems only possible to endure—and then only for a brief time. Thus, we are riveted by signs of physical distress and of imminent danger that lurk in all the classic images from the heroic age: Scott's exhausted and dejected 1912 polar party arranged around a flag that screams "Too late!"; Shackleton's 'Endurance' crushed to a pulp by ice in

1915, observed by stunned parties of men and dogs contemplating their fate. Even the most ordinary domestic scenes make us want to peer into the faces of those who would die, to wonder what they were thinking or feeling at that particular moment—Wilson and Scott bent over a pot of thin pemmican stew ("hoosh") in 1903; or Birdie Bowers and Titus Oates at leisure in their quarters at McMurdo during the 'Terra Nova' expedition. Or—entering completely different emotional waters—to wonder what Christopher and Weary Willie, Wolf and Lewis (to name a few of the ponies and dogs that were used up on these expeditions) experienced just before the bullet struck.

Is it not a strange and obsessive thing to know their names and fates, these men and animals from a century past who suffered and sometimes died in the most remote part of the planet? If it does not seem so, the reason is because of the imagery—caught by emulsion, immediately accessible, as if it all happened in some nearby yesterday.

ORGANIZING THE EXPEDITION

In conception and execution the National Antarctic Expedition was thoroughly nineteenth century. Indeed, the NAE marked not so much the beginning of a new tradition in exploration as the last gasp of the old. That the expedition came to pass in the way that it did was essentially due to the brute-force personality of one man: Clements Markham. For example, it was he who insisted, from the start, that it had to be a Navy-run project with limited civilian participation, because in Markham's experience this was the only model that worked. In this he was opposed, also from the start, by the Royal Society, which the Admiralty had paired with the RGS to work out the organization of the expedition. It was the view of the gentlemen of the Royal Society that the only justification for an expensive Antarctic undertaking would be to increase scientific knowledge. This reasoning meant that the enterprise had to be run by and for scientists. Little or no attention should be paid to pointless adventurism like polar flag-planting; the only role for the Navy was to ferry the land parties in and to retrieve them when their jobs were done.

For a time it seemed that the Royal Society might get its way; the cumbersome committee structure designed to examine the feasibility of the expedition favored substantial civilian participation. But Sir Clements was a born intriguer. Working behind the scenes and ruthlessly manipulating committee memberships, he literally forced the NAE into existence on his terms. A gouty, *fin-de-siecle* John Bull, possessed of the most spectacular social and class prejudices, Markham was determined to claim The Bottom for Britain according to his design.

Trouble was, the country couldn't have cared less about the proposed expedition. Even the force of Markham's exceptionally excessive personality was not enough to spark interest: polar adventures were regarded by the government as a waste of money, by the Navy as a waste of men and equipment, and seemingly by everybody else as a waste of time. Yet, Sir Clements was not deterred; throughout the late 1890s he pursued his project doggedly, with lectures, dinners, letters, and circulars designed to raise money for his enterprise. Virtually nothing came of any of it.

Then in March 1899 the fortunes of the NAE were completely turned around: Llewellyn W. Longstaff, a textile manufacturer with no known interest in Antarctic exploration, promised £25,000 toward the effort. (Later on, this same benefactor proposed that a certain Mr. Ernest Shackleton, late of the Merchant Marine, be hired on as third officer. Such is fate.) This act of generosity was quickly followed by the patronage of the Prince of Wales, and, finally, by the interest of the Balfour government, which offered £45,000 as a matching grant in June 1899. By August 1901, when 'Discovery' sailed, Markham had raised, by his own reckoning, slightly more than £93,000—more than half a million in current dollars. Actual resources were considerably greater, because Sir Clements had successfully pressed the Navy to pay the salaries and allowances of thirty petty officers and men—"this was most important," he said in his usual deeply prejudiced way, "as it would be quite impossible to get anything approaching the same class of men from the merchant service."

The expedition needed a leader and executive officers. But as the Royal Navy had done nothing of consequence in either polar region for decades, there was no one then serving who could assert a prior claim for command based on significant experience. It is only with this background as context that the choice of Scott makes any sense: if experience was vitiated as a factor, other considerations could come into play. Scott, like many officers of his relatively junior grade, was anxious for advancement. Polar service had traditionally provided a route for quicker promotion and more pay. Scott had a reputation for being workmanlike and had ruffled none of his superior's feathers by being cocky or too imaginative. And he had Sir Clements's support, somewhat guarded at first and then unbridled: "the best man for so great a trust, either in the navy or out of it."

This endorsement, ringing as it is, can hardly explain Markham's choosing Scott among dozens, if not hundreds, of equally likely prospects (including those from titled or influential backgrounds, whose company Markham preferred). One possibility is that Markham originally had several candidates in mind, but for one reason or another all of them had fallen into disfavor. By 1899, he was out of alternatives. In other words, it might have been anybody's lucky day that afternoon in June, but Scott got to the door first. He was of the right age and service ties, with some technical experience; he would take directives and was properly deferential to Markham's person; and he had declared himself available. That he had absolutely no relevant experience was of lesser concern.

By early 1900, Sir Clements had managed to push through Scott's nomination in committee—more through an excess of choler and bullying than persuasive reasoning. (Markham took everything immensely personally; in his diary he delighted in labeling his opponents as "wreckers," "sheep," "out & out jobbers," and "deserters now adrift." It is a wonder that the joint committee ever completed its task with so loose a cannon in its midst.) Scott, who had never shown any interest in high-latitude exploration prior to 1899, who had never commanded a vessel of any size, who had never worked outside the rigid confines of the navy hierarchy, now had just one year to get himself and everything else ready for departure. But the portents were good: straightaway he was raised in rank to Commander, with an increase in salary. The right stuff was working.

Directly or indirectly, Markham made many of the other important appointments on the 'Discovery' expedition. It is clear that he decided with only the most superficial reflection on a candidate's actual abilities and appropriateness for the work. Although Scott was consulted for his opinion, one has the feeling that—unsure of himself as always, especially in this new setting—he decided to be as complaisant as possible.

It is instructive to ponder some of Sir Clements's selection criteria. Second Lieutenant Michael Barne was "so zealous that he would have thrown up his commission rather than not go, and a relation of mine which is also in his favour." Reginald Koettlitz—selected as one of the surgeons and one of only two officers with any high-latitude experience whatsoever—was "anxious to do his best," even if "his mind perhaps works rather slowly, and he has no sense of humour." Blatant nepotism got an interview for Dr. Edward Wilson, nephew of Markham's friend Sir Charles Wilson. "I decided that he should be one of the Antarctic heroes"—a very odd way to certify the result of a selection process. But then Sir Clements was a romantic, and heroes there had to be.

Having said this, however, one also has to say that many of the choices worked out remarkably well, whatever they were based on. Edward Wilson, for example, seems at first glance to be the most unlikely of Antarctic explorers. Deeply religious and ascetic in habits, one wonders what physical, secular needs were fulfilled by going South. A medical doctor with no interest in practice, he spent most of his time absorbed in natural history projects. He was an able painter; his lively sketches and fragile watercolors adorn the pages of this book. In an era innocent of psychological counseling, "Uncle Bill" (as he was nicknamed on the 'Terra Nova' expedition) was mediator and confidant for many of the men. Indeed, it is his almost feminine compassion toward his companions, perhaps conveyed as much by the soothing tone of his voice as by anything he ever explicitly said, that especially commends him to us. Louis Bernacchi, the physicist on the 'Discovery', called him "intrinsically good." He was the one man to whom Scott could open up and not feel diminished. A confessor, in short; perhaps "Father Bill" would have been a better epithet.

Ernest Shackleton needs to be mentioned in this context as well. Strongly contrasting with Scott in matters of personal style and affect, it would have been impossible to be neutral about him. Scott certainly was not. Although describing Shackleton at first as an "excellent officer," and even selecting him, together with Wilson, for the nearly disastrous Southern Journey of 1902–1903, Scott must have found Shackleton's bluff and hearty Irish manner rather trying. Worse—much worse—he did not know his place. Calling someone a "bloody fool," as each described the other during one occasion out on the ice, would hardly seem to qualify as a cause for a major falling out, but Scott could be a terror if crossed or questioned in any manner that he regarded as impertinent. (In a famous incident he once put Brett the cook—a civilian—under arrest for "insubordination.") Although Shackleton and Scott may have exchanged other harsh words, the public record is largely silent about such matters. In any case, by the time the party, with all members near collapse, stumbled back into base camp in February 1903, Shackleton's position was already compromised. Immediately on returning—to find the relief vessel 'Morning' in the sound—Scott ordered Shackleton to prepare to evacuate, ostensibly out of concern for the latter's physical "break down" during the trip, but more likely because the Owner had had enough.

THE 'DISCOVERY'

As Scott relates in the opening chapters of his account, the 'Discovery' was purpose-built for the expedition—from wood, and powered by both steam and by sail. Choosing to build, in 1900, a vessel in wood for high-latitude exploration is not as quixotic as it may sound. The outer skin of 'Discovery' was laid in English elm and greenheart, the latter being one of the hardest woods known, so dense in structure and resistant to rot that it was long preferred to cement-coated steel for wharf pilings. The several kinds of woods used to form the hull, timbers, and crossbeams provided elasticity as well as strength. By itself, a steel-hulled vessel built at that time would have offered few advantages. Steel construction would certainly not ensure more rapid penetration of pack ice, as this was mostly a question of engine power.

It is of great interest that Scott closely compared the 'Discovery' to Nansen's 'Fram', which the great Norwegian explorer last used in his famous Arctic drift experiment between 1893–1895 (recounted in his polar classic *Farthest North*). Scott disparaged the 'Fram' for having been built with an overriding concern for "safety," and noted that it was quite unfit for the kind of high-seas sailing required in the Southern Ocean. For traversing that environment, one needed a vessel built on "good and well tried English lines." (An accurate statement indeed: Scott's 'Discovery', sixth of that name, was built based on plans originally developed for the fifth 'Discovery', used in the 1875–1876 Government Arctic Expedition and allegedly "the best ship that had ever been employed on Arctic service.") Scott sardonically concluded, "As yet the Southern Regions have shown no uses for the type which achieves safety at the expense of progress." It is, of course, more than ordinarily ironic that it was the 'Fram' that conducted Amundsen to and from Antarctica in 1911–1912. (In this regard, Amundsen deserves credit for an important innovation: he refitted the 'Fram' with a diesel engine for his secret voyage south in 1911. In this way he could get an instant response from his engine, rather than having to wait until steam pressure built up from banked coal fires.)

WORKING ON THE BOTTOM, 1902–1904

After passing through the Ross Sea in early 1902, the 'Discovery' touched at Cape Adare and passed along the Great Ice Barrier (now the Ross Ice Shelf) as far as Balloon Inlet (later Bay of Whales). Finding no better alternative for winter quarters than McMurdo Sound (originally discovered by Sir James Ross), Scott dropped anchor there on February 8, 1902. Here the 'Discovery' would remain, girdled by ice, for the next two years. During this period the NAE was only twice in contact with the rest of the world, when relief ships came down from New Zealand. On the second occasion, the Admiralty ordered Scott and his men home—with or without the 'Discovery', which ultimately had to be dynamited out of the ice.

A fair portion of Scott's chapters are taken up with recounting the day-to-day activities that Scott and his men performed during the next twenty-four months. Chief among those activities were operations connected with fulfilling the stated objectives of the NAE: to explore any lands that could be reached, and to undertake various scientific investigations.

The exploration activities of the 'Discovery' expedition are moderately well known. The most famous is the Southern Journey (from November 2, 1902 to February 3, 1903), in which Scott attained 82° 16′ (a new farthest south) and, in an eerie foreshadowing of the events of 1912, almost died from starvation, cold, and scurvy. This time everyone survived. Barely.

Nansen, who advised Scott on equipment, had long ago come to the sensible conclusion that, since the Inuit managed to avoid scurvy, it behooved high-latitude explorers to live in the same way they did. So Nansen recommended fresh, raw meat; big lungfuls of clean polar air; and the avoidance of canned goods—but only the first innovation had any significant impact on avoiding scurvy. At the time—at least in the Royal Navy—scurvy was viewed as some kind of infectious disease, caused by unknown pathogens that flourished in poorly prepared tinned foods or unwashed cooking utensils. Tearing away at raw meat was all right for aboriginals, but hardly the proper thing for Englishmen. Although Scott predictably mistrusted foreign wisdom, he nevertheless encouraged everyone to eat fresh (albeit cooked) meat.

There were other forays as well. The most important of these was the first Western Journey (from November 29, 1902 to January 19, 1903) to Victoria Land, in which a party under Lieutenant Armitage reached and returned from the untrodden Polar Plateau without mishap. Scott essentially repeated the feat the next summer (from October 12 to December 25, 1903), climbing up Ferrar Glacier with Petty Officer Evans and Leading Stoker Lashley. (A half century later, Sir Edmund Hillary used the same route to attain the South Pole during the Commonwealth Trans-Antarctic Expedition.) Scott—whose bad luck at times seems boundless—almost died on the return journey by falling through a crevasse. Several other trips of smaller duration serve to illustrate how dangerous The Bottom was for the unwary. On one jaunt (as it must be called in view of the serious lack of concern for safety measures), a seaman slipped to his death over a cliff edge into the sea because he was equipped with neither ice axe nor crampons. The seaman, George Vince, died only one month after the landing at McMurdo Sound—the only casualty of the Antarctic leg of the expedition.

The scientific results are much less remembered, partly because several disciplines were scantily or amateurishly pursued, and partly because the achievements of the NAE, although noteworthy at the time, were rapidly superseded by later, more professional expeditions. The science program involved dredging, seawater sampling, meteorological observation, geologizing, zoological collecting, and other such undertakings. Of all the works conducted, however, the most recondite for modern readers is the "magnetic survey." The survey was paired with exploration of new lands as the two most important goals of the NAE. This was not, as one might assume, primarily a hunt for the South Magnetic Pole (not actually reached until 1909, on Shackleton's 'Nimrod' expedition). It was the much more pedestrian effort of collecting and collating observations on compass declination (the tendency of a needle to depart from pointing toward true north, depending upon where you were on the earth's surface). In these days of GPS (Global Positioning Systems) and maps produced from space by sidescan radar, it is hard to appreciate how crucial a tool like a compass was in 1900, especially at sea. Although it had long been known that correction for declination was vital, variation does not occur in an easily interpretable, straight-line manner. As Edmond Halley conclusively demonstrated at the turn of the eighteenth century, the only option was to gather data by direct observation on site. In England it was the Navy's job to compile such information and make it available for navigators. Magneticians (as investigators of terrestrial magnetism were then called) connected with the Royal Society were eager to obtain data from the far south, where few observations had been made. Every chart of the Southern Ocean issued by the Admiralty for the next decade used the NAE's observations—small acclaim perhaps, but a real contribution.

SCOTT OBSERVED

It is appropriate to end this introduction with some reflections concerning Scott himself. According to some accounts, he was surpassingly charming, even witty; intelligent and a quick study; compassionate and empathetic to an extraordinary degree. According to others, Scott was almost perpetually out of sorts with everyone around him, even clinically depressed at times; opinionated beyond toleration; dreadfully under-prepared; a blubbering, unstable, incompetent who should never have been given command over a teacup, let alone a major expedition.

Louis Bernacchi, definitely an admirer, allowed in his book *The Saga of the Discovery* that Scott could be irritable and impatient at times, and that his " 'brown studies' might be mistaken for the depression, moodiness, and even illtemper hinted at during his second expedition." But outweighing these characteristics by far was Scott's dominant personality trait, which Bernacchi framed as his "sense of right and justice" combined with a "deep and reverent attitude towards nature and a most genuine love of science." All true, no doubt; but perhaps his men would have hoped that a concern for their welfare would have been rated as highly.

What chiefly comes across from a distance of nearly a century is that Scott was very much a Navy man of his time. He believed in—and accepted as natural—rigid lines of authority as the only way of getting things done. He was not by habit an innovator, although he did have occasional streaks of insight that—had they been combined with a capacity for practical implementation with the ability to motivate others—would have taken him very far toward his goals. What is hardest to come to terms with in Scott's personality was his extraordinary capacity to ignore good advice if it happened to go against the course he had already chosen.

Worse, he could not tolerate being told, no matter how diffidently, that he had made a poor or faulty choice; that he was following the wrong course; or that he should have done one thing rather than another. During the 'Discovery' expedition, he kept his plans almost entirely to himself until the last possible moment, when they would be presented in a defiant manner that ensured there would be no dissenting voices. There are too many examples, from too many sources, to think that such arrogance was purely an invention of his enemies. Refusal to listen to advice and failure to consult are grievous traits in a leader. They would eventually cost Scott his life.

All of this comes out clearly in Scott's position regarding the use of sled dogs. Even before leaving England, he had decided that he would not use dogs, or would use them only incidentally, to conquer the South Pole. He viewed sled dogs almost as an alien species, perverse and ungovernable except by the lash—not, in other words, the sort of beings that took orders in proper fashion. Also, Scott couldn't abide the effective-but-brutal method of travel that Arctic explorers favored: to periodically kill the weaker dogs and to feed them to the others over the course of a trip. The propensity of sled dogs to consume their own feces and to turn on each other with utmost savagery disgusted him. It was thus irrelevant that those who had immense experience crossing ice, explorers like Nansen and Amundsen, preferred dogs over any conceivable alternative. Of course, Scott took dogs anyway (and Siberian ponies as well on the second expedition), but except in a superficial way he did not require his men to be trained in their use. It was almost as though the dogs had a symbolic value: having them at all was enough to quell objections that he should have used them.

The other perennial issue that arises in discussion of Scott's capacities as a leader is his level of preparedness, or lack thereof, for his Antarctic expeditions. Much of the criticism is justified; much isn't. In fact, Scott was not a foolhardy man, whatever one wants to make of his disastrous, fatal push for the South Pole in 1911–1912. Indeed, his reputation was that of the meticulous planner (in contrast to Shackleton, who was unfairly regarded by many, including Scott, as being unable to concentrate on detail).

Consider the frenetic months leading up to *Discovery*'s sailing in August 1901. He had to bring the expedition from standstill to the peak of readiness in one year. Much of his time seems to have been spent perpetually rushing from here to there: from his office in Savile Row to Dundee to inspect the building of the 'Discovery'; to Norway to talk to Nansen; to Berlin to talk to the German expedition then preparing to depart for the Antarctic; and in the time left over, to pour over specifications for every sort of provision and supply. Although much of the equipment and supplies list for the 'Discovery' expedition may strike the modern reader as including peculiar or even ridiculous choices, one needs to imagine being asked to supply a polar expedition today with what can be found in your local supermarket or mall. In 1901 there were no synthetic, light-weight fabrics that could keep one warmer and drier than any natural product. So you wore wool, the Navy way. Energy bars? Well, there was cocoa and tea, plain sugar and sweets. Preserved foods? In cans or in the form of pemmican.

What is truly surprising is that Scott succeeded as well as he did. Indeed, the truth is that Scott cannot be regarded as particularly incompetent or negligent when compared to many other Arctic and Antarctic explorers of the time. If there was an odd man out in this group, it was Roald Amundsen, the supreme technocrat of high-latitude exploration who had previously conquered the Northwest Passage in 1903–06 and would go on to make the first dirigible crossing of the North Pole aboard the 'Norge' in 1926. A hard, inaccessible man who made no mistakes and planned for every contingency, it followed ineluctably that Amundsen would be the first to make Ninety South.

Ross MacPhee
New York, New York
March 2001

Ross MacPhee, Ph.D., was co-curator of the American Museum of Natural History's award-winning 1999 exhibition, "The *Endurance*: Shackleton's Legendary Antarctic Expedition." Since 1988 he has been Curator in the museum's Department of Mammalogy and has participated in many scientific expeditions to northern Siberia.

For Further Reading

Bernacchi, L. C. (1938). *The Saga of the Discovery*. Blackie & Son: London and Glasgow.

Fogg, G. E. (1992). *A History of Antarctic Science*. Cambridge University Press: London.

Huntford, Roland (1998). *Nansen: Explorer as Hero*. Barnes & Noble Books: New York.

—(1984). *Scott and Amundsen: The Race to the South Pole*. Atheneum: New York (Reprinted in 1999 under the title *The Last Place on Earth*, as part of the Modern Library's Exploration Series.)

—(1998). *Shackleton*. Carroll & Graf Publishers: New York.

Huxley, Elspeth (1978). *Scott of the Antarctic*. Atheneum: New York.

Neider, Charles, editor (1972). *Antarctica: Firsthand Accounts of Exploration and Endurance*. Doubleday Publishers: New York. (Reprinted by Cooper Square Press in 2000.)

—(1974). *Edge of the World: Ross Island, Antarctica*. Doubleday Publishers: New York. (Reprinted by Cooper Square Press in 2001.)

Ponting, Herbert G., (1922). *The Great White South* Robert McBride & Co.: New York. (Reprinted by Cooper Square Press in 2001.)

Pound, Reginald (1966). *Scott of the Antarctic*. Coward-McCann: New York.

Scott, Robert F., (1913, 1996). *Scott's Last Expedition: The Journals*. Carrol & Graf Publishers: New York.

Yelverton, Donald E. (2000). *Antarctica Unveiled: Scott's First Expedition and the Quest for the Unknown Continent*. University Press of Colorado: Niwot, Colorado.

FOREWORD

By his whole career, his achievements, his wonderfully heroic end, Robert Falcon Scott differs from all other travelers, and has a position of his own in the history of polar exploration. The message of his death in the great silence of the South Pole made a deep impression on the whole civilized world, and we felt, most keenly, the loss it was to humanity and to exploration. Since then the Great War has passed, and the world has been much altered. Does Scott look different after this deluge of events? To the writer it seems that his important achievements, the great results of his journeys, the deep noble qualities that distinguished him, and the beauty of his character, will be even more appreciated today than they were then.

It is strange to note that this man, who made such a mark in polar history and inaugurated a new era in Antarctic exploration, was led into this work quite accidentally. As he tells it himself, he had no predilection for polar exploration; he had not, like what we hear about so many other polar travellers, taken any keen interest in Arctic adventures ever since his boyhood. It was by mere chance that he happened one day in June 1899 to walk down the Buckingham Palace Road in London and meet Sir Clements Markham, who unbenownst to Scott had his eye on him ever since seeing him at work as a *mere lad*.

Scott learned then "for the first time that there was such a thing as a prospective Antarctic expedition." He had just served as first lieutenant of the *Majestic*, then flagship to the Channel Squadron; he was an unusually able, accomplished, and very promising young officer, who obviously had a great future before him in the Navy. Nevertheless, two days later, encouraged by Sir Clements, he "wrote applying to command the expedition and a year after that he was officially appointed."

His education hitherto had not prepared him for what was going to be his life's great work, and he had no training which made him especially fit for the task. He had not been a sportsman of the kind one may expect of a future Polar traveler; he had no experience in snow and ice, in cold and snowstorms, had never tried skiing or sledge-travelling or living in the snow. He was not a literary man who had studied the history of Arctic or Antarctic travelling and exploration. He was not a man of science who had studied the polar problems.

He was, however, something of more worth than all these things together: an excellent specimen of the human race, both physically and mentally, and he was a born leader of men.

When he was appointed leader of the expedition in June 1900, there was only a year left till the expedition was expected to start. He had nothing to do with the preparations of it before that time, and very little had been done, except that the building of the ship had begun in March 1900. Considering that he now had to study, from the beginning, the history of polar exploration, the technique of polar travel, and all the practical and scientific problems before him, one is filled with amazement and great admiration for the man who in that short time mastered all of the difficulties as he did and managed to outfit the expedition and set out only a year after he had taken over the command.

I have a vivid recollection of our first meeting when he came to my home in Norway with my friend Sir Clements Markham. I still can see him, a very attractive young naval officer who made an unusually good impression and at once inspired confidence. We discussed the problem of the Antarctic and all details of sledge-travelling, as well as polar and oceanographic research, etc. Although most of these subjects were more or less new to him, he at once grasped the principles and various details with his clear and well-balanced knowledge.

If one wishes to form a just opinion of the value of Scott's great achievements on the first expedition as compared with those of later explorers, one has to consider how much harder it was to prepare an Antarctic expedition when so little was known about the conditions and possible difficulties than it has been in later years when explorers could profit from Scott's discoveries and experiences.

Before the voyage of 'Discovery' our knowledge of the outer edges as well as the interior of the Antarctic was very scant indeed, and the views of the polar authorities differed widely. The prevailing idea was that perhaps the south polar region was covered by an extensive Antarctic continent, and according to the discoveries made during my own crossing of

the Greenland island ice, it was expected that this continent
was covered by a similar ice-cap, whose surface would rise
slowly inland from the outer continental coasts. Assuming
that the Antarctic continent had a great width, one of my
apprehensions was, that the surface of this ice-cap might rise
to considerable altitudes in the interior which might make
travelling difficult. On the other hand, it was to be expected
that this glacial surface would be very even and convenient
for sledge-travelling. Other authorities held, however, that
the Antarctic was probably not covered by one extensive continent, but by several different lands and groups of islands.
These lands were probably covered by great ice-caps, which
might extend more or less continuously across the interven-
ing sea, from one land to another. Little was also known
about the ice-conditions of the sea in the different seasons of
the year, along the Antarctic coasts and along the Great Ice
Barrier, and what the possibilities of navigation might be in
those waters.

Scott had to work out his plan and choose his equipment
with all possibilities in mind to be prepared for every eventuality. He did so in a masterly way, and his discoveries during
this first expedition, completed by those of his last great journey, have thrown an entirely new light upon the Antarctic.
His discovery of the Victoria Mountain range, which extends
inland with a low, almost horizontal glacial surface at its foot
and an extensive ice-cap covering the land behind, extending
towards the Pole; his examination of the ice surface and
determination of its altitudes; his discovery of King Edward
Land; and all of his other accomplishments have entirely

changed our views and have formed the foundation for a new understanding of the Antarctic.

It is remarkable that Scott, who was not a man of science by his education, had a perfect understanding of the importance of all kinds of scientific research in polar exploration; and of how the value of an expedition may be said to be proportional to its scientific results. This view grew so strong with him that, when he prepared for his last expedition, his ambition was that it should be as completely equipped for scientific work, with regard to both men and material, as possible. Resultingly, he had on board a fuller complement of scientists of different kinds and surveyors than ever before composed the staff of a polar expedition.

The scientific researches and results of that expedition are accordingly of great value to the different branches of science. Scott was unable to complete the projected scientific work and direct the presentment of it; thus a great loss was inflicted on science. Nevertheless, the work that was accomplished, the rich material of scientific observations collected , and the many important results obtained give this great expedition a unique, important, and—what will more and more prove to be a—fundamental knowledge of the Antarctic and its conditions.

It is also striking how Scott, who, as was mentioned before, had not the advantage of being educated, from his boyhood, in skiing and a life of snow, nevertheless learned to master the technicalities of sledge-travelling so perfectly that his last journey to the South Pole and back is really a unique feat in the history of travelling. It is strange that along with our common friend Sir Clements Markham he seemed to be opposed to the use of dogs for the more strenuous sledge-travelling. Had he used more dogs and less man haulage, he might have made an easy and brilliant journey to the Pole and back again. As it is, we are filled with admiration for the wonderful exploit accomplished, most of the enormous distance being covered on foot by him and his comrades without the help of any beasts of draught; and had it not been for the breakdown of some of his comrades, whom Scott could never think of leaving behind, he could easily have pulled through.

But Robert Scott was much more than a very prominent traveler and explorer: he was a great man with a noble and generous character. No one can read this book about his first expedition, and still less his diary written on his last journey, without being thrilled with admiration for this unusual man and his fine qualities. On every occasion we are struck by the startling selflessness of the man. His thoughts are for his country, his comrades, his navy, and for science; never for himself—a selflessness that does not fail even in the hardest moments.

When my memory goes back to the days when we met, I see him before me, his tight, wiry figure; his intelligent, handsome face; that earnest, fixed look; and those expressive lips so seriously determined, and yet ready to smile—the features of a kindly generous character, with a fine admixture of earnestness and humor. He was keen and intense in what he was doing but always ready to enjoy a joke or to lighten a strenuous moment with his whimsical humor. It is characteristic of him that his nearest never saw him lose his temper.

One understands how on his last death march he was able to cheer up his comrades almost to the last moment. The history of polar exploration has many a leaf that bears evidence of the noblest qualities of man in his struggle for unselfish goals, in his sacrifices for what he considers to be the aim of his life. But one of the most beautiful leaves is, in its tragic greatness, the one that tells about the last journey of Scott and his comrades. We find nowhere a finer revelation of the superiority of the spirit and will of man in his stubborn fight against the forces of Nature. Can one read anything more thrilling than Scott's simple narrative of the homeward journey after they had reached the Pole; how they, with one comrade already broken down and dying, with the difficulties piling up ahead of them, nevertheless carried out their scientific work, stopped to examine the rocks, to collect samples and important fossils throwing light on the origin and history of the great mountain range, which Scott had discovered. And then, further on, on their last terrible death march, in the cold and the blizzard and the snowdrift, they carried with them their journals and notes of observations, their instruments, and their valuable samples of rocks and fossils; they saved them for humanity while they themselves perished instead of throwing everything away and saving their lives.

For all future generations Scott has set an inspiring example of how a man takes struggle and suffering for a cause he has chosen as his own. From the leaves of his diary, written under the impression of the moment, from day to day, rises the picture of a great man, a great leader of the finest and noblest character that ever lived, and who never failed, even under the heaviest test, ever the same unbribable spirit, with

thoughts for others and none for himself, just to the end—
upright, and indomitable on the threshold to the long journey into eternal stillness. A *man* he was—a *man* wholly and
fully—a *man* till the last.

FRIDTJOF NANSEN

FRIDTJOF NANSEN (1861–1928) was a celebrated explorer,
winner of the Nobel Peace Prize, and author of the polar
classic *Farthest North*.

PREFACE

STRANGE as it may seem, the greater part of this story had been enacted before I realised that it would devolve on me to narrate it in book form.

When first I saw vaguely this unwelcome task before me there was fresh in my mind not only the benefit which we had derived from studying the records of former Polar voyages, but the disappointment which we had sometimes suffered from the insufficient detail which they provided. It appeared to me in consequence that the first object in writing an account of a Polar voyage was the guidance of future voyagers; the first duty of the writer was to his successors.

I have done my best to keep this object in view, and I give this explanation because I am conscious that it has led me into descriptive detail which will probably be tiresome to the ordinary reader. As, however, such matter is more or less massed into certain portions of the book, I take comfort from reflecting that the interested reader will have no difficulty in avoiding such parts as he may consider tedious.

I have endeavoured to avoid the use of technicalities, but in all cases this has not been possible, as the English language is poor in words descriptive of conditions of ice and snow. I take the opportunity, therefore, of defining some technical words that I have used freely.

Névé—the packed snow of a snow-field, an accumulation of minute ice-crystals. This word is, of course, well known to mountaineers.

Nunatak—an island of bare land in a snow-field. Where an ice-sheet overlies the land, the summits of hills thrust through the sheet present this appearance.

Sastrugus—an irregularity formed by the wind on a snow-plain. 'Snow-wave' is not completely descriptive, as the sastrugus has often a fantastic shape unlike the ordinary conception of a wave.

Ice-foot—properly applied to the low fringe of ice formed about Polar lands by the sea-spray. I have used the term much more widely, and perhaps improperly, in referring to the banks of ice of varying height which skirt many parts of the Antarctic shores, and which have no connection with sea-spray. Mr. Ferrar gives some description of these in his remarks on ice in Appendix I.

Beyond explaining these few words I make no apology for the style or absence of style of this book; I have tried to tell my tale as simply as possible, and I launch it with the confidence that my readers will be sufficiently indulgent to its faults in remembering the literary inexperience of its writer.

For me the compilation of these pages has been so weighty a matter that I must always feel the keenest gratitude to those who assisted me in the task. I cannot think that the manuscript would ever have been completed but for the advice and encouragement I received from its publisher, nor can I forget to thank Sir Clements Markham and other friends for hints and criticisms by which I profited, and Mr. Leonard Huxley for his judicious provision of the 'hooks and eyes' to many a random sentence. How much I owe to the artist, Dr. Wilson, and others of my comrades who are responsible for the originals of the illustrations, will be evident.

R. F. S.

August 28th, 1905.

CHAPTER XIII

JOURNEY TO THE FARTHEST SOUTH

Future Plans Modified by Reconnaissance Journeys—Trip to Cape Crozier —Start of the Southern Journey—Depot 'A'—Description of the Dog Team—Equipment of Sledges—Return of Supporting Party—Failure of the Dogs—Relay Work—Dog-driving—Dog-food—Atmospheric Phenomenon—Cracking of the Surface Crust—New Land in Sight— Beautiful Effects Produced by Snow-crystals—Dogs Weakening—Slow Progress—Depot 'B'—The Chasm—Pushing Southward—Increase of Hunger—Further Land—Scurvy Appearing—Cooking-arrangements— Soft Snow—Experiences with the Dogs—Christmas Day and its Good Cheer.

> Hold hard the breath and bend up every spirit
> To his full height. . . .
>   . . . Shew us here
> That you are worth your breeding, which I doubt not,
> For there is none so mean or base
> That have not noble lustre in your eyes.
> I see you stand like greyhounds in the slips,
> Straining upon the start.—SHAKESPEARE.

ALTHOUGH the gravity of our outbreak of scurvy was not underrated, and we had been busied in measures for the prevention of its recurrence, it must not be supposed that we had allowed it in any way to interfere with our plans for the future. Our preparations were pushed on as vigorously as though no such cloud had come to overshadow the brightness of our outlook.

The general results of the spring journeys had enabled
us to lay our plans for the summer with greater definition.
Our reconnaissance to the south had indicated that the
main party, after leaving the Bluff, would have to travel
directly over the snow-plain at a long distance from, and
possibly out of sight of, land ; the probability was that no
further depots could be established, and hence it was desirable that the party should be supported as far as possible
on their route. This theory added another object for
our sledging efforts, for if the coast ran sharply to the
west after rounding the Bluff it was evidently desirable
that we should gain some information concerning it. To
meet these requirements it was decided that Barne, with
a party of twelve men, should accompany the dog-team
until the weights were reduced to an amount which the
latter could drag without assistance. He was then to
return to the ship, and, after a short rest, to start again,
with a party of six, and endeavour to follow the coastline
west of the Bluff. With such a plan as I have outlined
it was hoped that there would be a good chance of solv-
ing the mysteries in a southerly direction ; and as soon as
this was in train Armitage was to have at his disposal all
the resources of men and material in the ship for his
attack on the western region.

In considering his earlier observations, Armitage had
come to the conclusion that it was impossible to force a
way through the entrance to New Harbour, where for
so many miles he had seemed to see a chaos of ice and
morainic material, and he thought his best chance lay in
ascending to the foothill plateau, in the neighbourhood of

the so-called 'Eskers,' as from this he hoped to find a pass which would lead him over the main ridge of mountains.

In busily preparing for this programme we did not forget the advantage we possessed in the fact that our surfaces and general travelling conditions were likely to improve rather than otherwise as the summer advanced ; we should have little of the sea-ice to cross, and we knew that with our cold summer this would not develop into the same treacherous condition that it does in the North, whilst the surfaces to the south or inland could not possibly grow moist and sludgy. With these conditions we could arrange our movements to take advantage of what we hoped to find the warmest and finest summer months ; and since there was no chance of the ship being released from the ice until February, there was little object in our sledge parties being back much before that date, while we should travel during the time that the sun was circling at its greatest altitude.

As a further result of our reconnaissance journeys, we were now better able to judge of the requirements of each individual party as far as smaller matters of equipment were concerned. It was evident that the western travellers would have to be provided with ice-axes, crampons, ropes, and other necessaries for climbing ; but it seemed that in going to the south we should be safe in omitting these accessories, and in preparing for a journey in which there was no formidable obstruction. As we proposed to begin our journey to the south at the end of October, it can be imagined that, with so many minor details to be attended to, the last weeks of the month were not a slack season for any of us.

On Friday, October 24, Royds and his party returned to the ship, having achieved the object of communicating with our 'Record' post at Cape Crozier. We now had the satisfaction of knowing that we had done all in our power to guide a possible relief ship to our winter quarters; should she make a diligent search on the northern slopes of Terror, as had been arranged, she would at least have a good prospect of receiving the latest information concerning us. It was also a very great source of satisfaction to find that the party returned in excellent health, for they had left us almost immediately after the outbreak of scurvy, and that they should have come back safe and well went far to show that hard sledging work would not necessarily cause a return of the disease.

From our experience of the previous season we had concluded that Terror Point, as the eastern extremity of the land mass was called, was an extremely windy region, and the adventures of this party left the matter beyond much doubt. Skirting the large bay south of Erebus to avoid the deeper snow, they had carried fine but cold weather with them on the outward march, and until October 10, when they were able to make their most advanced camp, ready to proceed over the bare rocks towards the rookery. The 11th proved a beautifully calm, bright day, and Royds, having injured his ankle, deputed the task of reaching the 'Record' to Skelton. The latter left the camp at noon with Evans, and by 6 P.M. returned, having accomplished his errand; in the bright, clear afternoon he had little difficulty in finding the spot, and came to the conclusion that they must have been within a very short distance of it in their autumn wanderings.

On the 12th Skelton set out again, with two companions, this time intent on photographing the immense ice disturbance caused by the barrier pushing around the land. After taking several photographs he returned, and the homeward route brought him close to the edge of the Crozier cliffs, where they rise with magnificent grandeur and form a frowning precipice more than 800 feet sheer above the sea; from this point of vantage he looked down directly on the barrier edge and into the small bay which breaks its outline near the land. Whilst he was admiring the beauty of the scene, his quick eye caught sight of numerous small dots on the sea-ice far below; it was not long before he decided that they must be Emperor penguins. He asked himself what they could be doing here in such numbers, and wondered if it were possible that at last the breeding-place of these mysterious birds had been discovered—it seemed almost too good to be true. Assurance must wait for some future occasion, and in the meanwhile he returned to the camp in no small state of excitement.

To-morrow the mystery must be cleared up; but to-morrow brought the wind, and not a yard from their tents could the party stir. This was the 13th. On the 14th the weather proved equally bad, save for a short lull when they were able to prepare a hot meal; directly afterwards, the blizzard swept down on them again and continued without intermission throughout the 15th, 16th, and 17th.

Before the gale they had built elaborate protecting snow walls to windward of the tents, and these almost proved their undoing; for the never-ceasing drift collected deeper and deeper behind these walls, and the occupants of the tents were conscious that the snow was gradually accumulating around them and that they were now powerless to prevent it. It soon reduced the light within to a mere glimmer, and then, becoming heavier and heavier on every fold of canvas, it diminished their interior space to such an extent that all were obliged to lie with their knees bent double. In the end they were practically buried in the heart of a snowdrift; but whilst the stout bamboos bent under the load and still further narrowed the space within, they luckily withstood the strain to the end.

It was now only by observing the extreme summit of their tents that the prisoners had any indication of what was happening without. Though in some respects this was a relief, yet for want of space they were unable to cook any food, they could barely turn from side to side, and they suffered a martyrdom from cramp. Their enclosed position brought them comparative warmth, but what advantage they gained in this way was largely discounted by the sodden dampness of articles which had thawed.

On the 17th the snow ceased to drift. The occupants of one tent were able to free themselves after some difficulty, but the other tent had literally to be dug out before

its imprisoned members could be got into the open;
whilst the sledges and all that had been left without
were buried completely out of sight. The tale of five
days spent in the manner which I have described is soon
told—Mr. Royds dismisses it in half a page of his report
—but I, and I believe the reader may, find that no great
effort of imagination is needed to grasp the horrible discomforts that it involved; and yet when this party were
recounting their adventures on board the ship, one might
have imagined that the incident was all extremely
amusing. The hardships had been forgotten, and all that
the men seemed to remember was how So-and-so had
launched out with the cramp and kicked someone else
fair in the middle, or how the occupants of one tent had
declared that they had been awakened by the snoring of
some particular member in the other.

It was not until the 18th that the wind ceased, and
they were able to make shift to dry their equipment and
to look out on the scene about them. When they had
arrived the whole Ross Sea had been frozen over as far
as their eyes could see, and now they gazed on a sheet
of open water. Not a scrap of ice remained in sight,
except in the bay to which Skelton had directed his
footsteps at an early hour; in this bay the ice still hung,
and it was doubtless the permanency of this sheet which
had caused the Emperor penguins to adopt it as a breeding place.

For Skelton had not been deceived in his observation: on reaching the sea-ice in this bay, after a stiff
climb over the high-pressure ridges, he found again

his colony of Emperors, numbering some four hundred, and, to his delight, amongst them several that were nursing chicks.

Upon the great interest of this find, and upon the many important notes which were made concerning the colony, both at this time and at a later date, I will not dwell, as these facts are dealt with in the excellent appendix which our zoologist, Dr. Wilson, has contributed to this volume, describing the habits of these extraordinary birds far more clearly than I could hope to do ; I will only testify to the joy which greeted this discovery on board the ship. We had felt that this penguin was the truest type of our region. All other birds fled north when the severity of winter descended upon us : the Emperor alone was prepared to face the extremest rigours of our climate : and we gathered no small satisfaction from being the first to throw light on the habits of a creature that so far surpasses in hardihood all others of the feathered tribe.

Full of their exploits the party started for home on the 19th, and, as I have said, reached the ship on the 24th.

Before the end of the month everything was prepared for the southern journey, instructions for various sledge parties and for the custody of the ship had been given, details of the conduct of affairs had been discussed and rediscussed. Every eventuality seemed to be provided for, and nothing now remained but to wait for the date which had been fixed for our departure.

The southern supporting party, as I have said,

consisted of Mr. Barne with eleven men ; and as it was expected that at first, at any rate, the dogs would outstrip the men, it was decided that this party should start on October 30, but that the dog team should not leave until a few days later. All were to meet at the depot which I had laid out, and which was now known as Depot ' A.'

Accordingly, on October 30 I record: 'The supporting party started this morning, amidst a scene of much enthusiasm ; all hands had a day off, and employed it in helping to drag the sledges for several miles. The sledges carried some decorations : Barne's banner floated on the first, the next bore a Union Jack, and another carried a flag with a large device stating " *No dogs need apply* " ; the reference was obvious. It was an inspiriting sight to see nearly the whole of our small company step out on the march with ringing cheers, and to think that all work of this kind promised to be done as heartily. Later Shackleton had a trial trip with the dogs to get our runners in better order, and the animals started so strongly that they carried away the central trace and started to gallop off; but luckily they all wanted to go in different directions, and so didn't get far, and, luckily also, there were a few of us about to prevent the worst effect of the inevitable fights.'

' *November* 2.— . . . We are off at last. By ten this morning the dogs were harnessed and all was ready for a start ; the overcast sky was showing signs of a break in the south. Every soul was gathered on the floe to bid us farewell, and many were prepared to accompany

us for the first few miles.   A last look was given to our
securings, the traces were finally cleared, and away we
went amidst the wild cheers of our comrades.   The dogs
have never been in such form ; despite the heavy load,
for the first two miles two men had to sit on the sledges
to check them, and even thus it was as much as the rest of
us could do to keep up by running alongside.   One by one
our followers tailed off, and by noon we three were alone
with our animals and still breathlessly trying to keep pace
with them.   Soon after lunch we saw a dark spot far ahead,
and about 5 P.M. we made this out to be our supporting
party ; we caught them up just as they were rounding
the corner of White Island, and learnt that they had had
very bad weather which had confined them to their tents.
Relieving them of some of their loads, we camped, whilst
they pushed on to get the advantage of a night march.'

'*November* 3.— . . . At 2 P.M. we came up with
Barne's people.   They are doing their best, but making
very slow progress.   The difficulty is the slipperiness of
the wind-swept snow, the surface being particularly hard
amongst the *sastrugi* opposite the gullies of the island.
They can get no hold with their fur boots, and find
their leather ski boots dreadfully cold for the feet ; the
result is that they scarcely cover a mile an hour.   The
only thing is for us to take life easy whilst they go on
in the best manner possible ; we have relieved them
of over 150 lbs. of weight, so that they now only help us
to the extent of 500 lbs.   I have told Barne to go on
quite independently of us.'

In this manner we journeyed slowly to the south

outside the White Island, the parties constantly passing
and repassing; it was impossible at this part to keep
together, as men and dogs took the march at quite a
different pace. To add to the slowness of our journey,
the weather proved very unpropitious, for the wind constantly sprang up and obliged us to camp, and we were
forced to lie up during the greater part of the 8th and
9th, whilst a heavy blizzard passed over us.

On the 9th I wrote: 'The wind still blows with
exasperating persistence, though the sun has been peep-
ing out all day; it adds to the trying nature of this inactivity to watch the sun pass pole after pole of our tent
and to know that the supporting party are cut off from
their slow daily progress. We are now south of the
Bluff, and cannot be more than eight miles from the depot.
To-night the wind is dying; the cloud mantle on the
Bluff has vanished, and for the first time for many days
one can catch a view of the western lands.

' On our outward track we have kept rather too close
to the White Island, and consequently have had to
traverse a good many undulations; it was curious to
watch the supporting party dipping out of sight on what
appeared to the eye to be a plain surface. Disturbed by
much barking from the dogs, we crawled out of our
bags to-night about eleven o'clock, to find, much to our
satisfaction, that our supporting party had arrived; they
camped close by, and Barne tells me they have had a
hard, cold pull up against the wind.'

' *November* 10.—Started early this morning, leaving
the supporting party quietly slumbering. Had much

difficulty in forcing the dogs along in face of a low drift and cutting wind, but managed to make good progress. At one o'clock, sighted the depot and were soon camped beside it, when the wind died away, the sky cleared, and we have again the whole splendid panorama of the northern and western mountains in full view.

'On the march to-day a small snow petrel suddenly appeared hovering above us, and later it was joined by a second; these are the first birds we have seen since the departure of the skuas in the autumn, and form a very pleasant reminder of summer. We are left in wonder as to why they should be so far from the sea. We were first apprised of their coming by the conduct of the dogs, and for a moment or two we could not understand why these animals should suddenly begin to leap about and bark furiously, but their wild dashes soon drew attention to our fluttering visitors.

'Already it seems to me that the dogs feel the monotony of a long march over the snow more than we do; they seem easily to get dispirited, and that it is not due to fatigue is shown when they catch a glimpse of anything novel. On seeing the men ahead they are always eager to get up with them, and even a shadowy ice disturbance or anything unusual will excite their curiosity. To-day, for instance, they required some driving until they caught sight of the depot flag, when they gave tongue loudly and dashed off as though they barely felt the load behind them.'

It would perhaps be as well to introduce the reader to our dog team, as they played so important a part in this journey, and before the tale of its ending will have disappeared from the scene for ever. Their origin and the names by which they had been formerly known are, as I have explained, mysteries which we could not penetrate, but long before the commencement of this journey each had learnt to answer to his own title in the following list :—

' Nigger,'	' Birdie,'	' Wolf,'
' Jim,'	' Nell,'	' Vic,'
' Spud,'	' Blanco,'	' Bismarck,'
' Snatcher,'	' Grannie,'	' Kid,'
' FitzClarence,'	' Lewis,'	' Boss,'
' Stripes,'	' Gus,'	' Brownie,'
	' Joe.'	

Each of these dogs had his own peculiar characteristics, and altogether they displayed as great a variety as could well be comprehended in a team of the size ; it can be imagined that what we did not know concerning their individuality we had ample opportunities of learning during the weeks that followed.

I have already given some idea of the dignity of character of our leader, ' Nigger.' He was a black dog with some tawny markings, and possessed the most magnificent head and chest, though falling off a little in the hinder quarters. A more perfect sledge dog could scarcely be imagined ; he chose his place naturally as the leader, and if put into any other position would make himself so unpleasant to his neighbours, and generally behave so ill, that he was very quickly shifted. In the happy times before sickness fell on our team, it was a delight to watch ' Nigger ' at his work : he seemed to know the meaning of every move. He would lie still as a

graven image till he saw the snow being shovelled from
the skirting of the tent, when up he would spring and
pace to and fro at his picket, giving out a low throaty
bark of welcome as any of us approached, and now and
again turning towards his neighbours to express his
opinion of them in the most bloodthirsty snarl.   A few
minutes later, as the leading man came to uproot his
picket, his keen eye would watch each movement, and a
slow wagging of his tail would quite obviously signify
approval ; then as the word came to start, he would push
affectionately against the leader, as much as to say,
' Now, come along,' and brace his powerful chest to the
harness.   At the evening halt after a long day he would
drop straight in his tracks and remain perfectly still with
his great head resting on his paws ; other dogs might
clamour for food, but ' Nigger ' knew perfectly well that
the tent had to be put up first.   Afterwards, however,
when one of us approached the dog-food, above the
howling chorus that arose one could always distinguish
the deep bell-like note of the leading dog, and knew that
if disturbance was to be avoided, it was well to go to the
front end of the trace first.

' Lewis was a big, thick-coated, brindled dog, a very
powerful but not a consistent puller ; always noisily
affectionate and hopelessly clumsy, he would prance at
one and generally all but succeed in bowling one over
with boisterous affection.   He was very popular with
everyone, as such a big, blustering, good-natured animal
deserved to be.

' Jim ' was a sleek, lazy, greedy villain, up to all the

tricks of the trade; he could pull splendidly when he chose, but generally preferred to pretend to pull, and at this he was extraordinarily cunning. During the march his eye never left the man with the whip, on whose approach ' Jim' could be seen panting and labouring as though he felt sure that everything depended on his efforts; but a moment or two later, when the danger had passed, the watchful eye would detect Master ' Jim' with a trace that had a very palpable sag in it. Yet with all his faults it was impossible not to retain a certain affection for this fat culprit, who was so constantly getting himself into hot water.

The general opinion of ' Spud' was that he was daft— there was something wanting in the upper storey. In the middle of a long and monotonous march he would suddenly whimper and begin to prance about in his traces; in dog-language this is a signal that there is something in sight, and it always had an electrical effect on the others, however tired they might be. As a rule they would set off at a trot with heads raised to look around and noses sniffing the breeze. It was 'Spud' alone who gave this signal without any cause, and, curiously enough, the rest never discovered the fraud; to the end he openly gulled them. On ordinary occasions ' Spud' would give one the impression of being intensely busy; he was always stepping over imaginary obstacles, and all his pulling was done in a jerky, irregular fashion. He was a big, strong, black dog, and perhaps the principal sign of his mental incapacity was the ease with which others could rob him of his food.

Amongst the team there had been one animal who was conspicuous for his ugliness : with a snubbish nose, a torn ear, an ungainly body, ribs that could be easily counted through a dirty, tattered coat, and uncompromisingly vulgar manners, he was at first an object of derision to all ; and being obviously of the most plebeian origin, he was named 'FitzClarence.' Kindness and good food worked wonders for 'Clarence,' and although he never developed into a thing of beauty or of refined habits, he became a very passable sledge dog.

'Kid' and 'Bismarck' were the only two dogs of the team that bore an outward resemblance, both being short-legged animals with long, fleecy, black-and-white coats. But the likeness was only superficial. Inwardly they differed much, for whereas Bismarck was counted amongst the lazy eye-servers, 'Kid' was the most indefatigable worker in the team ; from morn to night he would set forth his best effort. The whip was never applied to his panting little form, and when he stopped it was to die from exhaustion.

With all our efforts we could never quite tame 'Birdie, who had evidently been treated with scant respect in his youth. At the ship he would retire into his kennel and growl at all except those who brought him food, and to the end he remained distrustful and suspicious of all attempts to pet him. He was a large, reddish-brown dog, very wolfish in appearance, but a powerful puller when he got to understand what was required of him.

Of the rest of the team, 'Gus,' 'Stripes,' 'Snatcher,' and 'Vic' were nice, pleasant-mannered dogs, and good average pullers. 'Brownie' was a very handsome animal, but rather light in build. He was charming as a pet, but less gifted as a sledge-puller, and always appealed to one as being a little too refined and ladylike for the hardest work; nor did he ever lose a chance of utilising his pleasing appearance and persuasive ways to lighten his afflictions.

'Wolf' was the most hopelessly ill-tempered animal his character seemed to possess no redeeming virtue. Every advance was met with the same sullen, irreconcilable humour, and the whip alone was capable of reducing him to subjection.   On the principle that you can lead a horse to the water but you cannot make him drink, 'Wolf' had evidently decided that we might lead him to the traces but nothing could make him pull; and, as a consequence, from start to finish no efforts of ours could make him do even a reasonable share of his work.   We should have saved ourselves much trouble and annoyance had we left him behind in the first place.

To the effort to swell the numbers of our team Bernacchi had sacrificed his own property, 'Joe,' and poor 'Joe' had a history.   He had been born in the Antarctic Regions at Cape Adare; later in life he had learnt to behave himself with proper decorum in a London drawing-room; and now he had returned, no doubt much against his will, to finish his career in the land of his birth.   He was a very light dog, with a deceptively thick coat; much pulling could not be expected from his weight, and he certainly gave but little.

Such was our team as regards the dog element; but

a word may be added about the three of the other sex, whom at first I was very reluctant to take. 'Nell' was a pretty black animal with a snappish little temper but attractive ways; 'Blanco,' so called because she ought to have been white, had few attractions, and was of such little use that she was sent back with the supporting party; and poor 'Grannie' was old and toothless, but lived and died game on the traces.

Whilst the loads for this dog team had been heavy from the start, it had not been proposed to bring them up to full weights till after our departure from Depot 'A,' and from that spot we proposed to assist by pulling ourselves; it may be of some interest, therefore, to note the weights which we actually dragged.

The following table was one of a number of sheets which I prepared in order that we might know at each place exactly how we stood, and it seemed to simplify matters to draw rough diagrams of the sledges on the margin. The total of 1,850 lbs. was of course a heavy load for our team of nineteen, especially as the team possessed a few animals which were of little account; but it must be remembered that we expected to pull ourselves, and that each night, after the first start, would see a reduction of between thirty and forty pounds by the time all creature comforts had been attended to.

The load here shown allows for nine weeks only for our own food, and it was in order that we might increase this allowance to thirteen that the supporting party was arranged to accompany us for some part of our journey.

On the afternoon of the 11th the supporting party

Weights on Leaving 'A'

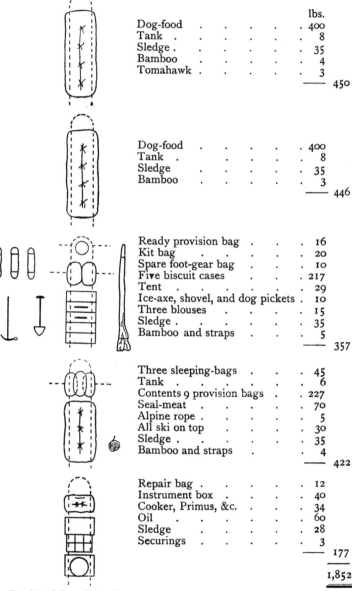

		lbs.	
Dog-food	. . . . .	400	
Tank .	. . . . .	8	
Sledge .	. . . .	35	
Bamboo	. . . .	4	
Tomahawk .	. . . .	3	
		——	450

Dog-food	. . . .	400	
Tank .	. . . .	8	
Sledge	. . . .	35	
Bamboo	. . . .	3	
		——	446

Ready provision bag	. . .	16	
Kit bag	. . . . .	20	
Spare foot-gear bag	. . .	10	
Five biscuit cases	. . .	217	
Tent	. . . . .	29	
Ice-axe, shovel, and dog pickets	.	10	
Three blouses	. . . .	15	
Sledge .	. . . .	35	
Bamboo and straps	. . .	5	
		——	357

Three sleeping-bags	. . .	45	
Tank .	. . . .	6	
Contents 9 provision bags	.	227	
Seal-meat	. . . .	70	
Alpine rope .	. . . .	5	
All ski on top	. . .	30	
Sledge .	. . . .	35	
Bamboo and straps	.	4	
		——	422

Repair bag .	. . .	12	
Instrument box	. . .	40	
Cooker, Primus, &c.	.	34	
Oil	. . . . .	60	
Sledge	. . . .	28	
Securings	. . .	3	
		——	177
			1,852

The dotted lines show plans
of sledges and straps.

hove in sight, and we were soon busily engaged in arranging matters for an early start on the morrow.

The 12th proved a misty, raw, cold day—not a happy omen for our start—but we got away betimes, and with a cheer set off for the first time on a due south course. The dogs were in such high feather that they quickly caught up the men, and little by little we had to increase their load until they were drawing no less than 2,100 lbs. When we camped for the night we had made $11\frac{1}{2}$ miles, and, in the slightly misty weather, already appeared to be lost on the great open plain. I note in my diary : ' The feeling at first is somewhat weird ; there is absolutely nothing to break the grey monotone about us, and yet we know that the mist is not thick, but that our isolation comes from the immense expanse of the plain. The excellent pulling of the dogs is likely to modify our plans, and I think of sending half the supports back to-morrow.'

' *November* 13.—Sights to-day showed us to be nearly up to the 79th parallel, and therefore farther south than anyone has yet been. The announcement of the fact caused great jubilation, and I am extremely glad that there are no fewer than fifteen of us to enjoy this privilege of having broken the record. Shackleton suggested that all should be photographed, whereat the men were much delighted, and we all gathered about the sledges with our flags fluttering over us. Then half our supporting party started to return, bearing the good news of our present success, and the other half stepped out once more on a due south line, with the dogs following.

' This morning it was very bright and sunny except

to the far north, where probably those on board the ship are not enjoying such delightful weather; behind us only the Bluff showed against a dark background, and that was already growing small in the distance. Away to the west the view was perfectly clear, and we now know that there is land beyond our western horizon; it is very distant, and appears in detached masses, but it is evident that the general trend of it is in a more southerly direction than we had supposed. At this great distance it looks to be completely snow-covered; we can only catch the high lights and shadows due to irregularity of shape, and can only say definitely that there must be many lofty mountains. I took a round of bearings with the prismatic compass, and then asked Barne to do the same; he got different readings, and on trying again myself I got a third result. The observations only differed by a few degrees, but it shows that these compasses are not to be relied upon where the directive force is so small.'

The needle of the prismatic compass carries a weighty graduated circle with it; it therefore bears heavily on the pivot, and the friction produced is sufficient to prevent accuracy of reading where the earth has such small influence on the needle. After this I depended for all bearings on the compass attached to our small theodolite, which possessed a simple light needle and seemed to give greater accuracy. I record this fact, because it was important that we should obtain accurate observations on our extended sledge journeys, and it would be well that this point should be more carefully considered in future expeditions.

On the 13th and 14th we pushed on to the south in spite of thick snowy weather which followed the fine morning of the 13th, and during those two days we managed to add fifteen miles to our southing. On the afternoon of the 14th I record : ' The men go ahead, and when they have got a good start we cheer on our animals, who work hard until they have caught up with them ; in this manner we get over the ground fairly well. The day has been murky and dull with a bad light, and we have come upon a new form of *sastrugus* : instead of the clean-cut waves about the Bluff, we have heaped-up mounds of snow with steepish edges. Heavily laden as they are, it is difficult work for the dogs when they come across the sudden rises. Now and then the clouds have lifted, showing the horizon line and glimpses of the land to the north, but for the main part the sky and snow-surface have been merged in a terrible sameness of grey, and it has been impossible to see the spot on which one's foot was next to be placed ; falls have been plentiful. The surface itself is getting softer, but the sledges run fairly easily. The dogs were pretty "done" when we camped to-night, but we are feeding them up, and I do not propose to overwork them whilst the load remains as heavy as at present. That we are travelling over a practically level surface was evident from our view of the supporting party to-day ; though we were often some distance apart they were always clearly in view, which would not have been the case had there been undulations.'

' *November* 15.—A beautifully bright, calm morning ;

the sun shone warmly on our tents, making them most
cheerful and comfortable within.   To the north the land
has become dim, to the west we have the same prospect
of distant detached snow-covered ranges, and in all other
directions the apparently limitless snow-plain.

'We were very busy this morning making arrangements for our last parting : the loads had to be readjusted,
the dog-harness attended to, observations taken, and
notes of farewell written.   All this was not finished till
after noon, when many willing hands helped us to pack
up our tent and make all ready for our final start.   If
former moments of parting have seemed unpropitious,
the same cannot be said of to-day ; the sun shone
brightly on our last farewells, and whilst behind us we
left all in good health and spirits, it is scarcely to be
wondered at that our hopes ran high for the future.
We are already beyond the utmost limit to which man has
attained : each footstep will be a fresh conquest of the
great unknown.   Confident in ourselves, confident in
our equipment, and confident in our dog team, we can
but feel elated with the prospect that is before us.

'The day's work has cast a shadow on our highest
aspirations, however, and already it is evident that if we
are to achieve much it will be only by extreme toil, for
the dogs have not pulled well to-day ; possibly it may be
something to do with the surface, which seems to get
softer, possibly something to do with the absence of
the men in front to cheer them on, and possibly something to do with the temperature, which rose at one
time to + 20° and made the heavy pulling very warm

work. Whatever the reason may be, by five o'clock we had only covered about three miles, and this is by no means up to expectation. We have decided that if things have not improved in the morning we will take on half the load at a time; after a few days of this sort of thing the loads will be sufficiently lightened for us to continue in the old way again.'

The above extract shows that our troubles were already beginning, but as yet we had no suspicion that they were likely to be as grievous as they soon became. On the following day we attempted once more to start our heavy loads, but after a few yards of struggling the dogs seemed to lose all heart, and many looked round with the most pathetic expression as much as to say we were really expecting too much of them; there was but one thing to be done—namely, to divide the load into two portions and take on half at a time. This meant, of course, that each mile had to be traversed three times, but as there was no alternative we were forced to start on this tedious form of advance. With this, even, we should have been content had the dogs shown their former vigour; but now, for some reason which we could not fathom, they seemed to be losing all their spirit, and they made as much fuss over drawing the half load as a few days before they had done over the whole one.

On November 18 I write : 'A dull day again, but we plodded on in the same monotonous style. Starting at 11 A.M., we pushed on for two and a half miles by our sledge-meter, with half the load, then returned for the

second half; the whole operation took about four hours and
a half, after which we had lunch and then repeated the
same performance.   It was 11 P.M. before we were in our
sleeping-bags, and at the end of the march the dogs
were practically " done."   What can be the cause it is
almost impossible to guess.   It cannot be wholly the
surface, though this is certainly much worse ; not only is
it softer, but all day long snow crystals are falling, and
these loose, light crystals enormously increase the
friction on the runners ; nor can it be altogether the
temperature, for even when it falls very chill there is no
sign of improvement in the pace.   I fear there must be
another reason which is at present beyond us.   We
gained five miles to-day, but to do it we had to cover
fifteen.'

These miles to which I refer are geographical, and
not statute miles ; in all our journeys we calculated in
the former unit for ease of reference to the degrees and
minutes of latitude, but it must be explained that there is
a considerable difference in these measurements : seven
geographical miles are equal to a little more than eight
statute.   In many cases I have reduced the mileage in
this book to the better-known statute mile for the convenience of the reader, but in some of my quotations I
leave the original figure unaltered; I think with this
explanation it will be clear when either is used.

A word may be added concerning the sledge-meter,
because it explains the curious-looking wheel which may
be seen in many of our photographs in rear of the
sledges.   Our engine-room staff cleverly manufactured

these instruments by applying the counter apparatus of some recording blocks to wheels of a certain definite diameter, and thus as one of these wheels trundled behind the sledge it revolved the mechanism of the counter so as to show the number of yards travelled. As I think I have said, at first we all thought we were walking very long distances through the snow, and when we adopted the sledge-meter and it showed us the chilling truth, many were inclined to be sceptical of its accuracy until it was found that when there was a difference of opinion between the party and the sledge-meter, astronomical observations invariably decided in favour of the latter, so that we were obliged to acknowledge that it was we, and not the sledge-meter, who were going too slowly.

After our experience one cannot help thinking that not a few sledging records would have been modified had this truth-telling instrument always been available ; it is to be recommended to future expeditions, not only for this reason, but on account of the excellent check it affords to the position of a sledge party for geographical purposes.

'*November* 19.—The sun was shining when we started to-day, and the fine snow was falling continuously ; it is a drizzle of tiny crystals, which settle on the sledges and quickly evaporate. The effect on the surface is very bad, and the dogs are growing more and more listless. We could only advance four and three-quarter miles, and that only by hard driving and going longer than we have yet gone. Two of us always pull

on the traces whilst the third drives ; the latter task is
by far the most dreaded. In going to the rear for the
second half-load, we always carry an empty sledge, and
up to the present, to prevent confusion of the traces,
someone has sat on the sledge, but to-day even this
appeared to be a perceptible drag on our poor animals.

'It is very tiring work. When one goes out in the
morning there is now no joyous clamour of welcome ; one
or two of the animals have to be roused up out of their
nests, then we start in a spiritless fashion. We take our
duties in turns ; one of us attaches his harness to the
head of the trace, and whilst he pulls he endeavours to
cheer on the flagging team. A second takes the best
position, which is to pull alongside the sledges, in silence ;
the third does not pull, but carries the whip and has to
use it all too frequently. Thus our weary caravan winds
its slow way along until the sledge-meter has reeled off
the required distance. When we halt, the dogs drop at
once, but when the lightened sledge is attached and we
start to wheel them round, they wake up and for the first
time display a little energy in trying to fight as they
circle about ; but this show of spirit soon fails, though
we naturally get back at a brisker pace. Then the second
half-load is joined up, and the whole thing has to be done
over again. When the dogs sight the advanced load,
however, there is a distinct improvement ; they know
that to get there means rest, and, encouraging this spirit
as much as we can, the last half-mile is done almost at a
trot. The afternoon march is of the same nature as that
of the forenoon, but is made worse by the increased

fatigue of our wretched animals.   It is all very heartbreaking work.

'This morning we sighted further land to the south-
west, and like the rest it appears as a detached fragment.
We now see three distinct gaps between the several
land masses, and the distance is too great for us to
make out any detail of the latter; to the south and
round through east to the north we have still the unbroken snow horizon.

'To-night we have been discussing our position
again; it is evidently going from bad to worse. We
have scarcely liked to acknowledge to ourselves that
the fish diet is having a permanently bad effect on the
dogs, but it looks very much like it; we saw that it
disagreed with them at first, but we have tried to persuade ourselves that the effect is only temporary. It
will be a terrible calamity if this is the cause of all our
distress, for there is no possible change of diet except
to feed the poor things on each other, and yet it is
difficult to account in any other way for the fact that
whilst they are receiving an ample amount of food they
should daily be growing weaker. One of the most
trying circumstances in our position is that we are
forced to spend hours in our tent which might be devoted to marching; it is the dogs, and not we, who call
the halt each night.'

Though it was only gradually that we could convince
ourselves that the dog-food was at the bottom of our
trouble, subsequent events proved it beyond a doubt,
and therefore it may be of interest to give some account

of that food. Originally I had intended to take ordinary dog-biscuit for our animals, but in an evil moment I was persuaded by one who had had great experience in dog-driving to take fish. Fish has been used continually in the North for feeding dogs, and the particular article which we ordered was the Norwegian stock-fish such as is split, dried, and exported from that country in great quantities for human food. There is no doubt about the excellent food-value of this fish, and in every way it seemed well adapted to our purpose ; and yet it was this very fish that poisoned our poor animals.

It is easy to be wise after the event, and on looking back now one sees the great probability of its suffering deterioration on passage through the Tropics, and, doubtless, had it been designed for human food we should have considered that point ; but, unfortunately for our dogs, this probability escaped our notice, and as there was no outward sign of deterioration it was carried on our sledge journey. As a result the dogs sickened, and in some cases died, from what one can only suppose was a species of scurvy. The lesson to future travellers in the South is obvious, in that they should safeguard their dogs as surely as they do their men. The dog is such a terrible scavenger that one is apt to overlook this necessity.

'*November* 21.—This morning the sun was shining in a cloudless sky, and to our surprise we found land extending all along our right ; probably it appears deceptively close owing to the mirage. At any rate, things are growing so bad that we have decided to edge towards it, and have altered our course to S.S.W. All things considered, this seems the best course, as our prospect of reaching a high latitude is steadily melting away. Our method of advance gives us at least the advantage of gauging the level nature of the surface over which we are travelling. To judge by one's feelings on the march, one might be climbing the steepest of hills all day, but the fact that we can always see our advanced or rear sledges from the other end shows that there must be an absence of inequality ; even the man who sits on the returning sledge with his eye not more than three feet above the surface rarely loses sight of these tiny black dots. It is surprising that although a sledge appears as a very minute object at two and a half miles, it can generally be seen clearly against the white background. On dull days, however, I am not sure but that it is a risk to advance them so far.'

'*November* 22.—The surface is becoming smoother, with less *sastrugi*, but the snow covering is, if anything, thicker ; one sinks deeper, and there is no reduction of friction on the sledge runners. After lunch we made a trial to start with full loads ; the dogs made a gallant effort, but could scarcely move the sledges, and we had to proceed as before. With this land ahead we ought to get some variation of the monotony of our present travelling, but there is a fear that the snow may get still softer as we approach it.

'We are growing very sunburnt, and noses and lips are getting blistered and cracked and extremely sore ; lips are especially painful, as one cannot help licking them on the march, and this makes them worse. With the constant variations of temperature and the necessary application of the hot rim of the pannikin they get no chance to heal; hazeline cream is in much request at night to deaden the burning. We have also had some trouble with our eyes, though we wear goggles very regularly. Our appetites seem to be increasing by leaps and bounds; it is almost alarming, and the only thing to be looked to on ŏur long marches is the prospect of the next meal.'

'*November* 23.— . . . There was a distinct improvement in the surface to-day, with a N.N.E. wind rolling the snow along like fine sand; in this way the old hard surface crust became exposed in patches, and the sledges drew easily over these. Altogether we have advanced 5⅓ miles, travelling over 15½ miles to do it. We raised the land considerably, and were able to see something more of the bold black headland for which we are making.'

'*November* 24.— . . . To-day we started a new routine, which eases us ánd gives a chance for odd jobs to be done. After pushing on the first half-load one of us stops with it, gets up the tent, and prepares for lunch or supper, as the case may be, whilst the other two bring up the second half-load.

' The land which appeared to be rising so quickly yesterday was evidently thrown up by mirage; I fear it is farther off than we thought.'

' *November* 25.—Before starting to-day I took a meridian altitude, and to my delight found the latitude

to be 80° 1'. All our charts of the Antarctic Regions
show a plain white circle beyond the eightieth parallel;
the most imaginative cartographer has not dared to cross
this limit, and even the meridional lines end at the circle.
It has always been our ambition to get inside that white
space, and now we are there the space can no longer be
a blank; this compensates for a lot of trouble.

'*November* 26.—Last night we had almost decided
to give our poor team a day's rest, and to-day there is a
blizzard which has made it necessary. We had warning
in the heavy stratus clouds that came over fast from the
south yesterday, and still more in Wilson's rheumatism;
this comes on with the greatest regularity before every
snowstorm, and he suffers considerably. Up to the
present it has been in his knee, but last night it appeared
in his foot, and though he ought to have known its significance, he attributed it to the heavy walking. To-day
it has passed away with the breaking of the storm, and
there can be no longer a doubt that it is due to change
of weather, and that he, poor chap, serves as a very
effective though unwilling barometer.'

'*November* 27.—To-day it is beautifully bright, clear
and warm, the temperature up to +20°; but, alas! this
morning we found that the dogs seemed to have derived
no benefit from their rest. They were all snugly curled
up beneath the snow when we went out, but in spite of
their long rest we had to drag them out of their nests;
some were so cramped that it was several minutes before
they could stand. However, we shook some life into
them and started with the full load, but very soon we

had to change back into our old routine, and, if anything,
the march was more trying than ever.   It becomes a
necessity now to reach the land soon in hopes of making
a depot, so our course has been laid to the westward of
S.W., and this brings the bold bluff cape on our port
bow.   I imagine it to be about fifty miles off, but hope
it is not so much ; nine hours' work to-day has only given
us a bare four miles.

' It was my turn to drive to-day ; Shackleton led and
Wilson pulled at the side.   The whole proceedings
would have been laughable enough but for the grim
sickness that holds so tight a grip on our poor team ;
Shackleton in front, with harness slung over his shoulder,
was bent forward with his whole weight on the trace ; in
spite of his breathless work, now and again he would
raise and half-turn his head in an effort to cheer on the
team.   " Hi, dogs," " Now then," " Hi lo-lo-lo . . ." or
any other string of syllables which were supposed to produce an encouraging effect, but which were soon brought
to a conclusion by sheer want of breath.   Behind him,
and obviously deaf to these allurements, shambled the
long string of depressed animals, those in rear doing
their best to tread in the deep footprints of the leaders,
but all by their low-carried heads and trailing tails showing an utter weariness of life.   Behind these, again, came
myself with the whip, giving forth one long string of
threats and occasionally bringing the lash down with a
crack on the snow or across the back of some laggard.
By this time all the lazy dogs know their names, as well
they ought ; I should not like to count the number of

times I have said, "Ah, you, 'Wolf,'" or "Get on there, 'Jim,'" or "'Bismarck,' you brute"; but it is enough to have made me quite hoarse to-night, for each remark has to be produced in a violent manner or else it produces no effect, and things have now got so bad that if the driver ceases his flow of objurgation for a moment there is a slackening of the traces. Some names lend themselves to this style of language better than others; 'Boss" can be hissed out with very telling effect, whereas it is hard to make "Brownie" very emphatic. On the opposite side of the leading sledge was Wilson, pulling away in grim silence. We dare not talk on such occasions—the dogs detect the change of tone at once; they seize upon the least excuse to stop pulling. There are six or eight animals who give little trouble, and these have been placed in the front, so that the others may be more immediately under the lash; but the loafers are growing rather than diminishing in numbers. This, then, is the manner in which we have proceeded for nine hours to-day—entreaties in front and threats behind—and so we went on yesterday, and so we shall go on to-morrow. It is sickening work, but it is the only way; we cannot stop, we cannot go back, we must go on, and there is no alternative but to harden our hearts and drive. Luckily, the turn for doing the actual driving only comes once in three days, but even thus it is almost as bad to witness the driving as to have to do it.

'To-night we discussed the possibility of getting some benefit by marching at night; it was very warm to-day in the sun, and the air temperature was up to $+25^{\circ}$.'

On the days which followed we gradually made our starting-hour later until we dropped into a regular night-marching routine ; we then used to breakfast between 4 and 5 P.M., start marching at 6 P.M., and come to camp somewhere about three or four in the morning.   Thus while the sun was at its greatest altitude we were taking our rest, and during the chiller night hours we marched. There were some advantages in this arrangement which scarcely need notice, but it was curious that with it we never quite got rid of the idea that there was something amiss, and it will be seen that it was likely to lead to confusion as to the date of any particular occurrence. Other drawbacks were that we were often obliged to march with the sun in our faces at midnight, and that sometimes the tent was unpleasantly warm during the hours of sleep.

'*November* 29,—Shortly after four o'clock to-day we observed the most striking atmospheric phenomenon we have yet seen in these regions.   We were enveloped in a light, thin stratus cloud of small ice-crystals ; it could not have extended to any height, as the sun was only lightly veiled.   From these drifting crystals above, the sun's rays were reflected in such an extraordinary manner that the whole arch of the heavens was traced with circles and lines of brilliant prismatic or white light.   The coloured circles of a bright double halo were touched or intersected by one which ran about us parallel to the horizon ; above this, again, a gorgeous prismatic ring encircled the zenith ; away from the sun was a white fog-bow, with two bright mock suns where it intersected the

horizon circle. The whole effect was almost bewildering, and its beauty is far beyond the descriptive powers
of my sledging pencil. We have often seen double
halos, fog-bows, mock suns, and even indications of
other circles, but we have never been privileged to
witness a display that approaches in splendour that of
to-day. We stopped, whilst Wilson took notes of the
artistic composition, and I altitudes and bearings of the
various light effects. If it is robbed of some of the
beauties of a milder climate, our region has certainly
pictures of its own to display.'

On our return to the ship I could find no account, in
such reference books as we had, of anything to equal
this scene, nor have I since heard of its having been
witnessed elsewhere. The accompanying drawing shows
more clearly than I can describe what we actually saw ;
our artist has shown it diagrammatically, and the observer
is supposed to be looking straight upwards towards the
zenith.

'*November* 29 (*continued*).—Both in the first and
second advance to-day we noticed that the points of starting and finishing were in view of one another, but that in
travelling between them either end was temporarily lost
to sight for a short time. This undoubtedly indicates
undulation in the surface, but I should think of slight
amount, probably not more than seven or eight feet, the
length of the waves being doubtful, as we cannot be
certain of the angle at which we are crossing them ;
they cannot exceed two miles from crest to crest, and
are probably about one.

'We had rather a scare to-night on its suddenly coming over very thick just as Wilson and I were coupling up the second load to bring it on ; all our food and personal equipment had been left with Shackleton in the advanced position, and, of course, we could see nothing of it through the haze. We followed the old tracks for some way, until the light got so bad that we repeatedly lost sight of them, when we were obliged to halt and grope round for them. So far we were only in danger of annoying delays, but a little later a brisk breeze sprang up, and to our consternation rapidly drifted up the old tracks ; there was nothing for it but to strike out a fresh course of our own in the direction in which we supposed the camp to lie, which we did, and, getting on as fast as possible, had the satisfaction of sighting the camp in about half an hour.   " All's well that ends well," and luckily the fog was not very thick ; but the incident has set us thinking that if very thick weather were to come on, the party away from the camp might be very unpleasantly situated, so in future we shall plant one or two flags as we advance with the first load, and pick them up as we come on with the second.'

'*December* 2. — We noticed again to-day the cracking of the snow-crust ; sometimes the whole team with the sledges get on an area when it cracks around us as sharply and as loudly as a pistol shot, and this is followed by a long-drawn sigh as the area sinks. When this first happened the dogs were terrified, and sprang forward with tails between their legs and heads screwed round as though the threatened danger was behind ; and, indeed, it gave me rather a shock the first time—it was so unexpected, and the sharp report was followed by a distinct subsidence. Though probably one dropped only an inch or two, there was an instantaneous feeling of insecurity which is not pleasant. Digging down to-night Shackleton found a comparatively hard crust two or three inches under the soft snow surface ; beneath this was an air space of about an inch, then came about a foot of loose snow in large crystals, and then a second crust. There is a good deal that is puzzling about these crusts.'

During the following year on our sledge journeys we frequently dug into the snow surface to see what lay below, and though we always found a succession of crusts with soft snow between, the arrangement was very irregular and gave us no very definite information.

'*December* 3.— . . . Our pemmican bag for this week by an oversight has been slung alongside a tin of paraffin, and is consequently strongly impregnated with the oil ; one can both smell and taste the latter strongly ; it is some proof of the state of our appetites that we really don't much mind !

'We are now sufficiently close to the land to make out some of its details. On our right is a magnificent range of mountains, which we are gradually opening out, and which must therefore run more or less in an east-and-west direction. My rough calculations show them to be at least fifty miles from us, and, if so, their angle of altitude gives a height of over 10,000 feet. The eastern end of this range descends to a high snow-covered plateau, through which arise a number

of isolated minor peaks, which I think must be volcanic ;
beyond these, again, is a long, rounded, sloping snow-
cape, merging into the barrier.   These rounded snow-
capes are a great feature of the coast ; they can be seen
dimly in many places, both north and south of us.   They
are peculiar as presenting from all points of view a perfectly straight line inclined at a slight angle to the horizon.
North of this range the land still seems to run on, but it
has that detached appearance, due to great distance, which
we noted before, and we can make little of it.   The south
side of the range seems to descend comparatively abruptly,
and in many cases it is bordered by splendid high cliffs,
very dark in colour, though we cannot make out the exact
shade.   Each cliff has a band of white along its top where
the ice-cap ends abruptly ; at this distance it has a rather
whimsical resemblance to the sugaring of a Christmas
cake.   The cliffs and foothills of the high range form the
northern limit of what appears to be an enormous strait ;
we do not look up this strait, and therefore cannot say
what is beyond, but the snow-cape on this side is evidently
a great many miles from the high range, and there appears
to be nothing between.   This near snow-cape seems to
be more or less isolated.   It is an immense and almost
dome-shaped, snow-covered mass ; only quite lately could
we see any rock at all, but now a few patches are to be
made out towards the summit, and one or two at intervals
along the foot.   It is for one of these that we have now
decided to make, so that we may establish our depot there,
but at present rate of going we shall be a long time before
we reach it.

'South of this isolated snow-cape, which is by far the nearest point of land to us, we can see a further high mountainous country ; but this also is so distant that we can say little of it. One thing seems evident—that the high bluff cape we were making for is not a cape at all, but a curiously bold spur of the lofty mountain ranges, which is high above the level of the coastline, and must be many miles inland. It is difficult to say whether this land is more heavily glaciated than that which we have seen to the north ; on the whole, I think the steeper surfaces seem equally bare. There is a consolation for the heavier surface and harder labour we are experiencing in the fact that each day the scene gets more interesting and more beautiful.

'To-day, in lighting the Primus, I very stupidly burnt a hole in the tent; I did not heat the top sufficiently before I began to pump, and a long yellow flame shot up and set light to the canvas. I do not think I should have noticed what had happened at first, but luckily the others were just approaching and rushed forward to prevent further damage. As it was, there was a large hole which poor Shackleton had to make shift to repair during our last lap ; it is not much fun working with a needle in the open at the midnight hours, even though the season happens to be summer.'

'*December* 4.—After a sunshiny day and with the cooler night hours there comes now a regular fall of snow-crystals. On a calm night there is nothing to indicate the falling crystals save a faint haze around the horizon ; overhead it is quite clear. Suddenly, and ap-

parently from nowhere, a small shimmering body floats
gently down in front of one and rests as lightly as thistle-
down on the white surface below. If one stoops to
examine it, as we have done many times, one finds that
it is a six-pointed feathery star, quite flat and smooth on
either side. We find them sometimes as large as a shilling,
and at a short distance they might be small hexagonal
pieces of glass; it is only on looking closely that one dis-
covers the intricate and delicate beauty of their design.

'The effect of these *en masse* is equally wonderful;
they rest in all positions, and therefore receive the
sun's rays at all angles, and in breaking them up reflect
in turn each colour of the spectrum. As one plods along
towards the midnight sun, one's eyes naturally fall on
the plain ahead, and one realises that the simile of a gem-
strewn carpet could never be more aptly employed than
in describing the radiant path of the sun on the snowy
surface. It sparkles with a myriad points of brilliant light,
comprehensive of every colour the rainbow can show,
and is so realistic and near that it often seems one has
but to stoop to pick up some glistening jewel.

'We find a difficulty now in gaining even four
miles a day; the struggle gets harder and harder.
We should not make any progress if we did not pull
hard ourselves; several of the dogs do practically
nothing, and none work without an effort. Slowly but
surely, however, we are " rising " the land. Our *sastrugi*
to-day, from the recent confused state, have developed
into a W.N.W. direction; it looks as though there was a
local wind out of the strait.'

'*December* 5.—At breakfast we decided that our oil is going too fast; there has been some wastage from the capsizing of the sledge, and at first we were far too careless of the amount we used. When we came to look up dates, there was no doubt that in this respect we have outrun the constable. We started with the idea that a gallon was to last twelve days; ours have averaged little over ten. As a result we calculate that those which remain must be made to last fourteen. This is a distinct blow, as we shall have to sacrifice our hot luncheon meal and to economise greatly at both the others. We started the new routine to-night, and for lunch ate some frozen seal-meat and our allowance of sugar and biscuit. The new conditions do not smile on us at present, but I suppose we shall get used to them.

' The events of the day's march are now becoming so dreary and dispiriting that one longs to forget them when we camp; it is an effort even to record them in a diary. To-night has been worse than usual. Our utmost efforts could not produce more than three miles for the whole march, and it would be impossible to describe how tiring the effort was to gain even this small advance. We have an idea we are rising in level slightly, but it is impossible to say so with certainty.

'Shackleton broke the glass of his watch yesterday afternoon; the watch still goes, but one cannot further rely on it, and I am therefore left with the only accurate timekeeper. It is a nuisance to lose a possible check on future observations, but luckily my watch seems to be a very trustworthy instrument; its rate on board the ship

was excellent, and I have no reason to suppose that it
has altered much since we left. My watch was presented to me by Messrs. Smith & Son, of the Strand,
and I believe it to be an exceptionally good one, but
the important observations which we take ought not
to depend on a single watch, and future expeditions
should be supplied with a larger number than we
carry.'

'*December* 6.— . . . A dire calamity to-day. When
I went outside before breakfast I noticed that "Spud"
was absent from his place. I looked round and discovered
him lying on the sledge with his head on the open
mouth of the seal-meat bag ; one glance at his balloon-
like appearance was sufficient to show what had happened. As one contemplated the impossibility of repairing the mischief and of making him restore his ill-gotten
provender, it was impossible not to laugh ; but the matter
is really serious enough : he has made away with quite a
week's allowance of our precious seal-meat. How he
could have swallowed it all is the wonder, yet, though
somewhat sedate and somnolent, he appeared to suffer no
particular discomfort from the enormously increased size
of his waist. We found of course that he had gnawed
through his trace, but the seal-meat bag will be very
carefully closed in future.

'Whilst we were making preparations for a start last
night we were overtaken by a blizzard and had to camp
again in a hurry. The barometer has been falling for
two days, and Wilson has had twinges of rheumatism ;
the former we took for a sign that we were rising in

altitude, but we ought to have been warned by a further drop of two-tenths of an inch whilst we were in camp. The blizzard was ushered in with light flaky snow and an increasing wind, and a quarter of an hour later there was a heavy drift with strong wind. We have been completing our calculations of what is to be left at the depot and what carried on to the south.'

'*December* 8.— . . . Our poor team are going steadily downhill; six or seven scarcely pull at all, perhaps five or six do some steady work, and the remainder make spasmodic efforts. The lightening of the load is more than counterbalanced by the weakening of the animals, and I can see no time in which we can hope to get the sledges along without pulling ourselves. Of late we have altered our marching arrangements; we now take the first half-load on for four miles, then return for the other half, eating our cold luncheon on the way back. To-day it took us three and a half hours to get the advanced load on, and I who remained with it had to wait another five and a half before the others came back—nine hours' work to gain four miles.

' Before supper we all had a wash and brush-up. We each carry a tooth-brush and a pocket-comb, and there is one cake of soap and one pocket looking-glass amongst the party; we use our tooth-brushes fairly frequently, with snow, but the soap and comb are not often in request, and the looking-glass is principally used to dress our mangled lips. Snow and soap are rather a cold compound, but there is freshness in the glowing reaction, and we should probably use them oftener if the

marches were not so tiring.   To-night the tent smells of
soap and hazeline cream.'

'*December* 10.—Yesterday we only covered two miles,
and to get on the second load at all we had to resort to the
ignominious device of carrying food ahead of the dogs.

' "Snatcher" died yesterday; others are getting
feeble—it is terrible to see them.   The coast cannot be
more than ten or twelve miles, but shall we ever reach it?
and in what state shall we be to go on?   The dogs have
had no hesitation in eating their comrade; the majority
clamoured for his flesh this evening, and neglected their
fish in favour of it.   There is the chance that this change
of diet may save the better animals.

'This evening we were surprised by the visit of a
skua gull; even our poor dogs became excited.   We are
nearly 180 miles from any possible feeding-ground it
may have, and it is impossible to say how it found us,
but it is curious that it should have come so soon after
poor "Snatcher" has been cut up.

'*December* 11.—Last night I had a terrible headache
from the hot work in the sun and the closeness of the
tent.   I couldn't sleep for a long time, though we had
the tent open and our bags wide; sleep eventually
banished the headache, and I awoke quite fit.   The
weather has improved, for although still hot a southerly
breeze has cooled the air.   In covering three and a half
miles we have altered several bearings of the land, so
that it cannot now be far off.   As we travel inward the
snow-covered ridges of our cape are blocking out the
higher range to the north.

'About 1 A.M. a bank of stratus cloud came rapidly up from the south ; it looked white and fleecy towards the sun and a peculiar chocolate-brown as it passed to the northward and disappeared. It must have been travelling very fast and about two or three thousand feet above us ; in an hour we had a completely clear sky.

'Hunger is beginning to nip us all, and we have many conversations as to the dainties we could devour if they were within reach.'

'*December* 14.—We have arrived at a place where I think we can depot our dog-food, and none too soon ; I doubt if we could go on another day as we have been going. We have just completed the worst march we have had, and only managed to advance two miles by the most strenuous exertions. The snow grows softer as we approach the land ; the sledge-runners sink from three to four inches, and one's feet well over the ankles at each step. After going a little over a mile things got so bad that we dropped one sledge and pushed on to bring some leading marks in line. Then Shackleton and I brought up the second half-load with the dogs some- how ; after which, leaving the dogs, we all three started back for the sledge that had been dropped. Its weight was only 250 lbs., yet such was the state of the surface that we could not drag it at the rate of a mile an hour.

The air temperature has gone up to + 27°, and it feels hot and stuffy ; the snow surface is + 22°. It would be difficult to convey an idea of what marching is like under present conditions. The heel of the advanced foot is never planted beyond the toe of the other, and of this

small gain with each pace, two or three inches are lost by
back-slipping as the weight is brought forward.   When
we come to any particularly soft patch we do little more
than mark time.

'The bearings of our present position are good but
distant.   To the west we have a conspicuous rocky patch
in line with one of three distant peaks, and to the north
another small patch in line with a curious scar on the
northern range.   The back marks in each case are
perhaps twenty or thirty miles from us, and, though they
will be easy enough to see in clear weather, one cannot
hope to recognise them when it is misty.   It is for this
reason that I propose to-morrow to take our own food,
on which our safety depends, closer in to the land, so
that there may be no chance of our missing it.'

'*December* 15 (3.15 A.M.).—As soon as we had
lightened our load last night we started steering straight
for the rocky patch to the westward.   The sky was
overcast and the light bad, and after proceeding about
a quarter of a mile we found that we were crossing well-
marked undulations.   Still pushing on, we topped a steep
ridge to be fronted by an enormous chasm filled with a
chaotic confusion of ice-blocks.   It was obvious that we
could go no further with the sledges, so we halted and
pitched camp, and after eating our meagre lunch set
forth to explore.   The light was very bad, but we roped
ourselves together, and, taking our only ice-axe and the
meat-chopper, descended cautiously over a steep slope
into the rougher ice below.   Taking advantage of the
snow between the ice-blocks we wended our way amongst

them for some distance, now and again stepping on some treacherous spot and finding ourselves suddenly prone with our legs down a crevasse and very little breath left.

'At first we could get some idea of where these bad places lay, but later the light grew so bad that we came on them quite without warning, and our difficulties were much greater, whilst the huge ice-blocks about us swelled to mountainous size in the grey gloom, and it was obvious that we could make no useful observations in such weather. We stumbled our way back with difficulty, and, cutting steps up the slope, at length caught a welcome view of the camp.

'The dogs were more excited than they have been for many a day; poor things, they must have been quite nonplussed when we suddenly vanished from sight. We can make little out of the chasm so far, except that it quite cuts us off from a nearer approach to the land with our sledges, so that we shall have to depot our own food with the rest of the dog food and trust to fortune to give us clear weather when we return.

'*December* 16.—There was bright, clear sunshine when we awoke yesterday afternoon, and we not only had a good view of the chasm, but Shackleton was able to photograph it. It looks like a great rift in the barrier which has been partly filled up with irregular ice-blocks; from our level to the lowest point in the valley may be about a hundred feet, and the peaks of some of the larger blocks rise almost to our level. The rift is perhaps three-quarters of a mile broad opposite to us, but it seems to narrow towards the south, and there is rather

a suggestion that it ends within a few miles. The
general lie of the rift is N.N.W. and S.S.E.; on the
other side the surface appears to be level again, and
probably it continues so for five or six miles to the land;
however, it is certainly not worth our while to delay
to ascertain this fact. In the sunlight the lights and
shadows of the ice-blocks are in strong contrast, and
where the sun has shone on blue walls, caverns have
been melted and icicles hang over glassy, frozen pools.
We found some of the icicles still dripping.

'Intent on wasting no more of our precious time, we got
back to our depot as quickly as possible, and set about re-
arranging the loads, taking stock, and fixing up the depot.
Whilst we were thus employed a very chill wind came
up from the south, and we did not escape without some
frost-bitten fingers; however, after luncheon we got
away and started head to wind and driving snow at
11 P.M. At midnight I got an altitude which gives the
latitude as 80.30, and at 1.30 we camped, as we have
decided now to start our marches earlier every day until
we get back into day routine.

'As I write I scarcely know how to describe the
blessed relief it is to be free from our relay work. For
one-and-thirty awful days have we been at it, and whilst
I doubt if our human endurance could have stood it much
more, I am quite sure the dogs could not. It seems now
like a nightmare, which grew more and more terrible
towards its end.

'I do not like to think of the difference between
the state of our party now and as it was before we

commenced this dreadful task ; it is almost equally painful to think of the gain, for during all this time we have advanced little more than half a degree of latitude, though I calculate we have covered 330 miles (380 statute miles).

'But it is little use thinking of the past; the great thing is to make the best of the future. We carry with us provisions for four weeks and an odd day or two, a little dog-food, our camp equipment, and, for clothing, exactly what we stand in.

'At the depot, which I have now called Depot " B," we have left three weeks' provision and a quantity of dog-food. This should tide us over the homeward march, so that the present stock can all be expended before we return to Depot " B " ; and all will be well if we can get back within four weeks, and if we have a clear day to find the spot.

'Poor " Vic " was sacrificed to-night for the common good.'

'*December* 17.—We roused out yesterday afternoon at 3 P.M. in very bright sunshine. To our astonishment, a couple of hundred yards behind us lay the end of the chasm which stood between us and the coast ; it gradually narrows to a crevasse, which in places is bridged over with snow, but in others displays a yawning gulf. We must have crossed it within a few feet of such a gulf; our sledge-track could be seen quite clearly leading across the bridge. Not suspecting anything of this sort we were quite regardless of danger during our last march, and unconsciously passed within an ace of destruction. It

certainly has been a very close shave, as we could scarcely
have escaped at the best without broken limbs had we
fallen into the hole, and one doesn't like to contemplate
broken limbs out here.

' This new light on the chasm seems to show that it is
caused by a stream of ice pressing out through the strait
to the north against the main mass of the barrier; this
would naturally have such a rending effect on either side
of the entrance. We have got the dogs on seven miles
to-night; they need a lot of driving, especially as the
surface has become irregular, with wavy undulations. It
is almost impossible to make out how these waves run.
As the chill of the evening comes on now, a mist arises
along the whole coastline and obscures the land; for
this reason we are the more anxious to get back into
day-marches, and we shall make a much earlier start
to-morrow.'

' *December* 18.—Started at 5 P.M. and finished at midnight. The short hours are to get to earlier marches,
but I begin to doubt whether we shall ever be able to
work the dogs for much more than eight hours again;
the poor creatures are generally in a healthier state with
the fresh food, but all are very weak and thin. With
such a load as we now have there would have been no
holding them when we left the ship; as someone said
to-day, " If only we could come across some good, fat
seals, we could camp for a week and start fair again." It
is curious to think that there is possibly not a living thing
within two hundred miles of us. Bad as the dog-driving
is, however, the fact that each mile is an advance, and

E 2

has not to be covered three times, is an inexpressible relief.

'We are gradually passing from the hungry to the ravenous; we cannot drag our thoughts from food, and we talk of little else. The worst times are the later hours of the march and the nights; on the march one sometimes gets almost a sickly feeling from want of food, and the others declare they have an actual gnawing sensation. At night one wakes with the most distressing feeling of emptiness, and then to reflect that there are probably four or five hours more before breakfast is positively dreadful. We have all proved the efficacy of hauling our belts quite tight before we go to sleep, and I have a theory that I am saved some of the worst pangs by my pipe. The others are non-smokers, and, although they do not own it, I often catch a wistful glance directed at my comforting friend; but, alas! two pipes a day do not go far, even on such a journey as ours.'

'*December* 19.—We are now about ten miles from the land, but even at this distance the foothills cut off our view of the higher mountains behind, save to the north and south. Abreast of us the sky-line is not more than three or four thousand feet high, though we know there are loftier peaks behind. The lower country which we see strongly resembles the coastal land far to the north; it is a fine scene of a lofty snow-cap, whose smooth rounded outline is broken by the sharper bared peaks, or by the steep disturbing fall of some valley. Here and there local glaciers descend to barrier level; the coast-line itself winds greatly, forming numerous headlands and bays; we are skirting these and keeping our direct course, a little to the east of south. The coast is fringed with white snow-slopes, glaciers, and broken ice-cascades; but in many places black rocky headlands and precipitous uncovered cliffs serve more clearly to mark its windings. Perhaps one of the most impressive facts is that we see all this above a perfectly level horizon line. Everywhere apparently there is as sharp and definite a line between the land and the level surface of the barrier as exists on an ordinary coastline between land and water. When it becomes at all thick or gloomy the rocks stand out and the white, snowy surfaces recede, giving rise to curious optical illusions. The high, curiously shaped rocky patches seem to be suspended in mid-air; there was one a few days ago, long and flat in shape, which appeared to be so wholly unsupported that it was named "Mahomet's Coffin," but when the weather cleared we could see that the snow about it was really closer than the rock itself.

'Wilson is the most indefatigable person. When it is fine and clear, at the end of our fatiguing days he will spend two or three hours seated in the door of the tent sketching each detail of the splendid mountainous coast-scene to the west. His sketches are most astonishingly accurate; I have tested his proportions by actual angular measurement and found them correct. If the fine weather continues we shall at least have a unique record of this coastline. But these long hours in the glare are very bad for the eyes; we have all suffered a good deal from snow-blindness of late, though we generally march with goggles, but Wilson gets the worst bouts, and I fear it is mainly due to his sketching.

' " Wolf " was the victim to-night. I cannot say " poor ' Wolf,' " for he has been a thorn in the flesh, and has scarcely pulled a pound the whole journey. We have fifteen dogs left, and have decided to devote our energies to the preservation of the nine best; we have done nearly eight miles to-day, but at such an expenditure of energy that I am left in doubt as to whether we should not have done better without any dogs at all.'

' *December* 20.— . . . Poor " Grannie " has been ailing for some time. She dropped to-day. We put her on the sledge, hoping she might recover, and there she breathed her last; she will last the others three days. It is little wonder that we grow more and more sick of our dog-driving.

' The sky has been overcast with low stratus cloud, but it is wonderfully clear below; we have had this sort of weather for some time. One looks aloft and to the east and finds the outlook dull and apparently foggy, when it is surprising to turn to the west and get a comparatively clear view of all the low-lying rocks and snow-slopes which are now ten or a dozen miles from us.

' My tobacco supply is at such " low water " that to-day I have been trying tea-leaves; they can be described as nothing less than horrid.'

' *December* 21.—We are now crossing a deep bay, but the sky is still overcast and our view obscured; the surface was particularly heavy to-day, and our poor dogs had an especially bad time. After a few miles we deter-

mined to stop and go on at night again, as the heat was
very great ; the thermometer showed 27°, but inside the
instrument-box, which is covered with white canvas, it
showed 52°. There must be an astonishing amount of
radiation, even with the sun obscured. Starting again
at 8 P.M., we found that matters were not improved at
all. Very few of the dogs pulled, whilst " Stripes " and
" Brownie " were vomiting. Things began to look very
hopeless, so we thought it would be wise to see what we
could do alone without assistance from our team. We
found that on ski we could just move our own sledges,
but only just ; on foot, after going for ten minutes, we
found we were doing something under a mile an hour,
but only with much exertion. After this experiment we
camped again, and have been discussing matters. We
calculate we were pulling about 170 lbs. per man ;
either the surface is extraordinarily bad or we are growing weak. It is no use blinding ourselves to facts : we
cannot put any further reliance on the dogs. Any day
they might all give out and leave us entirely dependent
on ourselves. In such a case, if things were to remain
just as they are, we should have about as much as we
could do to get home ; on the other hand, will things
remain just as they are ? It seems reasonable to hope
for improvement, we have seen so many changes in
the surface ; at any rate, we have discussed this matter
out, and I am glad to say that all agree in taking the risk
of pushing on.

' Misfortunes never come singly ; since starting we
have always had a regular examination of gums and legs

on Sunday morning, and at first it seemed to show us to
be in a very satisfactory condition of health, but to-night
Wilson told me that Shackleton has decidedly angry-
looking gums, and that for some time they have been
slowly but surely getting worse. He says there is
nothing yet to be alarmed at, but he now thought it
serious enough to tell me in view of our future plans.
We have decided not to tell Shackleton for the present :
it is a matter which must be thought out. Certainly this
is a black night, but things must look blacker yet before
we decide to turn.'

'*December* 22.— . . . This morning we had bright
sunshine and a clear view of the land ; the coastline has
receded some way back in a deep bay, beyond which the
land rises to the magnificent mountain ranges which
evidently form the backbone of the whole continent.
There are no longer high snow-covered foothills to
intercept our view of the loftier background ; it is as
though at this portion of the coast they had been wiped
out as a feature of the country, though farther to the
south where the coastline again advances they seem to
recur.

'But just here we get an excellent view of the
clean-cut mountain range. Abreast of us is the most
splendid specimen of a pyramidal mountain ; it raises a
sharp apex to a height of nine thousand feet or more,
and its precisely carved facets seem to rest on a base of
more irregular country, fully four thousand feet below.
With its extraordinary uniformity and great altitude it is
a wonderfully good landmark. Close to the south of

this is an equally lofty table mountain, the top of which is perfectly flat though dipping slightly towards the north ; this tabular structure is carried on, less perfectly, in other lofty mountain regions to the south ; we have not seen it so well marked on any part of the coast since the land we discovered south of Cape Washington, which seems to indicate some geological alliance with that part. We can now see also the high land that lies beyond the foothills we have lately been skirting ; it is more irregular in outline, with high snow-ridges between the sharper peaks.   To the south one particular conical mountain stands much closer to the coast than the main ranges.   It looks to be of great height, but may not be so distant as we imagine ; it will form our principal land-mark for the next week.   It is noticeable that along all this stretch of coast we can see no deep valley that could contain a glacier from the interior ice-cap (if there is one).

'The beauty of the scene before us is much enhanced when the sun circles low to the south: we get then the most delicate blue shadows and purest tones of pink and violet on the hill-slopes.   There is rarely any intensity of shade—the charm lies in the subtlety and delicacy of the colouring and in the clear softness of the distant outline.

'We have decided to cease using our bacon and to increase the seal allowance, as the former seems the most likely cause of the scurvy symptoms.   To Shackleton it was represented as a preventive measure, but I am not sure that he does not smell a rat.   The exchange is not quite equal in weight ; we again lose a little.   We cannot

certainly afford to lose more, as we are already reduced
to starvation rations.   Our allowance on leaving the
ship ran to about 1·9 lb. per man per day, but various
causes have reduced this.   At first we went too heavy
on our biscuit ; then we determined to lay by two extra
weeks out of eleven ; then " Spud " had his share of the
seal-meat bag ; altogether I calculate we are existing on
about a pound and a half of food a day ; it is not enough,
and hunger is gripping us very tightly.   I never knew
what it was like before, and I shall not be particularly
keen on trying it again.

' Our meals come regularly enough, but they are the
poorest stop-gaps, both from want of food and want of
fuel.   At breakfast now we first make tea—that is to say,
we put the tea in long before the water boils, and lift
and pour out with the first bubbling.   The moment this
is over we heap the pemmican and biscuit into the pot
and make what we call a " fry "; it takes much less time
than a *hoosh*.   The cook works by the watch, and in
twenty minutes from the time it is lighted the Primus
lamp is out ; in two or three more the breakfast is
finished.   Then we serve out luncheon, which consists of
a small piece of seal-meat, half a biscuit, and eight to
ten lumps of sugar.   Each of us keeps a small bag
which, when it contains the precious luncheon, is stowed
away in the warmth of a breast pocket, where it thaws
out during the first march.   Absurd as it may sound,
it is terribly difficult not to filch from this bag during
the hours of the march.   We have become absolutely
childish in this.   We know so perfectly the contents of

the bags that one will find oneself arguing that to-day's
piece of seal is half an inch longer than yesterday's ; *ergo,*
if one nibbles half an inch off, one will still have the
same lunch as yesterday.

'Supper is of course the best meal ; we then have a
hoosh which runs from between three-quarters to a
whole pannikin apiece, but even at this we cannot afford
to make it thick.   Whilst it is being heated in the central cooker, cocoa is made in the outer.   The lamp is
turned out directly the *hoosh* boils, usually from twenty-
eight to thirty-minutes after it has been lighted ; by
this time the chill is barely off the contents of the
outer cooker, and of course the cocoa is not properly dissolved, but such as it is, it is the only drink we can
afford.   We have long ceased criticising the quality of
our food ; all we clamour for now is something to fill up,
but, needless to say, we never get it.   Half an hour after
supper one seems as hard set as ever.

'My companions get very bad " food dreams "; in fact,
these have become the regular breakfast conversation.
It appears to be a sort of nightmare; they are either
sitting at a well-spread table with their arms tied, or they
grasp at a dish and it slips out of their hand, or they are
in the act of lifting a dainty morsel to their mouth when
they fall over a precipice.   Whatever the details may be,
something interferes at the last moment and they wake.
So far, I have not had these dreams myself, but I suppose they will come.

'When we started from the ship we had a sort of
idea that we could go as we pleased with regard to food,

hauling in automatically if things were going too fast; but we soon found that this would not do at all—there must be some rigid system of shares. After this we used to take it in turns to divide things into three equal portions; it is not an easy thing to do by eye, and of course the man who made the division felt called upon to make certain that he had the smallest share. It was when we found that this led to all sorts of absurd remonstrances and arguments that Shackleton invented the noble game of " shut-eye," which has solved all our difficulties in this respect. The shares are divided as equally as possible by anyone; then one of the other two turns his head away, the divider points at a " whack " and says, " Whose is this ? " He of the averted head names the owner, and so on. It is a very simple but very efficacious game, as it leaves the matter entirely to chance. We play it at every meal now as a matter of course, and from practice we do it very speedily; but one cannot help thinking how queer it would appear for a casual onlooker to see three civilised beings employed at it.'

' *December* 23.—We have been getting on rather faster than we thought, though we had a suspicion that the sledge-meter was clogging in the very soft snow. Our latitude is now about $81\frac{1}{2}°$ S. To-day I had to shift the balance-weight on the theodolite compass needle; the dip must be decreasing rapidly. Theodolite observations are now difficult, as the tripod legs cannot be solidly planted. I find it a good plan to leave it up for the night, as in the morning there is always a little cake of ice under each leg. The surface is so soft that one can push the shaft of the ice-axe down with a finger.

'The dogs of course feel it much, but the leaders have the worst time, for they have to make the foot-prints ; the others step carefully into them, and are saved the trouble of making their own. Several times lately, and especially to-day, the dogs have raised their heads together and sniffed at the breeze ; with a northerly wind one might suppose that their keen scent might detect something, but it is difficult to imagine what they can find in air coming from the south. Shackleton, who always declares that he believes there is either open water or an oasis ahead, says that the dogs merely confirm his opinion.

'We felt the chill wind in our faces much, owing to their very blistered state. We have especial trouble with our nostrils and lips, which are always bare of skin ; all our fingers, too, are in a very chapped, cracked condition. We have to be very economical with our eyes also, after frequent attacks of snow-blindness ; all three of us to-day had one eye completely shaded, and could see only by peering with the other through a goggle. But all our ailments together are as nothing beside our hunger, which gets steadily worse day by day.'

'*December* 24.—Wilson examined us again this morning. I asked him quietly the result, and he said, " A little more." It is trying, but we both agree that it is not time yet to say " Turn." But we have one fact to comfort us to-night—we have passed on to a much harder surface, and though it still holds a layer of an inch or

two of feathery snow, beneath that it is comparatively
firm, and we are encamped on quite a hard spot; the
sastrugi are all from the S.S.E. parallel to the land. If
the dogs have not improved, they have not grown much
worse during the past day or two; their relative strength
alters a good deal, as the following tale will show:
" Stripes " and " Gus " pull next one another; a week
ago one had great difficulty in preventing " Stripes "
from leaping across and seizing " Gus's " food. He was
very cunning about it; he waited till one's back was
turned, and then was over and back in a moment. Time
has its revenges: now " Gus " is the stronger, and to-
night he leapt across and seized " Stripes' " choicest
morsel. At other times they are not bad friends these
two; loser and winner seem to regard this sort of thing
as part of the game. After all, it is but "the good old
rule, the simple plan," but of course we right matters
when we detect such thefts.

    ' To-night is Christmas Eve. We have been think-
ing and talking about the folk at home, and also much
about our plans for to-morrow.'

    '*December* 25, *Christmas Day.*— . . . For a week
we have looked forward to this day with childish delight,
and, long before that, we decided that it would be a
crime to go to bed hungry on Christmas night; so the
week went in planning a gorgeous feed. Each meal
and each item of each meal we discussed and rediscussed. The breakfast was to be a glorious spread; the
Primus was to be kept going ten or even fifteen minutes
longer than usual. Lunch for once was to be warm and

comforting ; and supper !—well, supper was to be what supper has been.

'In fact, we meant this to be a wonderful day, and everything has conspired to make it so.

'When we awoke to wish each other "A merry Christmas" the sun was shining warmly through our green canvas roof. We were outside in a twinkling, to find the sky gloriously clear and bright, with not a single cloud in its vast arch. Away to the westward stretched the long line of gleaming coastline ; the sunlight danced and sparkled in the snow beneath our feet, and not a breath of wind disturbed the serenity of the scene. It was a glorious morning, but we did not stay to contemplate it, for we had even more interesting facts to occupy us, and were soon inside the tent sniffing at the savoury steam of the cooking-pot. Then breakfast was ready, and before each of us lay a whole pannikin-full of biscuit and seal-liver, fried in bacon and pemmican fat. It was gone in no time, but this and a large spoonful of jam to follow left a sense of comfort which we had not experienced for weeks, and we started to pack up in a frame of mind that was wholly joyful.

'After this we started on the march, and felt at once the improvement of surface that came to us last night ; so great was it that we found we three alone could draw the sledges, and for once the driver was silent and the whip but rarely applied. The dogs merely walked along with slack traces, and we did not attempt to get more out of them. No doubt an outsider would have thought our procession funereal enough, but to us the relief was inexpressible ;

and so we trudged on from 11.30 to 4 P.M., when we
thoroughly enjoyed our lunch, which consisted of hot
cocoa and plasmon with a whole biscuit and another
spoonful of jam.   We were off again at 5.30, and marched
on till 8.30, when we camped in warmth and comfort and
with the additional satisfaction of having covered nearly
eleven miles, the longest march we have made for a long
time.

'Then we laid ourselves out for supper, reckless of consequences, having first had a Christmas wash and brush-
up.   Redolent of soap, we sat around the cooking-pot,
whilst into its boiling contents was poured a double
"whack" of everything.   In the *hoosh* that followed
one could stand one's spoon with ease, and still the
Primus hissed on, as once again our cocoa was brought
to the boiling-point.   Meanwhile I had observed Shackleton ferreting about in his bundle, out of which he presently produced a spare sock, and stowed away in the
toe of that sock was a small round object about the size
of a cricket ball, which, when brought to light, proved
to be a noble "plum-pudding."   Another dive into his
lucky-bag and out came a crumpled piece of artificial
holly.   Heated in the cocoa, our plum-pudding was soon
steaming hot, and stood on the cooker-lid crowned with
its decoration.   For once we divided food without
"shut-eye."

'I am writing over my second pipe.   The sun is still
slowly circling our small tent in a cloudless sky, the air
is warm and quiet, all is pleasant without, and within we
have a sense of comfort we have not known for many

a day; we shall sleep well to-night—no dreams, no tightening of the belt.

'We have been chattering away gaily, and not once has the conversation turned to food.   We have been wondering what Christmas is like in England—possibly very damp, gloomy, and unpleasant, we think ; we have been wondering, too, how our friends picture us.   They will guess that we are away on our sledge journey, and will perhaps think of us on plains of snow ; but few, I think, will imagine the truth, that for us this has been the reddest of all red-letter days.'

CHAPTER XIV

RETURN FROM THE FAR SOUTH

Result of Shortage of Food—Nature of the Coastline—Snow-blindness—
Approaching the Limit of our Journey—View to the South—New Moun-
tains—Blizzard at our Extreme South—Turning Homeward—Attempt to
Reach the Land—The Passing of our Dog Team—Help from our Sail—
Difficult Surfaces—Running before a Storm—Finding Depot 'B'—Scurvy
Again—Shackleton Becomes Ill—The Last of our Dog Team—Bad Light
for Steering—Anxious Days—Depot 'A'—Over-eating—The Last Lap—
Home Again— Our Welcome.

> How many weary steps
> Of many weary miles you have o'ergone,
> Are numbered to the travel of one mile.
>   SHAKESPEARE.

' An' we talks about our rations and a lot of other things.'
                                        KIPLING.

OUR Christmas Day had proved a delightful break in the
otherwise uninterrupted spell of semi-starvation. Some
days elapsed before its pleasing effects wore off, and for
long it remained green in our memories. We knew by
this time that we had cut ourselves too short in the
matter of food, but it was too late to alter our arrangements now without curtailing our journey, and we all
decided that, sooner than do the latter, we would cheerfully face the pangs that our too meagre fare would cost.

Looking back now on the incidents of this journey,
the original mistake is evident, and even at the time,

apart from the physical distress which it caused us, it is clear that we suspected, what was indeed the case, that we were slowly but surely sapping our energies and reducing ourselves to the condition of our more willing dogs, who, with every desire to throw their weight on the traces, were incapable of doing so. Of course we never sank into the deplorable state of these poor animals, but there is no doubt that from this time on we were gradually wearing out, and the increasing weariness of the homeward marches showed that we were expending our energies at a greater rate than we were able to renew them with our inadequate supply of food, and thus drawing on a capital stock which must obviously have restricted limits.

Such a state of affairs is, as I have pointed out elsewhere, a false economy, and the additional weight which we should have carried in taking a proper allowance of food would have amply repaid us on this occasion by the maintenance of our full vigour.

A shortage of food has another great disadvantage which we experienced to the full : our exceptionally hungry condition caused our thoughts and conversation to run in a groove from which it was almost impossible to lift them. We knew perfectly well how ridiculous this was, and appreciated that it was likely to increase rather than diminish the evil, but we seemed powerless to prevent it. After supper, and before its pleasing effects had passed, some detachment was possible, and for half an hour or more a desultory conversation would be maintained concerning far-removed subjects; but it was ludicrous to observe the manner in which remarks gradually crept back to the old channel, and it was odds that before we slept each one of us gave, all over again, a detailed description of what he would now consider an ideal feast.

On the march it was even worse; one's thoughts were reduced to the most trivial details of the one unsatisfying subject. One would find oneself calculating how many footsteps went to the minute, and how many, therefore, must be paced before lunch; then, with a sinking heart, one would begin to count them, suddenly lose count, and find oneself mentally scanning the contents of the pemmican bag and wondering exactly how much could be allowed for to-night's *hoosh*. This would lead to the stock of pemmican on board the ship, and a recollection of the gorgeous yellow fat with which it was incorporated; the ship would recall feasts of seal, thick soup, and thicker porridge, and on one would speed to the recollection of special nights when our fare had been still more bountiful, and on again to all the resources of civilised life: the farewell dinner at So-and-so, what would it be like if it was spread out here on the barrier? One remembers declining a particularly succulent dish; what an extraordinary thing to do! What a different being one must have been in those days! And so one's thoughts travelled on from place to place, but always through the one medium of creature comfort.

It is natural that a diary kept through these long weeks should have reflected the subject that most fully occupied our thoughts and our conversation, and, as the

weakness of the dogs curtailed our marches and left
ample time for writing, I find copious allusions to the
somewhat distressing circumstances which attended our
experiences in this respect.

But it must not be supposed that we were wholly
absorbed by this subject ; if there were trials and tribula-
tions in our daily life at this time, there were also com-
pensating circumstances whose import we fully realised.
Day by day, as we journeyed on, we knew we were
penetrating farther and farther into the unknown ; each
footstep was a gain, and made the result of our labour
more solid. It would be difficult to describe with what
eagerness we studied the slowly revolving sledge-meter,
or looked for the calculated results of our observations,
while ever before our eyes was the line which we were
now drawing on the white space of the Antarctic chart.
Day by day, too, though somewhat slowly, there passed on
that magnificent panorama of the western land. Rarely
a march passed without the disclosure of some new feature, something on which the eye of man had never
yet rested ; we should have been poor souls indeed had
we not been elated at the privilege of being the first to
gaze on these splendid scenes.

On December 26 we had another brilliant, calm and
cloudless day, with a clear view to the west ; the coastal
ice-cape again obscured our view of the higher ranges
behind, but now it rose to a more considerable altitude,
being at least three or four thousand feet above our
level ; it undulated in long sweeping curves, with here
and there a black jagged outcrop of rock, and elsewhere

a steep crevassed fall. Our track had been taking us close
to the coast, and as we had skirted along, past pointed
snow-capes and rocky headlands, we had gradually
blocked out the remarkable tabular and pyramidal
mountains which had been abreast of us a week before ; behind us also we had left the sharp conical
peak which had been our principal landmark for many
days.

When, far to the north, we had first seen this mountain, we had exaggerated both height and distance,
and when things had gone badly with us we had wondered
if our fortunes would ever allow us to pass it. On Christmas Day, however, we were abreast of it, and though I
calculated its height to be under seven thousand feet,
this was no mean altitude for so remarkable a peak.
Since in preserving its uniform, sharp, conical appearance, it was still the most salient feature in our view,
we dubbed it 'Christmas Mountain' in honour of the
day. We passed within eighteen miles of it, according
to my calculations, and by the 26th it was 'abaft the
beam.' Whilst still retaining its pointed appearance, it
seemed from this new aspect to have assumed a certain
resemblance to the higher pyramidal hills of the north.

Perhaps the most interesting part of our view just at
this time was the coastline itself. We were from eight
to ten miles from it, and at such a distance one could
see very distinctly in that clear air ; it was comparatively
steep all along—that is to say, the undulating ice-cap fell
gradually to a height of one or two thousand feet and
then abruptly to the barrier level. In a few places this

fall was taken by steep but comparatively smooth snow-slopes, in others the snow seemed to pour over in beautiful cascades of immense ice-blocks, and in others, again, the coast was fringed by huge perpendicular cliffs of bare rock.   On this day we were abreast of the highest cliffs we had seen, and my angles, roughly computed, gave a height of 1,800 feet between their base and the white snow-line on top, and they were so impressive even in the distance that I cannot believe them to have been much under.   In many places the rock-face must have been sheer to this great height, for where it fell away a white splash showed where the snow had found lodgment.

Even at a distance of ten miles these cliffs were magnificent, and how grand they would have appeared had we been able to get close beneath them we could well imagine.   In colour they were a rich, deep red, though a little further to the south this rock was confusingly bedded with a darker, almost black one ; this alternation of black and red occurred along the whole coast south of our position at this time, always in the same irregular fashion, but always with a definite line between the red and the black.   At this time we were all under the impression that these rocks were of the same recent volcanic nature as those about the ship, but later on, after my visit to the western hills, I came to doubt this belief. It is possible that if at this time we had known more of the structure of the mainland to the north we should have been able to note points of similarity or difference which threw more light on this southern land, but it is doubtful whether in any case we could have discovered much that was definite at the distance from which we saw it.

It can be imagined that as we travelled onward our eyes were most frequently lifted towards the south. It is always bewildering to look along a coastline at such an oblique angle. Shortly before this the south had meant a long succession of dark rock-masses and hazy snow-capes, but during the last few days we had 'risen' a feature of noticeable distinction, and now we knew that we looked on a lofty mountain whose eastern slopes fell to the long snow-cape which for the present bounded our view.

The very gradual unfolding of its details told us that this mass of land was both distant and lofty, and as we approached the limit of safe endeavour we knew that here was an object that we could not hope to reach ; though we might approach it by many miles and be able to examine it with care, we should never know definitely what lay beyond. We felt that it was the most southerly land to which we should be able to apply a name, and we thought that the fine peak which for the present must remain the southerly outpost of all known lands could bear no more fitting title than one derived from the contributor whose generous donation had alone made our expedition possible. On the night of the 26th, therefore, we christened this distant peak 'Mount Long-staff,' but it was only on our return to the ship that I was able to fix its position as well beyond the 83rd parallel.

From a point of view of further exploration our position on the 26th did not promise great things. On our
right lay the high undulating snow-cap and the steep
irregular coastline; to the south lay a cape, beyond
which we could not hope to pass ; and to all appearance
these conditions must remain unaltered to the end of our
journey. We argued, however, that one never knows what
may turn up, and we determined, in spite of the unpromising outlook, to push on to our utmost limit. As
events proved, we argued most wisely, for had we turned
at this point we should have missed one of the most important features of the whole coastline ; it was only one
more instance of the happening of the unexpected.

In spite of the comforting nature of our Christmas
festivities, worry was never long absent from what was
now becoming rather a forlorn party, as the following
extract shows :

'*December* 26.— . . . Poor Wilson has had an attack
of snow-blindness, in comparison with which our former
attacks may be considered as nothing ; we were forced to
camp early on account of it, and during the whole afternoon he has been writhing in horrible agony. It is
distressing enough to see, knowing that one can do
nothing to help. Cocaine has only a very temporary
effect, and in the end seems to make matters worse. I
have never seen an eye so terribly bloodshot and inflamed
as that which is causing the trouble, and the inflammation
has spread to the eyelid. He describes the worst part as
an almost intolerable stabbing and burning of the eye-
ball ; it is the nearest approach to illness we have had,

and one can only hope that it is not going to remain serious.

'Shackleton did butcher to-night, and "Brownie" was victim. Poor little dog! his life has been very careworn of late, and it is probably a happy release.'

'*December* 27.—Late last night Wilson got some sleep, and this morning he was better; all day he has been pulling alongside the sledges with his eyes completely covered. It is tiresome enough to see our snowy world through the slit of a goggle, but to march blindfolded with an empty stomach for long hours touches a pitch of monotony which I shall be glad to avoid. We covered a good ten miles to-day by sledge-meter, though I think that instrument is clogging and showing short measure. The dogs have done little, but they have all walked, except "Stripes," who broke down and had to be carried on the sledge; he was quite limp when I picked him up, and his thick coat poorly hides the fact that he is nothing but skin and bone. Yesterday I noticed that we were approaching what appeared to be a deeper bay than usual, and this afternoon this opening developed in the most interesting manner.

'On the near side is a bold, rocky, snow-covered cape, and all day we have been drawing abreast of this; as we rapidly altered its bearing this afternoon it seemed to roll back like some vast sliding gate, and gradually there stood revealed one of the most glorious mountain scenes we have yet witnessed. Walking opposite to Wilson I was trying to keep him posted with regard to the changes, and I think my reports of this part must have sounded curious. It was with some excitement I noticed that new mountain ridges were appearing as high as anything we had seen to the north, but, to my surprise, as we advanced the ridges grew still higher, as no doubt did my tones. Then, instead of a downward turn in the distant outline came a steep upward line ; Pelion was heaped on Ossa, and it can be imagined that we pressed the pace to see what would happen next, till the end came in a gloriously sharp double peak crowned with a few flecks of cirrus cloud.

'We can no longer call this opening a bay ; it runs for many miles in to the foot of the great range, and is more in the nature of an inlet. But all our thoughts in camp to-night turn to this splendid twin-peaked mountain which, even in such a lofty country, seems as a giant among pigmies. We all agree that from Sabine to the south the grandest eminences cannot compare in dignity with this monster. We have decided that at last we have found something which is fitting to bear the name of him whom we must always the most delight to honour, and "Mount Markham" it shall be called in memory of the father of the expedition.'

'*December* 28.—Sights to-day put us well over the 82nd parallel (82.11 S.). We have almost shot our bolt. If the weather holds fine to-morrow, we intend to drop our sledges at the midday halt and push on as far as possible on ski. We stopped early this afternoon in order to take photographs and make sketches. Wilson, in spite of his recent experiences, refuses to give in ; whatever is left unsketched, and however his eyes may suffer, this last part must be done.

'It is a glorious evening, and fortune could not have provided us with a more perfect view of our surroundings. We are looking up a broad, deep inlet or strait which stretches away to the south-west for thirty or forty miles before it reaches its boundary of cliff and snow-slope. Beyond, rising fold on fold, are the great névé fields that clothe the distant range; against the pale blue sky the outline of the mountain ridge rises and falls over numerous peaks till, with a sharp turn upward, it culminates in the lofty summit of Mount Markham. To the north it descends again, to be lost behind the bluff extremity of the near cape. It seems more than likely that the vast inlet before us takes a sharp turn to the right beyond the cape and in front of the mountains, and we hope to determine this fact to-morrow.

'The eastern foothills of the high range form the southern limit of the strait; they are fringed with high cliffs and steep snow-slopes, and even at this distance we can see that some of the rocks are of the deep-red colour, whilst others are black. Between the high range and the barrier there must lie immense undulating snow-plateaux covering the lesser foothills, which seem rather to increase in height to the left until they fall sharply to the barrier level almost due south of us.

'To the eastward of this, again, we get our view to the farthest south, and we have been studying it again and again to gather fresh information with the changing bearings of the sun. Mount Longstaff we calculate as 10,000 feet. It is formed by the meeting of two long and comparatively regular slopes; that to the east stretches out into the barrier and ends in a long snow-cape which bears about S. 14 E. ; that to the west is lost behind the nearer foothills, but now fresh features have developed about these slopes. Over the western ridge can be seen two new peaks which must lie considerably to the south of the mountain, and, more interesting still, beyond the eastern cape we catch a glimpse of an extended coastline ; the land is thrown up by mirage and appears in small white patches against a pale sky.

' We know well this appearance of a snow-covered country ; it is the normal view in these regions of a very distant lofty land, and it indicates with certainty that a mountainous country continues beyond Mount Longstaff for nearly fifty miles. The direction of the extreme land thrown up in this manner is S. 17 E., and hence we can now say with certainty that the coastline àfter passing Mount Longstaff continues in this direction for at least a degree of latitude. Of course one cannot add that the level barrier surface likewise continues, as one's view of it is limited to a very narrow horizon ; but anyone who had travelled over it as we have done, and who now, like us, could gaze on these distant lands beyond its level margin, could have little doubt that it does so.

' It is fortunate to have had such glorious weather to give us a clear view of this magnificent scene, for very soon now we must be turning, and though we may advance a few miles we cannot hope to add largely to our store of information.

' It has been a busy evening, what with taking

angles, sketching, and attending to our camp duties, but hours so full of interest have passed rapidly ; and now the sun is well to the south, and from all the coast is rising the thin night mist exactly as it does after a hot day in England, so we are preparing to settle down in our sleeping-bags, in the hope that to-morrow may prove equally fine.

'A great relief comes to us in this distant spot at finding that our slight change of diet is already giving a beneficial result ; late to-night we had another examina tion of our scurvy symptoms, and there is now no doubt that they are lessening.'

' *December* 29.—Instead of our proposed advance we have spent the day in our tent, whilst a strong southerly blizzard has raged without. It is very trying to the patience, and to-night, though the wind has dropped, the old well-known sheet of stratus cloud is closing over us, and there is every prospect of another spell of overcast weather which will obscure the land. This afternoon for the third time we have seen the heavens traced with bands and circles of prismatic light, and, if anything, the phenomenon has been more complicated than before ; it was a very beautiful sight.

' Only occasionally to-day have we caught glimpses of the land, and it is not inspiriting to lie hour after hour in a sleeping-bag, chill and hungry, and with the knowledge that one is so far from the region of plenty.'

' *December* 30.—We got up at six this morning, to find a thick fog and nothing in sight ; to leave the camp was out of the question, so we packed up our traps and

started to march to the S.S.W. This brought us
directly towards the mouth of the strait, and after an
hour we found ourselves travelling over a disturbed surface with numerous cracks which seemed to radiate from
the cape we were rounding. After stumbling on for
some time, the disturbance became so great that we
were obliged to camp. If the fates are kind and give us
another view of the land, we are far enough advanced
now to see the inner recesses of our strait.

' After our modest lunch Wilson and I started off on
ski to the S.S.W. We lost sight of the camp almost
immediately, and were left with only our tracks to guide
us back to it, but we pushed on for perhaps a mile or
more in hopes that the weather would clear ; then, as
there was no sign of this, and we could see little more
than a hundred yards, we realised there might be considerable risk and could be no advantage in proceeding,
and so turned and retraced our footsteps to the camp.

' This camp we have now decided must be our last,
for we have less than a fortnight's provision to take us
back to Depot " B," and with the dogs in their present
state it would be impossible to make forced marches ; we
have, therefore, reached our southerly limit. Observations give it as between 82.16 S. and 82.17 S. ; if this
compares poorly with our hopes and expectations on
leaving the ship, it is a more favourable result than we
anticipated when those hopes were first blighted by the
failure of the dog team.

' Whilst one cannot help a deep sense of disappointment in reflecting on the " might have been " had our

team remained in good health, one cannot but remember that even as it is we have made a greater advance towards a pole of the earth than has ever yet been achieved by a sledge party.

'We feel a little inclined to grumble at the thick weather that surrounds us ; it has a depressing effect, and in our state of hunger we feel the cold though the temperature is $+15°$; but we must not forget that we had great luck in the fine weather which gave us such a clear view of the land two days ago.'

'*December* 31.—As we rose this morning the sun was still obscured by low stratus cloud, which rapidly rolled away, however ; first the headlands and then the mountains stood out, and we could see that we had achieved our object of yesterday in opening out the inlet ; but in this direction the cloud continued to hang persistently, so that it was to little purpose that we had obtained such a position. We could see now that the inlet certainly turned to the north of west ; on either side the irregular outlines of the mountains were clear against a blue sky and, descending gradually towards the level, left a broad gap between, but low in this gap hung the tantalising bank of fog, screening all that lay beyond. By turning towards the strait we had partly obscured our clear view of Mount Longstaff and quite cut off the miraged images of the more distant land, but we had approached the high cliffs which formed the southern limit of the strait, and in the morning sun could clearly see the irregular distribution of red and black rock in the steep cliff faces.

' In hope that the fog-bank to the west would clear, we proceeded with our packing in a leisurely manner, and when all was ready, turned our faces homewards. It was significant of the terrible condition of our team that the turn produced no excitement. It appears to make no difference to them now in which direction they bend their weary footsteps ; it almost seems that most of them guess how poor a chance they have of ever seeing the ship again. And so we started our homeward march, slowly at first, and then more briskly as we realised that all chance of a clearance over the strait was gone.

' In the flood of sunlight which now illumined the snow about us, we were able to see something of the vast ice upheavals caused by the outflow of ice from the strait ; pushing around the cape, it is raised in undulations which seem to run parallel to the land. We directed our course towards the cape with the hopes of getting to the land, but were obliged to keep outwards to avoid the worst disturbances ; this brought us obliquely across the undulation, and as we travelled onward they rose in height and became ridged and broken on the summit. Now, too, we came upon numerous crevasses which appeared to extend radially from the cape, and these, with the cracks and ridges, formed a network of obstruction across our path through which we were forced to take a very winding course.

' We extended our march until we had passed the worst of this disturbance, and by that time we were well to the north of the cape and abreast of one of the curious rocky groins that occur at intervals along the coast. This showed samples of both the red and the black rock, which seem to constitute the geological structure of the whole coast, and we decided to pitch our camp and make an excursion to the land on our ski. By the time that we had swallowed our luncheon the clouds had rolled away, leaving us in the same brilliant sunshine that we have enjoyed so frequently of late, and in which even at a distance of five or six miles every detail of the high groin could be distinctly seen.

' Not knowing what adventures we might encounter, we thought it wise to provide ourselves with a second luncheon, which we safely stowed in our breast pockets, and taking our ice-axe and Alpine rope, we set out for the shore. It looked deceptively near, nor was it until we had marched for nearly an hour without making any marked difference in its appearance that we realised we were in for a long job.

' By this time we were again crossing long undulations which increased in height as we advanced ; soon from the summits of the waves we could see signs of greater disturbances ahead, and at five o'clock we found ourselves at the edge of a chasm resembling that which had prevented us from reaching the shore farther to the north. This was not an encouraging spectacle, but on the opposite side, a mile or so away, we could see that a gentle slope led to the rocks, and that once across this disturbance we should have no difficulty in proceeding. On the near side the spaces between the ice-blocks had been much drifted up with snow, so that we found no great difficulty in descending or in starting our climb amongst the ice-blocks ; but as we advanced the snow became lighter and the climbing steeper. We could get no hold with our finneskoes on the harder places, and in the softer we sank knee-deep, whilst the lightly-bridged crevasses became more difficult to avoid, and once or twice we were only saved from a bad fall by the fact of being roped together. Constantly after circling a large block with difficulty we found in front of us some unclimbable place, and were obliged to retrace our steps and try in some new direction ; but we now knew that we must be approaching the opposite side, and so we struggled on.

'At length, however, when we thought our troubles must surely be ending, we cut steps around a sharp corner to find the opposite bank of the chasm close to us, but instead of the rough slopes by which we had descended, we found here a steep, overhanging face of ice, towering some fifty feet above us. To climb this face was obviously impossible, and we were reluctantly forced to confess that all our trouble had been in vain. It was a great disappointment, as we had confidently hoped to get some rock specimens from this far south land, and now I do not see that we shall have a chance to do so.

'Before starting our homeward climb we sat down to rest, and, of course, someone mentioned the provisions —it was to-morrow's lunch that we carried—and some-one else added that it would be absurd to take it back to the camp. Then the temptation became too great ; though we knew it was wrong, our famished condition

G 2

swept us away, and in five minutes not a remnant remained. After this we started our return climb, and at ten o'clock we reached the camp pretty well " done."

'There can be little doubt, I think, that the chasm we have seen to-day is caused by the ice pushing out of the southern strait against the barrier, and possibly it may end a little farther to the north, but I could not see any signs of its ending ; the blocks of ice within seem to have been split off from the sloping ice-foot—in fact, we saw some in the process of being broken away—and the fact that there is so much less snow towards the land seems to show that the inner ones are of more recent origin. The ice-foot is fed by the ice-cap on the hills above, which at this part flows over in a steep cascade. I do not see that we can make another attempt to reach the land before we get back to Depot " B " ; in fact, we shall have none too easy a task in doing that alone. We shall have to average more than seven miles a day, and the dogs are now practically useless ; but, what is worse, I cannot help feeling that we ourselves are not so strong as we were. Our walk to-day has tired us more than it ought.

'To-night Shackleton upset the *hoosh* pot. There was an awful moment when we thought some of it was going to run away on to the snow ; luckily it all remained on our waterproof floorcloth, and by the time we had done scraping I do not think that any was wasted.'

'*January* 1, 1903.—We have opened the new year with a march which is likely to be a sample of those which will follow for many a day to come. The state of our dog team is now quite pitiable ; with a very few exceptions they cannot pretend to pull; at the start of the march some have to be lifted on to their feet and held up for a minute or two before their limbs become stiff enough to support them. Poor " Spud " fell in his tracks to-day; we carried him for a long way on the sledge, and then tried him once more, but he fell again, and had to be carried for the rest of the journey tucked away inside the canvas tank. Towards the end of our day's march it has always been possible to get a semblance of spirit into our poor animals by saying, " Up for supper." They learnt early what the words meant, and it has generally been " Spud " who gave the first responsive whimper. This afternoon it was most pathetic; the cheering shout for the last half-mile was raised as usual, but there was no response, until suddenly from the interior of the sledge-tank came the muffled ghost of a whimper. It was " Spud's " last effort: on halting we carried him back to his place, but in an hour he was dead.

' The whole team are in a truly lamentable condition ; " Gus " and " Bismarck " are tottering; " Lewis " and " Birdie " may fail any moment; " Jim " is probably the strongest—he had reserves of fat to draw on, and has been a great thief; " Nigger " is something of a mystery : he is weak, but not reduced to the same straits as the others, and seems capable of surprising efforts.

' This afternoon a southerly breeze sprang up, and we improvised a sail out of our tent floorcloth ; it makes an excellent spread of canvas. Some time ago I fixed up our bamboo mast as a permanency by stepping it in the runner and binding it with wire to one of the standards.

On this we hoisted our sail, spreading it with two bamboo ski-poles.   This evening we saw the last of Mount Markham, and Mount Longstaff is already growing small in the distance.'

'*January* 3.—We are not finding our homeward march so easy as we expected, and we are not clearing a large margin over the distances which are actually necessary for each day ; it is plain that if there are blizzards now we must go on right through them.   But to-day we have done rather better than before.   This morning there was a hot sun, which brought the snow-surface nearly up to freezing-point, and we found the sledge drew easily. This afternoon there was a fresh breeze, when we got a great deal of help from our sail.   The dogs have not pulled throughout the day—we do not expect it of them now—and this afternoon Shackleton was ahead dragging on those who could not walk.   Wilson was carrying their long trace in rear to prevent it getting foul of the sledges, whilst I was employed in keeping the latter straight before the wind and in helping them over the rough places ; the sail did most of the pulling.   We have only two sledges left now, as we find this is sufficient to carry our much-lightened load.

'To walk eight or nine miles in a day does not sound much of a task for even a tired dog, yet it is too much for ours, and they are dropping daily.   Yesterday poor little " Nell " fell on the march, tried to rise, and fell again, looking round with a most pathetic expression.   She was carried till the night, but this morning was as bad as ever, and at lunch-time was put out of her misery.   This

afternoon, shortly after starting, "Gus" fell, quite played
out, and just before our halt, to our greater grief, "Kid"
caved in. One could almost weep over this last case; he
has pulled like a Trojan throughout, and his stout little
heart bore him up till his legs failed beneath him, and he
fell never to rise again.

'It is useless to carry all this dog-food, so we have
decided to serve it out freely, and the seven animals that
remain are now lying about quite replete; at any rate,
poor things, they will not die of starvation.

'Save for a glimpse of the sun this morning, a high
stratus cloud has hung over us all day. We see the land,
but not very clearly; we are inside our course in passing
down the coast, and about ten miles from the remarkable
cliffs we then noticed. To the north-west we recognise
well-known landmarks. In spite of our troubles we
managed to keep going for seven hours to-day, but we
feel that this is the utmost that we can do at present owing
to our poor team.'

'*January* 6.—This morning saw us start off in overcast
weather, but with a high temperature making very wet
snow, and in consequence a comparatively easy surface.
By lunch-time it had commenced to snow in large flakes,
and the temperature had risen to $+33°$ by the sling
thermometer; this is the first time the air-temperature
has been above freezing; the snow falling on us or on
the sledges immediately melted, so that the effect was
precisely the same as a shower of rain; and it was
ludicrous to see us trying to push things into holes and
corners where they would not get sopping wet. We wore

our gaberdine blouses this afternoon, and they had the appearance and the effect of mackintoshes. All this is a strangely new experience to us, and certainly one would never have dreamt that an umbrella might be a desirable thing on the Great Barrier. This wave of heat with thick foggy snow came from the south with a fairish breeze.

'We have been trying once or twice lately to go on ski as the snow is very soft and we sink deeply, but we find that we cannot put the same weight on the traces as we do on foot. On the whole our ski so far have been of little value. They have saved us labour on the rare occasions on which we have not had to pull, such as when we returned for the second load at our relay work; but the labour thus saved is a doubtful compensation for the extra weight which they add to the load. Another thing to be remembered is that one gets used to plodding, even in heavy snow, and, though it is very tiring at first, one's capacity for performance on foot ought not to be judged until one is thoroughly accustomed to the work.

'We have passed our old track once or twice lately; it is partly obliterated but much clearer than I expected to find it after the recent winds. We made sail again this afternoon, and the dogs, which have now become only a hindrance, were hitched on behind the sledges— a very striking example of the cart before the horse. " Boss" fell, and was put on the sledge.'

'*January* 7.—We have had a very warm and un- commonly pleasant day. The temperature at noon rose to 34° and the snow surface was just on the melting- point, a condition that is excellent for the sledge-runners.

We dropped all the dogs out of the traces and pulled steadily ourselves for seven hours, covering ten good miles by sledge-meter. " Boss," when we left, turned back to the old camp ; later he was seen following, but he has not turned up to-night though supper-hour is long past. The rest of the animals walked pretty steadily alongside the sledges. It is a queer ending for our team ; I do not suppose they will ever go into harness again, unless it is to help them along.

' But who could describe the relief this is to us ? No more cheering and dragging in front, no more shouting and yelling behind, no more clearing of tangled traces, no more dismal stoppages, and no more whip. All day we have been steadily plodding on with the one purpose of covering the miles by our own unaided efforts, and one feels that one would sooner have ten such days than one with the harrowing necessity of driving a worn-out dog team. For the first time we were able to converse freely on the march, and in consequence the time passed much more rapidly.

' We have seen little of the land of late, though occasionally our landmarks show up. The sun has been flickering in and out all day. Much cloud hangs above the coast ; this afternoon it developed into masses of rolled cumulus which clung about the higher peaks like rolls of cotton wool. It is the first time we have seen these to the south, and they are pleasantly reminiscent of milder climates ; they would certainly appear to have some connection with the wave of heat that is passing over us.

' We have been arguing to-night that if we can only get to the depot in good time we can afford to have an extra feed, a sort of revival of Christmas Day; at present we have gained a day on our allowance. We are positively ravenous, but this thought is sending us to bed in a much happier frame of mind.'

'*January* 8.—Truly our travelling is full of surprises. Last night we had a mild snow-storm depositing flaky crystals, but none of us guessed what the result would be. This morning the air temperature had fallen to 22°, the snow surface was 23°, and below the upper layer 26°; after breakfast the fog gradually cleared, the sun came out, and a brisk northerly breeze sprang up. We got into our harness in good time, and, lo! and behold, found we could scarcely move the sledges. We scraped the runners and tried again without any difference; somewhat alarmed, we buckled to with all our energy, and after three hours of the hardest work succeeded in advancing one mile and a quarter; then we camped to discuss the matter. It was evident that the surface had completely changed : last night we could have dragged double our present load with ease; this morning each step was a severe strain, we were constantly brought to a standstill and had to break the sledges away with a jerk. As the wind came up, the loose snow settled into little sandy heaps, and seemed actually to grip at the runners. We have decided to remain in camp until the surface changes, but the question one cannot help asking is, Will it change? I suppose it is bound to come right, but

we have less than a week's provisions and are at least
fifty miles from the depot. Consequently the prospect
of a daily rate of one mile and a quarter does not
smile on us—in fact, we are none of us very cheerful
to-night; and to add to his discomfort poor Shackleton
has another bad attack of snow-blindness.

'We got a clear view of the land this afternoon,
and I was able to get an excellent round of angles.
We are opposite the high pyramidal and tabular mountains once more, and get a good idea of the general
loftiness of the country.

' " Birdie " remained behind at the camp this morning, but came on later ; " Boss " has never rejoined—he
must have sunk like the rest from sheer exhaustion, but
with no one by to give him the last merciful *quietus* ;
" Joe " was sacrificed for the common good to-night.
It is fortunate that numbers will not permit these
massacres to continue much longer ; yet, after all, one
cannot help being struck with the extraordinary and
merciful lack of intelligence that these beasts display in
such tragic moments. We have had the most impressive
examples of this.

' When a decree has gone forth against any poor
wretch, it has been our custom to lead him some way
to the rear of the sledges and there, of course,
to put an end to him as painlessly as possible. As
the intended victim has been led away, the rest of
the team have known at once what is going to happen,
and as far as their feeble state has allowed they have
raised the same chorus of barks as they used to do

when they knew that we were going to fetch their food.
Of course the cause is precisely the same; they know
in some way that this means food.   But the astonishing
fact is that the victim himself has never known : he has
always followed willingly with his tail wagging, evidently
under the impression that he is going to be taken to the
place where the food comes from, nor, until the last, has
he ever shown the least suspicion of his end.

'Thus we have seen an animal howling with joy at
seeing his comrade led to the slaughter, and the next
night going on the same road himself with every sign of
pleasure ; it has a distinctly pathetic side, but it is good
to know clearly that they have not the intelligence to
anticipate their fate.

'I have used the pronoun "we" above, but I must confess that I personally have taken no part in the slaughter;
it is a moral cowardice of which I am heartily ashamed,
and I know perfectly well that my companions hate the
whole thing as much as I do.   At the first this horrid
duty was performed by Wilson, because it was tacitly
agreed that he would be by far the most expert; and
later, when I was perfectly capable of taking a share, I
suppose I must have shrunk from it so obviously that he,
with his usual self-sacrifice, volunteered to do the whole
thing throughout.   And so it has been arranged, and I
occupy the somewhat unenviable position of allowing
someone else to do my share of the dirty work.'

'*January* 9.—Late last night I was awakened by a
flapping of wings, and found a solitary skua gull hovering
round the camp.   One cannot guess how the creature

can have spotted us, especially as we had a northerly wind yesterday; but whatever has brought him, it is cheering to see a sign of life once more, as it is more than a month since we saw the last. It was anxious work trying the surface this morning, and we hurried over the breakfast to get into harness. We found the pulling hard work, but very much better than yesterday, and in the afternoon we were able to set our sail again. We have made a fairly good march, but now, unfortunately, cannot tell the exact distance covered, as this morning we found that the sledge-meter had refused duty. An examination showed that one of the cog-wheels had dropped off, so we detached the counter mechanism and abandoned the rest; it has done us good service, and we shall miss its exact record of our work.

' Our four remaining dogs roam around the sledges all day, sometimes lying down for a spell, but never dropping far behind. " Nigger " and " Jim " are moderately well, but " Birdie " and " Lewis " are very weak and emaciated. Poor " Nigger " seems rather lost out of harness; he will sometimes get close to our traces and march along as though he was still doing his share of the pulling.'

' *January* 10.—We started this morning at 8.25, with a moderately bright outlook and the land clear; the surface was a trifle better than yesterday, but with no helping wind we found it heavy enough until at eleven o'clock a high stratus cloud drifted up from the south and plunged us into gloom. With this the temperature rose and the surface improved as if by magic, and for the last hour before lunch we were able to step out briskly. Soon after this the wind came, and as we started our afternoon march it became evident that a blizzard was beginning. It is the first time we have marched in a blizzard, and though it has been very trying work, it has given us several extra miles.

'Almost immediately after lunch the sledges began to outrun us, and soon we were obliged to reef our sail, and even with the reduced canvas the mast was bending like a whip. The great difficulties were to keep the course and to run the sledges straight. At first we tried to steer by the direction of the wind, and only discovered how wildly we were going by the sail suddenly flying flat aback on either tack. The air was so thick with driving snow that one could not see more than twenty or thirty yards, and against the grey background it was impossible to see the direction in which the snow was driving. After this we tried steering by compass; Shackleton and Wilson pushed on before the wind, whilst I rested the compass in the snow, and when the needle had steadied directed them by shouting; then as they were disappearing in the gloom, I had to pick up the compass and fly after them. It can be imagined how tiring this sort of thing was to all concerned. At length I made up my mind that we could only hope to hold an approximate course, and getting Shackleton well ahead of me, I observed the manner in which the snow was drifting against his back, and for the remainder of the day I directed him according to this rough guide.

'As it was evident that, although we were not steering

straight, we were covering the ground quickly, we decided to go on for two hours extra and take every advantage we could from the wind. It was as much as we could do to hold out for this time, and when at length the halt was called we were all thoroughly exhausted. We had difficulty in getting our tent up in the heavy gale that was now blowing, and, as luck would have it, our wretched Primus lamp chose this occasion to refuse work, so that it was late before we could prepare our hot meal.

'The march has been the most tiring we have done; we are more or less used to steady plodding, but to-day we have sometimes had to run, sometimes to pull forward, sometimes backward, and sometimes sideways, and always with our senses keenly on the alert and our muscles strung up for instant action. Wilson and I are very much "done," though only to the extent that needs a night's rest; but Shackleton is a good deal worse, I think, and I am not feeling happy about his condition.

'We could very rarely spare our attention for the dogs to-day. Poor "Birdie" gave out early, and was carried on the sledge; as to-night he could not stand, we have had to give up hope of saving him, and he has breathed his last. "Nigger" and "Jim" have kept up well, but "Lewis" has only done so with great difficulty, and has sometimes dropped a long way behind.

'We cannot now be far from our depot, but then we do not exactly know where we are; there is not many days' food left, and if this thick weather continues we shall possibly not be able to find it.'

'*January* 11.—The surface has been truly awful to-day; with the wind swelling our sail and our united efforts we could scarcely budge the sledges. Nothing could be seen; not a sign of land; cold snow was driving at our backs, and it was most difficult to steer anything like a straight course. At noon the sun peeped out for a few minutes, and I got an altitude which gives the latitude as 80.44 S.; to-night, therefore, we cannot be more than ten or twelve miles from the depot.

' Our loads are ridiculously light, and that we should be making such heavy weather of them is very discouraging. It may be because we are overdone, but I cannot help thinking that the surface is getting consistently worse; and with no knowledge of our climate we have certain dismal forebodings that a snowy season has set in, which may be a regular thing at this time of year. With no sight of landmarks and nothing about one but the unchanging grey it is impossible to avoid a sense of being lost; never before have we entirely lost sight of the land for more than twenty-four consecutive hours, and looking at the diminished food-bag we are obliged to realise that we are running things very close. However, it is no use meeting troubles half-way; the only thing now is to push on all we can.

' We are not very comfortable in our camping equipment, as everything is wet through—clothes, sleeping-bags, and tent-gear. The canvas tanks and covers of the sledges are shrunk and sodden; the snow was melted as it drifted against one side of our sail to-day, and from the other hung long icicles.

' " Lewis " dropped farther and farther astern this morning, and as he has not come up to-night I fear we shall not see him again.

' *January* 12.—This morning as we breakfasted there was just a glimpse of landmarks, but before we could properly recognise them the pall of cloud descended once more ; we saw enough to show us that we cannot be very far from the depot. Thanks to a good southerly breeze we have done a good march, and with the help of another latitude sight I calculate the depot must be within a very few miles, but the continuance of this thick weather naturally damps our spirits.

' There is no doubt we are approaching a very critical time. The depot is a very small spot on a very big ocean of snow ; with luck one might see it at a mile and a half or two miles, and fortune may direct our course within this radius of it ; but, on the other hand, it is impossible not to contemplate the ease with which such a small spot can be missed. In a blizzard we should certainly miss it ; of course we must stop to search when we know we have passed its latitude, but the low tide in the provision-tank shows that the search cannot be prolonged for any time, though we still have the two dogs to fall back on if the worst comes to the worst. The annoying thing is that one good clear sight of the land would solve all our difficulties.

' For a long time we have been discussing the possible advantage of stripping the German silver off the sledge-runners. Once off it cannot be replaced, and therefore to strip them is a serious step ; the only way in which

we have been able to guess the relative merits of the
wood and metal runners is by contrasting the sledges
and the ski, and it has always seemed to us that the
latter are as likely to clog as the former, but the differing
conditions of their use make the comparison difficult.
However, the pulling has been so severe lately that I
cannot but think that, however bad the wood may be, it
cannot be worse than the German silver, and, though we
may not gain by stripping our runners, we cannot very
well lose ; so to-morrow morning I intend to strip one
of the sledges for trial, and we are looking forward with
some anxiety to the result of the experiment.'

'*January* 13, *noon.*—This morning we stripped a
sledge and then started on our march. Everything was as
bad as it could be. There was not a sign of the land ; the
whole outlook was one monotonous grey, and when we
started to march we found the surface in the most trying
condition. Steering could only be done by one person
pulling behind, catching the shadow of the others on the
light *sastrugi*, and constantly directing right or left ; we
were obliged to put every ounce of our strength on
the traces, and even thus advanced at a rate which was
something less than three-quarters of a mile an hour.
The whole thing was heartbreaking, and after three hours
of incessant labour we decided to halt. I am now writing
in the tent, and, I am bound to say, in no very cheerful
frame of mind. We have thought it wise to reduce our
meals still further, so that luncheon has been the very
poorest ray of comfort.

'And so here we lie, again waiting for a favourable

change. Little has been said, but I have no doubt we
have all been thinking a good deal. The food-bag is a
mere trifle to lift; we could finish all that remains in it
at one sitting and still rise hungry; the depot cannot be
far away, but where is it in this terrible expanse of grey?
And with this surface, even if we pick it up, how are we
to carry its extra weight when we cannot even make headway with our light sledges?

'I have been staring up at the green canvas and asking myself these questions with no very cheering result.'

'*January* 13, *midnight.*—Catching a glimpse of the
sun in the tent to-day, I tumbled out of my sleeping-bag
in hopes of getting a meridional altitude; it was one
of those cases which have been common of late when
observation is very difficult. Light, ragged clouds were
drifting across the face of the sun, and through the theodolite telescope at one moment one saw its blurred, indistinguishable image, and at the next was blinded with the
full force of its rays. After getting the best result that I
could, I casually lowered the telescope and swept it round
the horizon; suddenly a speck seemed to flash by, and a
wild hope sprang up. Slowly I brought the telescope
back; yes, there it was again; yes, and on either
side of it two smaller specks—the depot, without the
shadow of a doubt. I sprang up and shouted, "Boys,
there's the depot." We are not a demonstrative party,
but I think we excused ourselves for the wild cheer that
greeted this announcement. It could not have been
more than five minutes before everything was packed on
the sledges and we were stepping out for those distant

specks. The work was as heavy as before, but we were in a very different mood to undertake it. Throughout the morning we had marched in dogged silence; now every tongue was clattering and all minor troubles were forgotten in knowledge that we were going to have a *fat hoosh* at last. It took us nearly two hours to get up, and we found everything as we had left it, and not much drifted up with snow.

'We have had our *fat hoosh*, and again, after a long interval, have a grateful sense of comfort in the inner man. After supper we completed our experimental comparison of the two sledges, which have respectively metal and wood runners; we equalised the weights as nearly as possible, and started to tow the sledges round singly; we found that there was an astonishing difference: two of us could barely move the metalled sledge as fast as one could drag the other. We are wholly at a loss to account for this difference; one would have thought that if metal was ever to give a good running surface it would be now when the temperatures are high; but though the result puzzles us, we have of course decided to strip the second sledge.

'On the whole things stand favourably for us; we have perhaps 130 miles to cover to our next depot, but we have a full three weeks' provisions, and it looks as though we should not have great difficulties with our load, now that we are on wood runners. On the other hand, I am not altogether satisfied with the state of our health. There is no doubt that we are not as fit as we were: we are all a bit " done." In Shackleton's case especially

I feel uneasy ; his scorbutic signs are increasing, and he was again terribly done up when we camped to-night. All things considered, without knowledge of what may be before us, it is safer not to increase our food allowance for the present, more especially as in going north I want to steer inwards so as to examine more closely those masses of land which we have seen only in the far distance. But in spite of all, our circumstances are very different to-night from what they were last night ; the finding of the depot has lifted a load of anxiety, and I think we shall all sleep the better for it.

' We are all terrible-looking ruffians now ; the sun has burnt us quite black, and for many days our only bit of soap has remained untouched. It is some time, too, since we clipped our beards, and our hair has grown uncomfortably long ; our faces have developed new lines and wrinkles, and look haggard and worn—in fact, our general appearance and tattered clothing have been a source of some amusement to us of late.'

'*January* 14.—This morning we had a thorough medical examination, and the result was distinctly unsatisfactory. Shackleton has very angry-looking gums— swollen and dark ; he is also suffering greatly from shortness of breath ; his throat seems to be congested, and he gets fits of coughing, when he is obliged to spit, and once or twice to-day he has spat blood. I myself have distinctly red gums, and a very slight swelling in the ankles. Wilson's gums are affected in one spot, where there is a large plum-coloured lump ; otherwise he seems free from symptoms. Both he and I feel quite fit and well, and

as far as we are concerned I think a breakdown is very
far removed.

'Early this morning we reorganised our load, dropping everything that was unnecessary, overhauling mast
and sail, and generally putting everything ship-shape.
When we got away at last we carried, besides our own
belongings, a small quantity of food for our two remaining dogs, the whole amounting to a weight of 510 lbs., or
170 lbs. per man.   We made a fairly good march, and
to our surprise the sledges came easily ; the only marring
element was poor Shackleton's heavy breathing.   The
sky has been overcast all day, but for a short time we
had a good view of the lower land and could very clearly
see the leading marks on which we had placed the depot,
a sight which would have meant much to us a day or two
ago.

'Soon after coming to camp I went to the sledges to
feed the dogs, and, looking round, found that Wilson had
followed me ; his face was very serious, and his news still
more so.   He told me that he was distinctly alarmed
about Shackleton's condition ; he did not know that the
breakdown would come at once, but he felt sure that it
was not far removed.   The conversation could only be
conducted in the most fragmentary fashion for fear it
should be overheard, but it was sufficiently impressive to
make our supper a very thoughtful meal.   It's a bad
case, but we must make the best of it and trust to its
not getting worse ; now that human life is at stake all
other objects must be sacrificed.   It is plain that we
must make a bee-line for the next depot regardless of

the northern coast; it is plain also that we must travel as lightly as possible.

'It went to my heart to give the order, but it had to be done, and the dogs are to be killed in the morning. I have thought of the instruments, which are a heavy item, but some of them may be needed again, and I am loath to leave any until it is absolutely necessary.

'One of the difficulties we foresee with Shackleton, with his restless, energetic temperament, is to keep him idle in camp, so to-night I have talked seriously to him. He is not to do any camping work, but to allow everything to be done for him; he is not to pull on the march, but to walk as easily as possible, and he is to let us know directly he feels tired. I have tried to impress on him the folly of pretending to be stronger than he is, and have pointed out how likely he is to aggravate the evil if he does not consent to nurse himself. We have decided to increase our seal-meat allowance in another effort to drive back the scurvy.

'More than this I do not see that we can do at present. Every effort must be devoted to keeping Shackleton on his legs, and we must trust to luck to bring him through. In case he should break down soon and be unable to walk, I can think of absolutely no workable scheme; we could only carry him by doing relay work, and I doubt if Wilson or I am up to covering the distance in that fashion; it is a knotty problem which is best left till the contingency arises.

'It looks as though life for the next week or two is

not going to be pleasant for any of us, and it is rather curious because we have always looked forward to this part of the journey as promising an easier time.'

'*January* 15.—This morning " Nigger " and " Jim " were taken a short distance from the camp and killed. This was the saddest scene of all ; I think we could all have wept. And so this is the last of our dog team, the finale to a tale of tragedy ; I scarcely like to write of it. Through our most troublous time we always looked forward to getting some of our animals home. At first it was to have been nine, then seven, then five, and at the last we thought that surely we should be able to bring back these two.

'After the completion of this sad business we got into our harness, where another shock awaited us, for we put our weights on the traces without the least effect, and it was only when we jerked the sledges sideways the least movement followed. It was evident that something was wrong, and on turning the sledges up we found the runners solidly crusted with ice. It took us twenty minutes to clear them ; but afterwards we got on well and have covered nearly eight miles. As this caking of the runners is likely to happen whenever our sledges are left long in one position, we have decided to lift them off the snow every night.

'In the morning march we had bright sunlight, and it cheered us all wonderfully after its long absence. We could see the northern side of the high rounded snow-cape abreast of which we left our depot, and which we have always known as " Cape A." This northern side forms the southern boundary of the great glacier which occupies the strait, and it is very steep, with high frowning cliffs. We are now crossing more directly across the mouth of the strait, and there are already indications of ice disturbances ; we have been travelling over slight undulations and most confused *sastrugi.*

'Shackleton's state last night was highly alarming ; he scarcely slept at all and had violent paroxysms of coughing, between which he was forced to gasp for breath. This morning to our relief he was better, and this evening he is rather better than last, though very fagged with the day's work. We try to make him do as little pulling as possible until the pace is settled, and he can lean steadily forward in his harness.

'It is early to judge, but the double ration of seal-meat seems already to have a good effect : gums seem a trifle better. On the other hand, I have some stiffness in the right foot, which I suppose is caused by the taint, but at present I have not mentioned it, as my gums look so well that I am in hopes it will pass away.'

'*January* 16.—The sledges have been running easily, and we have made a good march, but the surface is getting more uneven, and under the dark, gloomy sky we could not see the inequalities and stumbled frequently. This sort of thing is very bad for Shackleton ; twice he slipped his leg down a deep crack and fell heavily, and on each occasion we had to stop several minutes for him to recover. He has been coughing and spitting up blood again, and at lunch time was very "groggy." With his excitable temperament it is especially difficult for him to take things quietly, and at the end of each march he is panting, dizzy, and exhausted.

' It is all very dreadful to watch, knowing that we can do nothing to relieve him ; if at the ship, he would be sent straight to bed, but here every effort must be made to keep him on his feet during the marches. There is now no doubt that the scorbutic symptoms are diminishing ; both Wilson and I have much cleaner gums, and my leg is vastly improved. Our seal-meat at the present rate will last another fifteen days, by which time we ought to be within reach of safety. Six weeks ago we were very much inclined to swear at the cook, who had been careless enough to leave a good deal of blubber in our seal-meat, but now we bless his careless-ness, and are only too eager to discover that our " whack " has a streak of yellow running through the dark flesh. I could not have believed it possible that I should ever have enjoyed blubber, and the fact that we do is an eloquent testimony to our famished condition.

' This afternoon we have had some glimpses of the land and have got some bearings, but there are still masses of cloud over the mountains. We can see the steep cliffs on the northern side of Cape A, and similar cliffs fringing the foothills on the opposite side of the strait, but what stands behind we cannot hope to know, unless the weather clears. So far as exploring is con-cerned, on these overcast days one might just as well be blindfolded.

' The sunlight this afternoon showed that we are cross-ing a very peculiar surface of hard, cracked, lateral ridges,

with softish snow between, due no doubt to the pressure
of the ice-mass pushing out through the strait.'

'*January* 17.— . . . The continuance of our overcast weather has brought a trouble which is now becoming
a serious matter, and that is the difficulty of steering.   I
take it on myself to do most of it now, sometimes by a
cloud, sometimes by the sun, and sometimes by *sastrugi*,
and in half an hour it often happens that each of these
methods has to be employed in turn.'

It would perhaps be as well here to make a short
digression to explain the difficulties connected with this
matter in such a journey as ours.   It will be understood
that we carried a compass in our instrument-box, but to
have held this in one's hand as one marched would have
been quite useless, as it was not until several minutes
after it was placed firmly on the snow that the card
ceased to swing and indicated a definite direction ; the
compass was therefore of little use to us on the march.

Knowing that this would be so, and expecting to travel
out of sight of land, I had prepared a device for steering
by the sun, and as this was constantly in use, and can be
highly recommended to future expeditions, it deserves a
short description.   It consisted of a small wooden dial
in the centre of which was a shadow-pin.   The edge
was marked with two circles, one showing the points of
the compass and the other a twenty-four hour clock-
face subdivided to half-hours ; the relation of these
circles involved a consideration of mean latitude and
equation of time, details which are somewhat techincal
but will be understood by the navigator.

The use of the instrument was extremely simple. It was held in the hand in such a position that the shadow of the pin fell on the hour, and when so held the outer circle showed the true north and south, or the true bearing of any object. Thus one could march straight on in any required direction by occasionally consulting one's watch and more frequently the dial. Whenever the sun was out, therefore, with this instrument we had no difficulty at all in keeping a straight course; and it served yet another practically useful purpose, for when it was put down correctly at night, it gave the time to anyone leaving the tent later on.

But when the sun disappeared this instrument was useless. Then it was that our troubles began, and we were reduced to all sorts of shifts and devices to steer a course. When possible we would take the bearing of a cloud and march on this for some time until we were conscious that its direction was altered and a fresh mark must be sought. Occasionally the low, rocky patches on the distant coastline formed a guide, but on the majority of overcast days the land was not visible, and the cloud-forms had no definite shape. At such times one looked on a monotonous, uniform sheet of grey which extended from under foot to the zenith. The leader could see nothing, but others might catch an idea of the direction of the snow-waves in his shadow. But the expedients to which we were reduced and the troubles they brought can be gathered from my tale, and it will be understood why the continuance of overcast weather should have caused them to be so frequently mentioned at this time.

January 17 (*continued*).—This morning we started with an overcast sky and an unshaded wall of grey ahead. A rapidly closing bright patch on our starboard beam was the only guide. After two hours I had to give up leading ; Wilson went ahead, but by lunch his eyes had had enough, and I finished the afternoon. It is difficult to describe the trying nature of this work ; for hours one plods on, ever searching for some more definite sign. Sometimes the eye picks up a shade on the surface or a cloud slightly lighter or darker than its surroundings ; these may occur at any angle, and have often to be kept in the corner of the eye. Frequently there comes a minute or two of absolute confusion, when one may be going in any direction and for the time the mind seems blank. It can scarcely be imagined how tiring this is or how trying to the eyes ; one's whole attention must be given to it, without relaxing for a moment the strain on the harness. At lunch to-day I fixed up a new device by securing a small teased-out shred of wool to the end of a light bamboo to act as a wind vane. The wind was light and shifty, but the vane relieved my eyes.

'*January* 18.—We started to-day on another abominable " blind " march. For half an hour I could just see some ridges and the slightest gleam in the sky to the north ; for another spell, a very light easterly breeze kept my vane on the flutter. The *sastrugi* under foot are light and confused, and when at last the wind fell we were left with no guide at all, and were forced to camp ; for the last ten minutes we had been four points off our course. Wilson says his eyes are on the point of going; mine, on which I see the party must principally depend, are not quite right, but not yet painful. The situation is startling, but we have not yet exhausted our resources. If there is no improvement after lunch, Shackleton will start on ahead with a flag, and when he has been directed for half a mile, Wilson and I propose to bring on the sledges; it promises to be slow work, but we must get on somehow.'

' *Midnight.*—All was going well with our march this afternoon, when Shackleton gave out. He had a bad attack of breathlessness, and we were forced to camp in a hurry; to-night matters are serious with him again. He is very plucky about it, for he does not complain, though there is no doubt he is suffering badly.'

' *January* 19.—Another long " blind " march. It is very distressing work, and the gloom does not tend to enliven our spirits; but Shackleton was better this morning and is still better to-night. We have now had overcast weather almost continuously for ten days.'

' *January* 20.—At luncheon we found ourselves in latitude 79.51 S., and on coming out of the tent were rejoiced to find a sight of the land on our left, though as yet but hazy. It rapidly cleared as we resumed our march, and soon a new scene was unfolded to our view. An opportunity of this sort was not to be missed, and we camped early, since which we have been busy taking angles and sketching. The temperature has fallen to zero, so that both these tasks have been pretty " nippy." The beautiful feathery hexagonal ice-crystals are falling again, and came floating down on our books and instruments as we worked.

'The land is a long way from us, but much closer than it was on the outward march ; the detached appearance which it then had is still maintained to some extent, but there is now every indication that a still closer view would show a continuous coastline, and that in the gaps between the nearer high mountain ranges would be found lower and perhaps more distant hills.

'Cape A is far behind us; we get a distant view up the strait on its northern side, and see only enough to show that it must penetrate deeply into the land before it rises in altitude to any extent.   If, as one cannot but suppose, it contains a glacier, that glacier must be the largest yet known in the world ; but with ice disturbance commencing nearly thirty miles from its mouth, one can imagine that to travel up it would not be an easy task.   Through the gap of the strait we get a distant view of more mountains—in fact, at any place on this coastline one is struck with the vast numbers of peaks that are within sight at the same moment.   There are far more than one could hope to fix on such a journey as ours : to plot the coastal ranges alone would be a big task, but wherever we get a view behind them it is to see a confusion of more distant hills.

'Northward of the strait we again see the high flanking range end on ; northward of this, again, are three distinct coastal ranges.   The farthest may possibly be the Royal Society range, though of this we cannot be sure at present ; but perhaps the most pleasing sight to-night is the glimpse we get of Mount Discovery; its conical peak rises just above our horizon, and the sight of that well-known landmark has seemed to bring us miles nearer to home and safety.'

'*January* 21.—The clouds have drawn down on us again, shutting out the land, but we have had a brisk southerly breeze, and, setting our sail, got along at a fine rate. For a time Shackleton was carried on the sledges, but for most of the march he walked along independently, taking things as easily as possible. Our sail did most of the pulling. I, hitched to the bow of the front sledge, kept it straight, and helped it over the rough places; Wilson hitched to the back of the rear sledge, and by hauling sideways acted as a sort of rudder. We got on fast, but it was by no means easy work, being so extraordinarily jerky and irregular. Shackleton is improving, but takes his breakdown much to heart.'

'*January* 22.—The southerly wind continued to-day; it is a godsend, and is taking us to the north faster than we ever hoped for. The masses of low heavy cumulus and stratus cloud and the higher cirro-cumulus, all hurrying to the north, have given us the most beautiful cloud effects. The sun has peeped forth occasionally, but the land is still heavily overcast. We are beginning to hope that we shall soon be able slightly to increase our food allowance.'

'*January* 23.—I think the fates have decided in our favour. We got off another excellent march to-day. The wind holds from the south, sometimes falling light, but on the whole giving us great help. This wind is the greater blessing because it was so wholly unexpected.

' We have slightly increased our food allowance, but we feel that it would take weeks of such feeding to make up for arrears. I went out late to-night and, as usual, inspected our biscuit tank ; it looked so healthy that I suggested a biscuit all round. There was loud applause from the tent, and we munched away at our small extra meal with immense joy.

' Ever since the warmer weather set in we have had to be very careful to keep our provisions out of the sun's rays. Our first warning was when an ominous splash on the canvas showed where the grease of the pemmican had melted its way through. Since then this class of food has been put in the middle and banked round with sugar and other non-meltable articles ; and after supper every night the ready provision-bag is buried under the snow. In spite of such precautions, we are rather afraid that our seal-meat has suffered from the heat, and that it is not so anti-scorbutic as it was ; our scurvy symptoms for the last few days have remained about the same, no better and no worse.'

' *January* 24.—Things are still looking well. Shackleton remains about the same ; he is having a cruel time, but each march brings us nearer safety. The overcast weather still holds, and we cannot see the main land, although, to our great joy, we caught a glimpse of the Bluff to the north this afternoon.

' We have got on to a new form of surface which makes the pulling very wearisome. There is a thin crust an inch or so beneath the soft snow surface ; this crust is almost sufficient to bear our weight, but not

quite ; the consequence is that as one steps on it, one is
held up until the whole weight comes on the advanced
foot, when the crust breaks and one is let down some
three or four inches.   To go on breaking the surface like
this throughout a long day is extremely tiring.   Such
work would finish Shackleton in no time, but luckily he
is able to go on ski and avoid the jars altogether.   In
spite of our present disbelief in ski, one is bound to
confess that if we get back safely Shackleton will owe
much to the pair he is now using.'

'*January* 25.—At last we have sunshine again and a
grand opportunity for sketches and angles.   The surface
is bad and the work increasingly heavy, but Wilson and
I are determined to leave as little as possible to chance
and to get our invalid along as quickly as his state will
allow.   We start him off directly our breakfast is over,
and whilst we are packing up camp he gets well ahead,
so that he is able to take things easy ; we follow on
and gradually catch him up, and after lunch the same
procedure is adopted.   At the night halt he sits quietly
while the tent is pitched, and only goes into it when all
is prepared.   He feels his inactivity very keenly, poor
chap, and longs to do his share of the work, but luckily
he has sense enough to see the necessity of such pre-
caution.

'The Bluff looks delightfully close in the bright
sunshine, but the depot must still be twenty or thirty
miles away.   Just before we camped to-night we could
see a little round cloud over the centre of the Bluff
ridge, and as we " rose " it further, we made it out to be

the smoke of Erebus ; it was cheerful to think that here was something which was beyond the ship ; it is more than a hundred miles away from us, but we are too well accustomed to see things at a distance to treat this fact as wonderful.'

'*January* 26.—Plodding on in our usual style this afternoon, we suddenly saw a white line ahead, and drawing closer found a sledge track ; it must have been Barne's, on his return from his survey work to the west. Thinking over it to-night, it is wonderful what that track told us. We could see that there had been six men with two sledges, and that all the former had been going sound and well on ski ; the sledge runners had been slightly clogged. From the state of the track it was evident that they had passed about four days before on the homeward route, and from the zig-zagging of the course we argued that the weather must have been thick at the time. Slight discolouration of the snow showed that two or three had been wearing leather boots, and so on : every imprint in the soft snow added some small fact, and the whole made an excellent detective study. The main point is that we know now, as certainly as if we had been told, that Barne and his party are safe and in good health, and this is no small relief after our own experiences.'

'*January* 27.—The temperature has again fallen to zero, but it has been brisk and pleasant in the sun. Old and familiar landmarks have been showing up one by one. Erebus raised its head above the Bluff range ; Terror opened out to the east ; the western range

developed into better-known shape. It has been grand
to watch it all. We calculate to get to the depot to-
morrow, and have been wondering whether we shall find
all the good things we expect.'

'*January* 28.—Things did not look so bright this
morning; low, suspicious-looking clouds came up from
the south with a bitterly cold wind, and soon they were
about us, obscuring everything. Shackleton had a bad
return of his cough, but said he thought he could
manage to get along; so we spread our sail and proceeded. One has to be prepared for very quick changes
in these parts, and by nine o'clock the whole sky had
cleared again, and the wind had gone round to W.S.W. ;
this was an awkward angle for our sail, and resulted
in frequent capsizes of the sledges, which brought
a considerable strain on our tempers. We hoped to
reach the depot by lunch, but it was an hour after that
meal before Shackleton, who was ahead, spotted the
flag, and we turned our course to make for it. As can
be imagined, the last of the march was as near a rush as
our tired legs could command. At length and at last we
have reached the land of plenty ; the one great and
pressing evil will grip us no more.

'Directly our tent was up we started our search
amongst the snow-heaps with childish glee. One after
another our treasures were brought forth : oil enough for
the most lavish expenditure, biscuit that might have
lasted us for a month, and, finally, a large brown provision-bag which we knew would contain more than food
alone. We have just opened this provision-bag and

feasted our eyes on the contents. There are two tins of sardines, a large tin of marmalade, soup squares, pea soup, and many another delight that already make our mouths water. For each one of us there is some special trifle which the forethought of our kind people has provided, mine being an extra packet of tobacco ; and last, but not least, there are a whole heap of folded letters and notes—*billets-doux* indeed. I wonder if a mail was ever more acceptable.

' All the news seems to be good ; the weather at the ship has been wonderfully warm and fine, and the glare of the sun so great that our people have had to wear goggles at their work. After long and trying labour Royds tells me he has succeeded in rescuing all the boats, though not without damage. Armitage has not returned, but is expected soon. So far there has been no sign of a return of scurvy. Blissett has discovered an Emperor penguin's egg, and his messmates expect him to be knighted. With all this to gossip about, we are a pretty cheerful party to-night, and I can only write scrappily. Meanwhile our *hoosh* is preparing ; we are putting a double " whack " of everything into the cooking-pot, and when in doubt as to what is double, we put in treble. The smell of this savoury mess is already arising, so I cease.'

' *January* 29.—I intended to finish writing up my diary last night, but I couldn't, and I'm afraid it's no use trying to disguise the fact that this was due to nothing but a condition of horrible surfeit. The tale is really lamentable ; we have got into a habit of eating our food

in the most wolfish fashion, and last night no sooner was
our first pannikin of *hoosh* served out than it was gone,
the unusual second pannikin vanished almost as quickly,
and even when it came to the hitherto unknown third,
there was not much slackening in the pace. Then, having
exhausted the contents of the inner cooking-pot, in
almost less time than it takes to tell, we passed on to
the thickest brew of cocoa with " lashings " of jam and
biscuit. Supper did not last more than twenty minutes,
but the amount we put away in that time would have
excited the envy of any gourmand.

' For the first half-hour everything was pure joy ; we
revelled in the sense of repletion, and read once more
all the good news that had come from the ship. But after
this there slowly crept on us a feeling that something
was going wrong ; our clothes seemed to be getting
extraordinarily tight, and the only conclusion we could
come to was that the concentrated food was continuing
to swell.

' For me at least discomfort speedily gave place to
acute suffering. From a sitting position I lowered myself
until I was stretched out at full length, but this did not
ease matters at all, and, with many groans, I was obliged
to hoist myself to my knees, and, later, to as near a
standing position as I could assume in the confined space
of our small tent. In this trying attitude I remained until
explosion seemed so imminent that I was forced to gasp,
" For heaven's sake, undo the door," and directly the
string was untied I dived out with a feeling that nothing
less than the vault of heaven could hold me.

'But if I expected relief outside it was very slow in coming. Round and round our small tent I paced with measured tread until the minutes grew into hours, a well-beaten track had been worn, and I began to wonder whether I should ever return to a sense of normal dimensions. I don't think I have ever spent a more unpleasant time, and it did not make matters easier to know that it was entirely the result of my own greediness. Moreover, although Shackleton had not been in a fit state to over-indulge himself as I had done, I felt distinctly aggrieved that Wilson had not been obliged to join me in my midnight walk, and such sympathy as I got from these others very thinly disguised their inclination to find the whole incident extremely amusing.

'However, when at length my pangs subsided sufficiently to allow me to return to the tent I had some revenge, for as I was about to enter, Wilson realised that his acutest suffering had only been deferred, and as I approached he burst into the open with a pea-green face, and I had some consolation in knowing that we had changed places. It will be a long time before any of us over-eat ourselves again, and it is certainly an object-lesson on the effects of hunger; but one of the most curious points is that at the worst, when we felt that we carried a great deal more than we ought, and were suffering in consequence, we still craved for more. Our appetites are in a state which it seems impossible to satisfy, and this morning we are as hungry as ever.

'A few hours of fitful sleep followed this uncomfort-

able experience, and we awoke to find a heavy blizzard
and the usual obscurity without. The first thought of
pushing onward was speedily abandoned when we found
that Shackleton had relapsed into the worst condition.
To the reaction from the excitement of last night is
added the most trying condition of weather. The result
is very dreadful. Our poor patient is again shaken with
violent fits of coughing and is gasping for breath ; it
looks very serious.'

' *Later*.—There is no doubt Shackleton is extremely
ill ; his breathing has become more stertorous and
laboured, his face looks pinched and worn, his strength
is very much reduced, and for the first time he has lost
his spirit and grown despondent. It is terrible to have
to remain idle knowing that we can do nothing to help.
I have talked to Wilson to-night, who thinks matters
are very critical, and advises pushing on to the ship at
all hazards. The only chance of improvement lies in a
change of weather, and if this blizzard continues the
worst consequences may ensue. We have enough food
now to carry him on the sledge, but to-night one may
well doubt whether he will be well enough for that. It
is a great disappointment ; last night we thought ourselves out of the wood with all our troubles behind us, and
to-night matters seem worse than ever. Luckily Wilson
and I are pretty fit, and we have lots of food.'

' *January* 30.—Shackleton scarcely slept at all last
night ; his paroxysms of coughing grew less only from
his increasing weakness. This morning he was livid and
speechless, and his spirits were very low. He revived a

little after breakfast, and we felt that our only chance
was to get him going again. It took him nearly twenty
minutes to get out of the tent and on to his ski ; everything was done in the most laboured fashion, painful to
watch. Luckily the weather had cleared, and, though
there was a stiff south-westerly breeze and some drift,
the sun was shining brightly. At last he was got away,
and we watched him almost tottering along with frequent
painful halts.

' Re-sorting our provisions, in half an hour we had
packed our camp, set our sail, and started with the
sledges. It was not long before we caught our invalid,
who was so exhausted that we thought it wiser he should
sit on the sledges, where for the remainder of the forenoon, with the help of our sail, we carried him. After
lunch he was better, and in one way and another we
have brought off a very long march. If he can only
sleep to-night there is a chance of further improvement ;
much depends on this. It is all very anxious work ; if
there is no improvement I half think of pushing on to
the ship for assistance. Wilson thinks that the relapse
is mainly due to the blizzard, and doubts if he can stand
another ; one would give much to ensure three or four
fine days. Nothing could be better than the weather
to-night, and the surface is excellent. Just here it is
swept hard by the wind, and the relief of treading on
something solid and firm is enormous. I did not fully
realise what terribly bad surfaces we have been struggling
with until we got back on this hard one.'

' *February* 1.—For two days the weather has been

glorious, and has had a wonderful effect on our invalid, who certainly has great recuperative powers. He managed to sleep a little last night, and to-day has kept going on his ski. After the last halt he had an attack of vertigo and fell outside the tent, which alarmed us greatly; but after about ten minutes it passed off, and to-night he is better again.

'All day we have been travelling along outside the White Island. So many parties have passed to and fro to the depot that there is now a regular beaten track, and one's eye can follow this highway for miles with a very cheering effect. This afternoon to the north we had a glorious view of Erebus and Terror; the smoke of the former trailed away in a long streamer to the east, and most curiously a second similar streamer floated away from the summit of Terror; one could have sworn that both mountains were active.'

'*February* 2.—Awaking to another fine day, we saw at last the prospect of an end to our troubles, and since that we have got off a long march and cannot now be more than ten or twelve miles from home. It was not till the afternoon that we surmounted a slight rise and altered our course in passing around the corner of the White Island; as we did so the old familiar outline of our friendly peninsula burst on our view; there stood Castle Rock like some great boulder dropped from the skies, and there to the left the sharp cone of Observation Hill. Almost one could imagine the figures on it looking eagerly out in our direction. Away to the west were all the well-known landmarks which led back to the vast

western range,. and to-night, therefore, on every side we
have suggestions of home.

' That it is none too soon is evident. We are as
near spent as three persons can well be. If Shackleton
has shown a temporary improvement, we know by experience how little confidence we can place in it, and
how near he has been and still is to a total collapse. As
for Wilson and myself, we have scarcely liked to own
how "done" we are, and how greatly the last week or two
has tried us. We have known that our scurvy has been
advancing again with rapid strides, but as we could do
nothing more to prevent it, we have not looked beyond
the signs that have made themselves obvious. Wilson
has suffered from lameness for many a day ; the cause
was plain, and we knew it must increase. Each morning he has vainly attempted to disguise a limp, and his
set face has shown me that there is much to be gone
through before the first stiffness wears off. As for
myself, for some time I have hurried through the task
of changing my foot-gear in an attempt to forget that
my ankles are considerably swollen. One and all, we
want rest and peace, and, all being well, to-morrow, thank
Heaven, we shall get them.'

At this point my sledge diary comes to an end, for
on the following day I had neither time nor inclination
to write, but the incidents of such a day leave too deep an
impression to need the aid of any note to recall them.

Nature wore its brightest aspect to welcome us home,
and early in the brilliant, cloudless morning we packed up
our camp for the last time, and set our faces towards

Observation Hill. We had plodded on for some hours when two specks appeared ahead, which at first we took to be penguins, but soon made out were persons hurrying towards us. They proved to be Skelton and Bernacchi. We had been reported early by watchers on the hills ; these two had hastened out to meet us, and soon we were gathered in our small tent whilst cocoa was made, and we listened to a ceaseless stream of news, for now not only had all our other travellers returned safe and sound with many a tale to tell, but our relief-ship, the ' Morning,' had arrived, bringing a whole year's news of the civilised world.

And so at our last sledging lunch, and during the easy march which followed, we gradually gathered those doings of the great world which had happened between December 1901 and December 1902, and, as can be imagined, these kept our thoughts full until we rounded the cape to see once more our beloved ship.

Though still held fast in her icy prison, our good vessel looked trim and neat. She was fully prepared to face again the open seas, and the freshly painted side glistened in the sunlight. A fairer sight could scarcely meet our snow-tried eyes ; and to mark the especial nature of the occasion a brave display of bunting floated gently in the breeze, while, as we approached, the side and the rigging were thronged with our cheering comrades.

But how can I describe this home-coming ; how we again clasped the hands of our friends ; how our eyes wandered about amongst familiar faces and objects ; how we dived into our comfortable quarters to find every want forestalled and every trouble lifted from our shoulders by our kind companions; how for the first time for three months we shaved our ragged chins and sponged ourselves in steaming hot water; how in the unwonted luxury of clean raiment we sat at a feast which realised the glories of our day-dreams; how in the intervals of chatter and gossip we scanned again the glad tidings of the home land; and how at last, in the comfort of our bunks, the closely written sheets fluttered from our hands and we sank into the dreamless sleep of exhaustion?

It was a welcome home indeed, yet at the time to our worn and dulled senses it appeared unreal: it seemed too good to be true that all our anxieties had so completely ended, and that rest for brain and limb was ours at last.

And so our southern sledge journey came to an end on February 3, 1903, when for ninety-three days we had plodded with ever-varying fortune over a vast snow-field and slept beneath the fluttering canvas of a tent. During that time we had covered 960 statute miles, with a combination of success and failure in our objects which I have endeavoured to set forth in these pages.

If we had not achieved such great results as at one time we had hoped for, we knew at least that we had striven and endured with all our might.

CHAPTER XV

WHAT HAD HAPPENED DURING OUR ABSENCE IN THE SOUTH

Royds' Journey to Cape Crozier—The King's Birthday—Athletic Sports—
The Western Journey—Difficulties amongst the Mountains—Ascent of
the Ferrar Glacier—Approaching the Summit—First Party on the Interior
of Victoria Land—Return of Western Party—Summer Thawing—About
the Islands to the South-West—Curious Ice Formations—Recovery of
the Boats—Preparing for Sea—History of the Relief Expedition—
Arrival of the ' Morning.'

Up along the hostile mountains where the
Hair-poised snow-slide shivers.— KIPLING.

As cold waters to a thirsty soul,
So is good news from a far country.—PROVERBS.

DURING our long absence in the south much work had
been done both on board the ship and by parties travelling in various directions, wherefore it can be imagined
that I set myself with no little eagerness to gather the
particulars of this employment, and especially to learn
how it had fared with those who had undertaken the
more extended journey to the west.

It was soon evident that since our departure the
sledging resources of the ship had been utilised to the
fullest extent ; the ship herself had become the centre of
the busiest activity, and throughout the summer parties
had been going and coming, ever adding something to
the knowledge of our surroundings.

On November 2, Royds had again journeyed to Cape Crozier to see how matters went with the Emperor penguins, and this short trip produced one or two interesting results. It can be seen from the chart that from the elevated land at this cape an excellent view of the Ross Sea can be obtained, and it will be remembered that Royds on his last visit, little more than a fortnight before, had seen this sheet of water swept clear of ice. We had thought that this was the last of the ice in this direction, and that it would have continued to drift to the north ; but now, to his astonishment, he found the whole sea thickly packed, and although the pack sometimes drifted away from the land, leaving some miles of open water, it was evident that no general exodus had yet commenced.

Descending to the Emperor rookery, he found several hundred adult birds, but not a single chick except those which lay dead on the floe ; this was a most surprising fact, as it seemed impossible that the small downy chicks of a fortnight before could have already taken to the sea. It was not until the following year that we learnt the interesting manner in which these small creatures leave their birthplace.

Pushing farther on, Royds found that he must have just missed the occupation of the Adélie penguin rookery. These small birds had returned in their thousands, and were just commencing to lay their eggs ; a few had laid their second, a larger number their first, but the majority had as yet laid none at all. From one point of view the moment could not have been more

opportune, and it was not long before the party were
enjoying the greatest delicacy which the Antarctic
Regions can afford.   In their good fortune, moreover,
they did not forget their comrades, but loaded their
sledges with a supply of eggs sufficient to provide at
least one feast for those on board the ship.   It was on
taking a last look at the spot where the Emperor
penguins had reared their young that Blissett called
Royds' attention to a rounded object almost buried
in the snow, which on being dug out proved to be an
egg—the first that had been found.   The joy was great,
and soon after the party hastened back with their
treasure.

Meanwhile on board the ship all efforts were devoted to the preparations of the western party, and it
was hoped that in spite of the difficulties of providing
for the large numbers who were to be employed, all
would be ready before the end of the month.   Progress
was so satisfactory that it was decided that, November 9
being the King's birthday, there should be a general
holiday, and it seemed no more fitting occasion could
present itself for holding the athletic sports which we
had often discussed.   Accordingly, in the early morning
the ship was dressed with flags, the large silken Union
Jack was hoisted at Hut Point, and marks were placed
and arrangements made for the various competitions.
The events were entered into with the keenest delight,
and as they were of a somewhat novel character for
English sports, some of them deserve notice.

Since our men had become expert on ski, competi-

JUNCTION OF THE BARRIER WITH THE LAND AT CAPE CROZIER.

TENT SNOWED UP.

PREPARED FOR CLIMBING OVER ROUGH ICE.

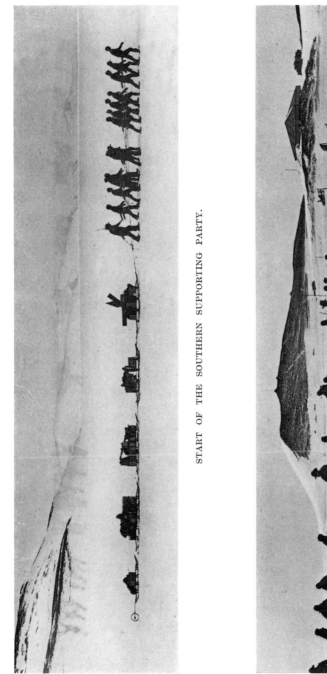

START OF THE SOUTHERN SUPPORTING PARTY.

THE SOUTHERN PARTY PREPARING TO START.

E. H. SHACKLETON.

R. F. SCOTT.

E. A. WILSON.

THE SOUTHERN PARTY.

DEPOT ' A.'

[See p. 51

CREVASSE WHICH ENDED THE CHASM WHICH WE CROSSED
IN THICK WEATHER.

'LEWIS' THE BOISTEROUS.

'FITZ-CLARENCE' THE PLEBEIAN.

'KID' THE COURAGEOUS.

'WOLF' THE ILL-TEMPERED.

CHASM AT DEPOT 'B.'

CHRISTMAS CAMP. THE CAMERA WAS WORKED WITH THE ROPE.

COASTLINE IN L

Mount Longstaff.

FARTHE

EREBUS AND TERR

LOOKING S.W.

Mount Markham.

Mount Lister.

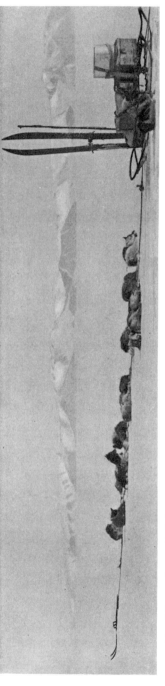

Mount Longstaff, very indistinct.

Mount Markham.

FARTHEST SOUTH.

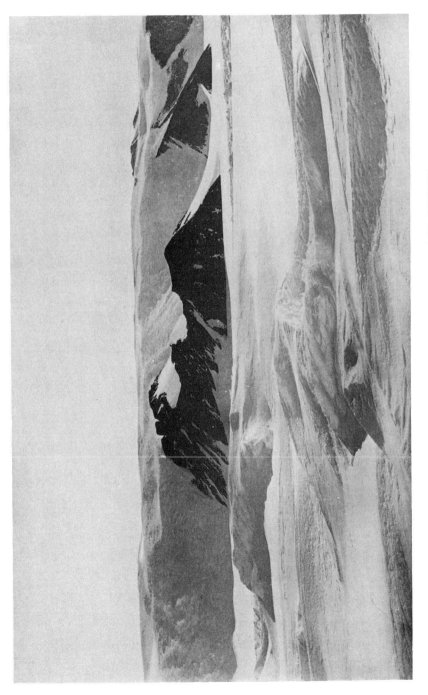

GROIN WHICH WE ATTEMPTED TO REACH, CHASM JUST SHOWING.

CHASM WHICH PREVENTED US FROM REACHING THE LAND.

CAMP AT WHICH WE PARTED WITH THE LAST OF OUR FOUR-FOOTED FRIENDS, SHOWING THE HEAVY NATURE OF THE SURFACE.

TOWARDS HOME LANDMARKS.   THE BLUFF FROM THE SOUTH.

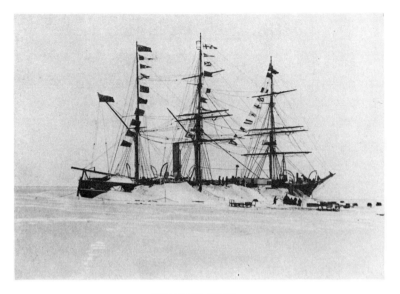

WELCOME HOME.

RETURN OF THE SOUTHERN PARTY.

HOME AT LAST.

CAPE CROZIER'S RECORD IN SUMMER.

LUXURIES FROM THE PENGUIN ROOKERY.

THE NEST.

TARGET PRACTICE. ANTARCTIC SPORTS.

APPROACHING THE WESTERN LAND.

A STIFF RISE.

HAULING UP WITH TACKLES.

FERRAR GLACIER FROM ABOVE. WIND IN THE VALLEY.

ON THE FERRAR GLACIER.

CHRISTMAS CAMP AMONGST THE ICE-BORNE BOULDERS.

A SWEEP OF THE GLACIER. SANDSTONE CLIFF WITH INTRUDED BASALT.

THE HIGHEST DEPOT (7,500 FEET).

LAKE FORMED BY THAW.

EFFECT OF THAW ON SIDE OF GLACIER.

'LIKE A TUMULTUOUS FROZEN SEA,' BROWN ISLAND AND MOUNT DISCOVERY IN DISTANCE.

A GIANT ICE-TABLE.

SHELTERED BY A SNOW-DRIFT.

FREEING THE BOATS. SAWING UNDER DIFFICULTIES.

THE FIRST BOAT APPEARS.

RESCUED, BUT NOT WITHOUT DAMAGE.

THE 'MORNING.'

tions connected with them were bound to be included; in the flat ski race it was impossible to say who would win, as so many could now go at a great pace; for the first half mile this event was wildly exciting, the leaders passing and repassing one another; but after that, staying powers showed up, and the race was won by Evans 'in a canter.' Next came a ski race down one of the steep hill-slopes which had given us so much amusement in the previous autumn; here of course it was skill and dexterity rather than strength which won the prize.

A very sporting event was the half-mile race on foot between teams of officers and men dragging heavy loaded sledges; at the start the teams went off at a gallop, but this pace was very soon reduced, and as the officers staggered back and won by a small margin they felt that they had had enough racing to last them for a long time.

Perhaps the keenest interest had been taken in the toboggan race. For this the men had entered in pairs, and each pair had been obliged to provide their own toboggan, subject to the rule that no sledge, or part of a sledge, and no ski could be used. The start was to be made from high up the hillside, and as the time for it approached there were gradually assembled perhaps the queerest lot of toboggans that had ever been seen together. The greater number were made from old boxes and cask staves, but the manner in which these were put together and the ideas they embodied were widely divergent; at last our canny Scotch carpenter's mate arrived with a far more pretentious article, though fashioned from the same material.   He had devoted his skill in secret to making what was really a very passable sledge, and when he and his companion proceeded to secure themselves to this dark horse the result seemed a foregone conclusion.   But after the start it was seen that these worthies had over-reached themselves, for though at first they shot ahead, the speed was altogether too great; in a brief space they lost control of their machine, and a moment after were rolling head-over-heels in clouds of snow, and whilst the hare thus disported itself the tortoises slid past and won the race.

Another competition that had to be arranged and managed with care was the rifle-shooting match ; the accompanying illustration shows the butts with the markers and the double target.   Considering the conditions under which these were prepared, I think it must be admitted that we generally did things pretty realistically in the 'Discovery.'   On this occasion there was keen competition to hit the bull's-eye, which the picture shows, and amongst the competitors was our redoubtable cook, who claimed to be a marksman of the highest order.   But by this time the cook's capacity for the narration of fables had become proverbial.   It first became evident from varying accounts of the number of places in which he had been born, and later, when the long hours of the winter had given him an opportunity of relating his adventures in many countries, one of the sailors computed that the sum total of these thrilling experiences must have extended over a period of five hundred and ninety years, which, as he said, was a fair age even for a cook.

So when this winner of many competitions possessed himself of a rifle at the firing-point, the markers disappeared
with extraordinary promptitude behind the butt, and after
the first two bullets had buried themselves in that
obstruction the cook was informed that whoever won the
the prize the honours of the day were certainly his, and
it would be quite unnecessary for him to exert himself
further.

And so the King's birthday was kept merrily on
board the ' Discovery,' and the first Antarctic athletic
meeting was pronounced by all to have been a distinct
success.

By November 29 the preparations for the western
journey had been completed, and it was a formidable
party that set out on that day to cross McMurdo Sound
and attack the mainland. In Armitage's own party were
included Skelton and ten men, whilst the supports consisted of Koettlitz, Ferrar, and Dellbridge, with six men.
In all twenty-one souls went forth to try to surmount
that grim-looking barrier to the west. I have already
pointed out that Armitage's plan, formed on the observations of his reconnaissance journey, was to attempt an
ascent of the mountain region in the vicinity of that vast
pile of morainic material which had erroneously been
termed the ' Eskers.'

In pursuance of this plan, late on December 2, the
party started to ascend the steep snow-slope which, as
can be seen on the chart, divides two masses of bare,
rocky foothills, and rises to a plateau separating them
from the higher mountains beyond.

As the party ascended the gradient became steeper, and it was soon necessary to divide the loads and make double journeys in the usual tedious manner of relay work. It was not until the 7th that they reached the summit of the slope and found themselves on a plateau with the lofty mountain range in front and the high granite foot-hills behind. They were now at a height of 5,000 feet. The *mer de glace* on which they stood seemed to have an outlet far to the south ; there was another over which they had ascended, and yet a third to the north-west, which appeared to them the most hopeful direction in which to find a pass to the west. To the south of this outlet there rose a mass of magnificent rocky cliffs, which Armitage named the Cathedral Rocks, and which he thought he recognised as being the southern boundary of the New Harbour Glacier ; it was this glacier which had appeared to him so unpromising in the lower reaches, and which he now hoped to reach at some higher point.

Advancing over a wavy, uneven surface of névé, they reached the vicinity of the outlet by the 9th. It was evident that it descended steeply into the New Harbour Glacier, which in future I shall call by its subse-quent name, the Ferrar Glacier ; but, in order to see its details more clearly, the officers were obliged to leave the camp and travel some distance to a more elevated position. On reaching this, they looked directly down on the Ferrar Glacier, and saw that it wound its way between high rocky cliffs far to the inland ; but the prospect of reaching this and of travelling on its surface did not at this time look hopeful.

To quote Armitage's report : ' After putting on the rope, which Koettlitz held, I went as close to the edge of the slope overlooking the pass as possible. It certainly did not look promising. Unfortunately, I could not see its juncture with the glacier. After consulting Dr. Koettlitz, I came to the conclusion that it would be best to seek a passage across the western range. . . . If we find it impossible to drag the sledges over the mountains, we must try the glacier, although Koettlitz considers that it would be madness to attempt it.' This was an unfortunate decision, and delayed the party greatly. It appears that in addition to the uncertainty of the steep road which led to it, the observers on this occasion were very distrustful of the appearance of the glacier itself ; the blue ice, with no snow on its surface, apparently promised great dangers and difficulties. However, the decision being made, on the 10th the parties separated, the supports turning towards the ship, whilst the main party continued to ascend the rising snow-slopes which led towards the higher mountains.

The slopes quickly increased in gradient, and the ascent became the most arduous and toilsome work. Armitage's report says : ' The following was our mode of procedure : two men carried the crowbar and two ice-axes up the slope to the available length of rope (about 180 feet). The crowbar was then driven into the ice, and the ice axes served as a backing ; a strong lashing connected the three. A small tailed block was made fast to the crowbar, the Alpine rope rove through it, and the

other end made fast to a sledge. Eight hands then
walked downwards with the upper end of the rope,
hauling the sledge upwards as they did so; two men
guided the up-going sledge, and when it arrived at the
top it was secured, and another was hauled up. Three
hauls made one fleet of the four sledges.' After proceeding for two days in this fashion and reaching a height of
6,000 feet, they suddenly found further progress barred
by an outcrop of rock; ' beyond this was an undulating
plain in which we could see large ugly-looking crevasses
and holes. To my intense disappointment there was no
route by which I could justifiably lead my party.' They
had little difficulty in descending the steep hillside
towards their former camps, but, delayed by blizzards, it
was not until the 16th that they could make a fresh
examination of the pass to the Ferrar Glacier, which
they were now obliged to consider the only possible
route to the west.

At this time the party were by no means in a pleasant
position. The plateau on which they stood was 1,800
feet above the glacier which they wished to reach; it
was evident that the pass which lay between, and which
they now called ' Descent Pass,' was filled with snow,
but how steep the slope might be, or how broken and
crevassed its surface, they could not guess. They
attempted to make a reconnaissance without the sledges,
but after descending a few hundred feet found the valley
so filled with cloud that they could see little except that
the slope appeared to get steeper as they proceeded.
In this quandary they determined to take their fortunes

in their hands, and, starting blindly with the sledges above, to trust to fortune to land them safely in the valley below.

Armitage says : ' I had the sledges lashed two and two, abreast of one another, rope breaks on each runner, and I told the teams to use the bridles as extra breaks on the steeper parts. Four men were told off to each sledge ; Skelton, Allan, Macfarlane, and I led the way. We started slowly, but the pace gradually increased until we were beyond all power of stopping ; it seemed but a moment before we were brought to rest on a much more gradual slope, and I stood up to find that we had descended 630 feet by aneroid. The other sledges came down after us with equal speed, and all arrived safely abreast of us. From this spot there was a long gentle slope, and then another fall of 400 feet, which, however, was not so steep as the first.' And so at length the party stood safely on the Ferrar Glacier at a spot whence its valley could be seen cutting deeply through the mountains, while its surface seemed to offer a gradual ascent to the interior. The place on which they stood was barely 2,000 feet above the sea level, but, as will be seen, in their pioneer efforts to reach it they had been forced to drag their heavy sledges over much difficult country, and had at one time reached an altitude of 6,000 feet.

The route taken by the party from this point was one which, as I shall relate in due course, I travelled myself in the following season. I was enabled then not only to observe it at first hand, but with much enlightenment which further experience had given us. The result of personal observation must ever be more satisfactory than an attempt to reproduce the impressions of others, and although this party were the first to see and describe the magnificent scenes of this glacial valley, I reserve an account of them until I can tell of that which I saw with my own eyes.

In the following year I was able to traverse this glacier at considerable speed and to treat its difficulties and obstacles lightly, but this, of course, was largely due to the fact that I was travelling over a route which was to some extent known. One is apt to forget the benefits conferred by the experience of others, and therefore, before recounting the slow and laborious progress of this party, I take the opportunity of acknowledging the debt which we owed to it.

On December 18 a start was made to ascend the glacier, and during the following days the party proceeded with great caution ; before the new track was broken Armitage went ahead, sounding at every other footstep with his ice-axe. Their route gradually ascended, but though the gradient was irregular it was never steep ; sometimes they were travelling over long stretches of blue ice where cracks and crevasses could be seen and avoided, but at others, the surface was covered with a thin and treacherous layer of soft snow, and here the greatest care had to be taken, as it was obvious that all dangers would be hidden. On such soft places, too, even a small gradient meant very heavy labour with the sledges, and nearly every day it was necessary to divide the loads and take the sledges on singly. The difficulty of advance was greatly hampered by the weather; though temperatures were high, the wind and snow-drift constantly swept down the valley with great force, and on many occasions masses of cloud hung about the valley and shut off all view of the surroundings. In bad weather it was almost impossible to proceed in a country which was so utterly unknown, and where it was necessary to direct a course with a view to avoiding obstacles which were sometimes seen a great distance ahead.

On the 23rd they had reached a plateau some 4,500 feet above the sea. Here the glacier, as may be seen on the chart, opens out into a broad basin turning towards the right; from this point a slight descent led them to a lower level, where a moraine of immense boulders ran transversely across the basin. Christmas Day was spent amongst the huge rocks of this moraine, but instead of the bright, cloudless weather which at this time we were experiencing in the south, here the sky was overcast with heavy nimbus cloud and all day long fierce squalls swept down the valley; nor had this party the sauce of hunger to give that full enjoyment of their Christmas fare which went so far to mark this day in our southern calendar. But in spite of these facts the season seems to have been celebrated with much merriment.

From this time the party still continued to ascend: at first over very rough wavy ice, where the sledges skidded but could be pulled with ease, and where neither fur nor leather boot could get a hold, and crampons armed with steel points had to be worn ; later they came again to snow surfaces, and on these they turned the corner and faced once more to the west to rise over the last stretch of the widening glacier. The rocky boundaries of the glacier were now comparatively lower. They had no longer frowning cliffs on each side ; gradually the bare land seemed to be sinking beneath the level of the great ice mass, and only the higher mountains showed as *nunataks* above the vast névé fields.

On December 31 they were abreast of one of the last of these isolated summits, and as it formed a most conspicuous landmark they determined to leave at its foot a depot of a week's provision. They were able to approach the high weathered basaltic cliffs with ease, and found a sheltered position amongst the rough talus heaps at its base. Continuing to the west, they were faced by a steep rise over which the surface was much broken ; but, selecting the smoothest route, they were able to surmount this obstacle, when, after crossing some wide bridged crevasses, they found themselves on a plateau which continued for many miles to a second steep rise.

New Year's Day found them on this plateau at a height of 7,500 feet ; the temperature had fallen to −2°, and a strong wind was blowing from the W.S.W. It was whilst they were marching under these conditions that one of their number, Macfarlane, suddenly collapsed. Armitage says : 'At first I was very much alarmed ; he could neither move nor speak, and his face, which had turned to a dull grey, looked positively ghastly. I had a tent pitched immediately, and soon the colour began to flow back into his face. He then complained of pains under his heart and shortness of breath, but these troubles gradually subsided. Being anxious to push on, after waiting some time, I decided to leave half the party in camp and continue to the west with the remainder. I came to the conclusion that Macfarlane's breakdown was due to some form of mountain sickness.'

Proceeding to the westward the advance party ascended another very steep rise, and then travelled over a gradual slope, at the top of which they camped on the night of January 3. This Armitage decided should be his last camp. They had now reached a height of 8,900 feet, and as far as they could see in every direction to the westward of them there extended a level plateau; to the south and north could be seen isolated *nunataks*, and behind them showed the high mountains which they had passed. On the 5th the party left their camp and proceeded to the south-west for some miles on ski. Armitage says : ' We ascended seventy feet in the first two miles; this was the highest elevation we reached, being about 9,000 feet. We then proceeded along a dead level for two miles, then we gradually descended thirty feet in a mile. At this point we stopped : the weather was beautifully clear, and observations showed that the horizon was rather below our level in every direction except to the north and north-east whence we had come. On all sides the surface was quite smooth, and there was very little sign of wind ; it looked as though the plateau on which we stood was the summit of the ice-cap.'

On the 6th the party started to return, and whilst descending the upper falls met with an incident which shows the treacherous nature of the irregular snow-slopes over which they were travelling. I quote the story from Armitage's report: 'We descended the upper falls with ease, and whilst crossing the smooth ice at their foot I was talking casually to Skelton when I suddenly became conscious that I was taking a dive, then I felt a violent blow on my right thigh, and all the breath seemed to be skaken out of my body. Instinctively I thrust out my elbows and knees, and then saw that I was some little way down a crevasse. It was about four feet wide where I was, but broadened to the right and left of me; below it widened into a huge fathomless cavern. Skelton sang out that my harness had held, and threw down the end of the Alpine rope with a bowline in it. I slipped this over my shoulders, and was hauled up with a series of jerks, and landed on the surface, feeling rather as though I had been cut in two and with not a gasp left in me. They told me that below my face had appeared to them to be covered in blood; the force of my fall had scattered everyone right and left and pulled the sledges up to the brink of the chasm, so that I was let down about twelve feet. It shook me up very much, and I could only hobble very lamely after the sledges as we proceeded on towards the camp where Macfarlane had been left.' After this the party continued to descend, following more or less the track by which they had come. Macfarlane,

who had shown some signs of improvement, had further
trouble with his breathing, and was carried for most of
the way on the sledges ; but it soon became evident that
there was nothing very wrong with him, and that he was
more alarmed about himself than others were for him.

On the way down, visits were made to the cliffs on
each side, and specimens of the rock were obtained *in
situ* as well as from the various moraines which were
passed. By January 11 the party were well on towards
the lower reaches of the glacier, and they found that the
temperature of the valley had risen considerably ; it was
frequently above 40°, and the air inside the tents was
often oppressively warm. This led to several minor and
unexpected troubles ; for instance, it was found that the
sleeping-bags gradually melted the surface of ice or snow
on which they were laid, and in the morning were surrounded with a pool of water.

The high temperatures also gave rise to a very
great amount of thawing in the valley. We never again
found it in this condition, and it is probable that it
only lasts for a period of a fortnight, or at the most
three weeks. This season of thaw is an extremely
interesting matter, and no doubt it plays an important
part in the denudation of the country. It will be remembered that before our arrival in winter quarters,
in February 1902, we had landed on the tongue of a
glacier and observed the beds of considerable glacial
streams, though at that time the thaw had ceased. It
may therefore be worth while to quote some remarks
from a report made by Skelton, who, as a member of this

party, saw the glacier in its most melting mood.   Skelton
writes : ' During the hot days of the latter part of December and early in January an immense amount of
melting goes on in the valley.   On the glacier surface
there is quite a loud " buzzing " sound, caused by the
air bubbles confined in the ice being freed and coming to
the surface through water.   On the way back we found
every boulder in the moraines standing in a large pool of
water, often three or four feet deep, and during the night
frequent rumblings could be heard as the boulders lost
their equilibrium and shifted their positions.   Some
boulders could be seen in the clear ice several feet below
the surface, having melted their way down.   There was
quite a torrent of water running down past the Cathedral
Rocks, where it flowed into a lake nearly half a mile
in diameter ; from there it ran in a rapid stream past
Descent Pass towards the sea.   The water in this stream
was about nine inches deep and seven feet across, and on
measuring its speed I calculated the flow of water to be
about fifty-three tons per minute ; this was only one of
many streams.'

On January 12 the party began to climb the steep
slopes of Descent Pass, and had to resort to their old
device of hauling the sledges up with the help of ropes
and blocks.   As some parts of these slopes stood at an
average angle of 45°, the task proved so laborious that
they did not reach the summit of the pass till the evening of the 14th.   From this time their work was easy,
and by the 17th they had again reached the sea level.
Here they were fortunate enough to find numerous seals

basking on the ice, and it was not long before they regaled themselves on fresh meat.

The remainder of the journey was uneventful, and on the 19th, when the party reached the ship, Macfarlane had practically recovered, whilst the remainder were in the best of health and condition. Some months elapsed before I was able to go closely into the results of this journey, and by that time unexpected circumstances had made it evident that we should have a further chance of exploring the interesting region which it had brought to our knowledge. By that time also the several rock specimens which had been secured had passed into the hands of the geologist. A rough map had been constructed and a series of photographs taken by Skelton had been developed, all going to show the valuable information which the party had collected, and opening an exceptionally interesting field of investigation for a second visit to the region.

There was no doubt that a practicable road to the interior had been discovered and traversed, and that the grim barrier of mountains which had seemed so formidable an obstruction from the ship had been conquered, but the portion of this road which led over the foothill plateau and down the steep slopes of Descent Pass still appeared as a serious impediment in the way of speedy approach to the ice-cap. It remained to be seen whether some easier route might not be found to the base of Cathedral Rocks, and, in spite of Armitage's observations, I could not help thinking that there must be some way by which sledges could be dragged from the New Harbour over the foot of the Ferrar Glacier.

It was evident that this party had reached the inland ice-cap and could claim to be the first to set foot on the interior of Victoria Land; but it was clear, too, that they had been forced to terminate their advance at an extremely interesting point, and to return without being able to supply very definite information with regard to the ice-cap. As I have already pointed out, the view of the sledge traveller on a plain is limited to an horizon of three or four miles; beyond this he cannot say definitely what occurs. This party appeared to have been on a lofty plateau, but the very short advance they had been able to make over it could not give a clear indication of what might lie to the westward; the nature of the interior of this great country was therefore still wrapped in mystery.

The photographs, the rock specimens, and the enthusiastic descriptions of the rugged cliffs which bordered the glacier valley showed that here lay the most promising field for geological investigations that we could possibly hope to find, and that at all hazards our geologist must be given the chance of exploring it. In the original programme it had been impossible to guess in what direction this important officer should direct his footsteps, and it had been decided that his ends would best be served by making short journeys in various directions. It was now evident that this deep glacier valley cutting a section through the mountain ranges was incomparably more interesting than any other region known to us, and what

could be learnt of it from the returned travellers only
went to show more clearly the extreme importance of a
second visit. But perhaps the most promising circum-
stance of all that pointed to the interest of this region was
that amongst the rock specimens brought back were fragments of quartz-grits. These, with other observations,
showed the strong probability of the existence of sedimentary deposits which might be reached and examined,
and which alone could serve to reveal the geological
history of this great Southern continent.

On the whole, therefore, the western party had done
excellent pioneer work; they had fulfilled their main
object, and in doing so had disclosed problems which
caused the greater part of our interest to be focussed in
this direction throughout the remainder of our stay in the
South.

The extensive preparations for the western journey
had almost denuded the ship of sledge equipment, and
the travellers who embarked on the shorter journeys in
the vicinity of the ship were obliged to do as best they
could with the little that remained. It was of course a
rule that everything must give way to the extended efforts.
However, this did not baulk the energies of other
travellers, who were willing to resort to all sorts of shifts
and devices rather than forego their share of exploration, and, in consequence, many short journeys were
made which added much to our knowledge of the very
interesting region about the ship.

A glance at the chart will give some small idea of
the confused conditions which existed to the south-west

of our winter quarters, and it can be imagined that before
our sledging commenced this district, on which we gazed
at a distance of twenty or thirty miles, seemed to hold
many mysteries. We could not tell whether the closer
masses of land were connected, or whether, as seemed
more probable, they were detached islands. Far away
we could see long lines of irregular debris-strewn ice,
but we could not say whence they came or what they
indicated.

Taken as a whole, from the point of view of the map-
maker, the general outline of the coast of Victoria Land is
simple. The land is bold and well marked, and the coast
is of a nature that lends itself to rough contouring ; but,
in marked distinction, the region of Ross Island has very
intricate geographical features. The complication seems
to start with that very curious formation which we called
the Bluff, and which runs out in such a singularly
thin, straight strip from the isolated volcanic cone of
Mount Discovery. North of this, as will be seen, there
are three large volcanic islands and a number of smaller
islets, amongst which lie the rock-strewn remains of an
ancient ice-sheet, with numerous vast and partly hidden
moraines; while finally comes the great upheaval of Ross
Island itself. The land masses as a whole, with their
thousands of craters, great and small, show the result of
a very remarkable volcanic outburst. For such light as
was thrown on this region during the summer of 1902-3
we had to thank Koettlitz, Ferrar, Hodgson, Bernacchi,
and others, who managed from time to time to collect a
rough sledging outfit and to make short trips of a week

or ten days towards the various points of interest. In this manner Koettlitz proved the insularity of the Black Island by surmounting the obstacles which had checked the first reconnaissance party, and succeeded in walking completely round it. On another occasion he examined the northern side of the Bluff, and on a third traversed much rough ice and ascended to the summit of Brown Island (2,750 feet), whence he and his companions were able to get some idea of what lay beyond.

In journeying to the south-west our travellers found it advisable to make for the northern coast of Black Island. As I have mentioned before, on such a track after crossing some four or five miles of recently formed ice, they rose from ten to fifteen feet in level to the surface of an older ice-sheet. The travelling continued good till within two or three miles of the island, when disturbances were met with, and it was necessary to cross lines of morainic material which streamed north from the eastern end of the island. This morainic material was principally composed of the black volcanic rock of the island, but amongst it could be found numerous blocks of granite, altogether foreign to the region. The island was surrounded by a well-marked tide-crack, which showed that the ancient sheet of rubble-strewn ice to the north was afloat. Amongst the huge heaps of rock material which it bore were found numerous remains of marine organisms, shells, polyzoa, worm-casts, and sponge spicules. There could be no doubt that in some manner the movement of the ice had lifted this material from below the water-level to its present elevation of perhaps fifteen or twenty feet above ; but precisely how this had been accomplished it was impossible to say.

From any of the small peaks which fringed the Black Island the travellers could get a good view of the surface of the strait which separated them from the Brown Island, and this was a very impressive sight.   From the base of Mount Discovery in the south, long ridges of morainic material spread out and entirely filled the strait, where they were disposed in wonderfully regular parallel lines which at first ran towards the north-east, but later swept round with perfectly uniform curves towards the north, in which direction they continued for some fifteen miles to the sea.   Here, then, was the origin of that rough, water-worn tongue on which we had landed on our way to winter quarters.

The finer material of these long lines of rock debris was naturally blown by the wind in all directions, and, settling liberally between the lines, it had caught the rays of the sun, melted deep and irregular channels, and left standing a wild confusion of fantastic columns and pinnacles of ice.   Seen from the distance the whole, as Koettlitz says, 'appeared like a tumultuous frozen sea with high crested waves curling towards us.'

To cross this confusion was no easy matter : long distances had to be done by portage, and in the thaw season the travellers had sometimes to take off shoes and stockings to cross rapid streams of water two and three feet in depth.

Whilst Black Island was formed of a very hard black

volcanic rock, Brown Island was principally composed of lava and volcanic ash. The rock was much weathered, and had a deep, reddish-brown appearance, while scattered over this island to a height of 500 or 600 feet were found erratic blocks of granite.

There seemed every reason to suppose that Brown Island is joined to Mount Discovery, and at least our travellers were certain that there was no flow of ice between the two; away to the west they could see the long sweep of the Koettlitz Glacier growing rough and disturbed as it fell to the level of the sea.

The snow plateau to the south of Black Island was found to be from 100 to 150 feet above the level to the north, rising to the general barrier level; it afforded a comparatively smooth, easy crossing, undisturbed until within two miles of the Bluff, to reach which the travellers had again to cross lines of morainic material in which the volcanic rocks of the region were mixed with numerous boulders of granite. Taken together, these various observations gave a moderately clear outline of the ice condition in this region. The space inside the Brown Island is governed locally by the Koettlitz Glacier, but it is evident that the ice of the barrier itself is moving, or has moved, around the end of the Bluff, and close along its northern shore; thence it is pressing, or has pressed, northward through the two channels which separate the islands, the greater part passing around to the west of Black Island.

All this led up to a highly important and interesting discovery. We could not doubt that the decayed and water-worn ice on which we had landed on February 8, 1902, marked what was nothing less than the end of the lateral moraine of the Great Ice Barrier. When it is considered what a colossal agent for transportation this moraine must be, it is curious to find that it ends in such a tame manner.

Whilst these efforts at exploration had been going on in various directions, the ship had been left in the charge of Mr. Royds. With people constantly going and coming, the numbers on board varied much ; sometimes there might be ten or a dozen hands available for work, at others no more than four or five could be got together ; but, whatever the number, all were kept steadily employed on the one most important task—that of freeing the boats.

I have already explained the calamity that had befallen us in this respect—how these indispensable articles of the ship's furniture had been placed on the ice, how they sank below the water level, and how we were forced to shovel away the snow to prevent them from going still deeper. This work of clearance was continued well on into the sledging season, as it was hopeless to attempt extrication until the night temperature had risen sufficiently to prevent the work of the day being wasted. This condition was not reached until the middle of December, and even then it was rarely that the thermometer stood above the freezing-point of salt water throughout the whole of the twenty-four hours, so that the work was greatly retarded.

When it was decided that the time had come to make

an effort to free the boats, many shifts and expedients were tried. At first it was thought that something might be done by sprinkling ashes and dark volcanic soil over the ice, but it was found that the sun's rays were not sufficiently powerful or constant to make this device a success. As a next step, after all the snow was cleared off the surface of the floe, the ice-saw was brought into action, and a complete cut was made around that part of the ice-sheet in which the boats were embedded; but when this cut was finished it was found that, contrary to our hopes, the centre square refused to rise. Then efforts were concentrated on a single boat; the saw-cut was completed about it, not altogether without injury to the boat, but even this small detached piece was held down in some inexplicable manner. Finally, in order to bring it up, small tins of gun-cotton had to be employed, and it was only after several explosions that the block was successfully brought to the surface.

In this position, the men, working knee-deep in slush, were able to dig out the inside of the boat, and bit by bit to clear away the ice which clung to the outside; then with shears and tackles she was slowly dragged from her icy bed. In this manner the first boat was got out, and then one by one the rest were extricated in like fashion.

As can be imagined, with so much sawing and blasting going on in the unseen depths of the ice below, it was not likely that the task could be accomplished without considerable injury to the boats, and when at length they had all been brought to the surface they presented a very dilapidated appearance, very different from that which they had possessed when first they had been incautiously placed on the floe. Of all our staunch whale-boats two only were in a condition to float, and it was evident that there would be many weeks of work for our carpenter before the remainder could be made seaworthy. Still, even the skeleton of a boat is better than no boat at all, and when on January 17 the last had been raised it was justly felt that a big load of anxiety had been removed.

Long before my departure to the south I had given instructions that the 'Discovery' should be prepared for sea by the end of January ; consequently after the boats had been freed, and as the sledge parties returned, everyone was very busily employed. To the non-nautical reader it may not be very clear what preparations for sea may mean in such circumstances, nor is he likely to understand what a lot of work they entailed on the few men who were available.

From the deck, tons and tons of snow had to be dug out with pickaxes and shovelled over the side ; aloft, sails and ropes had to be looked to, the running-gear re-rove, and everything got ready for handling the ship under sail ; many things which we had displaced or landed near the shore-station had to be brought on board and secured in position ; thirty tons of ice had to be fetched, melted, and run into the boilers ; below, steam-pipes had to be rejointed, glands repacked, engines turned by hand, and steam raised to see that all was in working order. But, not doubting that the ice would soon break up and release us, all this work was pushed forward vigorously, and in consequence, as I have remarked, on returning to the ship I found her looking trim and smart, and was told that all was ready for us to put to sea again.

But meanwhile the great event of the season had happened. The ' Morning,' our relief ship, had arrived ; and here, perhaps, I may be permitted to make a digression in order to explain how this had come about.

I have already shown the manner in which the necessary funds were raised for the ' Discovery,' and how, after arduous efforts, enough money was collected to equip our expedition in a thoroughly efficient manner. This being the case, and there being no reason to suppose that the ' Discovery ' was in distress, it may not be quite clear why it was thought necessary to send a relief ship in the following year. Indeed, the reason will probably not be plain to anyone who is incapable of putting himself into the position of those who bore the responsibility of the expedition.

Taking any general case where an expedition is sent forth to the Polar Regions, it is evident that when it has passed beyond the limits of communication, the authorities who despatched it must bear some burden of anxiety for its safety ; whilst they may hope that all will be accomplished without disaster, they cannot blind themselves to the risks that have been taken, and must inevitably ask themselves whether on their part they have done everything possible to avert mischance. If the expedition has departed without any definite plan, or has passed into a region in which it would be hopeless to search, those at home can do nothing; if, on the other hand, it has planned to pass by known but un-visited places, then it is obvious that its footsteps can be traced with the possibility of ascertaining its condition and of relieving distress.   In this last case the proper action of the authorities is clear : they must endeavour to take no risk of their relief arriving too late, but do their utmost to despatch it as early as possible in the track of the first venture.   Such has always been the attitude of those responsible for North Polar voyages, and in the South there is a further reason for its obser-vance in the fact that the Antarctic Regions are sur-rounded by a belt of tempestuous ocean, across which it would be impossible for explorers to retreat should they have suffered the loss of their ship.

As soon as the 'Discovery' had departed on her long voyage all these facts began to be practically con-sidered, and the necessity of safeguarding the enterprise by the early despatch of relief was realised.

To raise the necessary funds for this second venture was no light task, but the Geographical Society recog-nised its responsibility and energetically supported its President in the campaign which he immediately opened with his customary energy and pertinacity.   Urgent appeals were issued; a subscription list was opened and graciously headed by H.M. the King and H.R.H. the Prince of Wales ; Mr. Longstaff again came to the front with an addition of 5,000*l.* to his former munificent donation ; Mr. Edgar Speyer most generously subscribed a like sum.

From this start the fund gradually grew by the arrival of gifts from the most diverse and interesting quarters—from five great City Companies,[1] from boys at school, from members of the Stock Exchange collected by Mr. Newall, from sub-lieutenants at Greenwich, from officers of a Gurkha regiment in Chitral, from the New Zealand Government, from officers in South Africa, and from a thousand private individuals who gave what they could afford. But, great as was the interest shown, as always on such occasions, its manifestation was slow, and there were times when it seemed almost impossible that the urgency of the case could be met. Sir Clements Markham, however, refused to acknowledge defeat; as usual, having set his shoulder to the wheel, he worked on in good times or bad with the same untiring zeal and singleness of purpose, and, as all who know of this troublous time most freely acknowledge, it was due to this alone that the sum of 22,600l. was eventually raised in time to make the despatch of the projected relief expedition possible.

Even this sum did not admit of elaborate plans in the equipment of the relief expedition; the greatest economy was necessary.

A stout wooden whaler named the 'Morgenen,' or 'Morning,' was purchased in Norway, and after being thoroughly refitted and overhauled by Messrs. Green, of Poplar, was stored with the requisites for the voyage.

At an early date her commander had been appointed, and this proved in every respect a most fortunate selec-

---

[1] Goldsmiths, Fishmongers, Drapers, Mercers, and Skinners.

tion.   Lieutenant William Colbeck, R.N.R., was at this time in the employment of Messrs. Wilson, of Hull, who generously lent his services ; he had already been in the Antarctic Regions, having spent a winter at Cape Adare with Sir George Newnes's expedition, and he was therefore chosen as the most fitting person to command this new venture.   Colbeck selected some of his officers and most of his men from amongst those with whom he was personally acquainted ; many had served at one time or another in the Wilson Line.   The Admiralty showed their interest in the enterprise by permitting two naval officers to join the expedition.

At length, all being prepared, the 'Morning' left the London Docks on July 9, 1902, and after a long sea voyage, in which she rounded the Cape of Good Hope without touching land, on November 16 she duly arrived at Lyttelton, New Zealand, the base of all our operations. Here she received the same generous treatment which had been accorded to the 'Discovery,' and on December 6 made her final departure for the South, stored with many an additional present supplied by the kindly thought of our New Zealand friends.

Here perhaps it is necessary to pause for a moment to consider the work which lay before Captain Colbeck and his crew.

Long before the 'Discovery' had left New Zealand the idea of a relief ship had been mooted, and although I saw the great difficulties that were to be overcome in sending her, I felt confident that if the thing was to be done, Sir Clements Markham would do it.   From any point of view it was desirable to leave as much information as possible in our track, and with this idea I had foreshadowed the positions at which I hoped to be able to leave records and had laid down a rough programme for any ship which might follow us.   These instructions could only be indefinite ; but such as they were, they stated that attempts would be made to leave information at one or more of a number of places—Cape Adare, Possession Islands, Coulman Island, Wood Bay, Franklin Island, and Cape Crozier.   Especially in the last place, as the most southerly, I hinted that news of us might be looked for ; the relief ship was to endeavour to pick up such clues as might be found in this way, but if this was unproductive or signified that we had passed to the eastward without returning, she was to turn homeward after having landed provisions and stores at certain definite spots.

It will be seen, therefore, that it was in order to act up to this pre-arranged plan that we had left records at such of the named places as we could approach, and that I had been so anxious to establish sledge communication with the record at Cape Crozier.   For this enabled me to start south with the knowledge that a relief ship might gather meagre information at Cape Adare and Coulman Island, whilst, should she recover the Cape Crozier record, she would at once ascertain our whereabouts.

Captain Colbeck's instructions were to fall in with the purport of my letter, but the manner in which he should do so was left entirely to his discretion, and wisely, for with such slender information as was available no one could have acted more promptly or with greater discretion.

Thus it came about that whilst we were surmounting the difficulties of the great snow-plain and finding a way amongst the mountain ranges, the gallant little ' Morning' was hurrying towards us, eager to perform her helpful mission and bring us news of our distant home.

Small as she was, and without the ability to force a way through heavy pack-ice, her voyage to the South was full of adventure, and is a record of difficulties overcome by sturdy perseverance ; but of this I hope that Captain Colbeck will himself tell one day. On December 25 he crossed the Antarctic Circle, and a short way to the south, to his great surprise, discovered some small islands which he has since done me the great honour of naming the Scott Islands. The pack was negotiated successfully, if slowly, and on January 8 a landing was effected at Cape Adare, where the notice of the ' Discovery's ' safe arrival in the South was found. The Possession Islands were drawn blank, since we had not been able to land there. South of this the whole coast was found thickly packed ; it was impossible to approach Coulman Island or Wood Bay, and the ship was obliged to keep well to the eastward to get any chance of an ice-free sea.

Franklin Island was visited on January 14, but without result, and again quantities of pack had to be skirted in making a way to Cape Crozier, so that it was not

until 1 A.M. on the 18th that a landing was effected at
this spot.   Captain Colbeck himself joined the landing
party, which spent some hours in searching for a sign of
us.   He had almost given the matter up in despair, and
was despondently wondering what to do next, when
suddenly our small post was seen against the horizon ; a
rush was made for it, and in a few minutes the contents
of the tin cylinder were being eagerly scanned.   It can be
imagined with what joy the searchers gathered all the
good news concerning us and learnt that they had but to
steer into the mysterious depths of McMurdo Sound to
find the 'Discovery' herself ; their work seemed practically accomplished.

  But though they got hastily back to their ship,
and started westward with a full head of steam, the
goal was not yet reached.   The channel between
Beaufort Island and Ross Island was filled with an
ugly pack in which the ' Morning' could do little
more than drift idly along, but fortunately this drift
carried her steadily to the west, and on the 23rd our
friends were able to free themselves from the ice, and,
turning south, to round Cape Royds and recognise the
landmarks which had been described and sketched for
their instruction.

  On board the ' Discovery' the idea that a relief ship
would come had steadily grown.   For no very clear
reason the men had gradually convinced themselves that
it was a certainty, and at this time it was not uncommon
for wild rumours to be spread that smoke had been seen
to the north.   It was therefore without much excite-

ment that such a report was received on the night of the
23rd ; but when, shortly after, a messenger came running
down the hill to say that there was a veritable ship in
sight, it was a very different matter, and few found much
sleep that night whilst waiting and wondering what news
that distant vessel might bear.

Early on the 24th a large party set out over the floe,
and after marching a few miles could see clearly the
masts and yards of the relieving vessel, which lay at the
limit of the fast ice some ten miles north of the 'Discovery,' and comparatively close to the Dellbridge Islets.
The last mile was covered with difficulty, as here the ice
was only a thin sludgy sheet which had formed since
August and which would only bear those who were fortunate enough to be wearing ski. There was much
shouting and gesticulation, and one or two of the most
eager, sinking waist-deep in the treacherous surface, had
to be rescued with boards and ropes ; but at last our
party stood on the deck of the 'Morning,' and the greetings which followed can be well imagined. Those who
had remained in the 'Discovery' were not forgotten,
and soon the sledges were speeding back, dragged by
willing hands and stacked high with the welcome mail-
bags.

During the last week of the month the weather
remained gloriously fine ; some of the treacherous thin
ice broke away, allowing the 'Morning' to approach us
by about a mile ; otherwise all was placid. In the bright
sunshine parties were constantly passing to and fro, and
all gave themselves up to the passing hour in the de-

light of fresh companionship and the joy of good news
from the home country, and with an unshaken confidence
that the ' Discovery ' would soon be freed from her icy
prison.

It was thus that I found things on my return on
February 3, and when I and my companions, the last to
open our letters, could report that all was well, we had the
satisfaction of knowing that the ' Morning ' had brought
nothing but good news.

CHAPTER XVI

OUR SECOND WINTER

Effects of the Strain of the Southern Journey—Communication with the
' Morning '—Change of Weather—Stores Transported—Delays in the
Break-up of the Ice—Closing of the Season—Departure of the ' Morning '
—Making Provision for the Winter—Settling down—Hockey—Depar-
ture of the Sun—Fishing Operations—Record Temperatures—The Elec-
trometer—Midwinter Feast—Our Growing Puppies—Hodgson at Work
—The ' Flying Scud '—Return of the Sun—Signs of Summer—Plans for
the Future—General Good Health.

> And so without more circumstance at all
> I hold it fit that we shake hands and part.
> > SHAKESPEARE.

> Come what come may
> Time and the hour runs through the darkest day.
> > SHAKESPEARE.

IT was a curious coincidence that Colbeck should have
chosen the night of our return for his first visit to the
' Discovery.' Up to this time he had felt reluctant to
leave his ship, not knowing when a change of weather
might occur, but on this day he had decided to visit the
company to which he had brought such welcome intelligence, and soon after I had emerged from my first
delicious bath and was revelling in the delights of clean
garments, I had the pleasure of welcoming him on board.

In those last weary marches over the barrier I had
little expected that the first feast in our home quarters

would be taken with strange faces gathered about our festive table, but so it was, and I can well remember the look of astonishment that dawned on those faces when we gradually displayed our power of absorbing food. As we ate on long after the appetites of our visitors had been satisfied, there was at first mild surprise ; then we could see politeness struggling with bewilderment ; and finally the sense of the ludicrous overcame all forms, and our guests were forced to ask whether this sort of thing often happened, and whether we had had anything at all to eat on our southern journey.

But although we found our appetites very difficult to appease, for a fortnight after our return from the south our party were in a very sorry condition. Shackleton at once took to his bed, and although he soon made an effort to be out and about again, he found that the least exertion caused a return of his breathlessness, and more than once on entering or leaving the living-quarters he had a return of those violent fits of coughing which had given him so much trouble on the journey ; now, however, after such attacks, he could creep into his cabin and there rest until the strain had worn off and some measure of his strength returned. With Wilson, who at one time had shown the least signs of scurvy, the disease had increased very rapidly towards the end. He had slightly strained his leg early in the journey, and here the symptoms were most evident, causing swelling and discolouration behind the knee ; his gums also had dropped into a bad state, so he wisely decided to take to his bed, where he remained perfectly quiet for ten days. This final collapse showed the grim determination which alone must have upheld him during the last marches.

If I was the least affected of the party, I was by no means fit and well : although I was able to struggle about during the daytime, I had both legs much swollen and very uncomfortable gums. But the worst result of the tremendous reaction which overcame us, I found to be the extraordinary feeling of lassitude which it produced ; it was an effort to move, and during the shortest walks abroad I had an almost unconquerable inclination to sit down wherever a seat could be found. And this lassitude was not physical only ; to write, or even to think, had become wholly distasteful, and sometimes quite impossible. At this time I seemed to be incapable of all but eating or sleeping or lounging in the depths of an armchair, whilst I lazily scanned the files of the newspapers which had grown so unfamiliar. Many days passed before I could rouse myself from this slothful humour, and it was many weeks before I had returned to a normally vigorous condition.

It was probably this exceptionally relaxed state of health that made me so slow to realise that the ice conditions were very different from what they had been in the previous season. I was vaguely surprised to learn that the ' Morning ' had experienced so much obstruction in the Ross Sea, and I was astonished to hear that the pack was still hanging in the entrance of the Sound, and as yet showed no sign of clearing away to the north ; but it was long before I connected these facts with circumstances likely to have an adverse bearing on our position, and the prospect of the ice about us remaining fast throughout the season never once entered my head.

My diary for this month shows a gradual awakening to the true state of affairs, and I therefore give some extracts from it, more especially as when the news of our detention first reached England it was half suspected that the delay was intentional, and it is doubtful whether that view has been entirely dissipated even yet.

'*February* 8.—We are expecting a general break-up of the ice every day, but for some reason it is hanging fire. This is the date of our arrival at Hut Point last year, and then the open water extended as far as the Point; it is evident that this season is very backward, and I do not like the way in which the pack is hanging about in sight of the " Morning." It must go far to damp all prospects of the swell necessary for a general break-up. The " Morning " is eight miles away ; very slowly she is creeping closer, but I do not think that she has advanced more than a quarter of a mile in the last week. We have been arranging the stores which are to be transferred, but it will be rather a waste of labour to transport them whilst the distance remains so great.

'To-day England, Evans, and nine men came from the " Morning," bringing us a fresh load of papers and some more luxuries, especially potatoes. At present I feel that if I had the power of poetic expression I should certainly write an ode to the potato. Can one ever forget that first fresh " hot and floury " after so long a course of the miserable preserved article ? '

'*February* 10.—To-day we gave a dinner party, the invitation being delivered across six miles of ice through the medium of the semaphore. Colbeck, Doorly, Morrison, and Davidson arrived as guests clad in good stout canvas suits and quite ready for the feast. They brought good news, for they reported that more than a mile of ice has broken away yesterday and this morning. We entertained our guests principally on the luxuries they had brought us, and there was little to be complained of in the fare; we had giblet soup, skua gull as an entrée, then our one and only turkey, and a joint of beef, with plum-pudding and jellies to follow. Truly we are living high in these days, and I ask myself whether it was really I who was eating seal blubber a fortnight ago. After dinner we had the usual musical gathering, to which our guests brought a great deal of fresh talent. We have had a right merry night, and now all are coiled down to sleep; those who cannot find berths are snoring happily on the wardroom table.'

'*February* 12.—The weather has changed very much for the worse. The day of our return seemed to mark the last of the fine sunny summer; since that it has been almost continuously overcast, and our old enemy the wind returns at all too frequent intervals. Colbeck was weather-bound yesterday, but it gave us an opportunity of discussing the situation. If the ice is to be very late in breaking up, I think it is advisable that the 'Morning' should not delay to await our release; she at least should run no risk of being detained, and it is to be remembered that she has little power to push through the young ice. We have decided to commence the transport of stores to-morrow; it will be tiresome work, but we ought to get it over in less than a fortnight.'

On February 13 the work of transferring the stores was commenced; it was arranged that the loads should be taken half-way by the 'Morning's' men, and from thence brought in by our own. It seemed at first that the 'Morning,' with her smaller company, would have the heavier task, but this was avoided by a very liberal interpretation of the half-way point; in fact, the distance they covered gradually became little more than a quarter of the whole, whilst our parties took $3\frac{3}{4}$ hours to fetch the load in from the junction. The loads ran from 1,500 lbs. to 1,800 lbs., and in good weather two could be got across in the day, but the biting cold east wind was a great hindrance, and was felt more keenly at the 'Discovery' end. It was in general especially strong about Hut Point, showing that, as we had suspected, chance had placed our winter quarters in the most windy spot in the vicinity.

Owing to this interference of the weather, by the 20th only eight loads had been brought in; on that day, therefore, we started an extra party, which went to the 'Morning' in the forenoon and returned with a whole load in the afternoon. In this manner ten more loads were transported by the evening of the 23rd, and this completed the work except for sundry light articles. The manner in which the officers and men of the relief ship stuck to this very monotonous task was beyond praise; if anything had been wanting to show their ardent desire to assist us by every means in their power, this surely would have proved it. On our side, our people laboured for their own comfort, though, whatever the cause, they were little likely to jib at hard work; in fact, on this occasion there were not a few who, like Mr. Barne, volunteered to make the double journey each day—a matter involving eleven or twelve hours of solid marching.

The goods which we thus obtained from our relief ship were none of them necessary to our continued existence in the South, but they were such as added greatly to the comfort of our position, and I do not use the word 'necessary' here in its strictest sense; as far as food is concerned, the absolute necessities of life are very limited, and in the South they were amply provided by the region in which we lived, for life could have been maintained on the seals alone. But although existence may be supported in this simple fashion, it is scarcely to be supposed that civilised beings would willingly subject themselves to such limitations, and therefore it is reasonable to include as necessaries such articles as not only make existence possible, but life tolerable.

From this broader point of view we were well equipped in the 'Discovery,' and experience had taught us that we could continue to live with comparative comfort on very modest requirements. We had an ample stock of flour—enough to have lasted us for at least three years. To this might be added a large store of biscuit, which had been rarely used except on our sledge journeys. We were well provided with sugar, butter, pea-

flour, tea, chocolate, jam, and marmalade, and had a
moderate supply of lard, bottled fruits, pickles, cheese,
and milk. With our holds thus stored we should have
had little cause for anxiety for at least two or three years
to come, but with the relief ship so well stocked it can
be imagined that we were not long in considering how
we might still further increase our comfort and provide
for a greater variety in our fare. Our vegetables, both
tinned and dried, had been a distinct failure, and it was
in this, therefore, that we made our first call on the
resources of the ' Morning.' But besides this we had
run very short of sauces, herbs, tinned soups, and articles
of this nature, which were particularly desirable for
cooking and seasoning our dishes of seal-meat. Our
cheese, too, was not very satisfactory, whereas that
brought by the ' Morning ' from New Zealand was in
excellent condition ; and although our tinned butter was
very good, we were not long in discovering that the fresh
New Zealand butter brought by the ' Morning ' was a
great deal better.

The sledge loads which were dragged across the ice
with so much hard labour during this month of February
went, therefore, as far as food was concerned, to supplying minor deficiencies and to ensuring for us in the
second winter a greater degree of comfort than we had
enjoyed in the first ; but, besides food, they contained
other stores which, although we could have done without, we were exceedingly glad to have. In this manner
we took the small quantity of engine-oil which the
utmost generosity could spare, nearly a hundred gallons

of paraffin, some finneskoes, mits, and socks, and some
canvas and light material to repair our tattered garments.

'*February* 18.— . . . Yesterday I paid my first visit
to the " Morning," and although I took the journey very
slowly, I found it an awful grind.   Hodgson accompanied
me and shared in a royal welcome.   During the night
the ship broke away twice and had to steam up and re-
secure to the floe ; it was strange to feel the throb of the
engines once more.   A few small pieces of ice are
breaking away, but there is practically no swell, and the
pack can still be seen on the northern horizon.   At this
time last year we had a constant swell rolling into the
strait, but as I returned to-day the ice conditions were so
stagnant that one begins to wonder whether our floe is
going to break up at all.   It is rather late in the day,
but I have arranged to send some people down to the
ice-edge to try the effect of explosions.'

'*February* 22.—Yesterday I took the explosive party
down to the " Morning."   We made a hole about three
hundred yards from the ice-edge, and sank a charge of
19 lbs. of gun-cotton about six feet below the surface.
It blew up a hole about twenty feet in diameter, but the
effect was altogether local ; there were no extending
cracks.   We next tried closer to the edge, and sank
the charge about thirty feet.   The effect was better ; a
similar hole was made, but from it a few long cracks
ran to right and left.   To-day two more charges were
exploded near the cracks already formed ; the cracks
were increased in length and number, but no part of the

floe was detached. I came to the conclusion that it was only a waste of material to continue these experiments further, and sent the party back. On the whole, I think, something might be done in this way towards breaking up the ice, but, if so, the business must be undertaken in a thoroughly systematic manner; we must be prepared to employ everyone at the work, and to expend gun-cotton with a lavish hand; it is far too late to commence such a big undertaking this year.'

'*February* 25.— . . . There is no doubt things are looking serious. The ice is as stagnant as ever; there has been scarcely any change in the last week. I have had to rouse myself to face the situation. The "Morning" must go in less than a week, and it seems now impossible that we shall be free by that time, though I still hope the break-up may come after she has departed. I have been busy all day writing despatches, and have drawn up a summary of our proceedings, as well as a more detailed description of our present position.

' Some time ago I decided that, if we are to remain on here, it will be with a reduced ship's company, and certainly without the one or two undesirables that we possess.

' Yesterday I had a talk to the men. I put the whole situation before them; I told them that I thought we should probably get out after the "Morning" had left, but it was necessary to consider the possibility of our not being able to do so, and to make arrange-ments for such a contingency at once. I said that I wished nobody to stop on board who did not do so

voluntarily, and I hinted that I should be glad for a
reduction in our numbers; anyone who wished to leave
would be given a passage in the "Morning."

'To-day a list has been sent round for the names of
those who desire to quit, and the result is curiously
satisfactory. I had decided to reduce our number by
eight, and there are eight names on the list, and not
only that, but these names are precisely those which I
should have placed there had I undertaken the selection
myself.

'As regards the mess-deck, therefore, we shall be
left with the pick of our company, all on good terms,
and all ready, as they say, to stand by the ship whatever betides. Of course, all the officers wish to remain;
but here, with much reluctance, I have had to pick out
the name of one who, in my opinion, is not fitted to do
so. It has been a great blow to poor Shackleton, but
I have had to tell him that I think he must go; he
ought not to risk further hardships in his present
state of health. But we cannot afford to lose officers,
and Colbeck has already kindly consented to replace
Shackleton by his Naval sub-lieutenant, Mulock, and
the latter is most anxious to join us.'

'*February* 26.—We have 84 tons of coal left in the
"Discovery." This will be enough for more than one
winter, but will not be sufficient to allow us to do any
further exploration if, as I hope, we get out of the ice;
so I asked Colbeck to leave 20 tons on the Erebus
glacier tongue. He came on board to-night with
Skelton and Davidson to say that this was done yester-

day. It appears that they had a great excitement last night, for as they came back to the ice-edge, for the first time they found a northerly swell rolling into the strait, and the ice was breaking up with extraordinary rapidity. In little more than half an hour nearly a mile and a quarter went out, and bets were being freely made that they would be up to Hut Point in the morning; but, alas! the swell lasted little beyond the half-hour, and after that all was quiet again.'

'*February* 28.—Colbeck has spent the last few days with us; he goes back to-morrow early, and with him go those of our party who are homeward bound. Then in the evening we are invited to a last feast before our gallant little relief ship turns her bows to the north.'

'*March* 2.— . . . Yesterday early our guests left us, and our returning members soon followed with their baggage. In the afternoon all our company, except two or three men and Wilson, set forth for the "Morning," there to be entertained for the last time by our good friends; there was much revelry on the small mess-deck forward, and at the eight-o'clock dinner aft seats had to be found for no fewer than sixteen; as the utmost seating capacity of the wardroom table was eight, the overflow had to be accommodated in the tiny cabins at the side, but this in no way detracted from the excellence of the dinner or the merriment of the evening. After a most satisfying meal we all gathered about the piano, the air became thick with tobacco smoke, and for the last time we raised our voices in the now familiar choruses. It was well into the small hours before this final merry-making came to an end, and the occupants of the crowded wardroom rolled themselves into blankets to snatch a few hours' rest.

'During the night the temperature had fallen to zero, and young ice had formed over the open water; it needed no great experience to see that it was quite time that our farewells were said. The morning proved overcast and gloomy, and as we snatched a hasty breakfast a strong south-easterly wind sprang up, drifting thick clouds of snow across the floe and dissipating the young ice to seaward. It was not a cheering scene for our leave-taking, but delay was impossible.

'At length we of the "Discovery," with our belongings, were mustered on the floe ; the last good-byes had been said, and the last messages were being shouted as the "Morning" slowly backed away from the ice-edge ; in a few minutes she was turning to the north, every rope and spar outlined against the black northern sky. Cheer after cheer was raised as she gradually gathered way, and long after she had passed out of earshot our forlorn little band stood gazing at her receding hull, following in our minds her homeward course and wondering when we too should be permitted to take that northern track.

'Then we turned our faces to the south, and, after a long and tiring walk against the keen wind, have reached our own good ship ; so now we must settle down again into our old routine. If the ice does not break up, we are cut off from civilisation for at least another year, but I do not think that prospect troubles anyone very much. We are prepared to take things as they come, but one wonders what the future has in store for us.'

'*March* 13.—I have abandoned all hope of the ice going out. The most optimistic members of our community still climb up the Arrival Heights in hopes of bringing back favourable reports, but it is long since they have been able to return with cheerful faces. We had a strong north-easterly blow on the 5th and 6th, during which hope ran high, and was followed by much excitement when Dellbridge dashed on board to say that nearly all the ice had gone out, and that the open water was little more than a mile from us. We ran out to see this pleasing prospect, but only to find that the report was based on a curious mirage effect, and that it would have been nearer the mark to have given four miles instead of one as the distance of the open sea. Since this incident there has been no change; heavy pack has again been seen to the north, and it is evident that there is no swell entering the strait.

'The weather is a great deal worse than it was last year; we have had much more wind and much lower temperatures; the thermometer has not been above zero since the 6th, but possibly this is due to the absence of open water about us. We were frozen in last year on the 24th, but the old ice had ceased to break away some time before that, and so I fear the chance of more ice going out now is very small.

'But meanwhile we have not been idle; we have determined to stick rigidly to our fresh-meat routine throughout the winter, and whenever the weather has permitted, our seal-killing parties have been away on their murderous errand. Already the snow-trench larder contains 116 frozen carcases. We have now thirty-seven mouths to feed, and an average seal lasts about a day and a half; later, when appetites fall off, it ought to run to two or two and a half days, so that we shall be safe in allowing an average of two days per seal.

'Our sportsmen, too, have been adding to our food supply, and have succeeded in killing over five hundred skuas; one would not have thought there were so many to be killed. These birds will form a good change to the regulation seal. Our ideas and customs have certainly changed: last year we regarded the skua as an unclean, carrion-feeding bird. It was Skelton who first discovered the error of our ways. Whilst sledging to the west he caught one in a noose, and promptly put it into the pot; the result was so satisfactory that the skua has figured largely on our *ménu* ever since. In summer each appetite demands its whole skua, but in winter a single bird ought to do for two people; the legs and wings are skinny, but the breast is full and plump. Like all polar animals it is protected with blubber, and unusual precautions have to be taken to prevent the meat being impregnated with its rancid taste. The birds that have been shot for the winter have been cleaned and hung in the rigging, with their skins and plumage still on. It is found that when they are taken below and thawed out the skin can be removed without difficulty.

'Summing up our food supply for the winter, therefore, we seem to be in pretty good case:

116 seals should last about 230 days
551 skuas   „   „   „   25   „
20 sheep   „   „   „   20   „

                Total   275   „

Of course some of the seal-meat will be required for sledging operations, and we must allow margins for accidents, but on the whole I think we ought to steer through the winter without difficulty. We deplore very heartily that we cannot add penguins to the variety of our fare, but it is long since any have approached the ship, and they are not likely to come now, across so many miles of ice.

'*March* 14.—We have admitted the certainty of a second winter, and to-day orders have been given to prepare the ship for it. It is like putting the clock back : all our care and trouble in getting ready for the sea voyage are wasted. The boilers will be run down again, the engines pulled to pieces, small steam-pipes disconnected, ropes unrove and coiled away, the winter awning prepared, and snow brought in on the decks. The awning is in a very dilapidated state, and looks anything but fit to face the rigours of another season, but I suppose we shall be able to patch it up somehow. One thing we shall not do this year, and that is, place the boats out on the floe ; those in the way of the awning will be carried over on to the land, in which it is to be hoped they will not sink out of sight.'

'*March* 20.—To-day I went out on ski to Cone Hill, close to Castle Rock. The day has been fine, calm, with a bright sun, but the temperature has fallen to $-20°$. From the hill it was clear that the old ice had

broken away a good deal since the " Morning " left, but
it is still a long way from the ship—quite three and a half
miles.   The young ice nearly covers the sea, and must
be getting pretty solid.   There were a good many
open leads in it, but very few seals were up, which is
curious on such a fine day ; yesterday we added twenty-
eight to our stock, which ought now to be ample.

'On my walks I can rarely think of much else
but our position and its possibilities.   What does our
imprisonment mean?   Was it this summer or the last
which was the exception ?   Does the ice usually break
away around the cape, or does it usually stop short to
the north ?   For us these must be the gravest possible
questions, for on the answers depend our prospects of
getting away next year or at all.   It is little wonder that
I think of these things continually and scan every nook and
corner in hopes of discovering evidences to support my
views ; for I hold steadily to a belief that the answers are
in our favour, and that our detention is due to exceptional
conditions.

'The Ross Sea has certainly never been found in
such a heavily packed state as it was this year, but
how far this bears on the question one can only surmise.   Coming more immediately to our neighbourhood,
we have but one thing which can help us in the comparison of the two seasons—namely, the state of the old
ice on our arrival.   If this was one year's ice, as we
supposed, then there must have been open water round
the cape for two years in succession, and we could reasonably complain of ill fortune if there are many close

seasons to follow ; but the question is, Was what we found one year's ice ? On our arrival we never doubted the fact, but for this reason we never looked critically at it, and now it is most difficult to remember the indications which we observed so casually more than a year ago. All sorts of complicated difficulties arise in thinking out this problem, yet if it were purely an academic one, I should long ago have given my opinion unhesitatingly in the direction I have indicated. But, alas ! it is far too serious to be disposed of by the strongest expression of opinion, and no certain answer will come until we have waited to see what happens next year.

'So at the end of all my cogitations on this most important matter, I get little further than the knowledge that patience is an invaluable quality, and that it is not the least use worrying about the question now. I think this is pretty well the attitude of everyone on board, for although the subject sometimes crops up in conversation, it is generally dismissed as unprofitable : all are content to make the best of the present and hope for the best in the future.

'It is certainly a great matter for congratulation that we are rid of the undesirable members of our community ; although they were far too small a minority to cause active trouble, there was always the knowledge that they were on board, mixing freely with others, ready to fan the flame of discontent and exaggerate the smallest grievance. No doubt it would have been possible to suppress this element as effectually during a second winter as during the first, but one grows tired of keeping a sharp eye on disciplinary matters, and it is an infinite relief to feel that there is no longer the necessity for it. With such an uncertain future before us, it is good to feel that there is not a single soul to mar the harmony of our relations, and to know that, whatever may befall, one can have complete confidence in one's companions.

' It is not until lately also that I realised how easily we could spare the actual services of those who have left ; in fact, the manner in which the work is done now seems to show that they were a hindrance rather than a help to it. For instance, though I was unaffectedly glad to see the last of our cook, I was a little doubtful as to how we should manage in the galley department, but as things have turned out, we are doing infinitely better. It has been arranged that the cook's mate, Clarke, should be nominally the cook, and that volunteers from the crew should take spells of a fortnight or more as his assistant ; this means practically that Clarke continues to make the excellent bread and cakes which we have always enjoyed, whilst the cooking is conducted more or less by a committee of taste, who collectively bring considerable knowledge to bear on the subject and take a huge delight in trying to make pleasing dishes. Of course, as is natural with such an arrangement, there are occasional failures, but on the whole it works admirably ; the men are delighted with what might be termed the freedom of the galley, and at least they know now that everything is prepared with a proper regard for cleanliness.'

' *March* 23.—The sun is sinking rapidly, and already lamps are lit for dinner. It is curious to observe the

varying effect which the summer has had on the ice
about us.   At the end of the winter it was from six to
seven feet thick, but now at its thickest, in Arrival Bay,
it is only five feet, whereas a few hundred yards away off
Hut Point at one time it was almost melted through,
while off Cape Armitage there was a large hole where it
had disappeared altogether.   Under this hole we have
recently found a shallow bank of three fathoms, and we
know there is another bank off Hut Point ; there can be
no doubt, therefore, that the melting takes place where
the current runs rapidly over shallow places.   In our
small bay the ice is eight or nine feet thick, and in some
places much more, but this is due to the quantity of snow
which has fallen on its surface.

'It is strange how the tracks of footsteps remain
indicated in the snow round about ; as a rule, the com-
pressed snow under each footprint remains firm, and is
left like a small islet after the surrounding deposit has
been swept away by the wind.   In this manner the whole
nature of the surface about our colony has been altered ;
it is surrounded by a hard trodden area from which
radiate beaten highways in all directions.   The hill-slopes
round about are quite spoiled for skiing purposes.'

'*Abril* 7.—With the exception of spreading the
awning our preparations for winter are now pretty well
completed.   Snow has been brought in and distributed
liberally over the decks, and has been banked up on
each side opposite the living-quarters ; guide ropes to
the screen and to the huts have been erected ; one of the
boats has been placed on the ice-foot, and the remainder

so secured that they will be clear of the awning ; leading away in various directions can be seen long lines of sticks and cask staves, which go to different fishing holes and other outlying stations for work.   All these are due to the industry of Hodgson and Barne.

'The great game for the season is hockey ; whenever the weather permits all hands join in the keen contests we hold on the floe.   The game is played with light bandy-sticks and a hard ball made on board ; it is just as well we have not the heavier sticks, as few rules are observed and figures can be seen flying about with sticks held high above their heads ready to deliver the most murderous blows, back-handed or front, as suits best.   There is really no time to consider rules, and although there is the proper organisation of backs and forwards on each side, no one wants to take the part of umpire.   Occasionally there is a cry of " Off side ! " but no one pays very much attention.

'However, in spite of this, we have very exciting matches.   Sometimes the officers play the men, some-times we divide by an age limit, and sometimes in other ways.   To-day it has been " Married and Engaged v. Single," and as the former side lacked numbers we had to include in it those who were accused of being engaged, in spite of protest.   The match was played in a tempera-ture of −40°, and it was odd to see the players rushing about with clouds of steam about their heads and their helmets sparkling with frost.   We played half an hour each way, which was quite enough in such weather.   We shall, I hope, keep to this capital exercise until the light fails.'

'*April* 24.—On Wednesday the sun left us, and darkness is coming on apace; and so we are entering on the course of our second winter, but withal in the highest spirits, just as happy and contented a community as can be. It would be agreeable to know what is going to happen next year, but otherwise we have no wants. Our routine goes like clockwork; we eat, sleep, work, and play at regular hours, and are never in lack of employment. Hockey, I fear, must soon cease, for lack of light, but it has been a great diversion, although not unattended with risks, for yesterday I captured a black eye from a ball furiously driven by Royds.

' Our acetylene plant is now in full swing, and gives us light for twelve hours at an expenditure of about 3 lbs. of carbide. The winter awning is spread, and all is as snug as we can make it; but the temperature is extremely low, and we have the old trouble with the ice inside our living-spaces.'

' *May* 6.—A brilliant idea struck us a fortnight ago. We thought of putting our large fish-trap down on the shallow bank off the cape, and weighing it every few days to see what it contained. Visions of supplying our whole company with this delightful luxury were before our eyes. The fish-trap consists of a large pyramidal frame, six feet square on the base, and covered with wire netting, in which there are cone-shaped openings.

' In accordance with our idea, this trap was taken out to the bank, which is about a mile from the ship, and over which the ice is still comparatively thin. Here a high tripod was erected, a hole made, and the trap lowered; two days after it was got up again, and to our great joy we found it contained 105 fish. Our visions seemed realised; down went the trap again, and without a moment's delay we set about making another and digging a second hole close to the ship. This was no light task, and the workers were lost to view from above long before they reached the bottom of our solid ice, which proved to be more than eight feet thick. However, at length both traps were down, and since that we have been getting them up every other day; but, alas! there has been a most terrible falling-off in the catches. The outer trap fell from 105 to thirty, then to ten, and lately we are lucky if we find more than five or six. The inner has never had more than this last number, and sometimes comes up empty. One of the reasons for the failure of the outer trap is, I think, that the seals have found it, and feel that they ought to have first choice of the fish that it attracts, and this would naturally not be encouraging to the latter. Sometimes the seals must run full speed into the trap, because it often comes up badly dented; one can only hope it gives them a bad headache. Another great enemy to our fishing industry is the small shrimp-like amphipod; these small creatures collect in millions, and eat things up with extraordinary rapidity; they are submarine locusts, and vast armies of them settle on the bait, or even on the live fish, and in a few hours not a remnant remains of what they have attacked.

'The small bottom fish which we catch are very ugly little creatures; they have an enormous head, a

protruding under lip, and a gradually tapering body—
rather the shape of a whiting, only exaggerated. They
are extremely good eating, but unfortunately the
majority are very small; it takes two of the largest
to make a decent meal for one person, and of the
average size four or five will scarcely suffice. They
are of the genus *Notathenia*, and I believe there is
more than one species; the Weddell seals feed principally on these, but they also catch other sorts, whose
present habitat we cannot discover by any of our fishing methods. Besides what we may call the Antarctic
whiting, our people caught a quantity of a surface fish
that frequented the pools and cracks in the ice during
the summer. This was whilst I was absent from the
ship, and I have neither seen nor tasted this fish, but I
hear that it gave very good sport. Some of the men
would go out for an hour or two with quite a short
line and bread for bait, returning with a dozen or two
decent-sized fish, which report declares to have been
much better eating than even the whiting. Now that
all the cracks are frozen over we do not get a glimpse
of these fish, except when they are brought to view
from the interior of a seal. We know that there must
be lots of fish about from the continuance of the seals in
our region, and we have strong reason for supposing
that there must be some of a much greater size than any
we have caught, but we have tried all sorts of methods
and all sorts of baits without success in capturing anything but our whiting.

'The seal is certainly the best fisherman, and very

frequently when one is captured our people have the benefit of its latest prey as well as the animal itself.

'As far as our fish-traps are concerned, I'm afraid as the darkness deepens our catches are likely to get smaller and smaller. Recently we have been saving up, so that the mess-deck should have a fish breakfast one Sunday and the officers the same on the next, but this will not continue, as we cannot hope to keep up the supply for so many months.

'Our winter routine of feeding is now pretty well fixed. We shall have mutton on Sunday as long as it will last, skua on Tuesday, seal's heart on Thursday, and plain seal on the other days. The kidneys are used to make seal-steak pie, an excellent dish; the liver comes at breakfast twice a week; and the sweetbreads I suppose pass as cook's perquisites, as we never see them aft. I am thinking of having cold tinned meat one night a week, so as to give the galley people a night off.'

'*May* 16.—We are getting record temperatures. Yesterday the minimum at the outer thermometer was $-66°$, and to-day I read it myself at $-67.7°$; the screen thermometer has not been below $-55°$, showing that we still enjoy the shelter of our comparatively warm corner. It would appear that this year is going to be much colder than last, but since March we have had far less wind than during the corresponding period of last year, and we could welcome a far severer cold if it assures us an absence of this scourge.

'Some of our costumes this year are very quaint. Our

gaberdine wind clothes are badly worn, and what remains of them is being reserved for sledging ; to take the place of these we have served out all sorts of odd scraps of material together with a large green tent which was brought south by the 'Morning.' This has resulted in the most curious outer garments, and one may see a figure approaching in a pair of gaily striped and patched trousers and a bright green jumper, a combination of colour which in any other place could scarcely fail to attract marked attention.'

'*June* 12.—This week we have had the first blizzard for the winter, with some rather novel features. The wind has come and gone with surprising rapidity. Sometimes it has been blowing with extreme violence, harder than I have ever known it; at others it has been almost calm, with the air still filled with snow. The barometer has been hurrying down and up over a range of nearly an inch, and the thermometer rose at one time to $+17\frac{1}{2}°$. Last night the floor of the entrance porch was a swamp, whilst water was dripping from the sides and roof. It has never been in this state before during the winter. In many respects the gale has been the worst we have had, and yet, thanks to experience, we have weathered it without any of the minor mishaps of last year, except the temporary loss of our stove-pipe exhaust. From without the ship looks to be completely buried in snow.

' We are still at a loss for any warning of our approaching blizzards. The barometer only commences its vagaries after the storm is on us. There has been a suggestion that strong mirage is a sign of bad weather to come, but this fortunately is not the case, as very extraordinary mirage effects are constantly seen. At one time we had an idea that the electrometer might be taken as a guide, but this, again, seems to show little until the gale has actually begun.

'But although the electrometer may not serve us in this way, it has yielded some extremely interesting results. Bernacchi has continued to take regular observations with this instrument; he mounts it on a tripod and takes observations with the match conductor just above it, or hoisted on a pole fifteen feet high. He is thus able to discover the electrical potential at both these heights, though the task is not always a pleasing one, as the small screws of the instrument have to be manipulated with bared fingers. Once or twice Skelton has assisted Bernacchi in taking hourly observations over a considerable period. Perhaps the most interesting point is that there is almost continuously a negative potential in our regions, whereas in temperate regions the air is generally electro-positive to the earth.

'The observations at four feet and fifteen feet show that the difference of potential increases considerably with the altitude. During the summer months there is a perceptible daily range, with a maximum at midnight and a minimum at noon, and the potential is higher than in winter when there is no measurable range. When the air is filled with falling or drifting snow the potential becomes very large and the tension is often great enough to discharge the instrument.'

'*June* 23.—Our second midwinter day has come and
gone, finding us even more cheerful than the last. We
made a great night of it last night ; the warrant officers
dined aft, and we had soup made from a real turtle sent
to us by our kind friend Mr. Kinsey, of Christchurch,
and brought over in the last sledge-load from the
" Morning." After this came tinned halibut, roast beef
with artichokes, devilled wing of skua as savoury, and
the last of our special brand of champagne. On ordinary
nights we are now reduced to enamelled plates and mugs,
but we still hold in reserve some crockery and glass for
these special occasions, and it adds to our cheer to see
our table well appointed again.

After dinner we felt we must have some novelty, so
someone suggested a dance. The table was got out of
the way, Royds went to the piano, and the rest of us
assembled for a set of lancers, one of the most uproarious
in which I have ever indulged. Then came cock-fighting
and tugs of war, and altogether we had as festive an
evening as we have ever spent.'

'*July* 3.—Our winter is speeding along in the pleasantest fashion, and all are keeping in good health and
spirits. Our puppies of last year are puppies no longer,
but have developed into dogs, showing all the unmerciful,
bullying traits of character of their parents. In all there
are eight survivors of last year's litters : " Blackie,"
" Nobby," " Toby," and " Violet " are descendants of poor
" Nell," " Roger " and " Snowball " of " Blanco," and
" Wolf " and " Tin-tacks " of " Vincka." The different
families are not at all fond of one another, nor is there

any wild attachment between members of the same. However, we have decided they must take care of themselves and settle their own grievances as, although they may be useful next year, we do not propose to take them on long journeys ; they are therefore allowed to roam about as they please, though kennels are provided for them, and of course they are regularly fed. The result of this freedom is that there are already new families of puppies arriving on the scene. The greater number of these must be removed, as it cannot be hoped that they will be anything but poor creatures ; meanwhile there has been a searching for names, and the latest suggestion is a series including " Plasmon," " Somatose," and " Ptomaine " !

I am taking rather longer walks over the hills than I did last winter, as I want to be thoroughly fit for the sledging. As a rule four or five of the dogs come with me, and my appearance outside is the signal for a chorus of welcome ; as we go up the hills my companions scrimmage, playfully or otherwise, the whole time ; then their delight is for me to roll stones down the steeper slopes, when they dash after them at a prodigious speed and in a smother of snow. They are wonderfully sure-footed, and will sometimes bring themselves up in mid-career with extraordinary suddenness, and come trotting up the slope as though it was the easiest of feats.'

' *July* 13.—Yesterday Wilson reported an eruption of Erebus, a considerable sheet of flame bursting forth and lighting up the rolls of vapour, so that he could clearly see the direction in which they were going—a fact impossible to distinguish either before or after; the flare only lasted for five or ten seconds. These eruptions have been seen before, and possibly many have occurred without being seen, but they are certainly not frequent, and never last for more than a few seconds. I myself have never seen more than a red glare on the cloud of vapour immediately over the crater.'

'*July* 16.—Hodgson has been working away throughout the winter in the same indefatigable manner as before. His fish-traps and tow-nets merely go down through a hole in the ice, and there is no great difficulty about working them; but the manner in which he has carried out his dredging is really very cunning, and deserves description. Now and again, and especially after a cold snap, fresh cracks are formed in the ice-sheet across the strait, and these open out perhaps two or three inches. Before the space left has time to freeze thickly, Hodgson goes out with a long line, and presses the bight down between the sides of the crack until it is hanging in a long loop between points two or three hundred yards apart. Then at each end of the loop he starts to dig a large hole; this is the work of several days, and meanwhile the ice along the crack has become solid and thick, but this does not matter when once he has got what he wants—namely, two holes connected by a line which passes underneath the ice.

'Later on, when the holes are completed and shelters have been erected about them, the more important work commences. A net is secured to the line and lowered to the bottom at one hole, whilst at the other the line is manned and gradually hauled in ; thus the net is dragged along the bottom to the second hole, where it is hoisted out and its contents emptied into a vessel. Then the process is repeated by hauling the net back to the first hole. Finally the vessel, usually an old tin-lined packing-case, with its precious contents of animals buried in a mass of hardening slush, is sledged back to the ship and deposited close to the wardroom fire.

'On the following day the table is littered with an array of glass jars and dishes, with bottles of alcohol, formalin, and other preservatives, and soon we are able to examine the queer denizens of our polar sea-floor, and to watch their contortions as they are skilfully turned into specimens for the British Museum.'

'*July* 31.—For some days there has scarcely been any wind, and we have been able to enjoy delightful walks in the light noontide. The northern horizon at this hour is dressed in gorgeous red and gold, and the lands about are pink and rosy with brightness of returning day. I am not sure that a polar night is not worth the living through for the mere joy of seeing the day come back.

'The latest addition to our forces, in the shape of Mulock, has been a great acquisition. In one way and another we have collected a very large amount of surveying data, but the trouble was that we none of us had sufficient knowledge to chart it. Mulock came in the nick of time to supply the deficiency ; he has been trained as a surveyor, and has extraordinary natural abilities for the work. He has done an astonishing amount this winter, first in collecting and reworking all our observations, and later in constructing temporary charts. A special table was fixed up for him in my cabin, where he now spends most of his time. The result of his diligence is most useful to me, as I can now see much more clearly what we ought to try to do during our next sledging season.'

'*August* 1.—Walks over the hills are now delightful. However cold one may be on starting, by the time one reaches the crest one's blood is circulating freely, and the rest is wholly enjoyable. A good look at the glorious scene round about, a long trot over the hill plateau, an observation of Erebus with its gilded coil of smoke, a half slide, half shuffle down some convenient snow-slope amidst two or three scrambling, skylarking dogs, a sharp walk back over the level, and a glorious appetite for tea to follow : there is not much hardship about this sort of life.

'Perhaps Barne has enjoyed himself as much as anyone this winter in his own queer way. The improved weather has given him a chance to spend many a day at his distant sounding holes, and he has constantly departed soon after breakfast to vanish from our ken until dinner. But this winter he has rigged his small sledge with sails, and if it has not aided his work much, it has given him a deal of extra amusement. The sledge carries a small sounding machine, mounted high on a box in the centre. The box contains a miscellaneous collection of sinkers, thermometers, &c., together

with the owner's light midday repast.   In front of and
behind the box are the main and mizen masts, to which
are hoisted a dashing suit of sails, made from the drop
scene of the Terror Theatre.   There is also a drop keel
or lee board, made from a piece of boiler-plate, and a
wooden outrigger, which can be placed on either side
and weighted with a sinker to increase the stability of
the machine.   Barne declares that if there is any breeze
his noble craft sails like a witch, on or off the wind, but
this is scarcely the opinion of others who have watched
his movements.   However, when the " Flying Scud,"
as she is called, is lying astern of the " Discovery " with
sails neatly furled, or when with all canvas spread she is
prepared for her voyage over the floe, she at least looks
a very imposing and business-like tender.'

'*August* 13.—For three days we have had a furious
blizzard, which has kept us closely confined.   On the few
occasions when we attempted to reach the ship side we
found it almost impossible to stand, and there was a
curious suffocating feeling in battling with the whirling
drift.   Some gusts were so violent that the ship was
shaken, and things hanging in the wardroom were set
on the swing, notwithstanding that the ice must now be
from eighteen to twenty feet thick immediately around
us.   On Tuesday, with a lull, the glass rose three-quarters
of an inch in six hours—about the steepest gradient we
have known.   It then fell again sharply, and the wind
returned in full force.   To-day it is quite calm again,
and we can see that there has been an immense deposition of snow ; the ice-sledges are covered, and the

surface has risen to the level of the meteorological screens. From the hills I could see no sign of open water—a curious difference from last year, when after such a gale the sea would certainly have been open up to the Northern Islets.'

'*August* 20.—Some time ago poor little "Tin-tacks," who has a litter of pups in the after deckhouse, was found with her mouth covered with blood; she was unable to eat, and on examination Wilson found that her tongue had been torn or cut off within an inch or two of the root. The only fitting theory seems to be that the poor beast got it frozen to a tin and then became frightened, and jagged or bit it off. It was a horrible accident, but it shows the astonishing vitality of these dogs that within a few days she was able to eat and ran about as though nothing had happened; she had evidently quite ceased to suffer pain. But although she can feed herself she cannot keep herself clean, and she is likely to get into such a bad state in this way that I fear we shall have to kill her.

'Wilson has found a hard, calcareous growth in the seals' hearts which appears to show that these animals suffer from gout!

'We have seen some very beautiful "mother-of-pearl" clouds to the north lately—little patches of yellowish-white close to the horizon, edged with pale green passing to red and yellow, this bordering extending all around. The prismatic colouring we have hitherto seen in the light high cirrus has been horizontal only. The Danish Lapland Expedition noted prismatic clouds as having a height of thirty miles ; ours are certainly nothing like so high.'

' *August* 21.—The rim of the refracted sun could just be seen above the northern horizon at 12.30 to-day. I climbed Arrival Heights and got a view of the golden half-disc. It was a glorious day ; everything was inspiriting. For the first time for many a month the sun's direct rays were gilding our surrounding hills ; little warm, pink clouds floated about, growing heavier towards the south, where the deepening shadow was overspread with a rich flush ; the smoke of Erebus rose straight in a spreading golden column. It was indeed a goodly scene ! One feels that the return of day is beyond all power of description—that splendid view from the hills leaves one with a sense of grandeur and solemnity which no words can paint.

' And now our second long polar night has come to an end. I do not think there is a soul on board the " Discovery " who would say that it has been a hardship. All disappointment at our enforced detention has passed away, and has been replaced by a steady feeling of hopefulness. There is not one of us who does not believe that we shall be released eventually, however difficult he might find it to give his reasons. All thoughts are turned towards the work that lies before us, and it would be difficult to be blind to the possible extent of its usefulness. Each day has brought it more home to us how little we know and how much there is to be learned, and we realise fully that this second year's work may more than double the value of our observations. Life in these

regions has lost any terror it ever possessed for us, for
we know that, come what may, we can live, and live well,
for any reasonable number of years to come.'

'*August* 25.—The earth shadows on the southern
sky thrown by the sun as it skims along the northern
horizon have been very distinct this year, and there is
much that cannot be explained and therefore gives rise
to hot argument. Between nine and ten in the morning
a dark shaded line, inclined to the right at an acute
angle to the horizon, appears to the westward of the
Black Island; this line gradually rises to the vertical to
the east of Black Island, and then sinks to the left with a
diminishing angle. Just before noon its extremity rests
on the Bluff, when it is inclined well to the east, but
sometimes at about this time two other shadows spring
up, one vertical and the other inclined to the west;
the whole phenomenon then has the appearance of an
inverted broad arrow.

'It is very curious and interesting, and we have
failed to produce any sound explanation for it. It
must in some way be connected with Erebus, as it is
on the opposite side of it to the sun; but what particular parts of the mountain mass trace these confused
shadowy lines we cannot guess. Some of us have tried
to drag in the western mountains as reflecting agents,
but I think this theory has little to support it. Meanwhile we have all been busy with candles and sheets of
paper trying to reproduce the various effects, but so far
without much success.

'Beyond the region of our bay the snow which has

fallen during the winter is heaped into patches which are clearly distinguishable from the old surface, on which can still be seen in large numbers the pellets of the cartridges used in the skua *battues* of last autumn.   We have started our hockey matches again, and had some excellent games, but the ground is in very poor condition, with patches of soft snow where the ball gets half buried.

' *September* 3.—After the return of the sun there are some very pleasing signs of summer, for which we watch eagerly.   Amongst these are the first records of our solar instruments, one of which, the radiation thermometer, gave its first indication on the 28th, when there was an extremely slight difference between the black and silvered bulb thermometers.   This instrument faces the sun on Hut Point, and to-day it showed a very marked difference between the two readings ; and at the same time another instrument, the sunshine recorder, gave its first sign of life.   The sunshine recorder consists of a crystal sphere, by which the sun rays are focussed on a circular strip of graduated paper ; when the sun is out, the track of the focus is marked by a burnt line, and in this way the hours during which the sun shows are recorded.   Last year we got several papers burnt for the complete twenty-four hours, and doubtless we shall get the same again ; I believe this is the first time such a record has been got.'

Such extracts as I have given from my diary show that our second winter passed away in the quietest and pleasantest fashion.   Throughout the season the routine of scientific observations was carried out in the same

manner as it had been during the previous year, whilst
many new details of interest were added. The weather
on the whole, though colder, had been far less windy,
and this, together with the help which experience gave
to our methods of living, had greatly added to our comfort. Whilst everything was taken calmly and easily,
the work of preparation for the coming season had been
steadily pushed forward. An examination of our sledge
equipment showed that there was scarcely an article
which did not need to be thoroughly overhauled and
refitted, and throughout the winter our men had been
systematically employed in repairing the sledges, sleeping-bags, tents, &c., in weighing out and packing the
various provisions, and generally in preparing for the
long journeys which had been arranged. With our best
efforts, however, it was evident that our outfit for this
season would be a somewhat tattered and makeshift
affair compared with what it had been at the commencement of the last. For our sleeping-bags we were obliged
to employ skins that we knew to be of inferior quality ;
our tents were blackened with use, threadbare in texture,
and patched in many places ; our cooking-apparatus were
dented and shaky ; our wind clothes were almost worn
out ; and for all the small bags which were required
for our provisions we were obliged to fall back on such
sheets and tablecloths as could be scraped together.

As in the previous year, the plan of campaign for
the coming season had been drawn up in good time,
so that everyone might have ample opportunity of preparing himself for the work ; and in the peaceful quiet

of the winter it had been easy to see the weak places in our former explorations and the directions in which the future journeys should be made.

Perhaps here, therefore, it would be well to mention briefly the considerations which led me to the adoption of the programme of sledging carried out during our second year.

The first point was of course to review our resources ; as before, I knew that extended journeys could only be made by properly supported parties, and an easy calculation showed me that our small company would only admit of two such supported journeys, though numbers might permit of a third more or less lengthy journey without support.

The next thing was to decide in what direction these parties should go. In this connection, as I have already explained, the principal interest undoubtedly lay in the west ; to explore the Ferrar Glacier from a geological point of view and to find out the nature of the interior ice-cap were matters which must be attempted at all hazards.

In the south it was evident to me that however well a party might march, or however well they might be supported, without dogs they could not hope to get beyond the point which we had reached in the previous year ; but our journey had been made a long way from land, and had consequently left many unsolved problems, chief amongst which were the extraordinary straits which had appeared to us to run through the mountain ranges without rising in level. It was obviously absurd for us to pretend that we knew all about these places when we had only seen them at a distance of twenty or thirty miles; any further light thrown on these, or on the junction of the barrier with the land, must prove of immense interest to us. It was therefore with the main object of exploring one of these straits that I decided that the second supported party should set forth.

The credit for arranging the direction in which the unsupported party should go really belongs to Bernacchi, for it was he who first asked me what proof we had that the barrier surface continued on a level to the eastward. Since the previous year, and having regard to the barrier edge in this direction, we had assumed this fact, but when I came to look into it I found we really had no definite proof. The only way to obtain it was to go and see, and this was therefore named as the objective of the unsupported party, who affected to believe that they were destined to discover all sorts of interesting land arising through the monotonous snow-plains for which they were bound. Besides the longer journeys, the programme for the season included, as before, a number of short journeys for specific purposes. The most important of these were periodic visits to the Emperor penguin rookery, as we hoped that this year our zoologist would be able to observe the habits of these extraordinary creatures from the commencement of their breeding season.

The next step in this programme was the most difficult of all; it was to name the individuals for the various journeys. When all had supported me so loyally, and when all were so eager to go to the front, it can be imagined what a hard task lay before me in making a selection. However, this difficulty, like others, was gradually overcome by much thought, and the various parties were told off. The journey to the west I decided to lead myself, that to the south I entrusted to Barne and Mulock, whilst the two officers named for the south-eastern effort were Royds and Bernacchi.

Finally, it was decided that one important factor must dominate all our sledging arrangements. We knew that we were mainly at the mercy of natural causes as to whether the 'Discovery' would be freed from the ice in the coming year, but at least I determined that as far as man's puny efforts could prevail, nothing should be left undone to aid in the release of the ship. At the earliest date at which we could hope to make any impression on the great ice-sheet about us, the whole force of our company must be available for the work of extrication; consequently the last of the summer must be sacrificed, and it was ordered that all sledging journeys should start at such a date as to assure their return to the ship by the middle of December.

Thus when the sun returned again in 1903 it found us ready to start on our journeys once more, and only waiting with impatience for the light which was to guide us on our way. The story of these journeys I reserve for a future chapter, but in what state of health and spirits we undertook them can be gathered from the following :

' *September* 6.—To-morrow we start our sledging ; the Terror party go to Cape Crozier. The ship is in a state of bustle, people flying to and fro, packing sledges, weighing loads, and inspecting each detail of equipment. To judge by the laughter and excitement we might be boys escaping from school. The word " scurvy " has not been heard this year, and the doctor tells me there is not a sign of it in the ship. Truly our prospects look bright for the sledge-work of the future.'

CHAPTER XVII

COMMENCEMENT OF OUR SECOND SLEDGING SEASON

Parties Starting—Away to New Harbour—We Find a Good Road, Establish
a Depot, and Return—Sledging in Record Temperatures—Experiences in
Different Directions—Emperor Penguin Chicks—Eclipse of the Sun—A
Great Capture—Preparing for the Western Journey—Ascending Ferrar
Glacier—Our Sledges Break Down—Forced to Return—Some Good
Marching—Fresh Start—More Troubles with the Sledges—A Heavy
Loss—Wind from the Summit—The Upper Glacier—A Week in Camp
—We Break Away and Reach the Summit—Hard Conditions—Party
Divided—Eight Days Onward—An Awe-inspiring Plain—We Turn as
the Month Ends.

> Where the great sun begins his state
> Robed in flames and amber light.—MILTON.

> Path of advance ! but it leads
> A long steep journey through sunk
> Gorges, o'er mountains in snow.—M. ARNOLD.

WHEN the great sun had begun his state in 1903 we were
all, as I have said, eager to be off on our travels once
more.

Royds and Wilson were the first to get away, on
September 7 ; they had with them four men—Cross,
Whitfield, Williamson, and Blissett ; their mission lay on
the old track to Cape Crozier, and the object of going
thus early was to catch those mysterious Emperor penguins before they should have hatched out their young.

Barne and his party were timed to start some days

later, with the idea of laying out a depot beyond the White Island, in preparation for the longer journey to come.

On the 9th I got away with my own party, which included Mr. Skelton, Mr. Dailey, Evans, Lashly, and Handsley. Our object was to find a new road to the Ferrar Glacier, and on it to place a depot ready for a greater effort over the ice-cap. I pause a moment to recall to the reader the position of affairs in this region. The Ferrar Glacier descends gradually to the inlet, which we named New Harbour, but it will be remembered that Mr. Armitage had reported most adversely on this inlet as a route for sledges, and in conducting his own party had led it across the high foothills. I had not been to this region, but in the nature of things I could not help thinking that some practicable route must exist up the New Harbour inlet, and I knew that if it could be found our journey to the west would be made far easier. It was in this direction, therefore, that I set out with my party.

Half-way across the strait we had the misfortune to encounter a blizzard, which delayed us in our tents and effectually covered all our camping equipment with ice ; then the temperature fell rapidly, and we knew that our discomfort for the trip was ensured. Owing to the delay we did not reach the New Harbour until the 13th, and it took us the whole of the daylight hours of the 14th to struggle up the south side of the inlet to the commencement of the disturbances caused by the glacier.

The night of the 14th was an anxious one, and I

remember it well. On each side of us rose the great granite foothills. The light had been poor in the afternoon march, and now that the sun had sunk behind the mountains in a crimson glow, we were left with only the barest twilight. We had been forced to camp when we had suddenly found ourselves on a broken surface, and all about us loomed up gigantic ice-blocks and lofty morainic heaps. To-morrow was to decide whether or not these obstructions could be tackled ; meanwhile the temperature had fallen to $-49°$, and in the frigid gloom our prospects did not look hopeful.

On the following day, however, with cheerful sunshine to aid our efforts, we proceeded for some way up the bed of a frozen stream, still on the south side of the glacier. On our right was the glacier itself, distorted into a mass of wall faces and pinnacles, which looked unscalable, whilst on our left were the steep bare hillsides ; soon the glacier stream came to an end, and we were forced to consider what was next to be done.

As a result of our consultation some of the party climbed the hillside to prospect, whilst Skelton and I attacked the glacier. We fully expected to discover a mass of broken ice extending right across the inlet, but were agreeably surprised to find, first, that by carefully selecting our route we could work our way to the summit of the disturbance ; and, secondly, that beyond our immediate neighbourhood the high, sharp ice-hillocks settled down into more gradual ridges. This implied that to the north things were smoother, and after our short reconnaissance and a confirming report from the hills, we occupied the rest of the day in carrying our loads and sledges in the direction we had chosen across the disturbance. It was a difficult portage, but by night we were camped in a small dip well in on the glacier surface.

Those who have seen glaciers in a mountainous country will recall the regular and beautiful curves they present in sweeping around the sharp turns of the valleys they occupy. It was such a curve that the Ferrar Glacier now showed us as we looked westward on the morning of the 16th ; its surface, as we afterwards found, was comparatively regular, but in the distance it looked like a smooth polished road—a ribbon of blue down the centre of which ran a dark streak caused by a double line of boulders. On each side towered the massive cliffs and steep hillsides which limited its course. But the foot of this promising road was some way from us, and we had still four or five miles of unviewed surface to cross before we could reach it. Here, again, we were agreeably surprised, for instead of further ice disturbances we found our way gradually growing smoother, and in the afternoon we reached the incline without further difficulty.

What followed was easy. We proceeded to ascend the smooth icy surface of the glacier until we came abreast of Cathedral Rocks, and when their lofty pinnacles towered three or four thousand feet immediately above our heads we selected a conspicuous boulder in the medial moraine, about 2,000 feet above the sea, and, ascertaining its bearings, 'cached' the provisions which we had brought, and turned homeward.

The result of our short journey had been really

important. It had taken the western party of the previous year three weeks to reach the spot at which we had left our depot ; I knew now it would go hard with us if we could not get there well within the week, and if in the future we found a still easier road, avoiding the portage stage, we might hope to journey out in four or five days.

On our return, therefore, we steered more to the north, and to our further delight found that the route in that direction was much easier, so that eventually we reached the sea-ice without having to carry our sledges across any difficult places.

The fact which was thus discovered, and which was amply supported by further observations, is a general one that is highly important to future explorers. In all cases in the Antarctic Regions where glaciers run more or less east and west, the south side will be found very much broken up and decayed, whilst the north side will be comparatively smooth and even. The reason is a very simple one—so simple that it seems to argue some obtuseness that we did not guess its effect. The sun of course achieves its greatest altitude in the north, and consequently its warmest and most direct rays fall on the south side of a valley, and on the loose morainic material and blown débris that rest on that side of a glacier. Here, therefore, the greater part of the summer melting takes place with irregular denudation, causing the wild chaos of ice disturbance that I have described.

At the foot of the Ferrar Glacier, Armitage had seen the disturbance on the south side, and had concluded that it must extend right across ; our fortunate step had been to push over the southern disturbance and find the easier conditions beyond.

Throughout this short journey we had exceedingly low temperatures. Nearly every night the thermometer fell below −50°, and in the daytime it was very little above that mark. After the effects of our blizzard we were extraordinarily uncomfortable; it was partly for this reason, and partly to test the real marching capabilities of my party, that, our object attained, I decided to put on the speed in crossing the fifty miles of sea-ice which lay between us and our snug ship. We crossed this stretch in less than two and a half days; we were to do better marching still under better conditions, but at the time we were very pleased with this effort, and considering the excessive cold and our heavily clad and ice-encumbered condition, it was certainly worthy of note. It was on the night of the 20th, therefore, that we tramped into our small bay and saw the pleasantly familiar outlines of the ship.

We were inclined to be exceedingly self-satisfied; we had accomplished our object with unexpected ease, we had done a record march, and we had endured record temperatures—at least, we thought so, and thought also how pleasant it would be to tell of these things in front of a nice bright fire. As we approached the ship, how-ever, Hodgson came out to greet us, and his first question was, 'What temperatures have you had?' We replied by complacently quoting our array of *minus* fifties, but he quickly cut us short by remarking that we were not in it.   It was evident, therefore, that we should have tales to listen to as well as to tell.

For such tales I draw once more on my diary :

'*September* 22.—It is pleasant to be back in the ship again after our hard spring journeys.   They have awakened us all and given us plenty of fresh matter to talk about, so that there is a running fire of chaff and chatter all day.   Everything looks very bright and hopeful : the journeys have accomplished all that was expected of them, and there is not a sign of our old enemy the scurvy ; and this in spite of the fact that our travellers have endured the hardest conditions on record.

' It is no small tribute to our sledging methods that our people have come through temperatures nearly seventy degrees below zero without accident or injury ; a tent and a sleeping-bag have never protected men under such conditions before.

' Whilst we have been away there seems to have been a cold snap throughout our region.   Barne with his party got the worst of it, as they were away out on the barrier, where conditions are always most severe.   He was absent for eight days, and succeeded in laying out a depot to the S.E. of White Island.   His party consisted of Mulock, Quartley, Smythe, Crean, and Joyce ; all have tales to tell of their adventures, and agree that it was pretty "parky."   The temperature was well below $-40°$ when they left the ship ; it dropped to $-50°$ as they reached the corner of White Island, and a little way beyond to $-60°$; but even at this it did not stop, but continued falling until it had reached and passed $-65°$.

At $-67.7°$ the spirit-column of the thermometer broke, and they found it impossible to get it to unite again ; we shall never know exactly, therefore, what degree of cold this party actually faced, but Barne, allowing for the broken column, is sure that it was below $-70°$.

'Joyce was the only one who suffered seriously from these terribly severe conditions. After his features had been frost-bitten several times individually, they all went together, and he was seen with his whole face quite white. Though, of course, it is in a very bad state now, the circulation was restored in it at the time without much difficulty ; but worse was to follow, for on the march he announced that one of his feet was gone, and, having pitched the tents, Barne examined it, and found that it was white to the ankle. It was quite an hour before they could get any signs of life in it, and this was only accomplished by the officers taking it in turns to nurse the frozen member in their breasts.

'All the party, and especially the owner of the frozen foot, seem to regard this incident as an excellent jest ; but for my part I should be slow to see a joke when I had a frost-bitten foot myself, or even when I had to undo my garments in a temperature of $-70°$ to nurse someone else's. It appears that those who were giving the warmth found that they could keep the icy foot in contact with their bodies for nearly ten minutes, but at the end of that time they had to hand it on to the next member of the party ; they own that it was not a pleasing sensation, but think that it increased their appetites. However, their ministrations have brought Joyce safely back to the ship with his full allowance of toes, which is the main point.

' Royds and his party also had very low temperatures, as their thermometer often showed −60°, and at the lowest −62°. Blissett was the chief sufferer on this journey, as he also had his face very severely frostbitten ; the rest seem to have stood it well, and Whitfield is described as standing outside the tent with his pipe in his mouth, his hands in his pockets, and the air of cheerful satisfaction of one who contemplates his garden on a warm summer day at home.

' This party have had a great stroke of luck. On arriving at Cape Crozier it was found, in spite of calculations, that the Emperors had already hatched out their young ; about a thousand adult birds were seen, and a good number of chicks, but at first there appeared to be no eggs. The luck came when the travellers examined the ice towards the land and found that there had been a recent fall of ice-blocks ; close to this they discovered a number of deserted eggs. It seems evident that the avalanche frightened away the sitting birds, much to the benefit of our collection. Including the single find of last year we have now seventeen specimens of this new egg ; some are cracked, but a good number are whole ; they weigh about a pound apiece.

' As may be imagined, the party were highly elated with this find, and Wilson was glad of the opportunity of studying the chicks at a more tender age than they were seen last year. In spite of the severe temperature, Cross determined to try to bring two of these small mites home. He sacrificed his sleeping-jacket to keep them warm, and tended them with such motherly care that he has succeeded in his design, and now these small creatures are housed in Wilson's cabin, much to our amusement. They chirrup like overgrown chickens, and possess the most prodigious appetites.'

These chicks continued to afford us entertainment; they had no fear whatever, and when they thought that the time had come for more food, they clamoured loudly for it.

At first they were fed on crustaceans, and afterwards on seal-meat, but both of these were chewed up by the person who fed them, so that there should be no chance of indigestion. It will be seen from their shape that they were well designed as regards capacity for containing food, but even allowing for the fact that they did not study the symmetry of their waists, one paused aghast at the amount they swallowed. From the first we had to regard them as small tanks, but as they grew they almost seemed to be bottomless caverns, into which any quantity of material might be dropped without making any appreciable difference.

After meals their small heads would sink back on their round, distended little bodies, and they would go placidly off to sleep in their well-lined nest, when they were covered up and for the moment forgotten; but as the next meal-hour approached there would be a great 'to-do,' and the box would be uncovered to show the small heads bobbing up and down and giving forth shrill demands for more food, nor was there peace till they got it.

Things went on like this until our small friends suddenly took it into their heads that there was much too long an interval between supper and breakfast, and after this they used to go off like alarum clocks in the middle of the night. There was only one way of pacifying them, and their custodian had perforce to get out of his warm bed and to chew up more seal-meat until they were satisfied.

Of course we could scarcely hope to rear these birds under such artificial conditions, and we were not surprised when one of them pined away and died; but the other lived and throve for a long time, and only met his end when the warmer weather came on and he was incautiously put in one of the deck-houses for a short time; this exposure brought on the rickets, from which he never recovered.

During the interval between the return of our spring expeditions and the start of the longer summer ones we had several small excitements on board.

In one of these we suffered a grievous disappointment. Our nautical almanac told us that there would be an eclipse of the sun on September 21. It was not to be a total eclipse for us, but nine-tenths of the sun would be obscured. Bernacchi was especially busy in preparation for this event, and all placed themselves under his orders for the occasion. When the great day came all telescopes and the spectroscopic camera were trained in the right direction, magnetic instruments were set to run at quick speed, and observers were told off to watch the meteorological instruments, the tide gauge, and everything else on which the absence of sun could possibly have a direct or indirect effect. Everything, in fact, was ready but the sun itself, which obstinately refused to come out; from early morning a thick stratus cloud hung over our heads, and as the hours went by we were forced to abandon all hope of a clearance. There may have been an eclipse of the sun on September 21, 1903, as the almanac said, but we should none of us have liked to swear to the fact.

After our return from the spring journey, appetites had increased to such an alarming extent that we began to have renewed doubts as to the adequacy of our stock of seal-meat, and by this time all the especial luxuries in the shape of livers and kidneys had entirely disappeared. Seals rarely came up on the ice, and when they did our wretched dogs, the puppies of the previous year, did their best to worry them down again. It was at this juncture that our hunters were called upon, and their chief, Skelton, devised an excellent harpoon with hinged barbs which proved the most effective weapon. With a line attached, it was kept in readiness at one of the nearer fishing holes, and the keenest sportsmen would go out and wait by the hour, harpoon in hand, ready for the first unfortunate seal which should come up to breathe. The long wait in the cold was rather a drawback, but when at last a black snout appeared on the surface and the murderous weapon was plunged downward there was great excitement, and loud shouts were raised for assistance to haul in the line. In this way our larder was kept well supplied, whilst a few obtained feasts of the fish which we had long ceased to catch by our own efforts.

There was great excitement one day when one of the men went to this hole in the ice and, seeing a disturbance in the water, plunged the harpoon down. Evidently striking something, he rushed back to the ship to say that he had hit a big fish. There was a general stampede for the hole, and the harpoon line was soon being hauled in, in spite of the very lively something at the other end; but when at last this something was landed on the floe it was found to be nothing more unusual than a large seal, and naturally there was a chorus of jeers at the expense of the man who had claimed to have struck a big fish. In spite of ridicule, however, this individual stuck to his story that there had been a fish, and soon after it was proved that he had been quite accurate, for, searching amongst the brash ice in the hole, Skelton suddenly raised a shout, and in a moment or two produced the headless body of the large fish for which we had angled so ineffectually.

It was borne back in triumph to the ship and hung up for general admiration; in its mangled condition it was three feet ten inches in length and weighed thirty-nine pounds.

The importance of this capture deserves some description. Large fish are very uncommon in polar waters : as a general rule, the colder the water the smaller the fish. We had known, however, that large fish existed in our regions, as more than once we had found the skeletal remains of one on the ice.   But this was the first time we had actually seen the creature itself, and now, alas! it had no head, and therefore lacked the most important detail for its scientific classification.   The most scientific, and, in fact, the only account we ever had of the missing head was from the originator of the incident, who declared that 'it was like one of Mr. Barne's crampons.' This account, whilst it delighted those who not infre-quently entered into discussions with Barne as to the size of his feet, failed to supply the accuracy necessary for scientific description.   There was one consolation, however, in the fact that if the head had remained on, the fish would have sunk and we should have seen nothing of it.

Piecing together the facts of the capture, we came to see how it had all happened, and the whole makes a curious story.   We found that the seal was a female with young, and had not had food for a long time.   In this condition it had attacked the large fish, and evidently had had a tremendous tussle with it.   The seal must have been almost at the end of its diving powers when it had dragged its struggling prey to the surface, and at this point the harpoon must have transfixed both it and the fish.   Whether the seal had mutilated the head of the fish we could not tell, but close to the tail and on the tail-fin of the latter were found distinct wounds caused by the seal's teeth.   It shows the great swimming powers of the seal that it should have been able to capture so powerful a victim.

When we had safely got our big fish on board, a dreadful fear arose that our biologist would demand its preservation in spirit. I do not know whether it was the absence of the head or his own appetite that prompted his decision on this question, but to our relief he announced that as long as he had the skeleton, the rest, after he had examined it, could go to the cook. As we had no use for the skeleton, we were perfectly contented with this arrangement, and on the following day our fish provided the most sumptuous repast for our whole company. It is difficult to say exactly what this fish tasted like. Science would, I suppose, dismiss its qualities in this respect by the single word 'edible,' and we, whilst we could muster a good many adjectives to express our appreciation, found it difficult to liken it to anything we had previously tasted. It had a firm, white flesh, and a most deliciously delicate flavour, and that perhaps is all I can say of it.

Not long after this great capture the ship was once more busy with all the preparations for the coming sledging campaign. Barne and Mulock were the first to get away, on October 6. This was one of the two extended journeys of which our complement would allow. In the advance party with these two officers went the men who had accompanied them on their severe depot journey, whilst the supporting party consisted of Dellbridge, Allan, Wild, Pilbeam, and Croucher. The whole party were to journey south around the Bluff, and thence to strike across for the entrance to the big strait since called the Barne Inlet. After about a fortnight the supporting party were to turn back, whilst the advance party made the best of a ten weeks' absence from the ship.

By October 11 all preparations for my own western effort had been completed, and on the following day we started full of high hopes of penetrating far into the interior.

I have already pointed out what great interests lay to the west at this time, and how incomplete our knowledge was of this region. The long hours of our second winter had given me ample time to consider the importance of the problems which yet remained to be solved there, and these thoughts had not only resigned me to our detention in the ice, but had gradually shown me that if all went well in future, it might turn out to be an unmixed blessing.

If we could do all that I hoped in the Ferrar Glacier and beyond, during a second season's work, I knew that the value of our labours of the first year would be immensely increased. As I have said before, the interest centred in this region ; there were fascinating problems elsewhere, but none now which could compare with those of the western land. It was such considerations that made me resolve to go in this direction myself, and I determined that no effort should be spared to ensure success.

Rarely, I think, has more time and attention been devoted to the preparation of a sledge journey than was given to this one. I rightly guessed that in many respects it was going to be the hardest task we had yet undertaken, but I knew also that our experience was now a thing that could be counted upon, and that it would take a good deal to stop a party of our determined, experienced sledge travellers.

I am bound to confess that I have some pride in this journey. We met with immense difficulties, such as would have brought us hopelessly to grief in the previous year, yet now as veterans we steered through them with success; and when all circumstances are considered, the extreme severity of the climate and the obstacles that stood in our path, I cannot but believe we came near the limit of possible performance.

It is for this reason, and because the region in which much of our work lay was very beautiful and interesting, that I propose to take the reader into the details of one more sledging excursion.

The party with which I left the ship on October 12, 1903, numbered twelve members in all. It was really the combination of three separate parties. First came my own advance party, which I had selected with great care, and which included our chief engineer, Skelton, our boatswain, Feather, and three men, Evans, Lashly, and Handsley; secondly, there was a small party for our geologist, Ferrar, with whom went two men, Kennar and Weller; and thirdly, there were the supports, consisting of our carpenter, Dailey, and two other men, Williamson and Plumley.

The original scheme was that the whole party should journey together to the summit of Victoria Land, and as far beyond as could be reached within a certain limit of time ; then the advance party should proceed and the remainder turn back. An absence of nine weeks was calculated for the advance party. The supports were to return direct to the ship, but stores were to be so arranged in the glacier depots that Ferrar was allowed an absence of six weeks in which to make a geological survey of the region.

We started from the ship with four eleven-foot sledges, and with an outfit of permanent stores which the reader will find on referring to the chapter dealing with sledge equipment. Altogether our loads were a little over 200 lbs. per man ; but most of us were in pretty hard condition by this time, and we found little difficulty in dragging such a weight.

And so we started away with the usual cheers and good wishes, little thinking how soon we should be on board again.

As I had determined that from first to last of this trip there should be hard marching, we stretched across over the forty-five miles to New Harbour at a good round pace, and by working long hours succeeded in reaching the snow-cape on the near side early on the 14th—a highly creditable performance with such heavy loads.

This snow-cape was in future to be known as ' Butter Point.' It was here that on our return journey we could first hope to obtain fresh seal-meat, and, in preparation for this great event, a tin of butter was carried and left at this point for each party.

And here I fall back on my diary as may be required to continue the thread of my tale.

' *October* 14.—Had to camp early to-night as Dailey and Williamson are a bit seedy, probably a little overcome with the march. At supper the third member of this unlucky unit, Plumley, cut off the top of his thumb in trying to chop up frozen pemmican. He is quite cheerful about it, and has been showing the frozen detached piece of thumb to everyone else as an interesting curio. For the present we are comparatively comfortable; the temperature has not been below −20°, and I do not expect anything lower till we get to the upper reaches of the glacier.'

On the 15th we struck the glacier snout well on its north side, and found, as I had guessed, an easy road; from there on to the first incline of the glacier we crossed only mild undulations and had no difficulties with our sledges. It was extraordinary, after we had discovered and travelled over this easy route, to remember what a bogey it had been to us for more than twelve months.

On the 16th we reached our spring depot under the Cathedral Rocks, and after picking it up and readjusting our loads, proceeded a few miles higher to a spot where Armitage had planted some sticks in the previous year to mark the movement of the glacier. We camped in gloriously fine weather, and I wrote: ' To-night it is difficult to imagine oneself in a polar region. If one forgets for the moment that there is ice under foot, which it is not difficult to do as it is very dark in colour and there are many boulders close about us, one might be in any climate, for nearly all around is dark bare rock. We

are in a deep gorge, not narrow, as the glacier here is
probably four or five miles across, but the cliffs on either
side are so majestic and lofty that the broad surface of
the glacier is wholly dwarfed by them.

' We are on the south side of the valley, and towering
precipitously between three and four thousand feet above
our heads are the high sunlit pinnacles of the Cathedral
Rocks ; they were well named by Armitage, for their lofty
peaks might well be the spires of some mighty edifice.
Low down the rock itself is gneiss, I believe ; in colour a
greyish black, but veined and splashed with many a lighter
hue.   The high weathered pinnacles have a rich brown
shade ; this is basalt, which here directly overlies the
gneiss.   On the further side of our valley the hills rise
almost as abruptly as on this ; reddish brown is the predominant colour there also, but where the sunlight falls
on the steeper cliffs it is lightened almost to a brick red.
A little snow can be seen amongst the peaks and gullies
opposite to us, and here and there the sparkling white of
some hanging glacier is in marked contrast to the rich
tones of the bare rock.

' We are camped in the medial moraine, a long
scattered line of boulders of every form and colour.
Looking east one can see this line winding down with
graceful curves over the blue surface of the glacier,
towards the sea ; far away beyond is the ice-covered
sea itself, pearly grey in the distance.   One can follow
this highway of boulders to the west too, till it vanishes
over the undulating inclines above us ; in this direction the glacier wears a formidable aspect, for in its

centre is an immense cascade.   It is exactly as though this was some river which had been suddenly frozen in its course, with the cascade to show where its waters had been dashing wildly over a rocky shallow ; it is very beautiful, with its gleaming white waves and deep blue shadows, but we shall have to give it a wide berth when we travel upward.   The upper valley is perhaps our most beautiful view ; the dark cliffs form a broad V and frame the cascading glacier, and above it the distant solitary peak of the Knob Head Mountain and a patch of crimson sky.'

'*October* 17.—We have been climbing upward all day, at first over a gentle incline on smooth, hard, glassy ice, where the sledges came very easily but unsteadily, skidding in all directions ; later the incline increased and the surface was roughened with tiny wavelets like those formed by a catspaw sweeping over a placid lake.   We walked on without crampons, getting foothold in the hollow of these wavelets.   Later still we came to a stiffer rise, and transverse cracks appeared across our path, growing more numerous and widening out as we ascended till we found ourselves crossing miniature crevasses lightly bridged with snow.   We had to step across these, and often it meant a long step.   In this manner we steered round to the north of the cascade, and by lunch-time had ascended almost to the higher basin of the glacier.

' Immediately before lunch we had to get over a very stiff little bit, where the cracks were sometimes three or four feet across, and the ice very rough between ; it was heavy work getting the sledges up, and I rather feared someone would get a strain or sprain, but we all got over it in safety. In the afternoon, at a height of 4,500 feet, we topped the last rise that led to the glacier basin ; and then, on a surface covered with the usual tiny wavelets, and from which the cracks rapidly disappeared, we travelled over a stretch of seven or eight miles with a gradual fall of 600 or 700 feet, and at length reached a stream of enormous boulders which ran right across our track. This is what Armitage called the Knob Head Moraine. He was twenty-seven days out from the ship before he reached it ; we have got here in six.

' The changes of scene throughout the day have been bewildering. Not one half-hour of our march has passed without some new feature bursting upon our astonished gaze. Certainly those who saw this valley last year did not exaggerate its grandeur—indeed, it would be impossible to do so. It is wonderfully beautiful. As we came up the lower gorge this morning, we passed from side to side with frowning cliffs towering over us on either hand ; ahead between these dark walls the sky, perhaps by contrast, looked intensely blue, and here and there in the valley floated a little wisp of feathery white cloud ; again and again these appeared under some forbidding rock-face only to melt impalpably away. As we emerged into the great ice-basin we turned towards the north to face a new aspect of this wonderful country.

' To describe the wildly beautiful scene that is about us to-night is a task that is far beyond my pen. Away behind us is the gorge by which we have come ; but now above and beyond its splendid cliffs we can see rising fold on fold the white snow-clad slopes of Mount Lister. Only at the very top of its broad, blunt summit is there a sign of bare rock, and that is 11,000 feet above our present elevated position ; so clear is the air that one seems to see every wrinkle and crease in the rolling masses of névé beneath.

'The great basin in which we are camped has four outlets. Opposite that by which we have come descends what we call the south-west arm ; it is a prodigious ice-flow, but falls steeply and roughly between its rocky boundaries. Away ahead of us is the north-west arm ; we have some twisting and turning to get to it, but shall eventually round a sharp corner and steer up it to the westward. To the right of this and ahead of us also is the north arm, which seems to descend sharply towards the sea. Besides these main outlets or inlets, there are some places to the west of us where smaller ice-flows fall into our basin with steep crevassed surfaces, and in many places around are lighter tributaries descending from the small local névé fields. But for the main part we are surrounded with steep, bare hillsides of fantastic and beautiful forms and of great variety in colour. The groundwork of the colour-scheme is a russet brown, but to the west especially it has infinite gradations of shade, passing from bright red to dull grey, whilst here and there, and generally in banded form, occurs an almost vivid yellow. The whole forms a glorious combination of autumn tints, and few forests in their autumnal raiment could outvie it.

' The most curious feature about us is the great mass of rock immediately in front. It appears to form two islands, for the great body of ice which occupies the basin seems to join again beyond it. Armitage called these islands the " Solitary Rocks "; they are comparatively flat on top, and rich brown in colour, save where two broad bands of yellow run horizontally through them. These bands are so regular and uniform in thickness that one might almost imagine they had been painted on. Geologically all this should be of immense interest, for the bands which are broken off so sharply at the cliffs of these islands can be seen to appear again in the high hills beyond, and no doubt would appear everywhere if many of the hillsides were not covered with loose rubble. The whole structure of the country seems to be horizontal, but exactly what the rocks are, we have not yet ascertained ; the brown is probably basalt, and the yellow, Ferrar hopes, is the sedimentary rock which he has found in the moraines.'

As Mr. Ferrar has added an appendix to this volume dealing with the geological formation of this interesting region, I shall in future omit all remarks of mine which bear on the subject. I have only included the foregoing to give some idea of the task which Ferrar had before him. Both before and after this he found in the various moraines a large variety of rocks — granites, gneisses, sandstone, quartz, &c. — but as this was all transported material it told very little. It was only as we ascended this great glacier and saw the curious horizontal stratification of the hills that the problem gradually unfolded itself before him, and he arrived at some notion of the places to be visited when he commenced his investigations.

It was on the night of the 17th, whilst we were still absorbed in the beauty and novelty of the scene about us, that the first cloud of trouble loomed above our horizon, for it was on this night the carpenter reported that the German silver had split under the runners of two of our sledges.   As this matter was of the gravest import to us, it perhaps needs a little explanation. I have pointed out before that the wood runners of our sledges were quite capable of running on snow without protection ; on the hard, sharp ice, however, it was a different matter.   In such circumstances, a wood runner would be knocked to pieces in a very few hours, especially if the sledge was heavily laden.   At all hazards, therefore, it was necessary to protect our runners over this hard ice, but unfortunately the German silver protection had already stood one season's work, and this had worn it thin without giving any outward sign.   We only found out how thin it had become when it gave out on this journey, and hence the troubles which I am about to describe were quite unexpected.

From start to finish of the Ferrar Glacier there were about ninety miles in which hard ice might be expected, and the problem that soon came before us was how to get our sledges over this without damage.

On the 17th I scarcely realised myself the full importance of the carpenter's report, but on the 18th matters came to a crisis, as will be seen.

'*October* 18.—We got away early this morning, crossed the moraines and continued our ascent over hard, wavy ice. It was quite calm about us, with the temperature at about −20°, but a short distance ahead we could see the wind sweeping down from a gully on our left, carrying clouds of snowdrift. We did not at all like the look of this wind-swept area, but it had to be crossed, and we plunged into it after adjusting our wind-guards. It took us over an hour to get across, and several of us got badly frost-bitten, as immediately opposite the gully the wind was extraordinarily violent, and it was as much as we could do to hold up against it. Once past the gully, however, it was nearly calm and comparatively warm again ; by lunch-time we had reached a new meandering moraine, almost abreast of the Solitary Rocks, and had achieved a height of over 6,000 feet.

'I, with my party, was some way ahead when I decided to camp, but the supports soon came up, bringing, alas ! a woeful tale—another sledge had split its runners.

'After lunch I had all the sledges unpacked and the runners turned up for inspection, with horrid revelations. On two sledges the German silver was split to ribbons and the wood deeply scored, a third was only in slightly better case, whilst the fourth still remained sound. I could see nothing for it but to return home ; if we had two sound sledges we might struggle on with the advance party, but with one we could do nothing. It was no use even discussing the matter—there was only one course ; so we left the sound sledge with everything else except the half-week's provisions necessary to take

us back, and after crossing the windy area once
more, we are now back at our old encampment in the
Knob Head Moraine.   It is a bitter disappointment to
my hopes; everything will have to be reorganised, and
Heaven knows what sacrifices of time we shall have to
make.   However, there shall not be more than I can
help, and things which have gone fast in the past, will
positively have to fly in the future.'

On the following days we came as near flying as is possible with a sledge party.   We had eighty-seven miles to
cover on the morning of the 19th, when we were up and
away with the first streak of dawn; then we started our
rush, at first up the slight incline to the summit of the
pass, and then down through the steeper gorge towards
the sea.   We did not pause to pick a road, but went
straight forward, scrambling as best we could over steep
places and taking all obstacles in our stride.   Once only
we halted to snatch a hasty lunch, and then were off
again over the rugged, slippery ice.

That night we camped at sea level twenty-seven
miles below our starting-point.   The next morning
brought us a hard pull with our torn runners over
the long stretch of rough snow-covered glacier tongue,
but at lunch-time we had reached the end, and devoted
an hour to stripping the broken, twisted metal from
our sledges.

By this time I had determined to test my own party
to the utmost, but I did not see that the supporting
people need be dragged into our effort; so telling the
latter that they might take their own time, I started

away with my own detachment over the sea-ice towards the mouth of the inlet at the quickest pace we had yet attempted. When the brief night descended on us we camped with twenty-four miles to our credit for the day, and as our tents were being secured I looked round to find that the supporting party were still gallantly struggling on in our wake; seeing our tents go up, they halted about a mile and a half behind us.

At dawn on the 21st we were away once more, and stretching out directly for the ship; far away we could see Castle Rock and Observation Hill, small dots on the horizon. Hour after hour went by, but we never eased our pace till at our lunch hour we came on a fat seal and paused to eat our meal and to secure the certainty of a good supper from the animal that had been unwise enough to bask in our track. In the afternoon our home landmarks grew more distinct, and as the sun dipped we came on the last six miles of wind-tossed snow that skirted our peninsula. The semi-darkness found us struggling on over this uneven, difficult surface, but at half-past eight we were through and reached the ship, having covered thirty-six miles in the day.

We had accomplished a record for which the glow of satisfaction that we felt was excusable; but more was to follow, for later that night a shout of welcome announced that our undefeated supporting party had also struggled home. Ferrar soon told me his tale: at first they had not intended to come in at racing speed, but seeing the advance party striding off at such a pace, their feelings of emulation had been excited, and they had

felt bound to follow. On camping behind us on the previous night they had determined to catch us in the
early morning, but as they roused out with that intention
they saw that we also were preparing to be off. Then
followed the long march, when, despite all their efforts,
the leading party grew more and more indistinct. It
was not until late in the afternoon that they lost sight of
us altogether, and then there could be no doubt of our
intention to reach the ship before night.

In spite of their lame and exhausted condition, they
determined to follow. Once or twice they had halted to
brew tea to keep themselves going, but not one of them
had suggested that the halt should be extended. In the
hard struggle of the last few hours some of the men had
kept things going by occasionally indulging in some dry
remark which caused everyone to laugh. Kennar's attitude had been one of grieved astonishment ; presumably
referring to me, he had kept repeating, ' If he can do
it, I don't see why I can't : my legs are as long as his.'

And so it was that this party made the record march
of all, for they started more than a mile behind us, and
must have covered over thirty-seven miles in the day.

In spite of our marching, it was a blow to be back in
the ship so soon after we had made our first hopeful
start, and, as can be imagined, I did not allow time to
be wasted in preparing to be off again. Our carpenter
was soon at work repairing the sledges with all the
assistance that could be afforded him. Meanwhile I saw
that it would be necessary to reorganise our arrangements. Without going into the reasons which guided me,

I may say that I now thought the best scheme was for the advance party to start off on its own account, to pick up the glacier provisions, and to dispose of them on a new plan. I arranged that Ferrar should start with a small sledge of his own, and should be entirely independent; but as he signified his wish to remain with us as long as possible, it was still a party of nine that started out on October 26, five days after our flying return. Our material for repairing sledges was very scanty, but at length out of the parts of various broken ones we had succeeded in producing one sound eleven-foot sledge for our own party and a short seven-foot one for Ferrar's glacier work.

With these we once more started to cross the long stretch of sea-ice to the mainland. The night of the 27th found us at the end of the glacier tongue, and I wrote: 'We can fairly claim to be in good marching condition, having crossed the strait at an average of over twenty-five miles a day. This morning we met a small group of Emperor penguins; they were going south towards "the Eskers," for what reason one cannot guess, travelling on their breasts and propelling themselves with their powerful feet at a speed of at least five miles an hour. Of course when they saw us they made in our direction, and when quite close stood up and squawked loudly. They watched us for some time with every manifestation of amazement, and then started to follow in our wake, but of this they soon tired, and resuming their old course to the south, were shortly out of sight.'

In preparation for our renewed struggle with the hard ice of the glacier, we had brought with us some under-runners shod with German silver, and at the glacier tongue we picked up all the scraps of this metal which we had formerly discarded.

'*October* 28.—We are camped opposite Descent Pass after a hard day. This morning early we had a glorious view of the glacier valley. The sun shone brightly on the great gaunt cliffs which rose one above the other towards the inland, and every outline was sharp against the deep blue sky. Later, low sheets of stratus cloud spread across the valley and shimmered in the sunlight. This afternoon a nimbus cloud crept in over our heads, bringing a trifling snowfall; the sun struggled against it, but for the time the valley was clothed in mists.

'Troubles have already come upon us; the under-runners of our sledge split on the first incline, and we had to take them off. The metal on one of the runners on which we now rely is badly laminated, and may go at any moment. These difficulties are very annoying, but I have determined to get to the top this time, even if we have to carry our loads.'

From this time on we had constant worries with these wretched runners. On the 29th Ferrar's small sledge gave out, and we had a long delay to get it into working order again. Notwithstanding this we got within a few hundred yards of the Knob Head Moraine before we called a halt for the night. On the broad surface of this glacier there were few places in which we could camp for want of snow to secure our tents; for this reason we generally kept moderately close to the long lines of morainic boulders, as under the largest of these there was usually sufficient snow for our purpose.   In a few places elsewhere we found a thin sheet or isolated patches, but this was not common.

On the night of the 29th we camped in a calm, with the sun shining brightly, and had a fair view of grand hills that surrounded the glacier basin, but now also we again observed a fact which was not so cheering.   On each occasion when we were in this basin it was calm all about us, except in two regions where the wind evidently swept down with great and almost continuous violence.   One of these was what we called the 'Vale of Winds,' across which we had passed before, and the other was unfortunately the north-west arm, up which we proposed to go.   We had never seen the latter without clouds of drift pouring down over its surface, and we shrewdly suspected that we were in for a pretty bad time when we reached it.

'*October* 30.—We have grown a little careless in leaving our things about outside the tent, and this morning we had a lesson.   Our sleeping-bags, with socks, finneskoes, and other garments, lay scattered about on the ice whilst we were having breakfast, when suddenly the wind swept down on us; before we could move everything was skidding away over the surface of the ice.   The moment we realised what was happening the tents were empty and we were flying over the ice as fast as we could after our lost garments.   The incident would have been extremely funny had it not involved the possibility of such serious consequences. The sleeping-bags were well on towards the steep fall of the north arm before they were recovered, and by good luck the whole affair closed with the loss of only a few of the lighter articles.

'As soon as we had struggled back against the heavy wind that was now blowing, we packed our sledges, put on our crampons, and started onward ; but by this time the wind had increased to a full gale, and we could hardly stand against it, so we steered to the westward to get under shelter. This brought us on a slope which gradually grew steeper till it ended in the perpendicular side of the glacier. Proceeding down as far as we thought safe, we entered the moraine and pitched our camp again. I do not know what to make of this moraine, which, starting from the side of the glacier, runs directly across it, and, after first rising for several hundred feet, descends again steeply down the north arm towards the sea.'

I may here mention that these crampons to which I refer were manufactured on board the ship ; those used in the previous year were voted wholly unsatisfactory, and gave rise to many blisters, whereupon our chief engineer took the matter in hand, and with the assistance of the boatswain produced an article which rendered us excellent service on this journey. Each crampon had two steel plates studded with mild steel spikes, one for the sole and the other for the heel ; the plates were riveted on to a canvas overall half-boot which could be put on over a finnesko and kept tight with thongs. The device was heavy, but as quite the best sort of thing in the circumstances it is well worthy of imitation by future travellers in these regions.

The moraine which at this time bewildered us so much was one of those signs of a former greater extension of the ice to which I shall refer in my final chapter.

The wind kept us in this wretched moraine for two days—a tiresome delay—but we managed to get out for an hour or two and make an interesting excursion to the side of the glacier. After a short search we found a way by which, with some aid from a rope, we could climb down the steep ice-face and visit the land beyond.

The accompanying illustration shows the side of the glacier at this spot, and we afterwards found that this was more or less typical of other places. It must be understood that from the top of this wall the surface sloped rapidly up, whilst the bottom layer of ice would naturally have sloped down into the valley, so that in the middle the glacier must have been very many times as thick as at the side. It will be seen how curiously the ice was stratified ; the white part contained numerous air vesicles, the darker parts were in many cases due to included dirt, but the broad dark band in the middle had no dirt in it at all—it was the cleanest ice we saw. A piece split off it was like the purest crystal without a sign of grit or air bubble to obstruct its perfect transparency.

Between this ice-wall and the mountain side lay a deep trench, showing the smooth glassy surface of frozen thaw-water. The mountain side itself, except for one place lower down where there was an outcrop of red granite, was thickly strewn with boulders of every kind of rock which the region produced, whilst here and there could be seen enormous perched blocks ranging up to three or four hundred tons in weight.

All this vast quantity of débris had evidently been carried by ice, and it was now that we first realised to what vastly greater limits our glacier had once extended, for these thickly strewn boulders covered the mountain side to a height of three thousand feet above our heads, where a horizontal line signified their limit and the extent of the glacier at its maximum.

'*November* 1.—It was overcast and dull this morning, but the wind had fallen light and we decided to push on; although the air was comparatively still about us, close ahead the "Vale of Winds" was sending forth its snow-laden gusts as merrily as ever.   Before we came to this unattractive area we passed two more carcases of Weddell seals; the last was at the greatest altitude we have yet found one, nearly 5,000 feet above the sea; it grows more than ever wonderful how these creatures can have got so far from the sea.'   We never satisfactorily explained this matter.   The seal seems often to crawl to the shore or the ice to die, possibly from its instinctive dread of its marine enemies; but unless we had actually found these remains, it would have been past believing that a dying seal could have transported itself over fifty miles of rough steep glacier surface.

'We got safely past the "Vale of Winds" with only one or two frost-bites, and a few miles beyond found our depot without much difficulty.   At first we thought that everything was intact, but a closer examination showed us that the lid of the instrument box had been forced open and that some of the contents were missing. Evidently there has been a violent gale since we were here before. When we came to count up the missing articles, we found that Skelton had lost his goggles and that one or two other trifles had disappeared ; but before we could congratulate ourselves on escaping so lightly, I found to my horror that the " Hints to Travellers " had vanished.

'The gravity of this loss can scarcely be exaggerated ; but whilst I realised the blow I felt that nothing would induce me to return to the ship a second time ; I thought it fair, however, to put the case to the others, and I am, as I expected, fortified by their willing consent to take the risks of pushing on.'

I must here explain what this loss signified. In travelling to the west we expected to be, as indeed we were, for some weeks out of sight of landmarks. In such a case as this the sledge traveller is in precisely the same position as a ship or boat at sea : he can only obtain a knowledge of his whereabouts by observations of the sun or stars, and with the help of these observations he finds his latitude and longitude. To find the latitude from an observation of a heavenly body, however, it is necessary to know the declination of that body, and to find the longitude one must have not only the declination, but certain logarithmic tables. In other words, to find either latitude or longitude, a certain amount of data is required. Now, all these necessary data are supplied in an excellent little publication issued by the Royal Geographical Society and called ' Hints to Travellers,' and it was on this book that I was relying to be able to work out my sights and accurately fix the position of my party.

When this book was lost, therefore, the reader will see how we were placed ; if we did not return to the ship to make good our loss, we should be obliged to take the risk of marching away into the unknown without exactly knowing where we were or how to get back.

As will be seen, this last is precisely what happened, and if the loss of our ' Hints to Travellers ' did not lead us into serious trouble it caused me many a bad half-hour.

' Having decided to push on, we lost as little time as possible in packing our sledges, and in the afternoon we were off once more, steadily ascending over the rough ice. The Solitary Rocks have fallen behind us, and our camp to-night looks out on the broad amphitheatre above them where the glacier sweeps round from the upper reach. On our left is the Finger Mountain, a precipitous mass of rock showing the most extraordinary " fault " in that yellow-banded structure which now seems to surround us on every side.' The reader will see this fault clearly in the accompanying illustration, and will understand its significance from Mr. Ferrar's notes on the Beacon Sandstone formation.

' Finger Mountain forms the pivot about which the glacier turns, and the great difference in the level of the ice above and below the mountain is taken by two heavy broken falls. We are encamped under the lower

and smaller one, but the upper, some three or four miles
beyond, is a magnificent mass of twisted, torn ice-blocks.
To-morrow we have to rise over these falls, but I propose
to take a very roundabout way to avoid difficulties.

'The scene behind us is glorious; we look down
now on the great glacier basin with the dark rugged
mountains that surround it, and far away beyond,
the summit of Mount Lister shows above a bank of
twisted sunlit cloud. But, alas! pleasant as it is to look
at this beautiful scene, trouble is never far from us,
and this afternoon we have had our full share. First
one sledge-runner gave out and then another, and
we arrived at camp with three out of four disabled.
Now, however, there is a fixed determination in the
party to get through somehow, and each difficulty only
serves to show more clearly their resourcefulness. This
particular trouble has called on the metal workers, and
no sooner had we halted and unpacked the sledges than
Skelton and Lashly were hard at work with pliers, files,
and hammers stripping off the torn metal and lapping
fresh pieces over the weak places. They have established a little workshop in this wild spot, and for hours
the scrape of the file and the tap of the hammer have
feebly broken the vast silence.

'We have hopes of the lapping process which is now
being effected, but it needs very careful fitting; each
separate piece of metal protection is made to overlap
the piece behind it, like slates on a roof ; I should doubt
whether such work could be done by people unaccustomed
to dealing with these matters.'

' *November* 2.—This morning it was perfectly calm and still, with a bright sun and the temperature at $+2°$. There was little difficulty in finishing off our repairing work, and when the sledges were ready we started to march upwards again.

'We steered well to the eastward to make a wide circuit of Finger Mountain and its dangerous ice-falls, and on this course gradually approached the northern limit of the great amphitheatre beyond. The precipitous mountains that fringe this limit show in the clearest and most beautiful manner the horizontal stratification of their rocks, and now there can be no doubt that this simple, banded structure is common to the whole region about us, and that the sharp clear lines of the strata are singularly free from faulting.

'In ascending we gradually passed from hard ice to snow. Apparently there is a considerable snowfall in this amphitheatre ; it has made our pulling much harder, but, on the other hand, it saves our sledge-runners from injury, and the more we can get of it the better we shall be pleased. After lunch we passed on to ice again, and the wind sprang up. Coming at first in eddying gusts, it increased with great rapidity, and very soon we were all getting frost-bitten. It was obviously desirable to camp as soon as possible, but never a patch of snow could be seen, and we pushed on with all haste towards the base of the mountains and the fringing moraines of the glacier. We had to search long amongst the latter before we could find the least sign of snow, and when at length we found some, it was so hard that it took us nearly an hour to get our tents up.

' We are now at the base of the upper glacier reach.
From here it rises directly to the inland, and it is over
this broad surface that the wind seems to sweep perpetually.   The whole valley is very ugly with wind and
driving snow, and there cannot be a doubt that this is its
usual condition, and that we shall have a hard fight with
the wind in our teeth; it will be no child's play battling
with this icy blast from the summit.   We have had a fore-
taste of it this afternoon, and at the present moment it is
straining our threadbare tent in no reassuring manner.'

On the following day the wind was as strong as ever,
but we knew it was useless to wait, so pushed on once
more.   For a brief half-hour we got some shelter in a
curious horseshoe bay which we entered to repair
Ferrar's sledge-runners.   Here the cliffs rose perpendicularly, and immediately above our heads the broad band
of sandstone ran with perfect uniformity around the
whole bay.   On rising to the open glacier again, I struck
off for the south side, hoping to get better conditions,
and with very happy results, for shortly after lunch we
walked out of the wind as easily as we had walked into
it on the previous day.   And now I made an error, for I
started from this point to ascend directly upward.   It is
impossible to describe all the turns and twists which
were taken by this glacier, or to mention the numerous
undulations and disturbances which obliged us constantly
to alter our course from side to side, but it must not be
imagined that our route was all plain sailing and easy
travelling.

From a very early time we saw that it was desirable

R 2

to map out our course a long way ahead, and to do so with reference to the various land masses so as to avoid disturbances which we could not see, but at which we guessed. I mention this matter because it impressed on us a golden rule for travelling in this region, which was, 'Always take a long sweep round corners.' We were often tempted to break this rule when a shorter road looked easy, but we never did so without suffering. It was an error of this nature that I made on the afternoon of the 3rd, and which after an hour's work landed us in such a dangerously crevassed region that we were very glad to struggle back by the way we had come. The note I made at this time may perhaps be quoted : ' The whole of this glacier can be made easy by taking the right course—a course such as a steamer takes in rounding the bends of a river. The temptation to cut corners is excessive, but it is always a mistake. By walking round obstructions such as cascades, not only does one avoid danger to life and limb, but also the chance of relay work, which alone would allow the longer distance to be three times as far, without loss of time.

' Whilst we were in difficulties this afternoon there occurred one of those extraordinary climatic changes which are such a menace to sledge travellers. The cold had been so intense that we had been walking all day in our wind clothes and with our heaviest headgear ; but now we suddenly found ourselves perspiring freely, and within half an hour we had stripped off our outer garments, and the majority were walking bareheaded.'

That night we camped in gloriously fine weather,

after crossing to the south side of the glacier and finding another long stream of boulders. Here we had our usual trouble in repairing our battered, torn runners ; and, to add to this annoyance, we had come to the end of our scraps of metal, nails, and everything else necessary for repairing work. It was evident that we could not stand many more miles of this rough ice, and that it would be touch-and-go whether we ever reached the snow above without having to carry our belongings.

We had now attained a height of 7,000 feet, and whilst the summits of the mountains on each side still stood high above our level, they no longer overawed us or conveyed that sense of grandeur which we had felt so keenly at our former camps. The majestic cliffs of the lower valley were beneath us, and we gazed over the top of many a lesser summit to the eastward. To the west the glacier still wound its way upward, and we saw that there was a stiff climb yet to come ; but already the character of the valley was altering, the boundary cliffs were cut by the broad channels of tributary glaciers, the masses of dark, bare rock were becoming detached and isolated, whilst the widening snowfields were creeping upward with the ever-increasing threat to engulf all beneath their white mantle.

November 4 was such an eventful day that I quote its incidents from my diary :

'Started in bright sunshine, but with a chill, increasing wind in our teeth. At first we made good progress over hard, smooth ice, but soon came to a broad field of snow where a large tributary entered the main ice-

stream.   It was heavy pulling across this snow with our
ragged runners, and, to add to our discomfort, the wind
swept down the side valley with the keenest edge.
Beyond this valley lay the "Depot Nunatak," a huge
mass of columnar basalt, and at length we were able to get
our breath beneath its shelter.   Here Evans told me
that one of his feet was "gone."   He was foolishly wearing
a single pair of socks in remembrance of the warm march
of yesterday.   As soon as we had got his unruly member
back to life we proceeded.

'Ahead of us there showed up an immense and rugged
ice-fall, one of those by which the glacier signifies its
entrance into the valley ; at this I knew the bare blue
ice would come to an end, and with it our difficulties with
the sledge-runners, so I determined to push on to the
foot of this fall before camping.   The way led up a steep
crevassed slope of rough, blue ice, and before we had
even reached this slope the weather assumed a most
threatening aspect.   The sun was obscured by stratus
cloud, which drifted rapidly overhead, and the wind
momentarily increased.   We went on at our best speed,
but when we were half-way up the bare icy slope, which
proved much longer than I had expected, the full force
of the gale burst upon us, and the air became thick with
driving snow.

'We pushed on almost at a run to reach the summit
of the slope, and then started to search in every direction for a camping spot.   By this time things were
growing serious ; everyone was badly frost-bitten in the
face, and it was evident that the effects might be very

ugly if we did not find shelter soon. I shall not forget
the next hour in a hurry; we went from side to side
searching vainly for a patch of snow, but everywhere
finding nothing but the bare blue ice. The runners of
our sledges had split again, so badly that we could barely
pull them over the rough surface; we dared not leave
them in the thick drift, and every minute our frost-bites
were increasing. At last we saw a white patch, and
made a rush for it; it proved to be snow indeed, but
so ancient and wind-swept that it was almost as hard as
the solid ice itself. Nevertheless, we knew it was this
or nothing, and in a minute our tents and shovels
were hauled off the sledges, and we were digging for
dear life.

' I seized the shovel myself, for my own tent-party,
but found that I could not make the least impression
on the hard surface. Luckily, at this moment the boatswain came to my relief, and, managing the implement
with much greater skill, succeeded in chipping out a
few small blocks. Then we tried to get up the tent,
but again and again it and the poles were blown flat;
at last the men came to our assistance, and with our
united efforts the three tents were eventually erected.
All this had taken at least an hour, and when at length
we found shelter it was not a moment too soon, for we
were thoroughly exhausted, and fingers and feet, as well
as faces, were now freezing. As soon as possible we
made a brew of tea, which revived us greatly; afterwards
we got our sleeping-bag in, and since that we have been
coiled up within it.

'The temperature to-night is −24°, and it is blowing nearly a full gale ; it is not too pleasant lying under the shelter of our thin, flapping tent under such conditions, but one cannot help remembering that we have come mighty well out of a very tight place.   Nothing but experience saved us from disaster to-day, for I feel pretty confident that we could not have stood another hour in the open.'

Whilst we congratulated ourselves on the fortunate manner in which, in the nick of time, we had been able to find shelter in this camp, we little thought of the dismal experience that we were to suffer before we left it.   It was Wednesday, November 4, when we pitched our tents so hurriedly ; it was Wednesday, November 11, before we resumed our march ; and if I were asked to name the most miserable week I have have ever spent, I should certainly fix on this one.   Throughout this whole time the gale raged unceasingly ; if the wind lulled for a few brief minutes, it was to return with redoubled violence immediately after.   Meanwhile not a vision of the outer world came to us ; we were enveloped continuously in a thick fog of driving snow.

It is difficult to describe such a time ; twenty-two hours out of each twenty-four we spent in our sleeping-bags, but regularly in the morning and in the evening we rolled these up, prepared and ate a hot meal, and then once more sought the depths of the bag.   To sleep much was out of the question, and I scarcely know how the other long hours went.   In our tent had one book, Darwin's delightful ' Cruise of the " Beagle," ' and sometimes one or another would read this aloud until our freezing fingers refused to turn the pages. Often we would drop into conversation, but, as can be imagined, the circumstances were not such as to encourage much talking, and most of the commoner topics were threadbare by the end of the week. Sometimes we would gaze up at the fluttering green canvas overhead, but this was not inspiriting. I find I have written a great deal in my diary, obviously as an occupation; but the combination of all such things was far from filling a whole day, and therefore for the greater part of the time we lay quite still with our eyes open doing nothing and simply enduring. Communication between tents was only possible in the lulls; we therefore watched for these eagerly, and in the quietest, rushed round to shout greetings and learn how our comrades fared.

One task only we were able to perform throughout the time, and that on the first day of our imprisonment, when, thinking all would soon blow over, we hauled our sledges beneath one of the tents and stripped the German silver ready for the onward march.

At first, of course, we went to sleep each night with the comforting hope that the next morning would see a change for the better; but as day followed day without improvement, it was impossible to cherish this hope. And yet I do not believe we ever grew despondent; the feeling that there must be a change if we had the patience to wait never left us.

By the fifth day of our imprisonment, however, sleep threatened to desert us, and matters in general began to take a more serious aspect.   Our sleeping-bags were getting very icy ; some complained that they could no longer keep their feet warm in them, and there could be no doubt that the long inactivity was telling on our circulation and health.

On the evening of this day, therefore, realising that things were beginning to go badly for us, I determined that whatever the conditions might be we would make an attempt to start on the following morning.   To show the result of this attempt I again have recourse to my diary.

'*November* 10.—Before breakfast this morning we shifted our foot-gear ready for the march, and during a lull the boatswain and I dug out our sledges and provisions.   After breakfast the wind came down on us again, but we went out to complete our work.   In ten minutes we were back in the tent ; both my hands were " gone," and I had to be assisted in nursing them back. Skelton had three toes and the heel of one foot badly frost-bitten, and the boatswain had lost all feeling in both feet.   One could only shout an occasional inquiry to the other tents, but I gather their inmates are in pretty much the same condition.   I think the wind and drift have never been quite so bad as to-day, and the temperature is − 20°.   Things are looking serious ; I fear the long spell of bad weather is telling on us.   The cheerfulness of the party is slowly waning ; I heard the usual song from Lashly this morning, but it was very short-lived and dolorous.   Luck is not with us this trip, and yet we have worked hard to make things go right.

Something must be done to-morrow, but what it will be, to-morrow only can show. Weller complained of feeling giddy to-day, but Ferrar says it is because he eats too fast!

'*November* 11.—Thank heaven we have broken away from our " Desolation Camp" at last. It is imposible to describe how awful the past week has been ; it is a "nightmare" to remember. When we turned out this morning there was a lull, but the air was still as thick as a hedge. We hurried over breakfast, dreading each moment that the wind would return, then we bundled everything on to the sledges anyhow, seized our harness, and were away. I had just time to give a few directions to Ferrar, who turned back to seek shelter under the Depot Nunatak. Then we started for the ice-fall, and since that we have got to the top, but how, I don't quite know, nor can I imagine how we have escaped accident. On starting we could not see half-a-dozen yards ahead of us ; within a hundred yards of the camp we as nearly as possible walked into an enormous chasm ; and when we started to ascend the slope we crossed any number of crevasses without waiting to see if the bridges would bear. I really believe that we were in a state when we none of us really cared much what happened ; our sole thought was to get away from that miserable spot.

'At the top of the slope, after ascending nearly 500 feet, we passed suddenly out of the wind, which we could still see sweeping down the valley behind us, and here we halted for lunch, after which all six of us got in one tent whilst the other was hauled in for repairs, which it badly needed after its late ill-usage. While we were chatting over this work it would have been difficult to recognise us as the same party which had started under such grim circumstances in the morning.'

We rose nearly 700 feet on the 11th, and over another steep fall of about the same height on the 12th, but the 13th found us on a more gradual incline, and at the end of the day we camped with our aneroids showing an elevation of 8,900 feet above the sea. We had at length won our fight and reached the summit. We had nearly five weeks' provisions in hand, and I felt that things would go hard if we could not cover a good many miles before we returned to the glacier.

During these few days the weather had been overcast and dull, but on the 14th it cleared, and we got a good view of our surroundings. We found ourselves on a great snow-plain, with a level horizon all about, but above this to the east rose the tops of mountains, many of which we could recognise. Directly to the east and to the north-east only the extreme summits of the higher hills could be seen, but to the south-east Mount Lister and the higher peaks of the Royal Society Range still showed well above our level. It was a fortunate view, for it gave me a chance of fixing our latitude by bearings, and of noting the appearance of objects which would be our leading marks on returning to the glacier.

The latitude also assisted me in putting into execution a plan which I had thought out, and which, though it is somewhat technical, I give for the benefit of ex-

plorers who may be in like case in future. I have already
mentioned the loss of the tables necessary for working
out our observations, and the prospect which lay before
us of wandering over this great snow-plain without knowing exactly where we were. The matter had naturally
been much in my thoughts, and whilst I saw that there
was no hope of working out our longitudes till we got
back to the ship, it occurred to me that we might gather
some idea of our latitude if I could improvise some
method of ascertaining the daily change in the sun's
declination.

With this idea I carefully ruled out a sheet of my
note-book into squares with the intention of making a
curve of the sun's declination. I found on reflection
that I had some data for this curve, for I could calculate
the declination for certain fixed days, such as the day
when the sun had returned to us, and the day when it
first remained above our horizon at midnight; other
points were given by observations taken at known latitudes on the glacier. To make a long story short, I
plotted all these points on my squared paper, and joined
them with a freehand curve of which I have some reason
to be proud, for on my return to the ship I found it was
nowhere more than 4' in error. On the journey I did
not place so much reliance on my handiwork as it
deserved, for there is no doubt it gave us our latitude
with as great an accuracy as we needed at the time.

We had scarcely reached the summit of the ice-cap
and started our journey to the west, when troubles began
to gather about us once more. Our long stay in ' Deso-

lation Camp' had covered our sleeping-bags and night-
jackets with ice, and now the falling temperature gave
this ice little or no chance to evaporate, so that our camping arrangements were attended with discomforts from
which there seemed little prospect of relief.   Each night
the thermometer fell a trifle lower, until on the 16th it
had reached $-44°$, and although it rose slightly in the
daytime, the general conditions of our work were such
as we had experienced on the spring journeys at sea level.
The snow surface in places became extremely hard and
slippery, so that we were obliged to wear crampons, and
between the hard patches lay softer areas through which
we had the greatest difficulty in dragging our sledges.
But the worst feature of our new conditions was the
continuous wind ; it was not a heavy wind—probably
its force never much exceeded 3 or 4 in the Beaufort
scale—but, combined with the low temperature and the
rarefied air, its effect was blighting.   It blew right in our
teeth, and from the first it was evidently not the effect of
temporary atmospheric disturbance, but was a permanent
condition on this great plateau.

I do not think that it would be possible to conceive a
more cheerless prospect than that which faced us at this
time, when on this lofty, desolate plateau we turned our
backs upon the last mountain peak that could remind us
of habitable lands.   Yet before us lay the unknown.
What fascination lies in that word!   Could anyone
wonder that we determined to push on, be the outlook
ever so comfortless ?

And so we plodded on to the west, working long

WHERE NEWS OF US WAS AT LAST FOUND.

THE FIRST GREETINGS.

LEFT BEHIND.

A SKUA GULL.

SKUAS FEEDING.

PREPARED FOR OUTDOOR WORK IN WINTER.

WEDDELL SEAL AND FOUR SPECIES OF FISH.

BERNACCHI AND THE ELECTROMETER.

OUR BIOLOGIST IN HIS SHELTER.

[See p. 191.

FIRE-GLOW ON THE SMOKE OF MOUNT EREBUS.

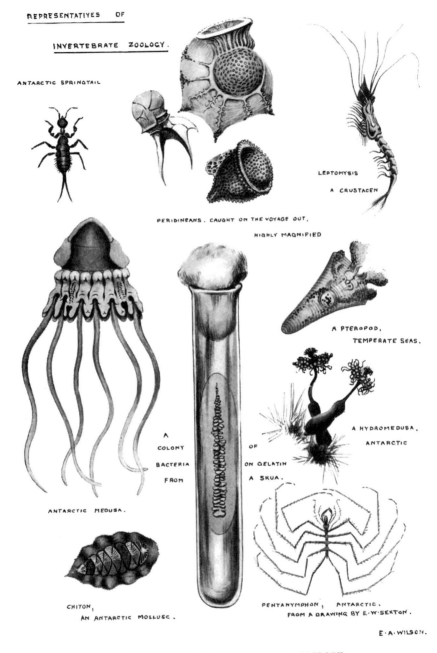

REPRESENTATIVES OF

INVERTEBRATE ZOOLOGY.

ANTARCTIC SPRINGTAIL

LEPTOMYSIS

A CRUSTACEN

PERIDINEANS. CAUGHT ON THE VOYAGE OUT,

HIGHLY MAGNIFIED

A PTEROPOD,

TEMPERATE SEAS.

A
COLONY
BACTERIA
FROM

OF
ON GELATIN
A SKUA.

A HYDROMEDUSA,

ANTARCTIC

ANTARCTIC MEDUSA.

CHITON,
AN ANTARCTIC MOLLUSC.

PENTANYMPHON, ANTARCTIC.
FROM A DRAWING BY E·W·SEXTON.

E·A·WILSON.

REPRESENTATIVES OF INVERTEBRATE ZOOLOGY.

THE 'FLYING SCUD.'

EARTH SHADOWS.

THE BLACK BULB THERMOMETER.

THE SUNSHINE RECORDER.

LOOKING UP FROM NEW HARBOUR.

THE SOUTH SIDE OF A GLACIER.

EMPEROR PENGUIN ROOKERY.

TOWARDS THE EMPEROR PENGUINS.

THE QUAINT PETS BROUGHT FROM CAPE CROZIER.

The Camel's Hump.   Cathedr

LOOKING DOWN ON THE LOWER G

Cathedral Rocks.

A TRIB

al Rocks.

ORGE OF THE FERRAR GLACIER.

The Camel's Hump.

TARY.

Solitary Rocks.   Mount Lister.

A

A

THE SOLITARY ROCKS.

A

A

PANORAMA FROM A POINT ABOVE

Finger Mountain.   Upper Reach of the Glacier.

WAITING FOR A SEAL TO COME UP TO BREATHE.

OUR GREAT CAPTURE—A FORTY-POUNDER.

THE SOLITARY ROCKS FROM THE GLACIER BASIN.

THE SIDE OF THE GLACIER.

BETWEEN GLACIER AND LAND.

FINGER MOUNTAIN.

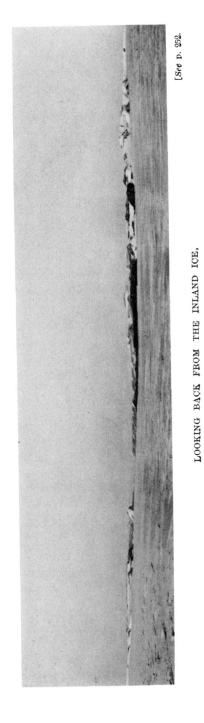

[See p. 252.

LOOKING BACK FROM THE INLAND ICE.

CASCADE IN THE FERRAR GLACIER.

DOWN A CREVASSE.

THE DEPOT NUNATAK.

[*See* p. 285.

DESCENT TO THE 'NORTH ARM.'

[*See* p. 290.

A HANGING GLACIER.

A VALLEY FROM WHICH THE ICE HAS RECEDED.

COOKING WITH SEAL BLUBBER.

PRESSURE RIDGE OFF CAPE CROZIER.

FROM THE FOOTHILLS NORTH

OF THE KOETTLITZ GLACIER.

THE TENT ISLAND.

THE SAWING TENT.

hours and straining at our harness with all our strength, but in spite of every effort our progress became slower. Up to the 17th we kept a fairly good pace, but on the 18th and 19th there was a visible slackening. By this time we had divided our sledges ; Feather, Evans, and I pulled one of them, whilst Skelton, Handsley, and Lashly pulled the other. It was customary for my sledge to pull ahead whilst the other followed as best it could, but soon I found that the second sledge was only keeping up with the greatest difficulty, and it was borne in on me that the excessive strain of our labour was beginning to tell on the party.

The realisation of this fact placed me in a rather amusing but awkward predicament, because, whilst I knew my own strength was unimpaired, I was forced to admit that some of my companions were failing, and in order to find out which of them it was, I was obliged to keep a constant watch on their actions. As was natural with such men, not one of them would own that he was 'done' ; they had come to see the thing through, and they would have dropped in their tracks sooner than give in. And so it was only by the keenest attention, and by playing the somewhat unattractive part of a spy that I could detect those who from sheer incapacity were relaxing their strain on the traces. Even when the knowledge came to me, my position seemed no clearer, for how could I tell these lion-hearted people that they must turn back ? Thus it came about that all six of us marched onward, though I knew that progress would have been bettered had the party been divided.

But this state of affairs came to a climax on the 20th, as the following extract shows :

'We have struggled on some miles to-day, but only with difficulty.   Late last night Handsley came to me to ask if there was anything in the medical bag to relieve a sore throat ; of course there was nothing.   I asked his tent-mates about it, and they told me that for some time he had suffered from his chest, and that on getting up in the morning he had been unable to speak.   This morning he could only answer my questions in a whisper, but declared that he was feeling perfectly fit and quite up to pulling all day.   I didn't like the look of things, but we pushed on.   After about two hours, however, Skelton ranged alongside to say that Handsley had broken down ; it appears that the rear sledge party is finding it terribly hard work to keep up with us, and Handsley has been overstraining himself in attempting to do so.   We camped and had lunch, after which Handsley said he felt sure he could go on, so we packed up, but this time I put all hands on a single sledge, marched it out about three miles, and leaving Handsley to pitch camp, went back to fetch the other one.   This sort of thing won't do at all, but what is one to do ?

'Handsley came to me to-night to beg that he might not be made an example of again.   I tried to explain that I had no intention of reflecting on his conduct, but apparently nothing will persuade him but that his breakdown is in the nature of disgrace.   What children these men are ! and yet what splendid children !   They won't give in till they break down, and then they con-

sider their collapse disgraceful.   The boatswain has been
suffering agonies from his back; he has been pulling just
behind me, and in some sympathy that comes through
the traces I have got to know all about him, yet he has
never uttered a word of complaint, and when he knows
my eye is on him he straightens up and pretends he is
just as fit as ever.   What is one to do with such people ?'

'*November* 21.— . . . There was nothing for it this
morning but to go on with relay work.   We started
over heavy *sastrugi*, but soon came to a space where
there was a smooth glazed crust, which made travelling
easier.   The wind blows continuously from the W.S.W.,
and the temperature has not been above $-30°$ all day;
conditions could not be more horrid.   Handsley is
better, but our whole day's work has only yielded four or
five miles.   Whatever disappointment it may entail, we
cannot go on like this.'

'*November* 22.—After a night's cogitation, I determined this morning on a separation of our party.   Till
lunch we went on in the usual order, but at that meal I
was obliged to announce my decision.   Those told off to
return took it extremely well ; they could not disguise
their disappointment, but they all seemed to understand
that it had to be.   The boatswain was transferred to the
other tent, and Lashly to mine.   After lunch the whole
party manned our single sledge and marched out with
us for two hours, then as the sky looked threatening, the
three returning members turned back to seek their own
camp, whilst I and my chosen two marched steadily on
to the west.'

We had now lost sight of landmarks for several days, and were marching as straight a course as we could, principally with the aid of a small steering dial such as I described as being in use on our southern journey. The error of our compass had passed from east to west, and was nearly at its maximum of 180°; although I could not calculate it accurately at the time, I could get a good idea of its amount by observing the direction in which the sun reached its greatest altitude. The reader will see that from a magnetic point of view this was a very interesting region. We were directly south of the south magnetic pole, and the north end of our compass needle was pointing towards the South (geographical) Pole.

To show what a practical bearing this reversal of the compass had, I may remark that in directing Skelton on his homeward track to the eastward, I told him to steer due west by the compass card. It is only on this line or the similar one which joins the northern poles that such an order could be given, and we were not a little proud of being the first to experience this distinctly interesting physical condition in the Southern Hemisphere.

From the date on which, so reluctantly, I decided that some of my party should turn homeward, there followed for us who remained, three weeks of the hardest physical work that I have ever experienced, and yet three weeks on which I cannot but look with unmixed satisfaction, for I do not think it would have been possible to have accomplished more in the time. I have little wonder when I remember the splendid qualities and physique of the two men who remained with me by such a severe process of selection. Evans was a man of Herculean strength, very long in the arm and with splendidly developed muscles. He had been a gymnastic instructor in the Navy, and had always been an easy winner in all our sports which involved tests of strength. He weighed 12 st. 10 lbs. in hard condition. Lashly, in appearance, was the most deceptive man I have ever seen. He was not above the ordinary height, nor did he look more than ordinarily broad, and yet he weighed 13 st. 8 lbs., and had one of the largest chest measurements in the ship. He had been a teetotaller and non-smoker all his life, and was never in anything but the hardest condition.

My own weight at this time was about 11 st. 6 lbs.; it fell so far short of the others that I felt I really did not deserve such a large food allowance, though I continued to take my full share.

With these two men behind me our sledge seemed to become a living thing, and the days of slow progress were numbered. We took the rough and the smooth alike, working patiently on through the long hours with scarce a word and never a halt between meal and meal. Troubles and discomforts were many, and we could only guess at the progress we made, but we knew that by sticking to our task we should have our reward when our observations came to be worked out on board the ship.

We were now so far from the edge of the plateau that our circumstances and conditions were such as must obtain over the whole of this great continental area at this season of the year. It is necessary, therefore, to give some description of them.

I used to read my aneroid with great regularity, and I find that the readings vary from 20·2 in. to 22·1 in., but both of these limits were under exceptional atmospheric conditions. By far the greater number of readings lie between 21·1 and 21·6 inches, and these differences were due to change of level to some extent, but, as will be seen, they do not admit of any considerable change in level. It was evident to us as we travelled onward that there were undulations in the plain; we could sometimes see the shadow of a rise and sometimes a marked depression, but these variations were so slight and so confused that we could make little of them, until we recognised a connection between them and the occurrence of the *sastrugi*. We then came to see that the summits and eastern faces of undulations were quite smooth with a very curious scaly condition of surface, whilst the hollows and the western faces were deeply furrowed with the wind. On our track, therefore, we met with great differences of surface. For long stretches we travelled over smooth glazed snow, and for others almost equally long we had to thread our way amongst a confused heap of sharp waves. I have rarely, if ever, seen higher or more formidable *sastrugi* than we crossed on this plateau. For instance, on November 24 I wrote : 'At first there were lanes of glazed surface leading to the W.S.W., but afterwards these disappeared, and we struggled over a sea of broken and distorted snow-waves. We were like a small boat at sea : at one moment appearing to stand still to climb some wave, and at the next diving down into a hollow. It was distressing work, but we stuck to it, though not without frequent capsizes, which are likely to have a serious effect on our stock of oil, for I fear a little is lost with each upset.'

Regularly each night, when the sun was low in the south, the temperature fell to −40° or below, whilst during the marching hours it rarely rose much above −25°, and with this low temperature we had a constant wind. At first it blew from the W. by S., and it was in this direction that most of the hard high *sastrugi* pointed, but we noticed that it was gradually creeping to the southward. Before we left the plateau it had gone to S.W. by W., and now and again it became still more southerly and brought a light snowfall which formed fresh waves in the new direction.

There can be little doubt, I think, that the wind blows from west to east across this plateau throughout the winter, and often with great violence, as the high snow-waves showed. What the temperature can be at that season is beyond guessing, but if the thermometer can fall to −40° in the height of summer, one can imagine that the darker months produce a terrible extremity of cold.

On November 26 I wrote : 'The wind is the plague of our lives. It has cut us to pieces. We all have deep cracks in our nostrils and cheeks, and our lips are broken and raw ; our fingers are also getting in a shocking state ; one of Evans's thumbs has a deep cut on either side of the nail which might have been made by a heavy slash with a knife. We can do nothing for this as long as we have to face this horrid wind. We suffer most during the first half-hour of the morning march before we have warmed up to the work, as then all these sore places get frost-bitten. There is a good deal of pain also in the tent at night, and we try to keep our faces as still as possible ; laughing is a really painful process, and so from this point of view jokes are not to be encouraged. The worst task of all is the taking of observations. I plant the theodolite as close as possible to the tent to gain what shelter I can, but it is impossible to get away from the wind, which punishes one badly at such times.'

' *November* 28.—To-day we have a new development in the weather. The sky has been overcast with a bank of stratus cloud ; the light has been very bad, and we have had the usual difficulty under such conditions in keeping our course. This is really serious. At this altitude I had expected at least the single advantage of a clear sky, but if we are to have overcast weather, our return journey will be a difficult matter. I almost thought of stopping to-day, but reflecting that days of this sort cannot be common, I resolved to push on to the appointed date.'

' *November* 29.—Started in moderately bad light, but in half an hour struggled through *sastrugi* to a decent surface and did a long march. Stopped for a minute or two to dig down in an apparent crevass, but found, as I expected, that the resemblance was superficial. We

have not seen a crack, crevass, or sign of ice-disturbance
since we reached the summit.

'Our finneskoes are getting very worn. Evans has
had to take to his spare pair, but Lashly and I still
have ours in reserve. One of the pair I am using,
however, is scarcely good for more than two or three
marches. We are all in excellent condition and health:
not a sign of the scurvy fiend has appeared, though I
watch narrowly for it.'

'*November* 30.—We have finished our last outward
march, thank heaven! Nothing has kept us going during
the past week but the determination to carry out our
original intention of going on to the end of the month,
and so here we have pitched our last camp. We made
an excellent march in the forenoon, and started well after
lunch, when we could see the sun gleaming on a more
than ordinarily steep incline ahead. I altered course a
little to take it square, and soon we were amongst heavy
sastrugi. I think it must have taken an hour and a half
to struggle through. It is not that it reduces our pace so
much, but it shakes us up dreadfully; falls are constant,
and the harness frequently brings up with a heavy jerk,
which is exasperating to a tired man. At last we got
through, and found on looking back that we must have
descended into a hollow, as the horizon was above us on
all sides. Ahead the slope was quite smooth, and, in
spite of all the dreary monotony of the plain we have
crossed, I felt distinctly excited to know what we should
see when we got to the top. I knew it was the end of
our effort, and my imagination suggested all sorts of

rewards for our long labours.   Perhaps there would be a gradual slope downward, perhaps more mountains to indicate a western coast for Victoria Land.

'Greenland, I remembered, would have been crossed in many places by such a track as we have made. I thought, too, what a splendid thing it would be to find a coast in this way.   All very vain imaginings, of course, for after 200 miles of changeless conditions there was a poor chance indeed of finding a difference in the last one.   But so it was.   I journeyed up this slope with lively hopes, and had a distinct sense of disappointment when, on reaching the summit, we saw nothing beyond but a further expanse of our terrible plateau.

'Here, then, to-night we have reached the end of our tether, and all we have done is to show the immensity of this vast plain.   The scene about us is the same as we have seen for many a day, and shall see for many a day to come—a scene so wildly and awfully desolate that it cannot fail to impress one with gloomy thoughts.   I am not an imaginative person, but of late all sorts of stupid fancies have come into my mind.   The *sastrugi* now got on my nerves ; they are shaped like the barbs of a hook, with their sharp points turned to the east, from which direction many look high and threatening, and each one now seems to suggest that, however easy we may have found it to come here, we shall have a very different task in returning.

'But, after all, it is not what we see that inspires awe, but the knowledge of what lies beyond our view.   We see only a few miles of ruffled snow bounded by a vague, wavy horizon, but we know that beyond that horizon are hundreds and even thousands of miles which can offer no change to the weary eye, while on the vast expanse that one's mind conceives one knows there is neither tree, nor shrub, nor any living thing, nor even inanimate rock—nothing but this terrible limitless expanse of snow. It has been so for countless years, and it will be so for countless more. And we, little human insects, have started to crawl over this awful desert, and are now bent on crawling back again. Could anything be more terrible than this silent, wind-swept immensity when one thinks such thoughts ?

' Luckily, the gloom of the outer world has not been allowed to enter the door of our tent. My companions spare no time for solemn thought ; they are invariably cheerful and busy. Few of our camping hours go by without a laugh from Evans and a song from Lashly. I have not quite penetrated the latter yet ; there is only one verse, which is about the plucking of a rose. It can scarcely be called a finished musical performance, but I should miss it much if it ceased.

' We are all very proud of our march out. I don't know where we are, but I know we must be a long way to the west from my rough noon observation of the compass variation ; besides which we cannot have marched so many hours without covering a long distance. We have been discussing this matter at supper, and wondering whether future explorers will travel further over this inhospitable country. Evans remarked that if they did they " would have to leg it," and indeed I think they would.'

CHAPTER XVIII

RETURN FROM THE WEST

Returning over the Great Plateau—Doubts about Provisions and Oil—
Harrowing Effect of Fresh Snowfall—Thick Weather—No Sight of
Landmarks—Sudden Descent into Glacier—Escape from a Crevass—
Exploration of North Arm—A Curious Valley—Return to the Ship—
Results of other Sledging Efforts—Ferrar's Journey—Barne's Journey—
Royds' Journey—Shorter Journeys—Review of Sledging Work.

Ceaseless frost round the vast solitude
Bound its broad zone of stillness.—SHELLEY.

THE interior of Victoria Land must be considered the
most desolate region in the world. There is none other
that is at once so barren, so deserted, so piercingly cold,
so wind-swept or so fearsomely monotonous.

I have attempted to give some idea of it in the last
chapter, but I feel that my pen has poorly expressed the
awe-inspiring nature of its terrible solitude. Nevertheless, when the reader considers its geographical situation, its great elevation, and the conditions to which we
were subjected while travelling across it, he will, I think,
agree that there can be no place on earth that is less
attractive. For me the long month which we spent on
the Victoria Land summit remains as some vivid but
evil dream. I have a memory of continuous strain on
mind and body lightened only by the unfailing courage
and cheerfulness of my companions.

From first to last the month was a grim struggle with adversity, and never a trouble was overcome but some fresh one arose, until an ever-increasing load of anxiety was suddenly and finally removed. Thus it was that on turning homeward on December 1, whilst we enjoyed the relief of having the biting wind at our back, new difficulties soon appeared. Scarcely had we started our return march when the weather again grew overcast, and, though we struggled on for the first part of the day, the sky eventually became so gloomy that we were forced to camp and sacrifice more than an hour of the afternoon. On December 2, this sort of thing was still worse and landed us at one time in what seemed a most serious position, as my diary shows:

'We started at seven o'clock this morning, the sky very overcast, but the sun struggling through occasionally. All went well until ten o'clock, when the sun vanished and the light became shockingly bad. We plunged on for an hour amongst high *sastrugi*; our sledge capsized repeatedly and we ourselves sprawled in all directions. At length we could see nothing at all, and our falls became so frequent and heavy that I felt that we were running too great a risk of injury to our limbs, and that there was nothing for it but to camp. So here we are in our sleeping-bag in the middle of the marching hours, and I don't like the look of things at all. We are about seventeen marches out from the glacier, but of course this includes the days when, with full numbers, we did poor distances. We have something over fourteen days' full rations left, and perhaps twelve days' oil allowance.

If we could get clear weather, I believe we have not over-estimated our marching powers in supposing we can cover the longer daily distance required to reach the safety of the glacier, but this overcast weather puts an entirely new complexion on the matter; it is quite clear that we cannot afford delay. I don't like to think of half rations; we are all terribly hungry as it is, and I feel sure that we cannot cut down food without losing our strength. I try to think that at this altitude there cannot be long spells of overcast weather, but I cannot forget that if this condition should occur frequently we shall be in "Queer Street." '

The reader will remember that this same difficulty with an overcast sky had been met by my southern party of the previous year, and therefore it was not new to me ; but, as I have pointed out, at the high altitude to which we had climbed, and with the low temperatures that prevailed, to find banks of cloud still above us was unexpected and added a most alarming circum-stance to our situation. For, as will be seen, we had placed ourselves in a position from which we could only hope to retreat by relying on our hard condition and util-ising all our marching powers ; a simple arithmetic sum showed that we could not afford an hour's delay, and to be forced to lie idle in our tent was one of the most serious misfortunes that could overtake us. But this black outlook was not to remain for long, and later this day I was able to make a more cheering entry :

' After we had lain for two hours in the bag in a highly disconsolate frame of mind, Evans suddenly put his head outside and in his usual matter-of-fact tones remarked that the sun was shining. We were up in a moment. I do not believe sledges have ever been packed so quickly ; it was certainly less than ten minutes before we were in our harness and away. As this meant shifting foot-gear, packing everything, and hoisting our sail, it can be imagined how we flew about. Strangely enough, by a good light we found the surface we had been struggling with in the morning was by no means bad, and now that we could see where to step, we got on at a great pace. In spite of our distressing delay we have covered a good distance. My companions are undefeatable. However tiresome our day's march or however gloomy the outlook, they always find something to jest about. In the evenings we have long arguments about naval matters, and generally agree that we could rule that Service a great deal better than any Board of Admiralty. Incidentally I learn a great deal about lower-deck life—more than I could hope to have done under ordinary conditions.'

' *December* 3.— . . . About an hour after lunch we suddenly came on one of our outward-bound night camps, and from that we followed our old track with some difficulty till we came to what I think must be our lunch camp of the 27th, which means that we have gained half a day on the outward march. Considering the bad light, this is good enough, but I shall hope to gain at a greater rate if the weather holds. The wind to-day was exceedingly cold, but with our backs to it it was not so much felt, except at packing and camp work, which were simply horrible. The old track we followed is being rapidly drifted up ; we are unlikely to see it again. Evans and Lashly have both been suffering a good deal from cold feet and fingers ; my feet keep well, though fingers easily go.'

'*December* 4.— . . . We were up before five o'clock and away early. Started marching along the faint remains of our old track but soon lost it. We kept a good surface for two hours, then fell amongst bad *sastrugi* which gave us the usual trouble ; by lunch we were fairly clear again. Returning now we can see more clearly the undulations of the surface ; they seem irregular depressions rather than waves. We cross the hollows sometimes and seem to skirt them at others ; they average anything from three to five miles across. The sledge has not capsized the whole day, which is a relief. The weather has been very threatening on several occasions during the last two days, but, thank heaven, it has come to nothing, and the sun only disappears altogether for very short intervals.'

'*December* 6.— . . . I am a little alarmed about our oil, so have decided to march half an hour extra each night. To-night the weather became overcast again, but luckily not until our camping time had arrived. It is still terribly cold work, but we all feel exceedingly fit. My trouble is want of sleep, or, rather, it doesn't seem to trouble me except as regards the nuisance of lying awake in the bag. I have had extraordinarily little sleep this last week, and none of us seems to want much ; after our long marches we ought to be in a fit state to go straight off into dreamland, but for some reason we are not.

'This afternoon two skua gulls were suddenly seen circling around us. It was such a pleasant sight that we could almost have cheered; but how in the world they can have found us at this great altitude and distance from the sea is beyond guessing. Hunger is growing upon us once more, though not to such an alarming extent as it did last year; still, we practise the same devices for serving out our rations, and are as keen at picking up the scraps as ever. It is curious that last year we used to think mostly of beefsteak pies and what Shackleton called "three-decker puddings," but this year there is ever before my eyes a bowl of Devonshire cream. If it was only a reality, how ill I should be! I think Evans's idea of joy is pork, whilst Lashly dreams of vegetables, and especially apples. He tells us stories of his youth when these things, and not much else, were plentiful.'

During this time we were making excellently long marches, and gradually as the days passed we were losing much of our fear of the overcast weather in its power of delaying us, though I still saw that the greatly increased amount of cloud might make it most difficult for us to recognise our landmarks when they should appear in sight.

Certainly the ups and downs of sledging life are wonderful; for instance, on the 8th, I find my record full of hope. We had marched long hours over a comparatively easy surface; I did not know where we were, but I knew that we must be up to date, and that if conditions held as they were, we should reach the glacier in good time, even if we had to spend some time in looking for landmarks. But on the 9th came a most serious change of surface which seemed to baffle all our hopes at one blow, for we knew well that this new condition had come to stay. I found out afterwards that at this time we must have been somewhere close to the spot which we had crossed on November 16 when outward bound. I have given some description of the surface at that time ; it was alternately hard and soft, but the hard places had been so slippery that we had been obliged to wear crampons to pull our sledges over them. Now all this was changed by a recent fall of snow, which had covered everything with a sandy layer of loose ice-crystals and brought terrible friction on the sledge-runners.

This layer grew heavier as we approached the edge of the plateau : apart from the difficulty which it presented to our travelling, this was an interesting observation, for it shows that the plateau snowfall takes place in December, and that it is far heavier on the edge than in the interior of the continent. Another interesting fact was observable in this connection, for whilst this light snow had been falling the wind had crept round to the south, sometimes to such an angle with our course that it was most difficult to trim our sledge sail to derive any benefit from it. In its most southerly direction it brought a desirable increase of temperature, and on some days we had a fair imitation of the mild southerly blizzards which were such a conspicuous feature at the ship. But at this time, as we plodded on with an eye on our diminishing stock of provisions, it can be imagined that we were not inclined to bless the climatic conditions which had wrought such a change in the surface. December 9, in fact, seemed to show everything going wrong for us, and the marches on that day and those which followed I can never forget. Our sledge weight was reduced almost to a minimum, and we ourselves were inured to hard marching if ever three persons were, yet by our utmost exertion we could barely exceed a pace of a mile an hour. I have done some hard pulling, but never anything to equal this. The sledge was like a log; two of us could scarcely move it, and therefore throughout the long hours we could none of us relax our efforts for a single moment— we were forced to keep a continuous strain on our harness with a tension that kept our ropes rigid and made conversation quite impossible. So heavy was the work that I may remark we once tried pulling on ski and found we simply couldn't move the sledge.

It was on the evening of the 9th that the seriousness of our position once more manifested itself, and I therefore resort again to my diary:

' . . . This afternoon the surface grew worse and worse, and at the end of the march we were all dog tired. The state of affairs is again serious, whereas this morning I thought it would only be a matter of hours before we should be able to increase our rations and satisfy the pangs of hunger, which are now growing very severe. I have had to think things out under this new development, and I don't find the task is pleasant; nothing is in sight ahead, and the prospect is gloomy. We have a week's provision in hand, but it looks mighty little in the midst of this horrible, never-ending plain ; but what is more alarming is that we are well into our last can of oil, and there is only a few days' allowance left, at the rate we have been using it.

'We have had a long discussion about matters to-night. I told the men I thought we were in a pretty tight place, and that we should have to take steps accordingly. I proposed that we should increase our marching hours by one hour, go on half allowance of oil, and if we don't sight landmarks in a couple of days reduce our rations. I explained the scheme for oil economy which we adopted last year, and when I came to the cold lunch and fried breakfast poor Evans's face fell ; he evidently doesn't much believe in the virtue of food unless it is in the form of a *hoosh* and has some chance of sticking to one's ribs. Lashly is to do all the cooking until we come to happier times, as he is far the best hand at the Primus, and can be relied upon not to exceed allowance.

'I have been struggling with my sights and devia-tions table, but although I believe we cannot be far off the glacier the sense of uncertainty is oppressive. We are really travelling by rule of thumb, and one cannot help all sorts of doubts creeping in when the consequences are so serious.

'*December* 10.—This morning we plugged away for five mortal hours on a surface which is, if anything, worse than yesterday. The pulling is so heavy that it is impossible to drag one's thoughts away to brighter subjects, and the time passes in the most wearisome manner. Then came our new routine of cold, comfortless lunch, and we started once more. We had not been going more than an hour in the afternoon, however, when Evans's sharp eye sighted the land, and soon some isolated *nunataks* appeared on both bows. This was very cheering, and we struggled on through the remainder of our march with renewed hope. Later we rose several mountain peaks to the S.E., but cloud hangs so persistently about them that I cannot recognise anything. I imagine we are too far to the south, but I am not at all certain. I rather thought that when we saw the land it would bring immediate relief to all anxiety, but somehow it hasn't. I know that we must be approaching the edge of the plateau, but now the question is, where? There must be innumerable glaciers intersecting the mountains, and one cannot but see that it will be luck if we hit off our own at the first shot, and that we cannot afford to make a mistake. I hope and trust we shall soon recognise landmarks; but the sky is most unpromising, and it looks very much as though we were about to have a return of thick weather.'

On the 11th we caught only the same fleeting glimpses of the land as on the previous day, but we marched stolidly on, hoping for clearer weather, and on December 12 I wrote:

'It has been overcast all day. Now and again this morning I caught glimpses of land, which seems much closer, but I am still left in horrible uncertainty as to our whereabouts, as I could not recognise a single point. The light became very bad before lunch; everything except the sun was shut out, and that was only seen through broken clouds. Lately we have been pulling for ten hours a day; it is rather too much when the strain on the harness is so great, and we are becoming gaunt shadows of our former selves. My companions' cheeks are quite sunken and hollow, and with their stubbly untrimmed beards and numerous frost-bite remains they have the wildest appearance, yet we are all fit, and there has not been a sign of sickness beyond the return of those well-remembered pangs of hunger which are now becoming exceedingly acute. We have at last finished our tobacco; for a long time Evans and I have had to be content with a half-pipe a day, but now even that small comfort has gone; it was our long stay in the blizzard camp that has reduced us to this strait. There is one blessing; the next day or two will show what is going to happen one way or the other. If we walk far enough in this direction we must come to the edge of the plateau somewhere, and anything seems better than this heavy and anxious collar work.'

'*December* 13.—Strong southerly wind with blinding drift when we started this morning. Marched steadily on for four hours, when Evans had his nose frost-bitten. Evans's nose has always been the first thing to indicate stress of frost-biting weather. For some weeks it has been more or less constantly frost-bitten, and in consequence it is now the most curious-looking object. He speaks of it with a comic forbearance, as though, whilst it scarcely belonged to him, it was something for which he was responsible, and had to make excuses. When I told him of its fault to day, he said in a resigned tone, "My poor old nose again ; well, there, it's chronic !" When this unruly member was brought round we found the storm increasing, and the surface changed to the hard wind-swept one which we encountered on our ascent. On this we slipped badly, and when we stopped to search for our crampons the wind had grown so strong that I thought it necessary to camp. Before this was accomplished we were all pretty badly frost-bitten, and we had to make some hot tea to bring us round. After waiting for an hour there were some signs of clearance, and as we cannot now afford to waste a single moment I decided to push on. We held steadily to the east, and towards the end of our march there could be no doubt that we were commencing to descend. But it was uncanny work, for I haven't any notion where we are, and the drift was so thick about us that for aught we knew we might have been walking over the edge of a precipice at any moment. To-night it is as thick as ever ; it is positively sickening, but, good weather or bad, we must go on now.'

' *December* 15.—We all agree that yesterday was the most adventurous day in our lives, and we none of us want to have another like it. It seems wonderful that I should be lying here in ease and comfort to write of it, but as it is so, I can give its incidents in some detail.

' Very early in the morning I awoke to find that the storm had passed, and that the land was all around us ; but the clouds hung about the higher summits, and I was still unable to recognise any peak with certainty. In this bewildered condition we packed our sledge, and I could see no better course than to continue our march due east. We had scarcely been going half an hour, however, when high ice hummocks and disturbances appeared ahead, and we found ourselves on a hard glazed surface, which was cracked in all directions. Hoping to avoid the disturbed area, we first made a circuit to the right and then another to the left, but in neither of these directions did the prospect look more hopeful ; we stopped and had a council of war, but by this time the wind had sprung up again, it was bitterly cold, and the only result of our deliberations was to show more clearly that we did not know where we were. In this predicament I vaguely realised that it would be rash to go forward, as the air was once more becoming thick with snowdrift ; but then to stop might mean another long spell in a blizzard camp, when starvation would soon stare us in the face. I asked the men if they were prepared to take the risk of going on ; they answered promptly in the affirmative. I think that after our trying experiences we were all feeling pretty reckless.

' At any rate, we marched straight on for the ice disturbances, and were soon threading our way amongst the hummocks and across numerous crevasses. After a bit the surface became smoother, but at the same time the slope grew steeper, and our sledge began to overrun us. At this juncture I put the two men behind the sledge to hold it back whilst I continued in front to guide its course ; we were all wearing crampons, which at first held well, but within a few minutes, as the inclination of the surface increased, our foothold became less secure.

' Suddenly Lashly slipped, and in an instant he was sliding downward on his back; directly the strain came on Evans, he too was thrown off his feet. It all happened in a moment, and before I had time to look the sledge and the two men hurtled past me ; I braced myself to stop them, but might as well have attempted to hold an express train. With the first jerk I was whipped off my legs, and we all three lay sprawling on our backs and flying downward with an ever-increasing velocity.

' For some reason the first thought that flashed into my mind was that someone would break a limb if he attempted to stop our mad career, and I shouted something to this effect, but might as well have saved my breath. Then there came a sort of vague wonder as to what would happen next, and in the midst of this I was conscious that we had ceased to slide smoothly, and were now bounding over a rougher incline, sometimes leaving it for several yards at a time ; my thoughts flew to broken limbs again, for I felt we could not stand much of such bumping. At length we gave a huge leap into the air, and yet we travelled with such velocity that I had not time to think before we came down with tremendous force on a gradual incline of rough, hard, wind-swept snow. Its irregularities brought us to rest in a moment or two, and I staggered to my feet in a dazed fashion, wondering what had happened.

'Then to my joy I saw the others also struggling to their legs, and in another moment I could thank heaven that no limbs were broken. But we had by no means escaped scatheless; our legs now show one black bruise from knee to thigh, and Lashly was unfortunate enough to land once on his back, which is bruised and very painful. At the time, as can be imagined, we were all much shaken. I, as the lightest, escaped the easiest, yet before the two men crawled painfully to their feet their first question was to ask if I had been hurt.

'As soon as I could pull myself together I looked round, and now to my astonishment I saw that we were well on towards the entrance of our own glacier; ahead and on either side of us appeared well-remembered landmarks, whilst behind, in the rough broken ice-wall over which we had fallen, I now recognised at once the most elevated ice cascade of our valley. In the rude fashion which I have described we must have descended some 300 feet; above us the snow-drift was still being driven along, but the wind had not yet reached our present level, so that all around us the sky was bright and clear and our eyes could roam from one familiar object to another until far away to the eastward they rested on the smoke-capped summit of Erebus.

'I cannot but think that this sudden revelation of our position was very wonderful. Half an hour before we had been lost; I could not have told whether we were making for our own glacier or for any other, or whether we were ten or fifty miles from our depot; it was more than a month since we had seen any known landmark. Now in this extraordinary manner the curtain had been raised; we found that our rule-of-thumb methods had accomplished the most accurate "land fall," and down the valley we could see the high cliffs of the Depot Nunatak where peace and plenty awaited us.

'How merciful a view this was we appreciated when we came to count up the result of our fall. Our sledge had not capsized until we all rolled over together at the end, but the jolting had scattered many of our belongings and had burst open the biscuit box, so that all that had remained in it lay distributed over the cascade; we had no provisions left except the few scraps we could pick up and the very diminished contents of our food bag. As well as our stiffening limbs would allow we hastened to collect the scattered articles, to repack the sledge, and to march on towards the depot. Before us now lay a long plateau, at the edge of which I knew we should find a second cascade, and beneath it the region of our Desolation Camp and a more gradual icy surface down to the Nunatak. By lunch-time we were well across the plateau, and we decided that our shaken condition deserved a hot meal, so we brewed cocoa and felt vastly better after swallowing it. By this time the wind had reached us again, and I had cold work in taking a round of angles, but I got through it, and in an hour we were on the march once more. We soon found ourselves at the top of the second cascade, and under conditions which prevented us from looking for an easy descent; however, fortune favoured us, and by going very slowly and carefully we managed to get down without accident.

'Though we were all much shaken and tired, we congratulated ourselves on having overcome the worst difficulties, and started off briskly to cover the last five or six miles which lay between us and our goal. Feeling quite unsuspicious of danger, we all three joined up our harness to our usual positions ahead of the sledge; this brought me in the middle and a little in advance, with Lashly on my right and Evans on my left. After we had been tramping on in this way for a quarter of an hour the wind swept across from the south, and as the sledge began to skid I told Lashly to pull wide in order to steady it. He had scarcely moved out in response to this order when Evans and I stepped on nothing and disappeared from his view; by a miracle he saved himself from following, and sprang back with his whole weight on the trace; the sledge flashed by him and jumped the crevass down which we had gone, one side of its frame cracked through in the jerk which followed, but the other side mercifully held. Personally I remember absolutely nothing until I found myself dangling at the end of my trace with blue walls on either side and a very horrid-looking gulf below; large ice-crystals dislodged by our movements continued to shower down on our heads.

'As a first step I took off my goggles; I then discovered that Evans was hanging just above me. I
asked him if he was all right, and received a reassuring reply in his usual calm, matter-of-fact tones. Meanwhile I groped about on every side with my cramponed
feet, only to find everywhere the same slippery smooth
wall. But my struggles had set me swinging, and at
one end of a swing my leg suddenly struck a projection.
In a moment I had turned, and saw at a glance that
by raising myself I could get foothold on it; with the
next swing I clutched it with my steel-shod feet, and
after a short struggle succeeded in partly transferring
my weight to it. In this position, with my feet firmly
planted and my balance maintained by my harness, I
could look about me.

'I found myself standing on a thin shaft of ice
which was wedged between the walls of the chasm—
how it came there I cannot imagine, but its position
was wholly providential; to the right or left, above or
below, there was not the vestige of another such support—nothing, in fact, but the smooth walls of ice. My
next step was to get Evans into the same position
as myself, and when he had slipped his harness well
up under his arms I found I could pilot his feet to the
bridge.

'All this had occupied some time, and it was only
now that I realised what had happened above us, for
there, some twelve feet over our heads, was the outline
of the broken sledge. I saw at once what a frail support remained, and shouted to Lashly to ask what he

could do, and then I knew the value of such a level-headed companion ; for whilst he held on grimly to the sledge and us with one hand, his other was busily employed in withdrawing our ski. At length he succeeded in sliding two of these beneath the broken sledge and so making our support more secure. The device was well thought of, but it still left us without his active assistance ; for, as he told us, directly he relaxed his strain the sledge began to slip, and he dared not trust only to the ski.

'There remained no other course for Evans and me but to climb out by our own unaided efforts, and I saw that one of us would have to make the attempt without delay, for the chill of the crevasse was already attacking us and our faces and fingers were on the verge of freezing. After a word with Evans I decided to try the first climb myself, but I must confess I never expected to reach the top. It is some time since I swarmed a rope, and to have to do so in thick clothing and heavy crampons and with frost-bitten fingers seemed to me in the nature of the impossible. But it was no use thinking about it, so I slung my mits over my shoulders, grasped the rope, and swung off the bridge. I don't know how long I took to climb or how I did it, but I remember I got a rest when I could plant my foot in the belt of my harness, and again when my feet held on the rings of the belt. Then came a mighty effort till I reached the stirrup formed by the rope span of the sledge, and then, mustering all the strength that remained, I reached the sledge itself and flung myself panting on to the snow beyond. Lashly said, " Thank God ! " and it was perhaps then that I realised that his position had been the worst of all.

' For a full five minutes I could do nothing ; my hands were white to the wrists, and I plunged them into my breast, but gradually their circulation and my strength came back, and I was able to get to work. With two of us on top and one below, things had assumed a very different aspect, and I was able to unhitch my own harness and lower it once more for Evans ; then with our united efforts he also was landed on the surface, where he arrived in the same frost-bitten condition as I had. For a minute or two we could only look at one another, then Evans said, " Well, I'm blowed " ; it was the first sign of astonishment he had shown.

' But all this time the wind was blowing very chill, so we wasted no time in discussing our escape, but turning our broken sledge end for end, we were soon harnessed to it again and trudging on over the snow. After this, as can be imagined, we kept a pretty sharp look-out for crevasses, marching in such an order as prevented more than one of us going down at once, and so we eventually reached the bare blue ice once more, and at six o'clock found our depot beneath the towering cliffs of the Depot Nunatak.

' As long as I live I can never forget last night. Our camp was in bright sunshine, for the first time for six weeks the temperature was above zero, but what we appreciated still more was the fact that it was perfectly calm ; the canvas of our tent hung limp and motionless, and the steam of our cooking rose in a thin, vertical shaft. All Nature seemed to say that our long fight was over, and that at length we had reached a haven of rest. And it has been a fight indeed ; it is only now that I realise what discomforts we have endured and what a burden of anxiety we have borne during the past month. The relief of being freed from such conditions is beyond the power of my pen to describe, but perhaps what brought it home to us most completely was the fact that the worst of our troubles and adventures came at the end, and that in the brief space of half an hour we passed from abject discomfort to rest and peace.

'And so we dawdled over everything. We were bruised, sore, and weary, yet Lashly sang a merry stave as he stirred the pot, and Evans and I sat on the sledge, shifted our foot-gear, spread our garments out to dry, and chatted away merrily the whole time. Evans's astonishment at the events of the day seemed to grow ever deeper, and was exhibited in the most amusing manner. With his sock half on he would pause to think out our adventures in some new light and would say suddenly, "Well, sir, but what about that snow bridge ?" or if so-and-so hadn't happened "where should we be now ?" and then the soliloquy would end with "My word, but it was a close call ! " Evans generally manages to sum a case up fairly pithily, and perhaps this last remark is a comprehensive description of our experiences of yesterday.

'This morning the sun shines as brightly as ever, and there is still no breath of wind. It is so warm in the tent that as I write I have had to throw open my jacket. Meanwhile outside I can hear the tap of the hammer as my companions are arming our sledge-runners for the hard ice of the glacier.'

We only found a very small quantity of food at the Depot Nunatak, but it was enough to carry us to the main depot, which lay several miles below, provided we marched hard, as we were quite prepared to do. Luckily, here also we found a new nine-foot sledge which had been left the previous year, and to which we could now transfer the greater part of our load. But one of our most pleasing discoveries at the Depot Nunatak was the small folded notes which told us of the movements of our fellow-travellers. By these I learnt to my relief that Skelton and his companions had safely reached the glacier, and that Ferrar's party was all well after it had left our Desolation Camp. According to previous arrangements I found these notes at various stated points in the glacier, and there were few pleasanter things for us returning wayfarers than to find these cheery documents.

Starting our downward march on the afternoon of the 15th, we stretched over the miles with ease. This sort of work was mere child's play to our hardened muscles, and that night we reached the broad amphitheatre below Finger Mountain. On the 16th we picked up the ample supply of food which we had left in our depot opposite the Solitary Rocks, and that evening took up our old quarters in the Knob Head Moraine. I mention these movements because at this

point I had determined to do a small piece of exploration which is of some interest.   The reader will see
that we were now in the large glacier basin which I
described, and will remember that I mentioned amongst
other outlets its northern arm.   This arm of the glacier
descended with a very steep incline to the right of the
Solitary Rocks, and then its valley seemed to turn
sharply to the eastward.   The direction of flow of the
ice-streams in the glacier basin had always been something of a mystery for us, and we had thought that the
main portion of the ice must discharge through this
valley.

On the 17th, therefore, we started to descend it to
see what the conditions actually were, and after rattling
down over a sharp gradient for several miles we found
ourselves turning to the east.   We followed a long string
of morainic boulders through a deep valley on a moderate
incline, but early in the afternoon the descent became
steeper and the surface of the ice much rougher, until
at length our sledge bumped so heavily that we thought
it wise to camp.

Our camp life by this time had become wholly
pleasant except to poor Lashly, who had a fierce attack
of snow-blindness.   We pitched our tent behind a huge
boulder which must have weighed at least five hundred
tons, and here we were pleasantly sheltered from the
wind, whilst close by us trickled a glacier stream from
which we were able to fill our cooking pot-and obtain
an unlimited quantity of drinking-water.   We had a
splendid view of the great ice masses sweeping down

from above, but looking downward we were much puzzled, for the glacier surface descended steeply, and beyond it stood a lofty groin of rock which seemed a direct bar to its further passage.   This sight made us very anxious to proceed with our exploration, and as we could not advance further with our sledge, it became necessary to arrange for a long absence from our camp. Accordingly we rose very early on the following day, and taking our coil of Alpine rope, with our crampons and a supply of food, we set off over the rough ice of the glacier.   As this walk had several points of interest, I give its outline from my diary :

'Started at seven o'clock with a supply of pemmican, chocolate, sugar, and biscuit in our pockets, and our small provision measure to act as a drinking-cup.   It is an extraordinary novelty in our sledging experience to find that one can get water by simply dipping it up. As we descended, the slope became steeper, and soon the ice grew so disturbed that we were obliged to rope ourselves together and proceed with caution.   The disturbance was of very much the same nature as that which we had found on the south side of the Ferrar Glacier ; the ice seemed to have broken down, leaving steep faces towards the south.   Here and there we found scattered boulders and finer morainic material, and the channels of the glacial streams became visible in places, to vanish again under deep blue arches of ice.

'At length we descended into one of these water-courses and followed it for some distance, until, to our surprise, it came abruptly to an end, and with it the glacier itself, which had gradually dwindled to this insignificant termination. Before us was a shallow, frozen lake into which the thaw-water of the glacier was pouring. The channel in which we stood was about twenty feet above its surface, and the highest pinnacles of ice were not more than the same distance above our heads, whereas the terminal face of the glacier was about three or four hundred yards across. So here was the limit of the great ice-river which we had followed down from the vast basin of the interior ; instead of pouring huge icebergs into the sea, it was slowly dwindling away in its steep-sided valley. It was, in fact, nothing but the remains of what had once been a mighty ice-flow from the inland.

'With a little difficulty we climbed down to the level of the lake, and then observed that the glacier rested on a deep ground moraine of mud, in some places as much as ten or twelve feet in thickness ; this layer of mud extended beyond the face of the glacier, where it had been much worn by water ; enough remained, however, for Lashly to remark, " What a splendid place for growing spuds! " Skirting the lake below the glacier, we found ourselves approaching the high, rocky groin which puzzled us so much last night, but we now saw that a very narrow channel wound round its base. At its narrowest this channel was only seventeen feet across, and as we traversed this part, the high cliffs on either side towered above our heads and we seemed to be passing through a massive gateway ; beyond this the valley opened out again, and its floor was occupied by a frozen lake a mile in breadth and three or four miles in length. As the snow surface of this lake was very rough, we were obliged to skirt its margin ; we were now 1,300 feet below our camp, and about 300 feet above sea level. The shores of the lake for several hundred feet up the hillsides were covered with a coarse granitic sand strewn with numerous boulders, and it was curious to observe that these boulders, from being rounded and sub-angular below, gradually grew to be sharper in outline as they rose in level.

'At the end of the second lake the valley turned towards the north-east; it was equally clearly cut, but the floor rose on a mass of morainic material. At first there was a general tendency for this to be distributed in long ridges, but later the distribution was disturbed, and it was easy to see that broad water-channels had made clean breaches in these vast piles of sand and boulders. Quite suddenly these moraines ceased, and we stepped out on to a long stretch of undulating sand traversed by numerous small streams, which here and there opened out into small, shallow lakes quite free from ice.

' I was so fascinated by all these strange new sights that I strode forward without thought of hunger until Evans asked if it was any use carrying our lunch further; we all decided that it wasn't, and so sat down on a small hillock of sand with a merry little stream gurgling over the pebbles at our feet. It was a very cheery meal, and certainly the most extraordinary we have had. We commanded an extensive view both up and down the valley, and yet, except about the rugged

mountain summits, there was not a vestige of ice or
snow to be seen; and as we ran the comparatively
warm sand through our fingers and quenched our thirst
at the stream, it seemed almost impossible that we could
be within a hundred miles of the terrible conditions we
had experienced on the summit.

'Proceeding after lunch, we found that the valley
descended to a deep and splendid gorge formed by
another huge groin extending from the southern side, but
as we approached the high cliffs we found our way again
obstructed by confused heaps of boulders, amongst which
for the first time we saw the exposed rocks of the floor
of the valley smoothed and striated in a manner most
typical of former ice action. My object in pressing on
had been to get a view of the sea, and I now thought
the best plan would be to ascend the neck of the groin
on our right. It was a long climb of some 700 feet over
rough, sharp boulders. We eventually reached the top,
but, alas! not to catch any glimpse of the sea; for the
valley continued to wind its way onward through deep
gorges, and some five or six miles below yet another
groin shut out our further view.

'But from our elevated position we could now get
an excellent view of this extraordinary valley, and a
wilder or in some respects more beautiful scene it would
have been difficult to imagine. Below lay the sandy
stretches and confused boulder heaps of the valley floor,
with here and there the gleaming white surface of a
frozen lake and elsewhere the silver threads of the
running water; far above us towered the weather-

worn, snow-splashed mountain peaks, between which in places fell in graceful curves the folds of some hanging glacier. The rocks at our feet were of every variety of colour and form, mixed in that inextricable confusion which ice alone can accomplish. The lower slopes of the mountains were thickly clothed with similar rocks, but the variety of colour was lost in the distance, and these steep slopes had a general tone of sober grey. This colour was therefore predominant, but everywhere at a height of 3,000 feet above the valley it ended in a hard line illustrating in the most beautiful manner the maximum extent to which the ice had once spread.

' I cannot but think that this valley is a very wonderful place. We have seen to-day all the indications of colossal ice action and considerable water action, and yet neither of these agents is now at work. It is worthy of record, too, that we have seen no living thing, not even a moss or a lichen ; all that we did find, far inland amongst the moraine heaps, was the skeleton of a Weddell seal, and how that came there is beyond guessing. It is certainly a valley of the dead : even the great glacier which once pushed through it has withered away.

' It was nearly four o'clock before we turned towards our camp, and nearly ten before we reached it, feeling that it was quite time for supper. The day's record, however, is a pretty good tribute to our marching powers, for we have walked and climbed over the roughest country for more than fourteen hours with only one brief halt for lunch.'

With this short expedition our last piece of exploration came to an end, and on the 19th we started to
ascend the north arm. By the night of the 20th we
had reached our second depot under Cathedral Rocks,
and here for the first time, and with anxious eyes, we
looked out towards the sea. Many a time we had
discussed this prospect, and agreed that we should not
have cared how far round we had to walk if only that
stubborn sheet of ice in the strait would break away.
But now, alas! it was evident that our homeward track
might be as direct as we chose to make it, for the great
unbroken plain of ice still bridged the whole strait.
Only in the far distance could we see the open water,
where a thin blue ribbon ran in from Cape Bird and
ended abreast of the black rocks of Cape Royds. We
saw with grief that there must be very many miles
between it and our unfortunate ship.

On rounding Butter Point we had another blow on
finding an entire absence of seals, but, thanks to the
kindness of Skelton and his party, we were not deprived
of our long-expected feast of fresh meat, for close to our
tin of butter we found a buried treasure in the shape
of some tit-bits of an animal which they had killed.
From Butter Point we turned our course south to those
curious moraine heaps which we had called the ' Eskers,'
and which I had not yet seen. We spent half a day in
rambling amongst these steep little hills, and in trying
to find skuas' eggs which were not hard set ; but fortune
was against us in this last respect, and we found that
we were at least a week too late.

On the afternoon of the 23rd we started to cross the strait for the last time, and late on Christmas Eve we saw the masts of the ' Discovery,' and were soon welcomed by the four persons who alone remained on board. And so after all our troubles and trials we spent our Christmas Day in the snug security of our home quarters, and tasted once again those delights of civilised existence to which we had so long been strangers.

And now, seated at my desk, I could quietly work out my observations, and trace the track which we had made. I found, to my relief, that my watch had kept an excellent rate, as far as my observed positions could check it. This was a matter of great importance, as the longitude of our position on the great plain of the interior depended entirely on its accuracy. This watch has since been given to me by its makers, and I value it highly, as I think few watches have done greater service ; and here, for the benefit of future explorers, I must again point out the importance of the manner in which a watch is carried on such a journey. I shifted my watch-pocket several times during my earlier experiences before I decided on its best position, and throughout my travels I never failed to treat my watch with the greatest care. The pocket was eventually sewn to my inner vest, in such a position that my harness could not touch it, and I never took the watch out of this warm place unless it was necessary ; when taking sights I held it in the palm of my hand, and as far as possible under the cover of a mit.

When I had worked out our various positions and

calculated the distances we had travelled, I had before
me an array of figures of which our party might justifiably feel proud.   In our last absence of fifty-nine days
we had travelled 725 miles ; for nine complete days we
had been forced to remain in camp, so that this distance
had been accomplished in fifty marching days, and gave
a daily average of 14·5 miles.

Taking the eighty-one days of absence which had constituted our whole sledging season, I found that Evans,
Lashly, and I had covered 1,098 miles at an average of
15·4 miles a day, and that, not including minor undulations,
we had climbed heights which totalled to 19,800 feet.

I started my account of this journey by saying that
I thought we came near the limit of possible performance in the circumstances, and I hope these figures
will be considered as justifying that remark.   What the
circumstances were I have endeavoured to show, but
when it is considered that to the rigours of a polar
climate were added those which must be a necessary
consequence of a great altitude, it needs little explanation to prove that they were exceptionally severe.

We may claim, therefore, to have accomplished a
creditable journey under the hardest conditions on record,
but for my part I devoutly hope that wherever my future
wanderings may trend, they will never again lead me to
the summit of Victoria Land.

The four persons whom we found on board the
'Discovery' on our return were Dr. Koettlitz, our ship's
steward, Handsley (who had not yet fully recovered from
his chest troubles), and Quartley (who had received a

slight injury on the southern journey). All the remainder of our company had gone to the north, in
accordance with our pre-arranged plan, to saw through
the ice. I purposed shortly to go in this direction
myself, but after our excessive work the usual reaction
set in, and I thought that my small party had earned a
few days' rest in which we might renew our energies.
Communications with the northern camp were of daily
occurrence, thanks to our new team of dogs, which had
been brought into capital working order by their driver,
Dell.

It was not long therefore before I learnt the outlines of the other sledge journeys, and was able to read
the reports of the officers who had led them and study
the advance which had been made in our knowledge
by the sledging work of our second season. Space
does not permit me to go in detail into these various
journeys, nor do I think that the reader would be grateful for the minute relation of more sledging adventures.
But this story would not be complete without a summary
of the material facts which these efforts produced, nor
could I omit to pay a well-earned tribute to those who
secured them by prolonged and arduous labour and
unfailing spirit.

I purpose, therefore, to give in brief the movements
of other members of the expedition during our absence
to the west.

It will be remembered that the party which had left the
ship with me towards the end of October had eventually
split into three units. At first our geologist, Ferrar, left

us to explore the glacier valley, and later Skelton and I parted company on the inland ice. Skelton, returning with his overworked party, had wisely taken matters easily, but on arriving at the Depot Nunatak he had picked up the half-plate camera, and, although he had only a very limited number of plates, he succeeded in taking some excellent photographs of the valley ; some of these are reproduced in this book, but there are many more of great interest for which I can find no space.

Ferrar with his two companions had also come down the valley slowly, not because he had lingered on his way, but because he had crossed and recrossed the glacier to examine the rocks on each side. I was quite astonished to learn the numbers of places he had visited and the distances he had traversed in pursuit of his objects, especially when I remembered that all had been done with one rickety little sledge which I knew must have broken down repeatedly and have given endless trouble to those who dragged it. The results of this journey are told by the geologist himself in the appendix which he has supplied to this volume, but he has not told of all the difficulties which he had to overcome and which in themselves might well form a chapter of this book. For each specimen of rock which Ferrar brought back was obtained only by traversing long miles of rough ice, by clambering over dangerous crevassed slopes, and by scaling precipitous cliffs ; and all this at a great distance from home, and where a strained limb might have led to very serious consequences.

It will be remembered that the main work of this

season was thoroughly to explore this valley and the ice-cap which lay beyond ; thus, when to the results of the longer journey were added Ferrar's survey and Skelton's photographic work we had the satisfaction of knowing that our object had been well accomplished.

The object before Barne and Mulock on their journey to the south has already been stated. They left the ship on October 6, and, passing around the Bluff, steered for the inlet which has since been named after the former.

But ill fortune dogged this party from the start. They were hampered by continual gales from the south, and again and again had to spend long days in their tents, as it was impossible to march onward with the wind directly in their faces. In this manner no fewer than ten days were wasted on the outward march, four of these being consecutive, and consequently it was not until the middle of November that they approached the entrance to the inlet, and here they became involved amongst numerous undulations and disturbances which greatly impeded their progress.

As they advanced these disturbances grew worse, and it was necessary to cross wide crevasses and clamber over steep ridges. On November 19, to their great disappointment, they were forced to turn, having barely passed the mouth of the inlet which they had hoped to explore. From their observations, however, it seems evident that the whole of this area is immensely disturbed, and it is doubtful whether a sledge party could ever cross it unless they were prepared to spend many weeks in the attempt. Although from their farthest position they could see no definite rise in the level of the ice in the inlet, as they travelled towards its northern side they found a moraine of large granite boulders which showed conclusively the general flow of the ice-stream and gave some indication of the nature of the land which lay beyond.

Thoughout this journey Mulock was indefatigable in using the theodolite. The result of this diligence is that this stretch of coastline is more accurately plotted than any other part of Victoria Land, and by the fixing of the positions and heights of more than two hundred mountain peaks a most interesting topographical survey of this region has been achieved.

But one of the most important results of this expedition was obtained almost by an accident. The reader will remember that in my early journey in 1902 I fixed on a position off the Bluff to establish what I called Depot 'A.' This position lay on the alignment of a small peak on the Bluff with Mount Discovery. On visiting this depot in 1903, Barne found to his astonishment that the alignment was no longer 'on,' and therefore it was evident that the depot had moved. Thirteen and a half months after the establishment of the depot he measured its displacement, and found it to be 608 yards. And thus almost accidentally we obtained a very good indication of the movement of the Great Barrier ice-sheet.

To this very interesting fact I shall refer in considering the results of the expedition. Barne and his party

safely reached the ship on December 13, after being
absent sixty-eight days.

I have already referred to the projected trip to the
south-east; it will be remembered that its object was to
ascertain whether the barrier continued level in that
direction. The conduct of this journey was undertaken
by Royds, and with him went our physicist Bernacchi,
Cross, Plumley, Scott, and Clarke; the track which was
taken by the party can be seen on the chart. It was a
short journey, as it only occupied thirty days, and for
those who took part in it it could not be otherwise
than monotonous and dull; yet it deserves to rank very
high in our sledging efforts, for every detail was carried
out in the most thoroughly efficient manner.

The party went on a very short food allowance, and
day after day found themselves marching over the same
unutterably wearisome plain, and on a surface of
such a nature as I described in my own southern
journey; yet they marched steadily on, and fully
accomplished the main object for which they were sent—
a negative but highly important result. It was on this
journey also that a most interesting series of magnetic
observations were taken by Bernacchi, who carried with
him the Barrow dip circle, an especially delicate
instrument. The great value of these observations lies
in the fact that they were taken in positions which were
free from all possible disturbance either from casual iron
or from land masses; the positions also run in a line
which is almost directly away from the magnetic pole,
and consequently the series is an invaluable aid to

mapping out the magnetic conditions of the whole of this region.

To Bernacchi belongs the credit of these observations, but a certain amount of reflected glory must be allowed to those who accompanied him, for whilst he wrestled with the usual troubles of the observer within the tent, his companions had to cool their heels outside; and as they consented to do this night after night for an hour or more, it may be considered that they showed considerable practical sympathy with his scientific aims.

On December 10 Royds and his party arrived on board the ship in an extremely famished state, but with the satisfaction of having accomplished an exceedingly fine journey.

Our sledging efforts of 1903 were not confined to the longer journeys, for, as in the previous year, many shorter trips were made. From October 12, Wilson was away for more than three weeks to pay yet another visit to the Emperor penguin rookery. It was on this occasion that he observed the extraordinary manner in which these penguins migrated with their young. It will be remembered that in the previous year these birds had been found with very young chicks in down, and that on a second visit, shortly after, all the chicks had vanished, though it was evident that they could not have been prepared to take to the water. Now this mystery was explained. Soon after Wilson's arrival the ice began to break away, and he watched the parent birds and their young leave their rookery and station themselves in batches near the edge of the ice-sheet. In due course a piece of ice on which a batch stood was broken off, and slowly sailed away to the north with its freight of penguins, and there can be no doubt that in this manner these curious creatures are transported for many hundreds of miles until the chicks have attained their adult plumage and can earn their own living.

Wilson spent twelve days at Cape Crozier, and probably at what is the most interesting season of the year in that region. Whilst the steady emigration of parties of Emperor penguins went on day after day, a little further to the west there was an equally steady immigration of Adélie penguins now coming south to lay their eggs on the lower slopes of Mount Terror. Both these movements were evidently dependent on the seasonal change which was taking place, for on his arrival Wilson found the Ross Sea frozen over, and on precisely the same date as on the previous year a series of S.W. gales commenced, and swept the sea clear, giving at once a chance for the Emperors to go and the Adélies to come. Such a long stay as this party made was only rendered possible by a lucky find of seals on the sea-ice, these animals providing them with food and fuel. As this was the only time that our sledge parties cooked their meals with a blubber fire, I quote from Wilson's report : ' We killed a seal and brought the whole skin to camp. It was cut into three long strips with all the blubber on, and to each was tied a piece of line. Each of us had one strip to manage in crossing the pressure ridges. When we reached camp a stove was improvised outside the tent by Whitfield and Cross ; it was made out of an old tin biscuit box, which had been left on a previous journey, and some stones, and in this we eventually succeeded in lighting a blubber fire over which we cooked our supper.'

Altogether this journey to Cape Crozier was more productive of information than any of its predecessors, for Wilson by no means confined himself to his zoological studies. He climbed high on the foothills of Mount Terror and discovered a curious ice-formed terrace 800 feet above the barrier level; he collected numerous geological specimens from this area, and found erratic boulders at great altitudes. Next he made a complete examination of the enormous and interesting pressure ridges which form the junction of the Great Barrier ice-mass with the land, and now and at a later date he spent much time in studying the curious windless area which exists to the south of Ross Island, and thus threw considerable light on meteorological facts that puzzled us, and on the ice condition of an extremely interesting region.

I cannot conclude a summary of our last sledging season without referring to an excellent little journey made by Armitage, Wilson, and Heald. This small party crossed the strait towards the end of November and then turned sharply to the south under the foothills of the mainland. In this manner they broke new ground, and reached and examined the Koettlitz Glacier. This had previously been seen only from Brown Island, and its closer examination was important not only to complete the topographical survey of our region, but to verify numerous observations taken in the Ferrar Glacier. Amidst a scene of wild beauty Armitage obtained some excellent photographs which give a good idea of the typical mountain scenery, and would alone prove the receding glacial conditions of the whole continent.

Thus it will be seen that whilst I had been away on my long journey to the west, my companions had been working diligently in every direction which promised to increase our store of information. All, however, had returned before myself, so that when I arrived at the ship on Christmas Eve, 1903, it was to ring the curtain down on the last of our sledging efforts in this Far Southern region.

When all things are considered, it must be conceded that no polar ship ever wintered in a more interesting spot than the 'Discovery.' It was good fortune which had brought us to our winter quarters in February 1902, and from the first we saw what great possibilities lay before us, and determined that no effort should be spared to take advantage of our opportunities. During one long season we had laboured hard to this end, but yet its finish found us with many important gaps in our knowledge. Then fortune decided that we should be given another season to complete our work, and we started forth once more to fill in those gaps. With what success this was accomplished I have endeavoured to show, and I trust it will be agreed that after the close of our second sledging season we were justified in considering that the main part of our work was done.

CHAPTER XIX

ESCAPE FROM THE ICE

Indigestion—Arrival at the Sawing Camp—Sawing Operations—Break-up of Sawing Party—The Open Water—Arrival of the Relief Ships—Unwelcome News—Stagnant Condition of the Ice—Depressing Effect—Preparations for Abandoning the 'Discovery'—Ice Breaking Away—Explosions—Anxious Days—Final Break-up of the Ice—Dramatic Approach of the Relief Ships—The Small Fleet Together—Final Explosion—The 'Discovery' Free.

And Thor
Set his shoulder hard against the stern
To push the ship through . . .
. . . and the water gurgled in
And the ship floated on the waves and rock'd.
M. ARNOLD.

ON the whole, the few days' rest which I allowed myself and my party after our return to the ship was enjoyable, and for such sensations as were not I had only myself to thank. I found that Ford had become cook for the few who remained on board, and that, as a result of studying Mrs. Beeton's cookery book, he was achieving dishes of a more savoury nature than we had thought possible with the resources at our command. It was unfortunate that the highest development of the cooking art should have occurred at this season, as it found us too morally weak to resist its allurements, and, as a consequence, we suffered from the most violent indigestion. Though my

limbs craved for rest, I was obliged to be up and doing
to silence the worst pangs of this complaint.

The ship at this time was in a more snowed-up condition than I ever remember to have seen her, and
Koettlitz told me there had been such heavy falls of
snow a week earlier that they had been obliged to dig
their way out of the lobby entrances.   Koettlitz had
remained on board to attend on the medical cases;
these were now practically off his hands, but he was de-
voting most of his time, as he had done throughout the
summer, to bacteriological studies.   He rather feared,
however, that his diligence in this line would prove of
little avail, as few less promising places could have been
found for pursuing such investigations than the wardroom of the 'Discovery.'

After two or three days on board I began to grow
restless to see what was doing to the north; moreover,
I saw that as I could not curb my appetite there was
little chance of being rid of my indigestion until I
was once more on the march.   Our inactivity was also
having a most obvious effect on my sledging companions.
It had to be acknowledged that they were 'swelling
wisibly'; each morning their faces became a more
ludicrous contrast to what I remembered of them on the
summit.   Lashly was a man who usually changed little,
and therefore he quickly fell back into his ordinary condition, but Evans continued to expand, and reached
quite an alarming maximum before he slowly returned to
his normal size.

On the morning of the 31st, therefore, we three, with

Handsley, who was now quite recovered, packed our sledge once more, and started away for the sawing camp, some ten and a half miles to the north ; in the afternoon we arrived at the camp, to be greeted with cheers and congratulations.

I may perhaps now explain how this camp came to be formed. The reader will remember that I had arranged that the sledging parties should return by the middle of December, and that in the meantime a special tent should be prepared and disposition made so that as soon as possible after this date all hands should be available for the projected attempt to saw through the great ice-sheet which intervened between the ' Discovery' and the open sea. In drawing out instructions I could not foretell, of course, how broad this ice-sheet would be when operations were commenced ; I could only assume that it would be about the same as in the previous year, when the open water had extended to the Dellbridge Islets, about eleven miles from the ship. I directed, therefore, that the camp should be made behind these islets, so that there might be no chance of its being swept away. I had hoped to be back in time to commence the operations myself, but the breakdown of my sledges had made this impossible, and in my absence the command devolved on Armitage. He made all preparations in accordance with my instructions, but was then met with a difficulty, for when the middle of December came the open water, instead of being up to the islets, ended at least ten miles farther to the north. In these circumstances he thought it dangerous to take the camp

out to the ice-edge, and decided to pitch it behind the
islets as had been previously arranged. But this, of
course, meant that the sawing work had to be commenced in the middle of the ice-sheet instead of at its
edge, with the result that I shall presently describe.

When I arrived at the camp the greater number of
our people had been at work for ten days; the work and
the camp life had fallen into a regular routine, so that
I was able to judge at once of past results and future
prospects. Life at this sawing camp was led under such
curious conditions that it deserves some description.
The main tent was a very palatial abode, judged by our
standards of sledging life. Its long pent-roof shape can
be seen in the accompanying illustration; it was about
50 feet long and 18 feet across, and had a door with a
small lobby at each end. The interior was divided into
two compartments by a canvas screen; the smaller, about
18 feet in length, was for the officers, whilst the larger
accommodated the men. Close to this screen in the
men's quarters stood a small cooking-range mounted on
boards. The floor of both spaces was covered with tar-
paulin as far as possible, and as time went on imposing
tables and stools were manufactured from packing-cases.
All the fur sleeping-bags were in use, but as these were
not sufficient for all hands, some slept between blankets.
However, this was no hardship, as very little covering
was needed and nearly everyone complained of the heat
of the tent. The temperature had been extraordinarily
high, sometimes rising to 35° or 36°, and when the sun
shone on the dark canvas of the tent a few found the

interior so oppressive that they sought outside shelter in the smaller sledging tents, or spread their sleeping-bags on a piece of canvas in the open.

Thirty people were at the camp when we arrived. They were divided into three parties of ten, which relieved one another on the saws. The work on the latter was exceedingly heavy, so that a four-hour spell was quite sufficient for one party. It took them twenty minutes to get to their work, and another twenty to get back to the tent when they were relieved ; then, after cooking and eating a meal, they would coil down for five or six hours, and rise in time for a fresh meal before the next spell of work. With three parties working in this manner the preparation of meals practically never ceased throughout the twenty-four hours, and cook succeeded cook at the small range. Luckily this was a land of plenty. The tent lay within 200 yards of the largest of the islets, where the working of the ice formed spaces of open water through which hundreds of seals rose to bask on the floe. Now and again also a small troop of Adélie penguins would hurry towards the tent full of curiosity—to find their way promptly into the cooking-pot. Every other day the dog sledge came from the ship laden with flour, biscuit, sugar, butter, and jam, so that supplies of all sorts were readily available—and constant supplies were very much needed, as my earliest impressions of the camp assured me.

'It is a real treat to be amongst our people once more and to find them in such splendid condition and spirits. I do not think there is a whole garment in the party ; judging by the torn and patched clothing, they might be the veriest lot of tramps, but one would have to go far to find such sturdy tramps. Everyone is burnt to a deep bronze colour by the sun, but in each dark face one has not to wait long for the smiles which show the white of teeth and clear healthy eyes. I have been sitting on a packing-case with everyone trying to tell me stories at once, and from the noise which has come from beyond the screen I know that my sledge companions have been in much the same position.

‘ It appears that the work on the saws was felt very much at first, and arms and backs became one huge ache. Everyone had felt that if it had been leg work there would have been no difficulty after the sledging experience, but the new departure exercised a different set of muscles altogether, so that after the first efforts people suffered much from stiffness ; but this soon wore off, and then there had come the emulation of one party against another to show which could complete the longest cut in a four-hour spell. There had been no reason to be alarmed about the appetites even before this work commenced, but as soon as it had settled down into full swing, it was as much as the dog team and the seal killers could do to keep up supplies. I could scarcely wonder at this from what I saw to-night : one of the returning parties first fell on an enormous potful of porridge, and it was gone before one could well look round ; next came a dish piled high with sizzling seal steaks, and very soon the dish was empty ; then came the jam course, with huge hunks of bread and “ flap Johnny ” cakes, the sort of thing that is produced on a griddle and which I hear is very popular. Finally, after their light supper, this party composed themselves to sleep, and very soon other people arose and inquired how their breakfast was getting on.

'Each party have four of these meals in the day, so that twelve meals altogether are served in the tent. Barne's party seem to hold the record; it appears that they possess an excellent cook in Smythe, and that a few days ago he prepared for them a splendid stew which took seven penguins in the making; after cooking this he turned his attention to making cakes, and not until these were finished did he demand his share of the first dish, and then he discovered that there was none left! Considering that a penguin is not far off the size of a goose, I think this party deserve to retain the palm.

'But, apart from this, I do not think I ever saw such exuberant, overflowing health and spirits as now exist in this camp. It is a good advertisment for teetotalers, as there is no grog, and our strongest drinks are tea and cocoa, but of course the most potent factor is the outdoor life with the hard work and good food. Apart from the work, everyone agrees that it has been the most splendid picnic they have ever had; the weather on the whole has been very fine and the air quite mild. But it is certainly well that the conditions have been so pleasant, for I hear on all sides that the work is hopeless. This is a matter I must see for myself, however; for the present I have decided that to-morrow, being New Year's day, shall be a whole holiday; this will be a treat for all, and will give me time to think what shall be done next.

'*January* 1.—Last night I was irresistibly reminded of being in a farmyard. Animals of various kinds were making the queerest noises all about us. I lay awake in my own small tent for a long while listening to these strange sounds. The Weddell seal is a great musician, and can produce any note from a shrill piping whistle to a deep moan, and between whiles he grunts and gurgles and complains in the weirdest fashion. As there were some hundreds of these animals on the ice, there was a chorus of sounds like the tuning of many instruments. To this was added the harsh, angry cawing of the skua gulls as they quarrelled over their food, and now and again one of the dogs would yap in his dreams, whilst from the main tent came the more familiar snores of humanity. At first I missed one sound from this Antarctic concert, but it came at last when the squawk of a penguin was borne from afar on the still air; then the orchestra was completed.

' Royds, Wilson, and I took a sledge and our lunch, and went out to the ice-edge. It was farther than we expected, and the sledge-meter showed close on ten miles before we came to open water. Everything looked terribly stagnant; a thick pack, two or three miles across, hung close to the fast ice. The day was beautiful, and one could not feel very depressed in such weather; but I cannot say that it is pleasing to think that there is a solid sheet of twenty miles between us and freedom.'

'*January* 2.—To-day I had all hands on the saws, and then went out to see how matters were going.'

Perhaps it would be well to pause here to describe the nature of an ice-saw. A typical saw such as we had is about 18 feet in length, 8 or 9 inches in depth, and $1\frac{1}{2}$ or 2 inches in thickness; the teeth are naturally very coarse. It has a wooden cross-handle at the top, and is worked with the aid of a tripod in a very simple and primitive fashion. A rope is attached close to the handle, and led through a block on the tripod; it then divides into numerous tails, to each of which a man is stationed. When all these men pull down together the saw is lifted, and as they release their ropes other men on the handles press the saw forward, and it makes a downward cut. From time to time as the saw-cut advances the tripod has to be shifted. The arrangement can probably be well understood from the accompanying illustration. The action of the men on the ropes is very much that of bellringers, and it can be imagined that four hours of this sort of thing is a very good spell.

I must now ask the reader to consider what the sawing of a channel through a solid ice-sheet actually means. It will be obvious of course that two cuts must be made, one on each side of the channel; but the rest is not so evident. It lies in the problem of how to get rid of the ice which remains in the channel. In order to do this cross-cuts must be made at intervals; but this is not sufficient, for it is impossible to make the two side-cuts exactly parallel, so that by a cross-cut alone an irregular parallelogram is left, which will be immovable without being broken up. The simplest manner in which this can be effected is to make a diagonal cut right through it. The net result of the foregoing is to show that, in order to make a channel a mile in length, it is necessary to cut through four miles of ice. What added difficulties there were in our case my diary shows :

'I found that the result of twelve solid days' work was two parallel cuts 150 yards in length, and as operations had been commenced in the middle of the ice-sheet, instead of at the edge, the ice between the cuts could not be detached, and in some places it seemed to have frozen across again. I started the saws to see how matters had been going, and was astonished at the small result of the work. The ice was between six and seven feet thick, and each stroke only advanced the saw a fraction of an inch. The plain Rule of Three sum before us was, as 150 yards is to 12 days, so is 20 miles to x; and we did not have to work this sum out to appreciate the futility of further operations. I therefore directed that everything except the large tent should be taken back to the ship. The men will attempt to make a cut around Hut Point, so as to ease matters at the end if the ice breaks up, and the officers will be freed for their usual scientific work. Our sawing efforts have been an experience, but I'm afraid nothing more.

'I have been much struck by the way in which everyone has cheerfully carried on this hopeless work until the order came to halt. There could have been no officer or man amongst them who did not see from the

first how utterly useless it was, and yet there has been
no faltering or complaint, simply because all have felt
that, as the sailor expresses it, " Them's the orders." '

'*January* 3.—Most of our company went back to
the ship yesterday afternoon ; some officers remain in
the large tent, Hodgson to do some fishing and Ferrar
some rock searching.   Twenty miles of ice hangs heavy
upon me, and I have decided we must be prepared for
another winter.   We have fifty tons of coal left and
an ample stock of provisions ; also we can now take
advantage of every resource that our region provides,
for there are evidently a large number of penguins to
the north which will make a most grateful addition
to our usual seal-meat.   I have therefore told off four
of the men—Lashly, Evans, Handsley, and Clarke—to
fix their headquarters in the large tent, and to make such
raids on the penguins as will assure us a winter stock.

' This afternoon, after making these arrangements,
I started away to the north with Wilson.   We are
off on a real picnic ; there is to be no hard marching,
and we have made ample provision for the commissariat.
We know there will be numberless seals and penguins,
and we have brought plenty of butter to cook our
unsuspecting victims ; and then also we have jam and
all sorts of unheard-of sledging luxuries.   Personally
I want to watch the ice-edge and see what chance
there is of a break-up ; Wilson wants to study the life
in that region.   There has also been a talk of trying to
get some way up Erebus, but this means hard work,
for which at present we are neither of us inclined.

' To-night we are camped near some rocks half way towards the ice-edge ; there are several seals close by, and small bands of Adélie penguins are constantly passing us. It is curious there should be so many, as we know of no rookery near, and it is still more curious why they should be making south, as there is no open water beyond the few cracks near the land. It gives us the idea that they don't quite know what they are doing, especially since we watched the movements of one small band ; they were travelling towards the south with every appearance of being in a desperate hurry—flippers outspread, heads bent forward, and little feet going for all they were worth. Their business-like air was intensely ludicrous ; one could imagine them saying in the fussiest manner, " Can't stop to talk now, much too busy," and so we watched them until their plump little bodies were mere specks, when suddenly, for no rhyme or reason, they turned round and came hurrying back just as fussy and busy as ever. I can't tell whether they saw us, but to our surprise they showed no curiosity. When they were about twenty yards beyond us again, three of them suddenly plumped down on their breasts, drew their heads close in, shut their eyes, and apparently went fast asleep. It was the queerest performance ; one can imagine that in an hour or two they will be up and off again without even giving themselves time for a shake.'

' *January* 4.—We pursued our leisurely way, skirting the land towards the ice-edge this morning. When within half a mile of the open water Wilson suddenly said, "There they are." I looked round, and, lo and behold! on the dark bare rocks of Cape Royds there was a red smudge dotted with thousands of little black-and-white figures—a penguin rookery without a doubt. It is wonderful that we should have been here two years without knowing of this, and it is exasperating to think of the feasts of eggs we have missed. We steered into a small bay behind the cape, climbed a steep little rock-face, and found ourselves on a small plateau, luckily to windward of the rookery. No place could be better for our camp, so we hauled our belongings up with the Alpine rope and pitched our tent on a stretch of sand.

'Words fail me to describe what a delightful and interesting spot this is. From our tent door we look out on to the open sea, deep blue but dotted with snowy-white pack-ice. Erebus towers high above us on our right, and to the left we look away over the long stretch of fast ice to the cloud-capped western mountains. We hear the constant chatter of the penguins, and find a wonderful interest in watching their queer habits; the brown fluffy chicks are still quite small, and the adult birds are constantly streaming to and from the sea. Close about us many skuas are nesting; they naturally regard us as intruders, and are terribly angry. The owners of one nest near by are perched on a rock; whenever we move they arch their necks and scream with rage, and when we go out of the tent they sweep down on us, only turning their course as their wings brush our heads. However,

if we do not disturb their nest no doubt they will soon
get used to us.

'We have seen facts to-day which throw some light
on the ferocious character of this robber gull. On
returning from our walk Wilson saw one of them swoop
down on the nest of another and fly off with a stolen
egg in its beak. The owner of the nest was only a few
yards away, and started in such hot pursuit that the thief
was forced to relinquish its prize, which was dashed to
pieces on the rocks. It is evident that there is not even
honour amongst thieves in the skua code of morality.

'To-night we watched another incident in connection
with the domestic life of these birds. Close by us there
is a nest with two tiny chicks ; they might be ordinary
barn-door chickens but for their already formidable bill
and claws, and it is quite evident that they have not
been hatched out more than a day or two. Suddenly
we saw the parent bird come from the sea with a
very fair-sized fish in its bill. It perched on a rock
and began to tear pieces from its prey and offer them
to its offspring ; the latter seized these tempting morsels
with avidity, and though they could scarcely stand they
tore and gobbled at the food with wonderful energy.
But after a bit both chicks found themselves wrestling
with the same piece, and for some time there was quite
a tug of war until both seemed to realise that this was
not the way to settle such a matter, and, as if by mutual
consent, they dropped the cause of contention and went
for one another. They became perfect little furies as
they staggered about clawing and pecking at each other.

Of course they were too feeble to do any harm, and soon fell apart exhausted, but the struggle shows that the youthful skua possesses a very full share of original sin.

'We had a charming walk to the north side of the cape this afternoon, where the sea is lapping lazily on a shelving sandy beach, and where also there are several ponds with weeds and confervæ. How delightful it is to look on the sea once more! Yet how much more delightful it would be if one could lift the 'Discovery' up and deposit her twenty miles to the north!

'On our return we got amongst the penguins, much to their annoyance. They swore at us in the vilest manner, and their feathers and temper remained ruffled long after we had passed them.

'Before supper we took soap and towels down to a small rill of thaw-water that runs within ten yards of the tent and had a delightful wash in the warm sunlight. Then we had a dish of fried penguins' liver with seal kidneys; eaten straight out of the frying-pan this was simply delicious. I have come to the conclusion that life in the Antarctic Regions can be very pleasant.'

'*January* 5.—This morning we got up in the most leisurely fashion, and after a wash and our breakfast we lazily started to discuss plans for the day. Our tent door was open and framed the clear sea beyond, and I was gazing dreamily out upon this patch of blue when suddenly a ship entered my field of view. It was so unexpected that I almost rubbed my eyes before I dared to report it, but a moment after, of course, all became bustle and we began to search round for our boots and other articles necessary for the march. Whilst we were thus employed, Wilson looked up and said, " Why, there's another," and sure enough there were now two vessels framed in our doorway. We had of course taken for granted that the first ship was the " Morning," but what in the name of fortune could be the meaning of this second one ? We propounded all sorts of wild theories of which it need only be said that not one was within measurable distance of the truth.

' Meanwhile we were busily donning our garments and discussing what should be done next. The ships were making towards the ice-edge some five miles to the westward ; our easiest plan would be to go straight on board, but then if we did so our companions on board the " Discovery " would know nothing of it, and it would mean a long delay before they could get their mails. Our duty seemed to be to consider first the establishment of communications, so, hastily scribbling some notes with directions for the dog team and a sledge party to be sent down without delay, we started southward to search for the penguin hunters in order that these notes might be delivered.

' We went on for a long time without seeing a sign of them, but after travelling some six miles we caught sight of their tent, though without any signs of life about it ; we had to come within a hundred yards before our shouts were answered and four very satisfied figures emerged, still munching the remains of what evidently had been a hearty meal. Of course I thought they had not seen the ships, but they had, only, as they explained, they didn't see there was any call for them to do anything in the matter. I said, " But, good heavens, you want your mails, don't you?" "Oh, yes, sir," they replied, "but we thought that would be all right." In other words, they as good as said that life was so extremely easy and pleasant that there was no possible object in worrying over such a trifle as the arrival of a relief expedition. And these are the people whom, not unnaturally, some of our friends appear to imagine in dire straits and in need of immediate transport to civilised conditions!

'However, once they got their orders they were off like the wind, and Wilson and I turned about and faced for the ships. We were quite close before figures came hurrying forth to meet us, but then we were soon surrounded with many familiar faces, and with many also that were quite strange. Of course I learnt at once that the second ship was the " Terra Nova," and that her captain, MacKay, was an old acquaintance whom I was more than pleased to welcome in this Far South region ; but it was not until I had had a long talk with my good friend Colbeck that I began to understand why a second ship had been sent and what a strangely new aspect everything must wear. Indeed, as I turn in to-night, amidst all the comfort that the kindness and forethought of my " Morning " friends have provided, I can scarcely realise the situation fully. I can only record that in spite of the good home news, and in spite of the pleasure of seeing old friends again, I was happier last night than I am to-night.'

And now I must briefly explain how it was that these vessels had descended upon us like a bolt from the blue, and what messages of comfort and discomfort they bore.

To do so I must hark back to March 2, 1902, when, as will be remembered, the 'Morning' left us bearing despatches which outlined the work we had done and described our situation and the prospect of our detention for a second winter. The 'Morning' arrived in New Zealand in April, and the general outline of affairs was flashed over the cables, but received in a very garbled form; it was not until six weeks later that the mails brought a clear account of the situation to those who had been so anxiously awaiting news at home. And now for a moment I must pause to explain what this account conveyed to those authorities at home who were responsible for the despatch of the expedition. My report informed them that the 'Discovery' and all on board her were safe and well and prepared for a second winter, but perhaps rather unfortunately it referred to the return of the 'Morning' in the following summer as a foregone conclusion and enumerated the stores which it was advisable she should bring; it spoke also of our attack of scurvy, though stating that there was little chance of its recurrence. I had been tempted to omit this matter as calculated to cause unnecessary anxiety, but, reflecting that the rumour might spread from some other source and become greatly exaggerated, I had finally decided to state the facts exactly as they were.

Such a report could leave only one impression on the

minds of the authorities to which I have referred—
namely, that at all hazards the 'Morning' must be sent
South in 1903. But this contingency, which could not
easily have been foreseen, involved a serious difficulty, as
the 'Morning' fund was found to be wholly inadequate
to meet the requirements of another year. There can
be little doubt, I think, that had time permitted an
appeal to the public and a full explanation of the necessities of the case, the required funds would have been
raised, but, unfortunately, time was very limited, and
already some weeks had elapsed since the reception of
the news. In these circumstances no course was left
to the Societies but to appeal to the Government, and
after some correspondence the Government agreed to
undertake the whole conduct of the relief expedition
provided that the 'Morning,' as she stood, was delivered
to it. These arrangements being made, the Government naturally placed the active management of affairs
in the hands of the Admiralty, and a small committee
of officers was appointed by this department to deal
with it.

It is scarcely necessary to point out that when the
Government undertakes a matter of this sort it must be
with larger responsibilities than can rest on private individuals. Had the Societies possessed the necessary
funds, they would have been quite justified in relying on
the 'Morning' to force her way to the South as she had
done before, but when the Government undertook that
relief should be sent, it could not afford to entrust the
fulfilment of its pledge to one small ship, which, however

ably handled, might break down or become entangled in the ice before she reached her destination.

It was felt, therefore, that to support the Government pledge and ensure the relief of the 'Discovery' two ships should be sent. This decision and the very short time which was left for its performance brought a heavy strain on the Admiralty Committee to which I have referred. It consisted of the Hydrographer, Sir William Wharton, Admiral Pelham Aldrich, and Admiral Boyes, and it is thanks to the unremitted labour of these officers that the relief expedition was organised to that degree of efficiency which the Government desired.

To meet the requirements of the case the 'Terra Nova,' one of the finest of the whaling ships, was purchased and brought to Dundee to be thoroughly refitted; whilst there, she was completely stocked with provisions and all other necessaries for the voyage, and a whaling crew, under the command of Captain Harry MacKay, was engaged to navigate her. Perhaps never before has a ship been equipped so speedily and efficiently for polar work, and it is a striking example of what can be done under able guidance and urgent requirement. Even when the 'Terra Nova' had been prepared for her long voyage in this rapid manner the need for haste had not vanished, and it appeared that the time still left was quite inadequate to allow her to make the long voyage around the Cape under her own motive power. The same high pressure was therefore continued, and her course was directed through the Mediterranean and Suez Canal, on which route cruiser after cruiser took her in tow and raced her through the water at a speed which must have surprised the barnacles on her stout wooden sides.

Thanks to this haste, however, she arrived in the South in time to make the final preparations for her Antarctic voyage, and towards the end of November she lay off Hobart Town in Tasmania. In December she was joined by the 'Morning,' and in the middle of the same month both ships sailed for the Ross Sea. Captain Colbeck was directed to take charge of this joint venture until such time as both ships should come under my command. And so it came about that, much to our surprise, two ships, instead of one, arrived off the edge of our fast ice on January 5, 1904.

Looking back now, I can see that everything happened in such a natural sequence that I might well have guessed that something of the sort would come about, yet it is quite certain that no such thought ever entered my head, and the first sight of the two vessels conveyed nothing but blank astonishment. But it was not the arrival of the 'Terra Nova,' whose captain I saw from the first was anxious to do everything in his power to fall in with my plans, that disconcerted me and prompted that somewhat lugubrious entry in my diary which I have quoted. This was caused by quite another matter, and one which I might equally have guessed had I thought the problem out on the right lines.

When the news of our detention in the ice became known in England, it is not too much to say that the majority of those who were capable of forming a competent opinion believed that the 'Discovery' would never be freed. There is no doubt the Admiralty inclined to this opinion, but whether they did so or not, it was equally their duty to see that the expense of furnishing a relief expedition on such an elaborate scale should not be incurred again in a future season, and consequently they had no other course than to issue direct instructions to me to abandon the 'Discovery' if she could not be freed in time to accompany the relief ships to the North.

When I came to understand the situation I could see clearly the reason which dictated these instructions, but this did little to lighten the grievous disappointment I felt on receiving them.

It does not need much further explanation, I think, to show that the arrival of the relief ships with this mandate placed me and my companions unavoidably in a very cruel position. Under the most ordinary conditions, I take it, a sailor would go through much rather than abandon his ship. But the ties which bound us to the 'Discovery' were very far beyond the ordinary ; they involved a depth of sentiment which cannot be surprising when it is remembered what we had been through in her and what a comfortable home she had proved in all the rigours of this Southern region.

In spite of our long detention in the ice, the thought of leaving her had never entered our heads. Throughout the second winter we had grown ever more assured that she would be freed if we had the patience to wait ; we could not bring ourselves to believe—and, as events proved, quite rightly—that the ice-sheet about us was a permanency. When the end of December came and we still found twenty miles between us and the open sea, we had small fits of depression such as 'my diary showed ; but, as is also shown, they did not interfere with the healthy, happy course of our lives, and any one of us would have scouted the idea that hope should be abandoned. We had felt that at the worst this only opened up for us the prospect of a third winter, and we had determined that if we had to go through with it, it would not be our fault if we were not comfortable.

It was from this easy and passably contented frame of mind that we were rudely awakened. The situation we were now obliged to face was that if the twenty-mile plain of ice refused to break up within six weeks, we must bid a long farewell to our well-beloved ship and return to our homes as castaways with the sense of failure dominating the result of our labours. And so with the advent of the relief ships there fell on the ' Discovery' the first and last cloud of gloom which we were destined to experience. As day followed day without improvement in the ice conditions, the gloom deepened until our faces grew so long that one might well have imagined an Antarctic expedition to be a very woeful affair.

As we were very human also, it may be confessed that not a little of our discontent arose from wounded vanity. By this time we considered ourselves very able to cope with any situation that might arise, and believed that we were quite capable of looking after ourselves. It was not a little trying, therefore, to be offered relief to an extent which seemed to suggest that we had been reduced to the direst need.   No healthy man likes to be thought an invalid, and there are few of us who have not at some time felt embarrassed by an excess of consideration for our needs.

Although the month that followed the arrival of the relief ships was on the whole a very dismal one, it was by no means uneventful ; in fact, it was a season which displayed the most extraordinary ups and downs in our fortunes, and therefore I take up the tale once more with extracts from my diary:

'*January* 7.—I write again in camp at Cape Royds, where I have joined Wilson to get some quiet in order to read my letters and consider the situation.   I don't know in what state the relief ships expected to find us, but I think they must have soon appreciated that we were very much alive.   The messages I sent back to the " Discovery " on the 5th were carried at such speed that by 10 P.M. the dog team arrived at the ice-edge.   This meant that my orders had been conveyed forty miles in twelve hours.   Early the next morning the first sledge team of men arrived and departed with a large load of parcels and presents.   These by arrangement were taken to the main camp, whence another party took them to the ship, and so our friends saw teams of our distressful company coming north with a swinging march, appearing on board with very brown faces and only waiting for their sledges to be loaded before they vanished over the horizon again.   The number of parcels sent by our kind friends in England and New Zealand is enormous, but as one cannot tell what each contains till the owner opens it, I decided to send all.

'Conditions at the ice-edge have been absolutely quiescent, the weather calm and bright, and the loose pack coming and going with the tide ; not a single piece has broken away from the main sheet. I asked Colbeck to start his people on an ice-saw to give them an idea of what the work was like ; a single day was quite enough for them. MacKay suggested that he should get up a full head of steam and attempt to break the ice up by ramming, or, as he says, "butting" it. He has little hope of success, but points out that the " Terra Nova " is a powerful steamer and may accomplish something ; for my part, except as regards damage to his ship, I think he might as well try to "butt" through Cape Royds. However, he is to make the attempt to-morrow or the next day, and it is perhaps as well that every expedient should be tried. We can but try every means in our power and leave Providence to do the rest ; but it looks as though Providence will have a very large share.

'There is a light snowfall to-night; the penguins are unusually quiet, and the skuas lie low on the rocks ; does this mean a blow ? It is a curious irony of fate that makes one pray for a gale in these regions, but at present bad weather seems the only thing that can help us.'

'*January* 9.—At the main camp. Came up from Cape Royds last night intending to reach the ship this morning. This resulted in rather a curious experience. I started early and trudged on towards the ship through snow that has become rather deep and sticky. Half-way across the air grew thick and misty.   I lost sight of all landmarks, but went on for some time guided by the sun, which showed faintly at my back.   After a while the sun vanished, but thinking I might make some sort of general direction I turned towards the land and plodded on ; for nearly an hour I saw nothing, but then suddenly came across fresh footsteps ; they were my own !   I naturally decided that this was not good enough, so turned to retrace the track towards the camp ; a mile back I fell across a sledge party, and on inquiring where they were going was told that they had been following my footsteps to the ship.   Needless to say, we are all back at the main camp again.'

'*January* 10.—Reached the ship this morning and this afternoon assembled all hands on the mess-deck, where I told them exactly how matters stood.   There was a stony silence.   I have not heard a laugh in the ship since I returned.'

'*January* 11.—I have decided to arrange for the transport of our collections and instruments to the relief ships.   To-day the officers have been busy making out lists of the things to be sent.'

'*January* 13.—For some time we have had a flagstaff on the Tent Islet, ten miles to the north, and a system of signals in connection with it descriptive of the changes in the ice conditions.   A flag or shape is hoisted on the staff each morning which has a special meaning in our code, and each morning our telescope is anxiously trained towards it.   Up to the present only one signal has been read : it signifies " No change in the ice conditions." I don't know whether it is worse to be on board the relief ships and observe the monotony of the change-less conditions or to be here and observe the terrible sameness of that signal. Our people have been steadily struggling on with the ice-saw off Hut Point; the work is even heavier than it was to the north, as the ice is thicker and more deeply covered with snow. I have kept it going more as an occupation than from any hope of useful result, but to-day it has been stopped.'

'*January* 15.—I thought for some time about the advisability of starting to transport our valuables. The distance is long, and with the recent snowfall the work will be very heavy, but what I think principally held me back was the thought that it might be taken as a sign that we are giving up hope. Bad as things are, we are not reduced to that yet. In the end, however, I reflected that, whether the " Discovery " gets out or not, there is no reason why the relief ships should not carry our collections and instruments back to civilisation, and meanwhile the work of transport will relieve the terrible monotony of waiting. There is, perhaps, nothing so trying in our situation as the sense of impotence. I have decided, therefore, to set things going; our parties will drag the loads down to the main camp, and the crews of the relief ships will share the work of taking them on. Royds has gone north to arrange the details, and also to try some experiments with explosives. I have told him not to use much of the latter, as the distance is so great that it would only be waste to undertake serious opera-tions of this sort at present. I merely want to know exactly how to set about the work when the time comes, if it ever does come.'

'*January* 21.—Wilson returned to the ship to-night after a long spell at the Cape Royds camp, and told me all about his great capture. It appears that one day he strolled over to the north beach to see what he at first took for a prodigiously large seal lying asleep on it. As he got closer he saw, however, that the animal was quite different from any of the ordinary Southern seals, and his excitement can be imagined. Two of the "Morning" officers were in camp with him, and when Wilson had seized the gun the three proceeded to stalk this strange new beast. Their great fear was that they might only succeed in wounding it, and that it would escape into the sea, so in spite of the temperature of the water they waded well round it before they attacked. These tactics proved quite successful, and their quarry was soon despatched, but it was far too heavy for them to move or for Wilson to examine where it lay. The following day, however, Colbeck came over in the "Morning," and with the aid of boats and ropes the carcase was eventually landed on his decks.

'On close examination Wilson came to the conclusion that the animal is a sea elephant of the species commonly found at Macquarie Island, but this is the first time that such a beast has been found within the Antarctic Circle ; and that it should now have been captured so many hundreds of miles beyond is a very extraordinary circumstance. The sea elephant is, I believe, a vegetarian ; the stomach of this one was empty.'

I may remark that we got to know this particular
sea elephant very well.   As a rule, skeletons which are
bound for the British Museum are not cleaned until they
arrive on the premises, in order that there may be no
difficulty in reassembling the parts.   In accordance with
this custom, the skeleton of this animal was carried on
the skid beams of the 'Discovery' in a partially stripped
state.   All went well until we arrived in the tropics, but
after that we had no chance of forgetting that we carried
the remains of a sea elephant.   Shift it from place to
place as we would, it made its presence felt everywhere.
In the end the Museum came very close to losing a
specimen, and I doubt if it possesses many that have
caused more woe.

'*January* 23.—Since the start of our transporting work
more than a week ago, the weather has changed.   We
have had a great deal of wind from the east and south-east
with drifting snow, and an almost continuously overcast
sky.   The work has been impeded, but by steadily
pushing on we have managed to accomplish a good
deal.   Our people go out all together and drag four
heavily laden sledges down to the main camp ; there
they remain for the night, and return on the following
day.   The relief ships work the remainder of the distance in much the same way.   We keep a cook at the
main camp to provide the necessary meals.   Hodgson,
Bernacchi, and Mulock have been down to the ships to
see to the storage of our belongings.   Most of them will
go in the " Terra Nova," which has the greater accom-
modation.

' From these sources or from notes which come every other day I receive accounts of the ice. I scarcely like to write that things are looking more hopeful. Nothing happened until the 18th, but on that day some large pieces broke away, and since that the ships have made steady but slow progress. I estimate from reports that they are four or five miles nearer than when I was down a fortnight ago. I learn that the " Terra Nova's " " butting " came to naught, as I expected ; she could make no impression on the solid sheet, though she rammed it full tilt.'

' *January* 24. – Our people report that the ships were again on the move last night, and this morning did not appear to be more than three miles from the camp. I have been calculating that for things to be as they were in the year of our arrival thirteen or fourteen miles of ice must go out in fifteen days—nearly an average of a mile a day, whereas I scarcely like to think what a difference this would be from what has happened in the last fifteen days. We are at present behind last year's date as regards the ice, but, on the other hand, the recent winds have swept the pack away—a condition that never happened last year.'

' *January* 27.—Yesterday the large tent was shifted two miles this way, and is now this side of the glacier tongue ; this is by way of equalising the distance for the transporting parties, but our people have still much the longer distance to travel. Advices from the relief ships inform me that the ice is still breaking away, but not so rapidly as at the beginning of the week. I fear, I much fear, that things are going badly for us.'

'*January* 28.—This morning as I lay in my bunk I was astonished to hear the ship creaking. On getting up I found that she was moving in the ice with a very slow rhythmic motion. After breakfast we all went out to Hut Point and found that the whole ice-sheet was swaying very slightly under the action of a long swell ; its edge against the land was rising and falling as much as 18 inches. This is the most promising event that has happened : we have not known such a thing since our first imprisonment. It is too thick to see what is happening to seaward, but one cannot but regard this as a hopeful sign. We are all very restless, constantly dashing up the hill to the look-out station or wandering from place to place to observe the effects of the swell. But it is long since we enjoyed such a cheerful experience as we get on watching the loose pieces of ice jostling one another at Hut Point.'

'*January* 29.—Still no definite news of what is happening to seaward. The ship worked loose yesterday, and moves an inch or two in her icy bed. This has caused a great increase in the creaking and groaning of the timbers. This pleasant music is now almost continuous, and one feels immensely cheered till one goes up the hill and looks out on the long miles of ice and the misty screen which hides the sea. I grow a little sceptical of reports which tell of the departure of a mile or half a mile of ice, for if all these distances could be added together the relief ships should have been at Hut Point by now.'

'*January* 30.—Went up the hill with Koettlitz, and

saw a most cheering sight. The ice has broken away well inside the glacier, and the relief ships are not much more than eight miles away. Through the telescope one can see the hull and rigging very distinctly, and even the figures of men walking about.

'Later came full reports from the ships with excellent news. Colbeck tells me that during the last few days there has been a great change. On the 26th the open water extended to the outer islet, on the 28th to the inner one, and now it has reached inside the glacier. The ice broke away in very large sheets and so rapidly that he was carried away to the westward. As if to show contempt for our puny efforts, the scene of our sawing labours was carried away in the centre of a large floe; our feeble scratches did not even help to form one of the cracks which broke up the ice-sheet about them. In the last five days fully six miles of ice have broken away, so that we are all inclined to be very cheerful again. There is only one drawback: the swell is slowly but surely dying away, and there is no doubt that we are entirely dependent on it.'

'*February* 1.—We seem to be hanging in the balance, with even chances either way. On the one hand, the swell has died away, the ice is very quiet again, and one remembers that we are not really further advanced than we were at this time last year; on the other, we hear the hopeful sign of a clear sea to the north, and the knowledge that a swell will have full freedom of action. It's a toss-up.

'The work of transport has been going on steadily,

and a few more days will see its finish. The main tent is now about five miles from the ship, so that the work progresses more speedily. All our scientific collections and most of the valuable instruments were taken across some time ago ; then followed the scientific library, a very heavy item ; and now some of our personal effects and the pictures, &c., from the wardroom are packed for transit. Our living quarters are beginning to look bare and unfurnished, but we shall not mind that a particle if we can only get out.

'I find myself growing ridiculously superstitious, and cannot banish the notion that if we make every preparation for leaving the "Discovery," Nature with its usual cussedness will free her.'

'*February* 3.—I imagine the ice all over the sound has been thinning underneath ; off the various headlands it has rotted right through to a greater extent than it did last year. There is a very large open pool off Cape Armitage, and another smaller one off Hut Point, beyond which the ice is very thin and treacherous for three or four hundred yards. The sledge parties have to go a long way round to avoid this, though unloaded travellers can climb over the land and down on to the firm ice in Arrival Bay.

'For some days now there has been practically no advance in the ice conditions. Our spirits are steadily falling again, and I am just off to the "Morning" to see if anything more can be done.'

'*February* 4.—On board the "Morning." The ships are lying about one and a half mile inside the glacier, where they have been without change for the last three days. I have discontinued transport work for the present. It has been a lovely calm, bright day—alas! much too calm and bright. I cannot describe how irritating it is to endure these placid conditions as the time speeds along. There being nothing else to be done, Colbeck took me round the glacier tongue in the "Morning," and we sounded on both sides, getting most extraordinarily regular depths of 230 to 240 fathoms, except at one inlet on the north side, where we got 170. In the afternoon we climbed to the top of the Tent Islet (480 feet) and brought down the telescope and flags left by the signalling party. The ice to the westward is not broken away so far as I expected; altogether the view was not inspiriting. Spent the evening with Captain MacKay, who is excellent company for a depressed state of mind.'

'*February* 5.—I did not want to begin explosions whilst the distance was so great, but on considering the stagnant condition of affairs I decided to make a start to-day. It has been evident to me for some time that if explosives are to be of any use, they must be expended freely, and so to-day we experimented in this direction. To explain matters, it is necessary to describe the condition of the fast ice. Its edge starts about a mile from the end of the glacier, and after a sweep to the south turns to the west, in which direction it runs for five or six miles before it gradually turns to the north; any point along this long western line is more or less equidistant from the "Discovery." As one approaches the open water from the south, one crosses a series of

cracks which run for miles parallel to each other and to
the ice-edge; this is the first step that the swell makes
towards breaking up the sheet. These cracks are from
50 to 150 yards apart, and according to the dimensions of
the swell there may be any number from two or three to
a dozen. They are constantly working, those near the
ice-edge of course more perceptibly than the others. After
one of the long strips thus formed has been working for
some time a transverse crack suddenly appears, and then
a piece breaks away, usually at the eastern end ; and
very soon after it is weakened in this manner the rest of
the strip peels away right across the bay. I have now
seen two or three strips go in this manner, and it appears
to me that what we require to do is to get ahead of
Nature by forming the transverse cracks. To-day, therefore, I planted the charges at intervals in line with the
" Discovery," and with a specially made electric circuit
blew them up together. On the whole the result was
satisfactory ; we formed a transverse crack and the strip
under which the charges had been placed went out within
the hour. It is not a great gain, and the expenditure of
material is large, but I think the result justifies an
attempt to continue the work on properly organised lines.
I have therefore sent to the " Discovery " for a party of
our special torpedo men who will continue to fit, place
and fire the charges whilst the men of the relief ships
go on digging the holes. I feel that the utility of these
explosives depends entirely on the swell ; we can do
nothing unless Nature helps us ; on the other hand, we in
turn may help Nature.

'*February* 6.—We have started our explosive work in full swing, and all hands are working very vigorously at it. We have had eight men from the "Terra Nova" and seven from the "Morning" digging holes. I went along first and planted small sticks where these holes were to be dug; then the men set to, three at each hole.

'The ice is from five to six feet in thickness, and the work is quite easy until the hole is two or three feet deep, but then it becomes hard and tiresome, and can be continued only by chipping away with long-handled implements and occasionally clearing out the detached pieces with a shovel. The worst part comes when the water is admitted, as this happens before the bottom of the hole can be knocked out, and it is most difficult to continue the chipping under water; in fact, towards the end of the day we gave up attempting to do this, and decided that it was better to blow the bottom out with a small charge. Whilst the holes were being dug, our own "Discovery" party were busily fitting and firing charges; this is dangerous work of course, and I have been very careful to see that proper precautions are taken. The charge fitters are isolated in a tent some way from the scene of action, and the fitted charges are brought up on a sledge under proper custody, and handled only by our own experts. The battery is kept on a small sledge of its own, and can thus be taken out of reach of the electric circuits when not in use.

'We are doing things on a large scale; three charges are fired together, and each charge contains 35 lbs. of guncotton. When three holes are finished, a charge is

taken to each with a small line five fathoms long attached
to it; then the electric wires are joined up and the
charges are lowered under water to the extent of their
lines, everyone clears away from the region, and the
battery is run up to the other end of the wires, a hundred
and fifty yards away. When all is ready the key is
pressed. Then the whole floe rises as though there
was an earthquake; three mighty columns of water
and ice shoot up into the sky, rising high above the
masts of the ships ; there is a patter of falling ice-blocks
and then quiet again. One might imagine that nothing
could withstand such prodigious force until one walks up
and finds that beyond three gaping blackened craters
there is nothing to show for that vast upheaval—at least,
nothing that can be detected with a casual glance ; but a
close scrutiny of the surface between the holes generally
shows that after all something has been effected, for
from each hole a number of minute cracks radiate, and
one can see that in two or three places these have joined.
At first these cracks are so thin as to be scarcely discern-
ible, but if one watches on for ten minutes or more, one
can detect the fact that they are very gradually opening ;
half an hour later they may be a quarter of an inch in
width, and then it is possible to see that the ice on each
side is moving unequally. This is the beginning of the
end, for in an hour or two the broken floe, small enough
in area but containing many hundreds of tons of ice, will
quietly detach itself and float calmly away to the north.

'It is in this manner, therefore, that we now hope to
reach the "Discovery," if only the swell will hold. We

have advanced about a third of a mile to-day, though how much is due to our own efforts, and how much to the ordinary course of Nature, we cannot tell, nor do we much care as long as the advance is made.'

'*February* 7.—We certainly have curious ups and downs of fortune. This forenoon nothing happened after our explosion, and I felt very despondent, but after lunch as I was sitting in Colbeck's cabin, he suddenly rushed down to say that an enormous piece was breaking away—and sure enough when I got on deck I found that a floe from a half to three-quarters of a mile across was quietly going out to sea. The men of the relief ships are working like Trojans at the hole-digging; they are taking a keen interest in the proceedings and are especially delighted with the explosions. There is a competition in cutting the holes, and some take particular care in making them very neat and round regardless of the fact that in half an hour their handiwork will be blown to pieces. The best implement for this work is a sort of spud with a sharp cutting edge at the bottom. We are short of good tools of this sort, but the " Terra Nova's " blacksmith and our own engineers are busy making more.'

'*February* 8.—Wretched luck to-day. It is quite calm, and the swell has almost vanished; the floes that broke away last night are still hanging about the ice-edge and damping what little swell remains. Barne has a bad attack of snow-blindness, and so Evans, of the "Morning," relieves him for the present in the charge of explosive operations.'

'*February* 9.—On board the "Discovery." Our hopes, which were high on the 7th, have fallen again to a low ebb. Last night a few of the broken floes cleared away, but the swell did not return. Explosions were continued, but with little result. However, I felt that we could do no more than work on systematically, and as that has now been arranged I saw no object in my staying on board the "Morning," whereupon, asking Colbeck to superintend operations, I journeyed homeward again.

' At this date two years ago the ice had broken back to Hut Point, and now it is fast for six miles beyond ; one never appreciates what a distance six miles is till one comes to walk over it, and as I plodded homeward for two hours to-day I am bound to confess my heart gradually sank into my boots. There would be nothing to worry about if we only had time on our side, but each day now the sun is sinking lower and the air getting colder. It is only a matter of days now before the season closes.'

' *February* 10.—To-day I have done very little but walk restlessly about. Twice I have been up to the observation station on Arrival Heights. On this vantage point some·500 feet up we have a large telescope with which we can see pretty clearly what is happening at the ice-edge, and sad to relate it is very little.

' The ice about Hut Point is now so thin as to be dangerous for a long way out. Crean fell in yesterday, and had a very narrow shave, as he could not attempt to swim amongst the sodden brash-ice. Luckily he kept his head, and remained still until the others were able to run for a rope and haul him out. To avoid this in

future we have constructed a roadway over the land
so that sledges can be hauled up the steep snow-slope
from Arrival Bay. Everyone now is making an effort to
be cheerful, but it is an obvious effort.

'I have made every arrangement for abandoning the
ship. I have allotted the officers and men to the relief
ships and drawn up instructions for the latter. The
" Morning," I think, ought to be outside the strait by
the 25th, but the " Terra Nova " with her greater power
can remain perhaps a week longer. I don't think I ever
had a more depressing evening's work.'

' *February* 11.—Awoke this morning to find a light
southerly wind and the air filled with snow. We could
see nothing but the dismal grey wall all around us,
and, as may be imagined, the general gloom was not
much lightened by the view of things without ; and yet,
as always seems to happen to us, when things looks
blackest the sun breaks through. This morning I sent
the dog team over with the laboured instructions which
I wrote last night. A few hours later it returned with
a note to say the ice was breaking up fast. A good
deal had gone out in the night and more in the morning.
At eight o'clock Doorly, of the " Morning," arrived with
a second letter to say that the afternoon had proved
equally propitious and to ask that more men might be
sent to dig holes for the explosives. Half an hour later
Royds was away with a party of ten men, and since
that I have been able to do nothing but record these
pleasant facts. I can't think that much excitement of
this sort would be good for us.'

'*February* 12.—The weather was clearer this morning, but the sky still overcast. We were out at Hut Point early, and the difference in distance of the ships was obvious at a glance, so from there we dashed up Arrival Heights. From our observation station we could now see everything. The "Terra Nova" was just picking up our large tent, which was a little over four miles from Hut Point, but the "Morning" was to the westward and quite half a mile nearer, and it was here that the explosive work was being pushed vigorously forward; one could see the tiny groups of figures digging away at the holes. This afternoon I went down to the "Morning," and arrived after a walk of three-quarters of an hour. I learnt that there had been a considerable swell, but that it was now decreasing rapidly and things were growing quieter again; the explosions to-day had not done much, and the broken ice was again hanging about the edge instead of drifting to the north. To-night matters are not quite so pleasing again; I don't fancy another long wait for a swell, yet one has to remember that appearances are very different from what they were two nights ago.'

'*February* 13.—Thick weather again to-day; have seen or heard nothing from the ice-edge. Very anxious for a clearance.'

'*February* 14.—So much has happened to-night that I have some difficulty in remembering the events of the day. This morning the wind was strong from the south-east and carried a good deal of drift; although one could see the relief ships, one could not make out what was happening with regard to the work, or whether the ice was breaking away. The afternoon found us in very much the same condition, and even by dinner-time we had no definite news.

'It was not until we were quietly eating this meal that the excitement first commenced, when we heard a shout on deck and a voice sang out down the hatchway, "The ships are coming, sir!"

'There was no more dinner, and in one minute we were racing for Hut Point, where a glorious sight met our view. The ice was breaking up right across the strait, and with a rapidity which we had not thought possible. No sooner was one great floe borne away than a dark streak cut its way into the solid sheet that remained and carved out another, to feed the broad stream of pack which was hurrying away to the north-west.

'I have never witnessed a more impressive sight; the sun was low behind us, the surface of the ice-sheet in front was intensely white, and in contrast the distant sea and its forking leads looked almost black. The wind had fallen to a calm, and not a sound disturbed the stillness about us.

'Yet in the midst of this peaceful silence was an awful unseen agency rending that great ice-sheet as though it had been naught but the thinnest paper. We knew well by this time the nature of our prison bars; we had not plodded again and again over those long dreary miles of snow without realising the formidable strength of the great barrier which held us bound; we knew that the heaviest battleship would have shattered itself ineffectually against it, and we had seen a million-ton iceberg brought to rest at its edge. For weeks we had been struggling with this mighty obstacle, controlling the most powerful disruptive forces that the intelligence of man has devised, but only to realise more completely the inadequacy of our powers. Even Nature had seemed to pause before such a vast difficulty, and had hitherto delivered her attacks with such sluggish force that we had reasonably doubted her ability to conquer it before the grip of the winter arrested her efforts.

'But now without a word, without an effort on our part, it was all melting away, and we knew that in an hour or two not a vestige of it would be left, and that the open sea would be lapping on the black rocks of Hut Point.

'Fast as the ice was breaking, it was not fast enough for our gallant relief ships; already we could see them battling through the floes with a full head of steam and with their bows ever pressing forward on the yet unbroken sheet; working this way and that, they saw the long cracks shot out before them and in a moment their armoured stems were thrust into them and they forged ahead again in new and rapidly widening channels. There was evidently a race as to which should be first to pass beyond the flagstaff round which our small company had clustered, but the little "Morning," with her bluff bows and weak engines, could scarcely expect to hold her own against her finer-built and more powerful competitor.

'By ten o'clock we could observe the details of the

game and watch each turn and twist with a knowledge
of its immediate cause. By 10.30 we could see the
splintering of the ice as they crashed into the floes and
hear the hoarse shouts of the men as, wild with excitement, they cheered each fresh success. Scarcely half-a-
mile of ice remained between us, and now the contest
became keener, and the crew of the " Terra Nova "
gathered together by word of command and ran from
side to side of their ship till she rolled heavily and
seemed to shake herself, as the force of each rush was
gradually expended and she fell back to gather way for
a fresh attack ; but in spite of all her efforts the persistent
little " Morning," dodging right and left and seizing every
chance opening, kept doggedly at her side, and it still
seemed a chance as to who should be first to reach that
coveted goal, the open pool of water at our feet.

' Meanwhile our small community in their nondescript,
tattered garments stood breathlessly watching this wonderful scene. For long intervals we remained almost spell-
bound, and then a burst of frenzied cheering broke out. It
seemed to us almost too good to be real. By eleven
o'clock all the thick ice had vanished, and there remained
only the thin area of decayed floe which has lately made
the approach to the ship so dangerous ; a few minutes
later the " Terra Nova " forged ahead and came crashing
into the open, to be followed almost immediately by her
stout little companion, and soon both ships were firmly
anchored to all that remains of the " Discovery's " prison,
the wedge that still holds in our small bay.

' It seems unnecessary to describe all that has followed :

how everyone has been dashing about madly from ship to ship, how everyone shook everyone else by the hand, how our small bay has become a scene of wild revelry, and how some have now reached that state which places them in doubt as to which ship they really belong to. Much can be excused on such a night.

'And so to-night the ships of our small fleet are lying almost side by side ; a rope from the " Terra Nova " is actually secured to the " Discovery." Who could have thought it possible? Certainly not we who have lived through the trying scenes of the past month.'

'*February* 15.—The rapid passage of events has caught us unprepared, and to-day all hands have been employed in making up for lost time. It has been a busy day; our own men have been on board making things ship-shape and trim, whilst parties from the other ships have been digging ice and bringing it on board to fill our boilers. The small wedge of sea-ice that still remains in our bay is cracked in many places, and no doubt it would go out of its own accord in the course of a few days, but I am now all impatience to be away, and therefore contemplate expediting matters by some explosions. To make the necessary holes in the ice I have been obliged to call in the assistance of the officers, who have been digging away busily, but it has been no light matter to get through, for the ice at the edge is twelve feet thick, whilst closer to the ship it runs from fifteen to seventeen feet. We shall work all night till our boilers are filled, but what a very different matter work is under these new conditions! Faces have regained the old cheerful expression, and already the wags are finding new subjects for their sallies.'

'*February* 16.—I felt much too restless to go to bed last night, and so after spending the evening with my fellow captains I wandered about to see how the work went, and presently mustered the explosion party and prepared a large charge containing 67 lbs. of gun-cotton. We lowered this carefully into a hole some fifteen yards ahead of the ship, and at 1 A.M., regardless of the feelings of the sleepers, blew it up. It shook the whole bay, and I fear awakened all those who slumbered, but its effects were much what I had hoped. The ice, which had been very solid about the " Discovery," now showed cracks in all directions, and I knew I could go to bed with the hope of finding many of these well open when I arose. After breakfast I found this had duly happened. Nearly all had opened out an inch or two, whilst one from the stern of the ship was gaping a foot or more in width ; our ship work was completed, and nothing remained but the last stroke for freedom.

' So the last explosive charge was borne out and lowered into the yawning crack astern of the ship, the wires were brought on board and everyone was directed to seek shelter. When all was ready, I pressed the firing key ; there was a thunderous report which shook the ship throughout, and then all was calm again. For a brief moment one might have imagined that nothing had happened, but then one saw that each crack was slowly widening ; presently there came the gurgle of water as it was sucked into our opening ice-bed, and in another minute there was a creaking aft and our stern rose with a jump as the keel was freed from the ice which had held it down. Then, as the great mass of ice on our port hand slowly glided out to sea our good ship swung gently round and lay peacefully riding to her anchors with the blue water lapping against her sides.'

Thus it was that after she had afforded us shelter and comfort for two full years, and after we had borne a heavy burden of anxiety on her behalf, our good ship was spared to take us homeward. On February 16, 1904, the 'Discovery' came to her own again—the right to ride the high seas.

CHAPTER XX

HOMEWARD BOUND

Memorial to our Lost Shipmate—Gale Commences—Ship Driven on Shore—
Gloomy Outlook—Sudden Escape—Coaling—Driven North—Departure
of 'Morning'—Wood Bay—Trouble with Pumps—Possession Islands—
Rudder Disabled—Robertson Bay—Rudder Replaced—Towards Cape
North—Heavy Pack—Skirting Pack—'Terra Nova' Parts Company—
Balleny Islands—Over Wilkes' Land—Turning North—The Last Iceberg
—Auckland Islands—Reassembly—New Zealand again—Voyage Home-
ward—Completion of our Work—Our First Monotony—Home.

> Now strike yr sails, yee jolly mariners,
> For we are come into a quiet rode
> Where we must land some of our passengers
> And light this wearie vessel of her lode.
> Here she awhile may make her safe abode
> Till she repaired have her tackles spent
> And wants supplied ; and then again abroad
> On the long voyage whereto she is bent
> Well may she speede and fairly finish her intent.—SPENSER.

I WISH I could convey some idea of our feelings when
the 'Discovery' was once more floating freely on the
sea, but I doubt if any written words could express how
good it was to walk up and down the familiar bridge, to
watch the gentle movement of the ship as she swung
to and fro on the tide, to feel the throb of the capstan
engine as we weighed one of our anchors, to glance
aloft and know that sails and ropes had now some
meaning, to see the men bustling about with their old

sailor habit, and to know that our vessel was once more able to do those things for which a ship is built.   It is sufficient to say that it would have been hard to find a prouder or happier ship's company than we were that day.

But with all our feelings of elation we did not imagine that our troubles were at an end; we knew that it was far from likely that after so long a period of disuse everything would be found to work smoothly, and we knew also that if we were to carry out the remainder of the programme which we had set ourselves there must be no delay in getting to work.   It had always been my intention when the 'Discovery' was freed from the ice to devote what remained of the navigable season to an exploration of that interesting region which lay to the westward of Cape North, but now, after two years' imprisonment, we lacked what constituted a primary necessity for such a scheme; our long detention had made a deep inroad into our coal supply, and after lighting fires in our main boilers and raising steam afresh we found ourselves with barely forty tons remaining—an amount on which it would have been most difficult for us to reach New Zealand, and which absolutely precluded all idea of further exploration.

One of my first inquiries, therefore, on the arrival of the relief ships had been to find out the amount of this valuable commodity with which they could afford to supply us in the event of our release.   At first they had been able to name a very satisfactory figure, but after the long month of combat with ice and wind which had just passed their powers of assistance had been greatly diminished ; and now I saw, to my disappointment, that even at the best we should only increase our stock by an amount which would ensure our safe return to New Zealand, without leaving any adequate margin for exploring work. However, it was no use deploring facts which could not be altered. I determined to get all that could be spared without delay, and to use it as far as possible in carrying out our original programme.

As the ' Discovery ' seemed to be lying very snugly at anchor, we decided to get in what we could whilst we remained in the shelter of our small bay, and on the afternoon of the 16th the ' Terra Nova ' came alongside us to hand over her supply. Thus a few hours after our release the two ships lay snugly berthed together, busily securing whips and yards for the transfer of coal which was to commence on the following morning. The afternoon was beautifully calm and bright, and the weather seemed to smile peacefully on the termination of our long and successful struggle with the ice. We little guessed what lay before us, and assuredly if ever the treacherous nature of the Antarctic climate and the need for the explorer to be constantly on guard were shown it was by our experiences of the succeeding twenty-four hours, of which my diary gives the following account:

' *February* 16.—We have felt that our last act before leaving the region which has been our home for so long should be one of homage to the shipmate who sacrificed his life to our work. We have had a large wooden cross prepared for some time ; it bears a simple carved

A A 2

inscription to the memory of poor Vince, and yesterday it was erected on the summit of Hut Point, so firmly that I think in this undecaying climate it will stand for centuries. To-day our small company landed together for the last time, and stood bareheaded about this memorial whilst I read some short prayers. It was calm, but the sky had become heavily overcast and light snow was falling on our heads. The little ceremony brought sad recollections, but perhaps also a feeling of gratitude for escapes from many accidents which might well have added to the single name which the memorial bears.

'The water was oily calm as we pulled back to the ship, and the sky very gloomy and threatening, but this sort of weather has been so common we thought little of it. It had been decided that as to-day was the first time Captain MacKay had set foot on board the "Discovery," we should show him and his officers what an Antarctic feast was like. Accordingly by dinner-time our cooks had prepared very savoury dishes of seal and penguin, and we sat down, a very merry party, to discuss them. In the midst of dinner word came down that the wind had sprung up, and although I did not expect to find anything serious I thought it as well to go up and see how the land lay. On stepping out into the open, however, I saw we were in for a stiff blow, and had reluctantly to inform our guests of the fact. MacKay took one glance at the sky and was over the rail like a shot, followed by as many of his people as could be collected at such short notice. In a minute or two the warps were cast off, and the " Terra Nova " was steaming

for the open, where she was soon lost in the drift. Since
that it has been blowing very stiff, and a good deal of
ice has come down upon us; but I have a pretty firm
reliance on our ground tackle—the anchor weighs over
two tons, and we have a fair drift of cable out. The
wind is from the south, and the sea, which has risen
rapidly, is dashing over the ice-bound land close astern,
but we have not yet dragged. Colbeck is on board with
two officers and six men of the " Terra Nova." I don't
altogether like the look of things, and shall get up steam
as soon as possible; but I don't want to hurry the
engine-room people, or we shall have all sorts of trouble
with our steam-pipes, &c.'

'*February* 17.—We have had a day and no mistake;
I hope I may never have such another. Early this
morning the wind lulled but the sky still wore a most
threatening aspect, and I sent word for steam as soon
as it could possibly be raised. At about 8 A.M. the
" Morning " appeared out of the gloom and sent a boat
for Colbeck, who got away as quickly as he could. He
had scarcely reached his ship when the wind came down
on us again with redoubled fury, the sea got up like
magic, and soon the " Discovery " began to jerk at her
cables in the most alarming manner. I knew that in spite
of our heavy anchor the holding ground was poor, and I
watched anxiously to see if the ship dragged.

' It came at last, just as Skelton sent a promise of
steam in half an hour. The sea was again breaking
heavily on the ice-foot astern and I walked up and down
wondering which was coming first, the steam or this

wave-beaten cliff.   It was not a pleasant situation, as the distance grew shorter every minute, until the spray of the breaking waves fell on our poop, and this was soon followed by a tremendous blow as our stern struck the ice.   We rebounded and struck again, and our head was just beginning to fall off and the ship to get broadside on (heaven knows what would have happened then) when steam was announced.   Skelton said he could only go slow at first, but hoped to work up.   I told him to give her every ounce he could, when he could, and he fled below to do his best.

' With the engines going ahead and the windlass heaving in, we gradually pulled up to our anchor and tripped it ; then we ceased to advance.   The engines alone would not send the ship to windward in the teeth of the gale ; we just held our own, but only just.   Once around Hut Point I knew we should be safe with an open sea before us ; the end of the Point was only a quarter of a mile out, but off the end, some twenty or thirty yards beyond, I knew there was a shallow patch which had also to be cleared to get safely away.   So finding we could make no headway I started to edge out towards the Point.   All seemed to be going well until we got opposite the Point itself, when I saw to my alarm that although there was no current in our bay there was a strong one sweeping past the Point.

' Nothing remained but to make a dash for it, and I swung the helm over and steered for the open.   But the moment our bows entered the fast-running stream we were swung round like a top, and the instant after

we crashed head foremost on to the shoal and stopped
dead with our masts shivering. We were in the worst
possible position, dead to windward of the bank with
wind, sea, and current all tending to set us faster ashore.

'We took the shore thus at about 11 A.M., and the
hours that followed were truly the most dreadful I have
ever spent. Each moment the ship came down with a
sickening thud which shook her from stem to stern,
and each thud seemed to show more plainly that, strong
as was her build, she could not long survive such awful
blows. As soon as possible I had soundings taken all
around and found the depth was 12 feet everywhere
except under the stern, where the line showed 18 feet ;
I sent for the carpenter to know our draught of water and
he reported $12\frac{1}{2}$ feet at the bows and $14\frac{1}{2}$ feet aft. This
signified that the midship section must be very hard
aground, and that the only chance of release was by the
stern, a direction in which we could not hope to move
under present circumstances.

' So things stood before the men's dinner, but by the
time it was finished we seemed to have worked another
fathom ahead and then the soundings all around were
12 feet except at the extreme bowsprit end, where 15 feet
was obtained. I knew the bank must be very small in
extent, and asked myself, would it be possible to force,
her clean over it ? I determined to try, and ordered sail
to be made. The wind had steadily increased in force,
and it was now blowing a howling gale ; the temperature
was low enough to make the water slushy as it fell on
board. In spite of this we got the foresail and foretop-

sail spread, and at the same time rang the telegraph to full speed ahead.   The ship began to move, but it was only to swing round till her bowsprit almost touched the rocks of the Point; the seas came tumbling over her starboard quarter and she herself listed heavily to port.

'In two minutes I saw that we were only making matters worse, and shouted for the sails to be clewed up; and at the same moment Skelton appeared on the bridge and reported that the inlets were choked and the engines useless.   Once more we sounded around the ship, to find that there was not more than 9 to 10 feet from the bows to the mainmast or from 10 to 12 feet beyond: she seemed to be hopelessly and irretrievably ashore.   After this, for a very short time, we hoped that her high position on the bank would bring less strain from the seas, but soon she had formed a new bed for herself, and within an hour she was bumping more heavily than ever.

' It was now about three o'clock.   We had come to the end of our resources ; nothing more could be done till the gale abated.   We could only consider the situation and wait for the hours to go by.

' And the situation seemed to have no ray of comfort in it.   On deck the wind was howling through our rigging, the ship was swaying helplessly and rising slightly each moment, to crash down once more on the stony bottom ; the seas were breaking heavily over the stern and sending clouds of spray high up the masts ; the breakers on the shore flung the backwash over our forecastle ; the water was washing to and fro on our flooded decks. Towering above us within a stone's throw was the rocky promontory of Hut Point ; on its summit, and clearly outlined against the sky, stood the cross which we had erected to our shipmate. I remember thinking how hard it seemed that we had rescued our ship only to be beaten to pieces beneath its shadow.

' If the situation on deck was distressing, that below fairly rivalled it. Each time that the ship descended with a sickening thud into her rocky bed the beams and decks buckled upwards to such an extent that several of our thick glass deadlights were cracked across, every timber creaked and groaned, doors flew to and fro, crockery rattled, and every loose article was thrown into some new position. With the heavier blows one could see the whole ship temporarily distorted in shape ; through all and directly beneath one's feet could be heard the horrible crunching and grinding of the keel on the stones below.

' When it was known that nothing more could be done it was curious to see how different tempera-ments took it. Some sat in stony silence below, some wandered about aimlessly, and some went steadily on with an ordinary task as though nothing had happened. I almost smiled when I saw our excellent marine Gilbert Scott dusting and sweeping out the wardroom and polishing up the silver as if the principal thing to be feared was an interference with the cleanly state in which he usually keeps all these things. For myself I could not remain still. How many times I wandered from the dismal scene on deck to the equally dismal one below I do not know, but what I do know is that I tasted something very near akin to despair.

'But if this afternoon was a horrible experience, it has at least shown me again how firmly I can rely on the support and intelligence of my companions. For, seeing the utter impossibility of doing anything at the time, I bethought me that the next best thing was to be prepared to act promptly when the weather moderated. Accordingly I first sent for Skelton to see by how much we could lighten the ship. I had scarcely asked him the question when he said, "I have been thinking that out, sir," and in a minute or two he produced a list of our movable weights. I next sent for the boatswain to discuss the manner in which we could lay out our anchors, and he also had his scheme cut and dried ; and so it went on with everybody concerned in this knotty problem, until I knew that if the gale left us with any ship at all we should at least be able to make a bold bid to get her afloat.

'And so hour after hour went by whilst we thought and planned as well as our dejected state would allow, and the ship quivered and trembled and crashed again and again into her rocky bed.

'The first sign of a lull came at seven o'clock, and then, though the seas still swept over our counter, there was a decided slackening in the wind. Soon after we all assembled for dinner—not that any of us wanted to eat, but because it never does to disturb a custom. It was a dreary meal, the dreariest and most silent I ever remember in the "Discovery." Yet we were not more than half-way through it, when the officer of the watch, Mulock, suddenly burst in and said, " The ship's working astern, sir." I never reached the bridge in less time. I found that the wind and sea had dropped in the most extraordinary manner, but what surprised me still more was that the current, which had been running strongly to the north, had turned and was running with equal speed to the south. I took this in at a glance as I turned to get a bearing on with the shore ; in a minute or two I was left without doubt that Mulock's report had been correct. Each time that the ship lifted on a wave she worked two or three inches astern, and though she was still grinding heavily she no longer struck the bottom with such terrific force. I had scarcely observed these facts when Skelton rushed up to say that the inlets were free again. Every soul was on deck, and in a moment they were massed together and running from side to side in measured time. The telegraphs were put full speed astern ; soon the engines began to revolve, and the water foamed and frothed along the side. For a minute or two the ship seemed to hesitate, but then there came a steady grating under the bottom, which gradually travelled forward, and ceased as the ship, rolling heavily, slid gently into deep water.

'To this moment I do not know how it has all happened, but thinking things over to-night a fact has been recalled to my recollection which I noticed without realising its full significance. It seemed to me that the level of the water at Hut Point, as far as I could judge it in its agitated state, was abnormally low this afternoon, and taking this in connection with the change in direction of the current, I am inclined to believe that events have come about much as follows. The heavy southerly wind tended to drive the water out of the Sound and lowered its level by some feet. We must have run ashore when it was at this low ebb ; then came the lull, and the water swept back again, with the happy result of floating us off.

' But whether things have come about in this natural manner or not, I cannot but regard it as little short of a miracle that I should be going to bed free from anxiety at the end of this horrid day. We were clear of our shoal none too soon, for an hour after the wind blew up from the south again. Early in the day we had caught a glimpse of the " Terra Nova" far away to the south, so we made in this direction to find her and to seek shelter. At midnight we got up to the edge of the fast ice, where we found our consort secured with ice-anchors, and where we have been able to return her officers and men. We are now anchored close by her ; I do not know what has become of the " Morning."

' We have been diligently sounding our wells for signs of extra leakage, but the carpenter reports there is nothing to speak of, and so apparently, beyond the loss of our false keel, we have suffered little damage. It is an eloquent testimony to the solid structure of the ship.'

When I subsequently came to compare the experiences of the three ships during this long gale, I found that the complete lulls, such as I have recorded, took place at different times in their various localities ; and I have no doubt that by this irregular action of the wind the

waters of the Sound were pressed down in some places and
heaped up in others in a manner that is well known in
inland lakes.   But, even when all the physical facts are
realised, the story of our grounding and release remains
a very extraordinary one.   Rarely, if ever, can a ship
have appeared in such an uncomfortable plight as ours
to find herself free and safe within the space of an hour.
Such a sudden and complete relief of our distress seemed
to argue that we had been rather unnecessarily and
foolishly alarmed at our situation, but on looking back I
remember that we had no reason to expect that the
forces of Nature would so suddenly come to our rescue :
the best we looked for was a period of calm when we
might lighten the ship and attempt to drag her from her
perilous position ; and such a prospect, with the weather
thoroughly unsettled and the season closing rapidly, was
not hopeful.   To be in ten feet of water in a ship that
draws fourteen feet cannot be a pleasant position, nor
can there be a doubt that the shocks which the ' Discovery' sustained would have very seriously damaged
a less stoutly built vessel.

On the 18th the wind was still blowing strong, but had
gone round to the south-east, bringing smoother water in
our Sound, and now, as we were most anxious to complete our coaling operations, I decided to seek shelter in
the inlets of the glacier tongue to the north.   So at a
comparatively early hour we uprooted our ice-anchors
and steered in that direction, closely followed by the
' Terra Nova.'   In half an hour we were passing close
by Hut Point, and the small bay in which we had spent

such long months, but which had tendered us such a treacherous farewell. As we sped along we looked for the last time with almost affectionate regard on the scene which had grown so familiar, on the hills of which we knew every ridge and fold, on the paths which our footsteps had so often trodden, and on the huts and other signs of human life which we were leaving behind us. One wonders what is happening now in that lonely solitude, once the scene of so much activity!

In the afternoon we ran alongside the ice-edge in an inlet on the north side of the glacier tongue; soon the 'Terra Nova' was rubbing sides with us, and our whips were rigged for coaling. The weather by this time had cleared and the wind had almost dropped, but we knew that these conditions were not likely to last long, and officers and men buckled to with a will to remedy the alarmingly empty state of our bunkers. Late in the afternoon the 'Morning' suddenly appeared around the corner. She had been driven far to leeward by the gale, but at length had worked up and found some shelter in the New Harbour, where also the ice had recently broken away for the first time for two years.

By midnight we had received fifty tons of coal from the 'Terra Nova,' and that ship stood out in the offing. A northerly breeze had sprung up, and we were now obliged to go round to the south side of the glacier to get alongside the 'Morning.' Notwithstanding the long hours which they had already worked, our people elected to go right on throughout the night, and soon more coal sacks were being tumbled on board.

Now, as always, the manner in which our people undertook a heavy task and worked on at it without rest was a sight for the gods. Perhaps the strongest support of this splendid spirit was the fact that on such occasions, by mutual consent, there was no distinction between officers and men. At such times our geologist could be seen dragging coal bags along the decks, whilst the biologist, the vertebrate zoologist, lieutenants and A.B.s, with grimed faces and chafed hands formed an indistinguishable party on the coaling whips. It did not matter how formidable might be the scientific designation of any officer: in time of difficulty and stress he was content to be plain John Smith and to labour in common for the general good.

The 'Morning' afforded us twenty-five tons of coal, and I have an ever grateful recollection of that kindly deed, for in giving us so much, Colbeck reduced himself to the narrowest margin, and voluntarily resigned himself to the necessity of having to return directly homeward without joining in any attempt at further exploration. I have already mentioned that I had determined to try to penetrate to the westward around Cape North, and now that it had become necessary to promulgate my plans, I saw that whilst the 'Terra Nova' could keep pace with us wherever we went, we were likely to be much hampered by the company of the small 'Morning,' with her feeble engine power. But whilst these facts were evident, I naturally felt a reluctance to except from our further adventures the ship which had stood by us so faithfully in our troubles.

But Colbeck needed no reminder to see the difficulty of my position ; his practical common sense told him he could be of little use to us, and with his usual loyalty he never hesitated to act for the best, at whatever sacrifice to his own hopes and wishes.

So before we left the glacier in McMurdo Sound our programme was arranged, and it was decided that the three ships should remain in company while we journeyed up the coast, but that afterwards we should separate, the ' Morning' proceeding to the north, whilst the ' Discovery' and the 'Terra Nova' turned west.   The companies of both our relief ships expressed a strong wish that, whatever separation took place, they might be permitted to be with us when we entered our first civilised port ; and as this seemed to me a most reasonable desire after all their efforts on our behalf, I fixed upon Port Ross, in the Auckland Islands, as a spot at which we might rendezvous before our final return to New Zealand.

In accordance with these plans, before we left McMurdo Sound, the captain of each relief ship was in possession of full instructions providing for all such eventualities as the premature separation of the ships or the failure of any to arrive at the rendezvous before a certain limiting date.

We finished our coaling from the ' Morning' at 6 A.M. on the 19th, and by seven were alongside the glacier for the purpose of getting in water, as our tanks were quite empty, and we had nothing to supply the wastage of the boilers.   Our people had now been almost continuously at work for thirty-six hours, but not a moment was lost in setting about this fresh task. Now, however, commenced all those small difficulties which were a natural result with complicated machinery which had so long been idle. It was beyond expectation that things would be found to work as efficiently as if they had been in constant use, and the engine-room staff especially knew that, as they expressed it, they would have to work 'double tides' to put their department in order again.

On this particular morning it was the steam-pipes of our ice-melters which gave out and caused a long and tantalising delay, so that by the afternoon, when we were preparing to start work, the wind had sprung up from the south again, making our position untenable. We got clear of the south side of the glacier with some difficulty, and steered round to the north side, but scarcely had we planted our anchors when the wind increased to a gale. So swiftly did it sweep down on us that the ship could be kept up to the ice only by steaming full speed, and we had barely time to recover our men and anchors before we were drifted out of the inlet altogether. There was nothing for it now but to run to the north and hope to get our water elsewhere, and away we flew with our consorts at our heels.

And so that night, running swiftly through the water with a howling gale behind, we saw the last of McMurdo Sound. It was a fine scene, for although the wind blew with great force, the sky was comparatively clear. Away to the south-west behind the ragged storm clouds could be seen the deep red of the setting sun, against which

there stood in sharp outline the dark forms of the western
mountains and the familiar cone of Mount Discovery.
On our right in a gloomy threatening sky rose the
lofty snow-clad slopes of Erebus and the high domed
summit of Cape Bird.   For the last time we gazed at all
these well-known landmarks with feelings that were not
far removed from sadness, and yet whatever sorrow we
may have felt at leaving for ever the region which had
been our home, it is not surprising that after our recent
experiences the last entry in my diary for this night
should have been, ' Oh! but it is grand to be on the high
seas once more in our good ship.'

February 20 saw us still speeding along the coastline to the north with a strong following breeze;
although the sky was overcast the land was clearly in
view and we were able to keep within ten miles of it in
a perfectly clear sea, though we could see a fringe of
pack-ice and numerous small bergs close to the coast.
It will be remembered that this stretch of the coast was
quite unknown until we had made our way south along
it, and that even then we had been obliged to keep a long
distance out in many places on account of the pack-ice.
Now we were able to fill in all the gaps which had
formerly been missed, and even more; for our indefatigable surveyor, Mulock, remained on deck day and night
during this run, taking innumerable angles to peaks and
headlands, whilst our artist, Wilson, was equally diligent
in transferring this long panorama of mountain scenery
to his sketch-book.

At three in the afternoon of the 20th we sighted the

white cliffs of the curious glacier tongue which, as may
be seen on the chart, runs out for many miles in a
strangely attenuated form.   At 10 P.M. we rounded the
end of this snout and bore up for Wood Bay ; the high
cone of Mount Melbourne and the bluff cliffs of Cape
Washington could be seen in the distance.

The main object in going to Wood Bay was to fill up
our water supply, but we had also come to the conclusion
that this place must be closer to the magnetic pole than
had been supposed, and for a long time we had cherished
the hope of being able to make a series of magnetic
observations on its shores, but in this respect we were
destined to be disappointed, as my diary shows :

'*February* 21.—At 2 A.M. the wind, still freshening
from the west, brought the " Morning " up on us again.
She looked very trim and snug under her canvas.   As she
approached she ran up a signal which we could not distinguish, but guessing that she wanted to take advantage
of the breeze and get away north, I hoisted " Proceed
on your voyage," and soon her answering pennant fluttered out, her helm went up, and she shot away to the
north-east ; and so our imposing little fleet is breaking
up.   At 6 A.M. we rounded the inner angle of Cape
Washington, and to our surprise found the whole bay
full of pack-ice.   We passed through one broad stream
and got well inside the headland, but beyond this from
the crow's-nest I could see no open water, and it was
obviously impossible to proceed into any of the inlets.
Signalling to the " Terra Nova " to remain outside, we
pushed in towards the southern shore, and tried to secure

B B 2

the ship to a small berg ; but there was a considerable swell running into the bay, and after some unsuccessful efforts to reach the berg we tied up to a small but solid floe. Then all hands, officers and men, tumbled over the side and started working like demons to get the ice on board ; by 3 P.M. we had finished, and I was sincerely glad, for some of our people are almost dropping with fatigue. They had little rest before we came out of the ice, but since, they have had practically none. We never quite appreciated what a lot of work there was to be done till we got to sea, but what with the bending of ropes and sails, the securing of movable articles, and the constant chipping away of ice from every conceivable place, there has not been a moment's peace for our over-worked crew.

'The day has been very fine and bright, with occasional south-westerly breezes, but quite warm when the wind fell. There was a good deal of young ice in the bay when we entered, but it vanished in the course of the day. Wood Bay was looking its best. The south side is fringed by the ice-cliffs terminating the slopes of Mount Melbourne, with rocky headlands and huge masses of black morainic material occasionally occurring. The north side is limited by splendid bare rocky cliffs intersected with deep glacier valleys.

'It was 5 P.M. before we could clear the pack by standing close along the southern shore, where we saw quantities of skuas, and one small Adélie penguin rookery, showing again how these birds take advantage of every available landing place. On arriving in the open water, Armitage swung the ship, but before he could complete his task the sun disappeared. At seven we steamed out of the bay, meeting a heavy swell from the south-east, which is causing us to roll heavily. I trust this does not mean a gale, as we are by no means prepared to meet one yet.'

'*February* 22.—Last night we had an exceedingly unpleasant experience, with some hours of serious alarm. I suppose such things must be expected to happen under the circumstances, but I shall be extremely glad when we have settled down into sea trim. As far as I was concerned the trouble began at 1 A.M., when Skelton called me and asked permission to stop the engines, as the pumps had refused duty, and the water was gaining on the ship. When we stopped, the ship dropped broadside on the swell and commenced to roll 30° each way. This was not a pleasing condition under which to contend with any difficulty, much less with such a one as now faced us, for on looking down into the engine-room I found that the water had risen well over the stokehold plates, and with the rolling of the ship, it was washing to and fro with tremendous force. It was evident that the fires in the main boilers would soon be swamped ; so to avoid accidents they were drawn, which of course put the steam pump out of action, even if it had been in working order.

' The next thing was to try the hand pumps, and the carpenter with the deck watch was soon heaving at these, but without any result. Examination showed that they were quite choked up with ice, so the next hour or two was spent in attempts to clear them. Meanwhile the water was obviously gaining, though to this moment we have failed to discover exactly why, as there is no serious leak to our knowledge. At 3 A.M. it was suggested that the small boiler under the forecastle should be lighted, and an attempt be made to work the steam pump with it. An hour later therefore one party was rushing to and fro with fuel for this boiler, and another was struggling with the refractory hand pumps, but the water was gaining as steadily as ever. Meanwhile Dellbridge, working up to his waist in water, had taken the steam pump to pieces, examined each part, and replaced it.

'It was 6 A.M. before we had steam in the small boiler, and this meant that it had been raised in the quickest time on record. At the same time Dellbridge reported the pump ready again. I asked somewhat needlessly if he thought it would work now, to which he grimly replied, "It's got to, sir." Nevertheless when it was started we found to our consternation that it did not. Then, and not till then, someone thought of examining the bilge suction, and here in a moment was found the cause of all the trouble. The pump, we discovered, had never been out of order, but the rose which drew the water from the bilges was quite choked up with fine ashes. When we left our winter quarters all this part had been a mass of ice, and it had therefore been impossible to clear out the bilges, which were still in a half-frozen condition. When this suction had been cleared we had the satisfaction of seeing a stream of water pouring out of the ship's side, and soon after the hand pumps brought their small power to aid in the relief. By eight o'clock everything was reported in working order, the fires were re-lit and I got to bed. The whole of our engine-room staff have been on duty for twenty-four hours without a spell. Our scare has been useful in one way, as we can rely on our pumps for any sudden call in future.'

The heavy swell continued throughout the 22nd, but gradually fell towards the evening. Somewhat to our surprise, it did not prove to be the forerunner of a gale, and on the 23rd the sky was comparatively clear and the wind light. In the middle of this day we approached and passed Coulman Island at a very short distance, getting a fine view of its high cliffs and of the mountainous mainland. The coast to the south of the island was heavily packed, as it had been on our former visit, and even on the outside of the island we were obliged to force our way through several loose streams, besides a quantity of young ice, broken into tiny rounded pancakes with frilled edges, caused by the chafe of the swell. In the evening a breeze sprang up from the west which enabled us to make sail and afforded us much relief from the continual heavy rolling. We had always thought that the 'Discovery' was a particularly lively ship, but we never appreciated it more than on this day, when we found ourselves lurching from side to side in the most uncomfortable fashion while our consort followed in our wake with scarcely a movement.

After passing Coulman Island we were able to hug

the coast much closer than we had done when travelling south, and it is worthy of note that, as we could see, both Tucker Inlet and another unnamed one north of Cape Hallet are much deeper than Ross supposed. Either would afford excellent shelter to a ship. The two inlets curve in such a manner that the mass of land on which Ross has placed the names of Wheatstone, Hallet, and Cotter forms a peninsula. Mowbray Bay is also a deep inlet.

Early on the 24th we sighted the Possession Islands, and later passed through the group. There are nine islands and islets, very various in size and shape. That on which Ross landed is the largest, and has a shelving beach on the western side, though it is steep and precipitous on the eastern. The smaller islets are mere rocks, but some are of very curious shape. One is an almost perfect column more than 300 feet in height; another which has a similar but broader appearance from the south, when viewed from the east or west is seen to be pierced with two huge arches, the larger of which must be nearly 150 feet in height. Altogether these islands are a curious and interesting group.

Directly after we had passed through the channels between them the carpenter came to me with a serious face to call my attention to the rudder, and I immediately went aft to inspect it. I found that the solid oak rudder-head was completely shattered, and that it was held together by little more than its weight; as the tiller was moved to the right or left the rudder followed it, but with a lag of many degrees, so that it was evident that the connection between the two was quite insecure. How we had come by such an injury I could not guess, unless it was on the freeing of the ship or from collision with some submerged spur of the glacier in McMurdo Sound ; but it was obvious that in such a condition we could not hope to weather a gale without losing all control over the ship, and therefore that the sooner we got our spare rudder shipped in place of the damaged one, the better. On looking back at this incident I cannot but recognise how exceedingly fortunate it was that the sharp eyes of our carpenter should have detected the fault at this time, for, as will be seen, a few days later we were in such a position that the loss of our rudder would have been a most serious matter, and the steps which we now took would have been almost impossible in the open sea. The fault, such as it was, was not easily seen, for the injured rudder head was below the level of the deck and partly submerged by the wash of the screw. I have had reason before to speak of the invaluable qualities of our warrant officers, and certainly this was a case that proved them. As it was, immediately I realised our crippled state, I determined to make for Cape Adare and to seek shelter in Robertson Bay ; the events which followed I quote from my diary :

'We signalled to the "Terra Nova" that our rudder was damaged and that we should anchor in the bay. There was now a brisk breeze, and with sail, steam, and current we approached Cape Adare at a rapid pace. As we came nearer we could see a very large number of bergs scattered about off the entrance of the bay ; nearly all were tabular, and they varied from 50 to 150 feet in height and from a quarter to three quarters of a mile in length. Streams of pack were lying inshore and stretching from berg to berg. It was not altogether pleasant turning and twisting amongst these immense masses of ice with the knowledge that the rudder might give out at any moment. At the entrance of the bay we were involved in a heavy pack, but it was noticeable that the floes were decayed and water-worn to an extent which we have not seen since we first entered the Ross Sea. As we came through this pack the leadsman suddenly got a sounding of five fathoms, but though we sounded repeatedly before and after, nowhere else could we get anything but deep water. It appeared as though there must be a submarine ridge or hill at this particular spot.

'Late in the afternoon we dropped our anchor in thirteen fathoms off the beach we had formerly visited ; a few officers went on shore to take magnetic observations and to secure bird specimens, but the majority, with the men, set to work at once to shift the rudder. In spite of the facilities which are afforded by our rudder-well, the task is not an easy one, as the rudder itself and all the fittings connected with it are very ponderous. By ten to-night, however, when the light grew dim, the damaged rudder had been hoisted on deck and the spare one prepared for lowering it into its place. Whilst we were at work the tide setting out of the bay brought down on us a heavy pack ; our anchor held well, but the "Terra Nova" evidently did not like the look of things, and has weighed her anchor and put out to sea.'

'*February* 25.—By 6 A.M. we were at work again. The weather fortunately remained quite calm and bright. At 9.30 the spare rudder was in place, and, after a hasty breakfast, at 10.15 we weighed our anchor and pushed out to sea. A snowstorm swept down upon us immediately after, and we lost sight of the "Terra Nova," but pushing out in the direction in which she had last been seen we had the satisfaction of finding ourselves close to her when the storm passed, and soon after we were steaming north-west in company. An almost incredible amount of work has been done in the "Discovery" since we left winter quarters; it has been one long fight to bring her into sea trim, and difficulty after difficulty has arisen in the most exasperating manner; but now, I think, thanks to the determined energy of our people, we may say that all things are in order again, and that our ship is prepared to face most emergencies. The only thing I am doubtful about is the steering power of our spare rudder, as it has scarcely half the area of the old one.'

It was of great importance that our ship should be in good sea trim at this time, because according to our programme we were now about to make the attempt to penetrate a new region, and we expected to find quite enough to occupy our minds in contending with the obstacles in our path without having to consider internal troubles.

Now, therefore, we turned to the west with high

hope that with our steam-power we should be able to pass beyond the point which had been reached by Sir James Ross in his sailing ships.   At first all went well with us, as, except for bergs and very loose streams of pack, there seemed nothing to obstruct our course.   The number of bergs was extraordinary ; it would appear that the current which runs up the east coast of Victoria Land continues to the north-west after passing Cape Adare, and leaves a region of slack water to the westward of Robertson Bay, and, as a consequence, many of the bergs which stream up the coast are carried by eddies into this area where they present such a formidable accumulation.

When pack-ice is entangled amongst icebergs it has to be navigated with some caution, as amongst the floes will always be found numerous fragments of the bergs themselves ; these pieces generally float low and are not easily seen, but as they are very solid and often possess sharp spurs it is eminently desirable to avoid them.

By the afternoon of the 25th we were in the thick of the bergs, and, to our disappointment, we found the pack-ice growing closer.   Having but a very limited supply of coal in our bunkers, it was necessarily our policy to avoid the pack as far as possible ; and as we could not afford to force our way through long stretches of it, we turned outwards in hopes of finding a clearer passage.   This took us a long distance from the land, but we trusted that we should soon be able to return towards it.

With the closing of the season and our advance to

AT WORK ON THE SAWS.

DESPERATE HURRY—NO TIME TO TALK.

TO GAZE AT THE STRANGE INTRUDER.

PATIENCE ON AN EGG.

'WANT YOUR DINNER? WHY, YOU HAVE ONLY JUST HAD
BREAKFAST.'

DOG POST READY TO START.

FITTING EXPLOSIVE CHARGES.

EXPLOSION OF THREE CHARGES.

WATCHING THE RELIEF SHIPS FROM THE HILL.

FREEING OF THE 'DISCOVERY.' THE RELIEF SHIPS
AT 10 P.M., FEBRUARY 14.

FREEING OF THE 'DISCOVERY.' THE RELIEF SHIPS
AT 11 P.M., FEBRUARY 14.

FREEING OF THE 'DISCOVERY.' WATCHING THE
RELIEF SHIPS, FEBRUARY 14.

FREEING OF THE 'DISCOVERY.' JUNCTION OF THE
FLEET AT MIDNIGHT, FEBRUARY 14.

FREEING OF THE 'DISCOVERY.' AFTER THE LAST EXPLOSION, FEBRUARY 16.

THE VINCE MEMORIAL.

[*See* p. 366.

' COALING SHIP.'

NEAR CAPE GAUSS.

A CORNER OF WOOD BAY.

MOUNT MELBOURNE.

POSSESSION ISLANDS.

SHIFTING RUDDER IN ROBERTSON BAY.

OVERTURNED ICEBERG.

ICEBERG.

TILTED BERGS OFF THE GREAT ICE BARRIER.

A TABULAR ICEBERG.

STURGE ISLAND, BALLENY GROUP.

BUCKLE ISLAND, BALLENY GROUP.

THE EFFECT OF THE WAVES.

WELCOME BACK TO NEW ZEALAND.

A NEW ICE-FACE.

A MEDIUM ICE-FACE.

AN OLD ICE-FACE.

TYPICAL BERGS, WITH 'TERRA NOVA' IN CONTRAST.

A TILTED BERG, SHOWING THE OLD SURFACE
INCLINED TO THE LEFT.

A PIECE OF THE ANCIENT ICE-SHEET NEAR CAPE CROZIER.

[*See* p. 429.

THE BEACON OF THE UPPER AIR CURRENTS.

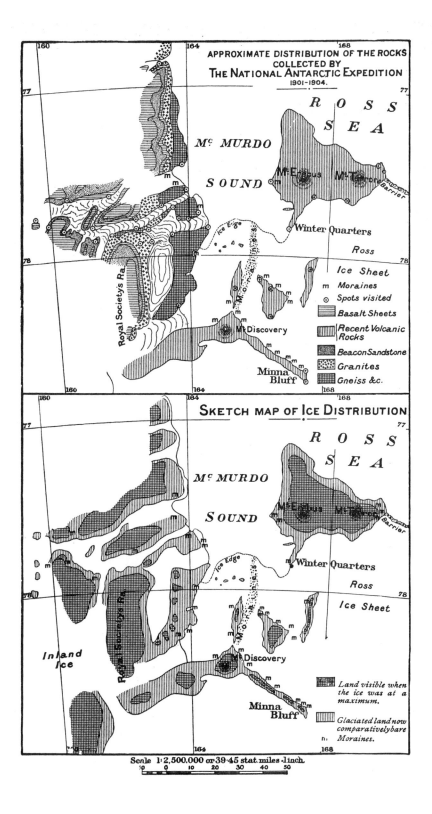

APPROXIMATE DISTRIBUTION OF THE ROCKS
COLLECTED BY
THE NATIONAL ANTARCTIC EXPEDITION
1901-1904.

R O S S
S E A

Mc MURDO

SOUND

Mt Erebus   Mt Terror

Terror Barrier

Ice Edge

Winter Quarters

Ross

Ice Sheet
m   Moraines
⊙   Spots visited
▤   Basalt Sheets
▥   Recent Volcanic
      Rocks
▦   Beacon Sandstone
▨   Granites
▧   Gneiss &c.

Royal Society's Ra.

Moraines

Mt Discovery

Minna
Bluff

SKETCH MAP OF ICE DISTRIBUTION

R O S S
S E A

Mc MURDO

SOUND

Mt Erebus   Mt Terror

Terror Barrier

Ice Edge

Winter Quarters

Ross

Ice Sheet

Moraines

Royal Society's Ra.

Inland
Ice

Mt Discovery

Minna
Bluff

▨   Land visible when
      the ice was at a
      maximum.
▥   Glaciated land now
      comparatively bare
n.   Moraines.

Scale 1: 2,500,000 or 39·45 stat. miles ·1inch.
10   0   10   20   30   40   50

NEAR CATHEDRAL ROCKS.

HOLLOWED BOULDERS.

[See p. 466.

THE NORTH SIDE OF THE UPPER VALLEY, FERRAR GLACIER.

HEAD OF A SEA LEOPARD.

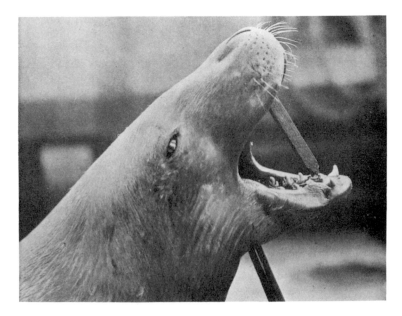

HEAD OF A CRAB-EATER.

Sooty Albatross.   Giant Petrel.   Mollymauk.

Antarctic Petrel.   Cape Pigeon.
       Wilson Petrel.   Snowy Petrel.   Wandering Albatross.

SOUTHERN OCEANIC BIRDS.

ADÉLIE PENGUINS.

THE FEEDING OF A YOUNG ADÉLIE PENGUIN.

ADÉLIE ROOKERY AT CAPE ADARE.

EMPERORS' ROOKERY UNDER BROKEN ICE-CLIFF AT CAPE CROZIER.

EMPEROR PENGUINS.

EMPEROR PENGUIN AND CHICK.

the north, our days were gradually drawing in, and already we had a night of four or five hours, when navigation amongst the ice promised to be anxious work.

For the incidents of the next few days I turn to my diary once more. On the night of the 25th I wrote :

'Shortly after 8 P.M. it became thick with driving snowstorms from the east. We are still surrounded with bergs, and thick weather is undesirable ; however, the snowstorms are like April showers, frequent but quickly over, and after they burst upon us it is not long before we see our consort and the bergs again. We are going half-speed for the night hoping that to-morrow will afford us a brighter outlook.'

'*February* 26.—I had scarcely lain down in my clothes last night, thinking of a clear sea ahead, when the pack was again reported. We pushed through several streams, hoping to escape, but to no purpose. At 5.30 we found ourselves completely embayed ; then the fog came down upon us, and we were obliged to stop engines. Whilst waiting about we took the opportunity to sound, and, to my surprise, got no bottom with 1,000 fathoms of line out. It is evident that the continental plateau slopes down very steeply off this coast. We were just preparing to get a net over when the weather cleared and we saw the land and clear water for some way towards it. We decided to waste no time in pushing on in this direction, but soon after noon our channel closed in again and we found ourselves surrounded with heavy pack. The weather was now quite clear, and from the crow's-nest one could get a good idea of our surroundings.

'From the high peaks of Mounts Minto and Adam the mountains gradually descend towards the west and grow more heavily glaciated ; the coastline abreast of us seems very indented and is marked with numerous dark outstanding cliffs behind which the comparatively low mountains are entirely snow-covered except where occasionally a sharp pyramidal peak thrusts its summit through the white sheet. Away to the west the land still descends, and all eminences are lost under the snowy mantle which slopes down gradually to the sea level at Cape North. A little ahead of us I could see the black headlands of Smith's Inlet, but between us and it, and, in fact, over the whole sea to the west, lay the broad expanse of a mighty field of pack-ice dotted with numberless bergs. Here and there towards the shore could be seen leads of open water, but they were nowhere continuous, and it was evident that at the best it would take us some days to reach the far cape.

'The temptation to push on was great, and I sent to learn how our coal supply stood ; the reply showed me that we had little over eighty tons remaining, an amount which would allow of sixteen days' steaming at our present consumption. I reflected that at least ten of these should be allowed for the return voyage, and I knew how little we could do with the six that remained if once we became involved in the pack. Reluctantly,

therefore, I decided to turn to the north-east and seek
a way around this formidable barrier; we must now look
for the first opening in it and reserve our small margin of
coal for more promising circumstances.   It is grievously
disappointing to find the pack so far to the east; Ross
carried the open water almost to Cape North.

'After being brought up by the pack, we sounded and
obtained bottom at 610 fathoms, and then devoted the
afternoon to getting a haul with our trawl.   Whilst this
operation was in progress a stiff breeze sprang up from
the west and the glass commenced to fall rapidly.
Hampered with our trawl-line we drifted alarmingly
close to several small bergs, so that I was not sorry
when we got our net on board again ; it produced some
new species, but the catch was not so satisfactory as we
could have wished.

' By the time we were ready to proceed the wind had
increased to a moderate gale, and the ice-streams began
to move with such rapidity that we made all possible
speed for the open sea.   We could not reach it, however,
without forcing our way through a broad belt of the
heaviest pack we have seen ; the floes were much hummocked, and rose almost to the level of our deck.   However, with a full head of steam we forced a way through,
and reached the open water just before dark.   We have
since made sail, and are now standing to the eastward
with a strong ice-blink on our port hand, but a comparatively open sea to leeward.   The sky has become very
overcast and the weather threatening, but the sea is
smooth.'

'*February* 27.—We are skirting this wretched pack; I cannot think what brings it so far to the east; last night we came through several streams, and were forced to turn to the south-east; but this morning we straightened up again, and are now going nearly due north.

'Before noon the wind gradually died away, and we now have a brisk and increasing breeze from the south. The glass, which had been steadily falling since noon yesterday, is slowing rising; we have passed away from this region of bergs, but the strong ice-blink is always on our port hand. If in no other way, we can guess our proximity to the pack-ice by the constant presence of the charming little snow petrels; they never seem to wander far from the pack. Last night we had a flight of Antarctic petrels around the ship; they came and went in the gloom in very ghostly, fashion, and this morning there were still a number about us. This morning brought more of the bird friends that we have missed for so long, and we saw again the fulmar petrel, the small *prion*, and a sooty albatross; these indicate, without doubt, a clear sea to the north. I wish one could say the same of the west.

'Our poor dogs are made very miserable by the wet. Born in the South, they have absolutely no experience of damp conditions, and at first they were much alarmed by them; they show the same horror of a wet deck or a wet coat as a cat might do. But the most curious result of their ignorance was the fact that they had to be taught to lap; they had never quenched their thirst except by eating snow, and when water was put before them they didn't know what to do with it ; in fact, they grew very thirsty before they could be persuaded to drink by thrusting their noses into the water tins.'

'*February* 28.—The S.E. breeze increased in force during the night, and by morning it was blowing a full gale with constant snowstorms. The night was not pleasant, as we got amongst the ice again, which kept us all on the *qui vive* ; at midnight we found it stretching across our bows, and the snow petrels had increased in number ; at 3 A.M. we passed through several loose streams, and immediately hauled to the north. With a strong breeze we now bowled along at a good rate. The "Terra Nova" was some distance astern, but turned in our wake ; in order that she might come up with us, I stopped the engines, and we stood on under sail alone. At six o'clock she was some two miles astern, but soon after a heavy snow squall blotted her out, and when this had passed nothing of her could be seen. I do not think there is any cause for anxiety, as the weather remained thick, but I cannot think why she did not keep close touch with us, as she should have found it easy to catch us after we stopped our engines.

'During the forenoon it blew very hard with a rapidly rising sea. I was very anxious about our foremost spars, as the hemp rigging is now quite slack and we have had no chance of setting it up. Our fore topgallant-mast was bending like a whip ; it must be a beautiful spar to have stood the strain.

'The ship has been kicking and plunging about in the most objectionable manner ; the upper deck has been

awash, and water has been pouring down through the
skylights and chimneys. It has been horribly stuffy below,
and the majority of us have been feeling extremely seasick. Altogether it has been a very unpleasant day, but
perhaps the most serious thing that it has disclosed is
the uselessness of our small rudder under such conditions ; it had so little effect on the ship that we could
only keep our course by constantly trimming our sails.
Had we met an iceberg, we should have had no choice
but to throw the yards aback. This is really a grave
matter, as the nights are long and we may fall across
bergs at any moment. Our deck watch is reduced to five
hands, moreover, and this is all too small a number to
deal with any sudden emergency ; as it is, they have to
be constantly on the alert to stand by the braces.

'The barometer ceased to fall at seven o'clock, and
the wind immediately slackened.'

'*February* 29.—We stood steadily on to the north last
night in hopes that the " Terra Nova " would catch us
up, but as there were no signs of her at 4 A.M. I
determined to go about. The wind had fallen light, but
there was a heavy sea running, and it was a good half-
hour before we could wear the ship round. We have
been standing due west all day about latitude 67½ ; the
glass has been rising, the wind dropping and the ship
kicking about most unmercifully. We passed a few bergs,
mostly small and flat-topped ; the seas were breaking over
them, dashing the spray to a height of 200 or 300 feet.
I fear there is no chance of seeing the " Terra Nova "
again until we reach the rendezvous.'

' *March* 1.—Last night we got amongst a number of bergs and some loose streams of pack, so we hove-to and kept a sharp look-out ; at four o'clock we got under way again with steam and proceeded steadily to the west. The weather has been thick, with an overcast, gloomy sky, and we have had a light breeze from the north ; there has been a steady ice-blink on our lee, sometimes appearing ahead, to be quickly followed by sight of a loose stream of pack. There can be no doubt that since leaving Victoria Land we have been skirting a continuous mass of pack which must cover the whole sea south of the Balleny Islands.

' That it should have lain so far to the eastward this year is very annoying ; however, if we can push on upon this course we ought to strike the islands. Birds have been plentiful all day, but to-night the albatrosses have left us ; snow petrels, Antarctic and fulmar petrels are our constant companions, and this afternoon we had the very unusual sight of a small flock of black-headed terns. We have also passed two or three sea leopards asleep on the floes : one we surprised greatly by ramming the floe on which he was taking his siesta, whereat he opened his formidable jaws and threatened us in the most ferocious manner.'

' *March* 2.— . . . Land was reported at 5 A.M., and on the port bow we could see black rock showing streakily through the mist. By 7.30 we were close up, and found on our port bow an island of considerable size. Our course took us just to the northward of its steep northern extremity. The general aspect of the land much resembled that of Coulman Island, but the glaciation was much heavier. High, precipitous, dark cliffs were capped by the sharp edge of the ice-cap, which undulated smoothly over the lesser slopes, and lay broken and crevassed on the steeper ones ; at places the vast snow-sheet descended to the sea, and spread out with immense fan-shaped glaciers fringed with high ice-cliffs. These conditions of the coast could be seen clearly, but above the height of 300 or 400 feet all was hidden in dense stratus cloud.

'By noon we were abreast of this forbidding land ; the clouds showed signs of lifting, but still enveloped the summit of the island. The coast was less than two miles from us, so that we could see each detail clearly, and twice, as we passed, an immense mass of névé became detached from the cliffs and fell with a huge splash into the sea. As I write we are standing to the west of the island, and, to our astonishment, with a clear sea. Once more we are treading untrodden paths. But before we turn our thoughts to the west we are puzzling over the question as to what this island and others we can dimly see to the north really are. We are about the latitude of the Russell Islands, yet we cannot follow Ross's description of them, nor can we understand where the Balleny Group lies. One thing is certain, however : whatever these islands may be, no one has ever seen them from this side before, and the sight of a clear sea to the west is most encouraging.'

It is as well perhaps to explain the dilemma we found ourselves in with regard to these islands. In 1839 Balleny discovered a group of islands in this region, but whilst the position of his ship was most carefully reckoned and the bearings of the land masses taken, he did not supply sufficient data accurately to fix the position of the various islands which he named. Three years later, Ross, when some way to the eastward of this position, saw land which he imagined must be to the southward of Balleny's discoveries; from the great distance at which he saw it he believed it to be divided into three distinct masses, and under this impression named them the Russell Islands. We came to this region, therefore, with the expectation of seeing two groups of islands, and were naturally much puzzled when we found that by no means could we reconcile the accounts of the two explorers to fit this theory; and at first the clouded condition of the land added much to this difficulty.

It was only after I had read the accounts many times, and compared them with what we actually saw, that the solution suddenly flashed upon me, and, as is so often the case, when the key was once supplied the matter became obvious to us all. We saw then that the island which we had just passed was Balleny's Sturge Island. Balleny had seen it from the north, in which direction it presents a comparatively narrow front; he could have had no idea of its length in a north-and-south line. At a later date Ross must have seen this same island, and, as we saw was quite possible, from a great distance he must have imagined it to be divided into three, and hence made the mistake of naming it as a separate group.

Later on this same day the cloudy screen about the islands gradually vanished ; we were able to see the land clearly both north and south of us, and Mulock obtained sufficient bearings to fix accurately the position of each island.

In the evening of the 2nd I wrote :

'This afternoon, as the weather cleared and the sun shone forth, we got a good view of the islands now falling behind us, and had no longer a doubt as to their identity. Looking astern, on our right was Sturge Island, more than twenty miles in length, with the lofty summit of Brown's Peak arising towards its northern end. The nearest island on the left was Buckle Island, its outline from this side being the exact reverse of that sketched by Balleny's mate from the other. The smaller island next to the north was Borrodaile Island, and this also could be recognised from the sketch. Young Island presented a high land to the left, though Peak Freeman, its highest point, was never wholly clear of cloud. The last of the group reported by Balleny, Row Island, we did not see, but this was not surprising, as it is stated to be comparatively low.

'Now that we have settled the knotty question as to the geography of these islands, our position seems extremely hopeful. This region to the westward has always been found heavily packed. We are the first to enter it, and to our delight we find an open sea ; it seems as though the pack has been driven to the southeast, into that area which we skirted. The wind has fallen, and we have furled our sails ; a long swell comes from the north-west, showing an absence of ice in that direction. We are standing directly to the west, towards Wilkes Land, and every eye is keenly on the alert for some new development—so keenly, in fact, that twice this afternoon has an excited person rushed up to me to report some imaginary discovery of land in the fantastical cloud forms that fringe our horizon. The night promises to be fine, though the glass is falling. Birds are gathering about us in numbers once more—the commonest to-day is the fulmar petrel; it looks as though it nested on the islands. Rorqual whales have been spouting in all directions, and altogether signs of life are plentiful and cheering.'

' *March* 3.—Early last night the sky clouded over, and towards the end of the middle watch it began to snow ; by the morning we found ourselves in a thick fog. We had made sail again to a northerly breeze, and at 5.30 A.M. we hove-to in none too pleasant a position, for we could not tell where we were drifting or when some monster iceberg might appear on our lee. At 11 A.M. there was a slight clearance, and we decided to push on, which we have since done, though every now and again the fog comes down on us as thick as ever. At noon to-day we estimated we were in longitude 159 E., and since that we have sailed some way to the west, so that we are now practically behind Wilkes' alleged land. But as there is a long swell from the north, it is plain that there cannot be any extent of land in that direction ; it is still possible that Wilkes may have seen some islands, but this we can only determine when the weather clears.

'It has cleared to some extent to-night, and has shown us more than one berg in our vicinity.   At seven o'clock we passed a large one that was slowly oscillating.   We could see it gradually tilt over until its flat surface was half submerged, then it slowly righted itself again ; this went on for some time, the oscillations growing larger, until suddenly it got beyond the point of recovery and with a huge splash turned turtle.   The sight of this immense mass rolling over in the foaming sea was very impressive, and we were grateful that it should have chosen such an opportune moment for our benefit.   We are longing for clear weather ; one cannot but believe there must be land somewhere in this region, especially on account of our soundings, but we know that we cannot go on like this much longer.   We have only sixty tons of coal remaining, a bare sufficiency to take us north ; no doubt the wisest plan would be to turn north now, but I have decided to go on as we are for another day in hopes that fortune may favour us with one clear sight of our surroundings.'

'*March* 4.—The wind failed us last night, and it has been calm all day.   The sky has been dull, but the horizon quite clear ; we could have seen land at a great distance, yet none has been in sight, and thus once and for all we have definitely disposed of Wilkes Land.   Both Armitage and I got good sights, and both fixed our noon position to be in latitude 67.23 S., longitude 155.30 E.   We have been standing N.W. true, and on such a course we should have sighted Eld's Peak and Ringold's Knoll on our right had these places existed.   It is therefore quite evident that they do not, nor can there be any land in this direction, as the long ocean swell has never ceased to roll steadily in from the north, and we have other signs of bird life which show a clear sea in that direction. To-night Cape Hudson should be in sight on the port bow, but that also is conspicuous by its absence. After reading Wilkes' report again, I must conclude that as these places are non-existent, there is no case for any land eastward of Adélie Land. It is a great disappointment to have to turn north at such an interesting time, but I feel that it is imperative; we have scarcely coal enough for ten days' steaming, and our late experiences have shown clearly how unmanageable the ship is under sail alone with our small spare rudder. There is nothing for it but to turn homeward, and even as it is we shall have to rely on favouring winds to reach our rendezvous.

'It is a curious fact that although we have sighted no land we are still on the edge of a continental plateau, and in comparatively shallow water. This morning we got 250 fathoms, and this afternoon 254 fathoms; the continental shelf would seem to extend as far as the Balleny Islands. This afternoon we put over a trawl and got a haul which delighted the heart of our biologist with quite a number of new species.'

'*March* 5.—During the night we passed close to the supposed position of Cape Hudson—except for a few bergs, in a perfectly clear sea. We had a full moon which, although usually hidden by clouds, gave a good light by which objects—and certainly land—could have been seen at a great distance. This morning there is not a sign of land, and remarkably few bergs. At 3.30 we got soundings in 245 fathoms, and at eight in 260 fathoms. The continental plateau must be extensive, and Wilkes certainly had the chance of being misled by his soundings. At noon to-day we were in latitude 66.23 S., longitude 154.7 E., and so we have crossed the Antarctic Circle again after an interval of two years and sixty-two days.

'This morning the breeze sprang up from the north-west, and we made sail, standing close-hauled to the N.N.E. Throughout the day the wind has freshened and hauled round to the west, so that we are now standing almost due north. I hoped to sound again to-night, but it is blowing too hard; I think we are in for a gale.'

On March 5, 1904, therefore, our exploring work came to an end, and we found ourselves entering once more that storm-swept area of the 'Westerlies' which separated us from civilisation. The programme with which I had hoped to close the season had been much hampered by our lack of coal, but if we had been unable to carry out our cherished plan of rounding Cape North, we had at least cleared up some geographical misconceptions in a more northerly latitude.

Two days later we saw the last of the Antarctic ice under conditions which made us exceedingly grateful that it was the last, as my diary shows:

'*March 7.*— . . . Since we shut off steam yesterday we have been progressing to the north, but in a very curious manner. In spite of all head sails being set, the ship has such a tendency to come up in the wind that the

helm has to be kept hard up, and so we plunge along
about five knots, with no power of control over the ship
except to stop her by throwing the yards aback. This
is not so bad as long as there are no bergs in sight, and
yesterday I thought we had seen the last of these unwelcome neighbours; but this morning, when it was blowing great guns, the boatswain came down and reported a
berg on the lee bow, and I dashed on deck to see a huge
mass of ice showing under the foot of the foresail. We
had either to go on or to "heave-to," as I knew we could
not alter course to pass to leeward. I decided finally to
go on, but the ship was labouring so heavily that it was
fully twenty minutes before we could be certain that the
bearing was changing in the right direction, and that we
stood a good prospect of weathering it. In another ten
minutes we passed close to windward of it, and could see
the mountainous waves dashing over its lofty pinnacles
and imagine the condition of the unfortunate vessel that
should run foul of it. It was an impressive farewell to
the Southern ice, for since that gaunt, wave-beaten mass
has dropped astern we have seen no more.'

With our last view of these formidable Southern
bergs my tale draws to a close, for what remains is little
more than the story of ordinary life on the high seas, and
may be told briefly.

The month of March is the most stormy season of
the year in the Southern Seas, and during the days which
we spent in travelling to the north the weather made no
exception in our favour. From the 6th to the 14th we
had continuous gales with conditions of greater physical

discomfort than we had ever experienced on board the 'Discovery.' The ship was in very light trim and was tossed about on the mountainous seas like a cork. There are few things more exasperating than the unceasing pitching and plunging of a very lively ship. Many of us were very seasick, and, to add to our distress, our decks were leaking badly, so that we lived in a perpetual drip below. The wind blew almost constantly northward of west, so that we were obliged to remain close-hauled. Our crab-like motion under sail soon showed us that we should be drifted to leeward of our rendezvous, and on the 9th we were obliged to start our engines again. Even with steam and sail it was touch and go whether we lay our course until the 13th, when a lucky slant of wind sent us well to windward. On the 14th we sighted the Auckland Islands on our lee bow, and early on the following morning we furled our sails off the entrance of Ross Harbour, and steamed into the calm waters of the bay.

It is not easy to forget that morning when, weary and worn with all our long struggle with the ice and the tempests of the South, we steered into this placid shelter and, for the first time for more than two years, feasted our eyes on hillsides clothed with the green of luxuriant vegetation.

Ross Harbour is a splendidly protected winding inlet, and it was in its deepest arm, shut off from all view of the sea, that we finally came to an anchor, within a hundred yards of the thick scrub which grows down to the water's edge. A glance at our bunkers was alone sufficient to show by how narrow a margin we had accomplished our work, for less than ten tons remained of our stock of coal, and yet not an ounce had been wasted on our northward voyage. Our plans had barely carried us to this uninhabited island, and with such a remnant we could not have made the longer journey to New Zealand.

It was with great surprise, and not altogether without anxiety, that I found neither of our consorts had yet arrived at the rendezvous. However, I reflected that it was quite possible that by going to the west we had achieved a windward position and thus got ahead of them in spite of their long start, and this conjecture proved to be correct.

Meanwhile we settled ourselves down to wait, determined to enjoy our new surroundings thoroughly, and to make our ship as smart as possible for her first appearance to the eyes of the multitude. It was a curious idea this last, but it was very strongly held by us all; it seemed a point of pride with us that the good ship which had carried us so well should not be allowed to display any untidiness in public, and so all hands fell to with a will. There was much scrubbing of decks and cleaning of paint work; then came a fresh coat of paint to cover up all the travel stains, and in a few days the ' Discovery' looked as though she had spent her three adventurous years in some peaceful harbour.

On March 19 the ' Terra Nova ' hove in sight, and on the following day we were still more relieved by the safe arrival of the 'Morning.' Both ships had the same tale to tell—a tale of continuous adverse gales which had blown so heavily that at times they had been obliged to 'heave-to,' and throughout had had a long and hard struggle in beating up to the islands. The little 'Morning' had had an especially dismal experience. She had been nearly a month fighting this terribly hard weather, with all sorts of added troubles in connection with her ramshackle engines and pumps, and her ill-ballasted condition. Captain Colbeck will no doubt tell of the adventurous incidents of this month, but none of us is likely to forget the utterly worn-out condition in which his small company arrived at Ross Harbour, or the universal testimony of officers and men that disaster had only been averted by the consummate seamanship with which their small vessel had been handled.

The few days which we remained in Ross Harbour after the arrival of our consorts were spent in ballasting the 'Morning' and in giving a much-needed rest to her crew; we were also able to obtain from the 'Terra Nova' the addition to our coal supply necessary for the last stage of our journey to civilisation.

On March 29 our small fleet set sail once more, and now everything favoured our prosperous voyage; with a strong breeze from the south-west and a moderate sea, we set all our canvas and ran rapidly to the north. On the 30th we sighted Stewart Island, and later the coast of the mainland; the following day found us running up the coast, and at length with the well-remembered outline of the Bankes Peninsula before us.

At daybreak on Good Friday, April 1, we were off the Heads of Lyttelton Harbour, and before noon we were safely berthed alongside the jetty from which we had sailed with such hearty good wishes more than two years before.

I have found my pen inadequate to describe many an incident in this narrative, but perhaps I never realised its inadequacy so completely as when I set about to picture the warmth of the welcome which we received on our arrival in New Zealand. Those who have been patient enough to follow the course of this story will remember the kindness with which our small party of adventurers were treated before our departure for the South, and how each visit of the relief ship brought us not only welcome news from the Old Country, but greetings and presents from this newer land. It is little wonder, therefore, that as we entered Lyttelton Heads after so long an absence, each one of us felt that we were returning to what was very nearly our home—to a place where we should find rest and peace after our wanderings, and to people who would greet us with sympathetic friendship. And all this we found in fullest measure ; New Zealand welcomed us as its own, and showered on us a wealth of hospitality and kindness which assuredly we can never forget, however difficult we may have found it to express our thanks. In these delightful conditions, with everything that could make for perfect rest and comfort, we abode for two full months before we set out on our last long voyage ; and even though that voyage was to carry us to our homeland, there was many a sad heart when for the last time we steamed out of Lyttelton Harbour and waved our fare-wells to those who had taken so deep an interest in our fortunes.

June 8 found us at sea again. The 'Morning' sailed with us, but soon parted company; the 'Terra Nova' had left more than a fortnight earlier. We did not sight land again until July 6, when we first saw the mountains of Tierra del Fuego. Meanwhile, how-ever, our voyage had not been without interest, as it had enabled us to accomplish some tasks of importance. Amongst these was the completion of our magnetic survey, which was thus carried about the greater part of the circumference of the Antarctic area, as well as to such regions as we had visited within it.

After leaving New Zealand we gradually increased our latitude until the greater part of our track lay between the parallels of 56° and 60°. This was a route which had often been taken by ships, but one in which the depth of the ocean was entirely unknown. So far as the weather and the circumstances of the voyage would permit, we endeavoured to supply this deficiency, and although we were not able to sound so frequently as I had hoped, the few soundings which we took are of great interest, as they constitute our only knowledge of the depth of the Pacific in high Southern latitudes. On the whole, these soundings showed a fairly uniform depth of something over 2,000 fathoms. The shallowest, 1,710 fathoms, was ob-tained on the meridian of 136 W., whilst the deepest, 2,738 fathoms, occurred on that of 106 W. close down on the

6oth parallel.   This is only a step, and a very small one, towards what is greatly needed—namely, a complete oceanographic survey of the seas about the Antarctic Circle.

Another point of geographical interest occurring in this voyage may be noted : on two occasions an island named Dogherty Island has been reported approximately in latitude 59 S., longitude 120 W., but later observations have thrown some doubt upon its existence.   On June 25 we arrived on the supposed position of this land, and found a depth of 2,318 fathoms.   It was remarkably clear both before and after we took this sounding, and had there been an island within any reasonable limits of its assigned position we could not have failed to see it. The case for the retention of an oceanic island on the chart after it has been proved absent from its supposed position is that the original discoverer may have largely miscalculated that position, but the evidence against the existence of Dogherty Island is now too strong to allow of this explanation.

I had originally intended to round Cape Horn on our homeward voyage, but as we approached this longitude we were driven to the northward by S.E. winds, and consequently altered our plans to pass through the Magellan Strait.   We entered this beautiful channel on the evening of July 6, and on the following night anchored off Puntas Arenas ; the 9th found us racing out through the Eastern Narrows on the strong ebb tide, and three days later we anchored in Port Stanley (Falkland Islands). Here we replenished our stock of coal and took the last

series of magnetic observations in connection with our
Southern Survey.

On the 20th we put to sea and turned our head to
the north, to face the last long stage of our journey;
and now for the first time we found our life on board
contained the elements of monotony. Our work was
done—nothing remained but to hasten homeward—and
we realised how poor a show of haste the 'Discovery'
was capable of displaying. We would willingly have
spirited our good ship from the southern to the northern
hemisphere, and chafed at the long weeks at sea which
resulted from our slow progress.

And so our passage to the north was somewhat
wearisome, but slowly and surely the miles were traversed,
and we passed from the wild and stormy seas of the
Westerlies to the mild regions of the gentle S.E. trade
wind, and from this to the sweltering heat of the Doldrums.

On August 13 we recrossed the line, and a week
later struggled slowly through the N.E. trade towards
the Azores; here I decided to take in a small stock of
coal, and on the last day of the month we anchored off
Punta Delgada, in the island of San Miguel.

On September 2 we put to sea for the last time, and
now, with favouring breezes, made comparatively rapid
progress towards the Channel.

Early on the morning of the 9th we sighted the homeland once more, after an interval of three years and one
month, and as we slowly steamed up the Channel it can
be imagined there were not many eyes that did not
gaze longingly over our port bulwarks. All Nature was

smiling to welcome us, and all day long we passed in clear view of that glorious panorama of the south coast which every sailor knows so well ; one wonders how many hearts have swelled at that sight !

At daylight on the 10th we were south of the Isle of Wight, and before noon the ' Discovery ' lay at Spithead, surrounded by many craft, whilst on board we welcomed those who had waited so long and so patiently for this moment.

There seems little to add. To attempt to describe the hearty welcome which we received from our country-men, and the generous tributes which have been paid to our efforts, would be beyond the scope of this book, which purports to deal only with the simple narrative of our voyage. For me, and for the small band who laboured so faithfully together in the ' Discovery,' there has been one cloud to dim the joy of this home-coming, for there was not one of us, I think, who did not feel the sadness of the day which brought the end of our close companionship and the scattering of those ties which had held us together for so long.

Yet although this inevitable parting has taken place, we hope that as the years roll on we may meet again, and we know that when such meetings come they will renew old friendships and recall some of the pleasantest memories of our lives.

GENERAL SURVEY OF OUR OBSERVATIONS

They that have wrought the end unthought
Be neither saint nor sage,
But men that merely did the work
For which they drew the wage.—KIPLING.

IT is impossible at this date to give anything like a complete summary of the results of our Antarctic Expedition, for until the scientific collection and observations have been thoroughly examined by experts, all deductions that can be drawn from them must be open to doubt. But in addition to the mass of important matter which cannot be safely discussed until it has been completely investigated, there is a large field of more general interest which does not need the close study of records, and concerning which ideas can be advanced without prejudice. In this field lie the purely geographical problems which we set forth to solve, as well as the outlines of others which formed the main objects of our various sledge journeys.

In the course of the narrative of our voyage I found it impossible to give in connected fashion all the observations of irregular occurrence which, when pieced together, form the main facts of our discoveries and exhibit problems of the greatest interest for future explorers.

At this point I propose, therefore, to collect these facts and observations in more connected form, partly to give a clearer idea of the physical conditions of the field of our labours, but mainly that those who follow in our footsteps may have the full benefit of our experience. In considering these objects the reader will readily understand the order in which I present the following paragraphs.

Pack-ice.—The ice conditions in the Ross Sea have been observed in the course of five different seasons. Although differences in date make it impossible to compare these seasons closely, one is led to believe that four were very similar and constitute the normal condition, whilst one—the summer of 1902-3—was exceptional. The normal condition seems to be that the sea becomes completely frozen over in the winter, the movement of the ice-sheet leaving narrow spaces of open water only at its edge, in such places as the northern face of the Great Barrier, and possibly in rents which are speedily refrozen.

The gales at Cape Crozier grow excessively violent towards the end of September and in October, and by this time the ice-sheet has probably commenced to weaken. The general break-up which results was witnessed on two occasions by our sledge parties; on one day they saw the sea completely covered with ice, and on the next looked forth on a clear sheet of open water. The ice thus freed drifts to the north,

and forms that belt of pack through which ships must
pass to reach the sea in the early summer. Drifting
under the influence of wind, loose pieces will always
travel faster than the main pack, and consequently the
southern edge of the belt will generally be a hard and
fast line where loose pieces are crowding on the main
pack, and the northern edge will be free where loose
pieces are tending to detach themselves from it.

Towards the end of December and the early part of
January this belt extends from the Antarctic Circle for
about 200 miles to the south and is probably best
attacked on the meridians of 178° to 180° E. To the
westward of this the pack would be augmented by the
coastal ice of Victoria Land, and to the eastward by
conditions which are not well known, but on which the
discovery of Scott Island and the difficulties experienced
by Ross throw some light.

The ice probably leaves the Ross Sea in large fields
and is broken by the ocean swell, which penetrates the
pack for a great distance ; and this accounts for the fact
that the floes increase in size as one approaches the
southern edge, though nowhere exceeding one or two
miles in length. The character of the ice in the main
pack frequently changes, giving the impression that a
quantity of ice of a previous season is caught when
the sea freezes over ; but none of the floes met with
is formidable—all are more or less rotten and decayed.

The exceptional ice conditions of the summer of
1902–3 seem to have arisen from causes commencing
at a very early date in the winter of 1902. What

must be considered an abnormal succession of southerly gales again and again broke up the ice in McMurdo Sound, and even late in the winter there was open water within a few miles of the 'Discovery.' The continual formation of fresh sheets of ice must have tended to congestion, which the exceptionally fine weather conditions of December and January failed to relieve, so that the greater part of the Ross Sea remained filled with ice ; and not only had the 'Morning' great difficulty in getting to the south, but the sea was never sufficiently open to admit of the swell on which we depended to break up the ice in McMurdo Sound and release the 'Discovery.'

In connection with this fact it is interesting to note that, though the main pack usually drifts to the north early, there is an eddy in McMurdo Sound in which a mass of ice is detained throughout December and January. At the end of January in 1902 and 1904 this mass was suddenly carried to the north, but it did not disappear until nearly a month later in 1903. When this occurred there was a noticeable change in the drift of the surface waters through the Sound.

Continuing to drift northward, the main pack is dissipated by the beginning of February, and during this month a ship, by coming directly south on the 178th meridian could reach the Great Barrier without encountering any pack-ice. It is strange to think that there may be a season in the year when the enterprising tourist steamer may show its passengers the lofty smoke-capped form of Mount Erebus as easily as it now does the fine scenery of Spitzbergen.

The sea-ice met with on the coast of Victoria Land is of a different character from that found in the main pack. It is very solid and hard, comparatively free from snow, and, except where dust and grit have settled on the surface, little decayed. Its uniform smoothness shows that there is very little pressure. The pack-ice met with in the vicinity of King Edward's Land was very heavy also, but the floes were much hummocked and many were evidently more than one season old. It appears probable that a large quantity of pack is detained amongst the numerous grounded bergs and ice-islands in this region, where also the snowfall seems heavier than to the west. The region south of the Balleny Islands will probably always be found heavily packed owing to the constant drift from the Victoria Land coast, but it is evident that the exact position of this pack is uncertain, as although in February 1904 we found it far to the east, Ross at the same season in 1841 observed an open sea to the eastward of the 168th meridian.

The pack-ice is, of course, the main obstruction to exploration in the far South. A study of its disposition and movement is therefore of great importance to the navigator. Mr. Ferrar has added some interesting notes on the physical properties of sea-ice in his geological summary.

Icebergs.—The main supply of icebergs in the Ross Sea is from the Barrier and King Edward's Land. The glaciers on the coastline of Victoria Land are in an extraordinary condition of stagnation, and nearly all the bergs met with along its coast have undoubtedly come from the east.   From Cape Adare to Cape Crozier there are only two ice-flows capable of giving off a clean tabular berg of any dimensions, and our observations went to show that the supply from these is extremely small.   In this connection it is instructive to note that the rate at which bergs are given off in various regions can be gauged to some extent by the comparative new-ness of the exposed faces of the ice-cliffs.   As a rule, the cliffs of the Barrier exhibit a smooth uniform face, whereas those on the coast of Victoria Land are honeycombed with the action of the sea and the weather.

It will be remembered that we found innumerable bergs aground on the shoals off King Edward's Land, and that some were very large.   We saw one or two small ones in the act of calving from the high cliffs in that direction, but we did not see any being detached from the Barrier itself, and I am under the impression, after our examination of its edge, that it must break away in very large pieces.

A stream of small bergs, with an occasional large one, sets along the Barrier and turns north along Victoria Land.   Many of these are delayed in the larger bays and inlets of the coast and hung up on such shoal patches as exist off Cape Crozier, Cape Washington, and Cape Adare.   From the latter especially there ex-tends a long string of grounded bergs which appear to have run ashore in an attempt to round the corner too sharply.   To the westward of Cape Adare, stretching on to Cape North, we found immense quantities of bergs, but after turning to the north we saw none until we had passed to the westward of the Balleny Islands, when they were again fairly numerous. I cannot think that the bergs we saw before entering the pack in January 1902 can have had any connection with the Ross Sea. I imagine they must have come from further east.

The size of Antarctic icebergs, as I mentioned in my narrative, has been much exaggerated, though when the formidable appearance of these objects is considered there is every excuse for such exaggeration. Of the many hundreds seen by us, very few exceeded a mile in length or 150 feet in height; the vast majority were less than a quarter of a mile across and less than 120 feet high. The largest we saw were aground off King Edward's Land, and here too, it will be remembered, we found some exceedingly tall ice-cliffs. We had various devices for measuring the heights of icebergs and ice-cliffs when we cruised alone, but it was easier still to get a true estimate of these when the 'Terra Nova' was in company with us, as then a direct comparison could be made with the height of the masts.

Another very important point to be determined with regard to Antarctic icebergs is the proportion of the submerged to the visible part. Sir John Murray has estimated this as about 7 to 1, but I am inclined to think that it is much less. My opinion is founded, firstly, on general observations of the depths in which bergs ground (120 to 150 feet bergs do not touch bottom in more than 100 to 120 fathoms of water); secondly, on an eye estimate of the proportion as indicated in an overturned berg ; and, thirdly, on the nature of the ice itself as exposed in the face of the berg on the cliff from which it has come. The transition from snow to ice is very gradual and strongly impresses one that the mass throughout must contain large quantities of air—an impression supported by the examination of some ice taken from the bottom of an overturned berg. It would be difficult, if not impossible, to ascertain exactly this proportion by actual measurement, but for the reasons which I have adduced I believe that it is not greater than 5 to 1.

I regard this factor as highly important. It would be of interest if it only enabled the mass of these great floating islands to be calculated but it does much more ; for it must be remembered that the bergs are detached from ice-sheets covering or connected with the land, and that the dimensions of the bergs give the thickness of the sheets from which they have come. In fact, from these data we can make an extremely interesting statement. If the average height of bergs be taken as 150 feet, and the proportion of the submerged to the visible part be accepted as 5 to 1, we can say that 900 feet is the average thickness of the ice-sheet extending over a very large area of the Antarctic Regions.

Current.—The general drift of the current in the Ross Sea is indicated by the direction taken by the bergs, to which I have referred. It will be remembered that on our return along the Barrier we had the good fortune to recognise a berg which we had seen on our outward journey. It had drifted seventy miles to the west in twelve days, but the surface water had been moving at a greater speed, as we could tell by its effect on the ship. The tidal streams do little more than accelerate or retard this current, and it was only occasionally that we were helped in our journey to the south and east by a favouring stream. To the eastward of the Balleny Islands the surface water is moving towards the north, but the absence of bergs seems to show that there is no deeper stream in this direction. To the westward of the Balleny Islands we did not notice any marked current, and the bergs were much scattered. On the whole, there seems little doubt that the water is circulating from east to west about the Antarctic lands, and therefore I think that, apart from other considerations, exploring efforts in the Far South should be directed to the west. I may remark that had the 'Discovery' been released from the ice after her first season it was my intention to ask permission to go south on the meridian of Cook's farthest position, and from there to work to the west, in hopes of making King Edward's Land.

I have touched so far on those results of our experience which may serve to aid the explorer to reach the Far South; I pass now to matters more immediately connected with our work. The main geographical interest of our expedition lies in the practical observation of a coastline from Mount Melbourne in latitude $74\frac{1}{2}°$ to Mount Longstaff in latitude $83°$, and of the conditions which lie to the east and west of this line. Our previous knowledge extended only to that part which lies between

Mount Melbourne and McMurdo Sound ; and of this we had but the vaguest description. This great region, which constituted the principal field of our labours, afforded interests of a most varied description, as I trust the reader of this book will have gathered.

It remains to give some connected account of these interests, and as the most extensive problems, here as elsewhere in polar regions, depended on conditions of glaciation, it is well first to consider this governing factor.

The Inland Ice.—The extent and uniformity of this great sheet must necessarily be matters of some doubt ; it is therefore desirable to marshal all the evidence concerning them.

The outline of the coast which limits the ice-cap and the position and heights of the mountain ranges are shown on the chart. It will be seen that these coastal ranges are comparatively low between Mount Melbourne and the Ferrar Glacier, whence one might be led to suppose that the ice-cap was also lower at this part. But low as the mountains are, in one place only does the inland ice pour any of its volume into the sea, whilst the mountains themselves form an effective screen to the con- ditions which exist behind them. I have only one note that throws light on these ; as we journeyed down the coast we looked back over the ice-river in latitude 75° and saw its surface rise sharply to a ridge between the mountains. I wrote : ' Beyond this the surface still seemed to rise, and bare patches of rock could be seen at a greater altitude, but it was impossible to estimate the exact distance or height of these.'

Turning now to our journey up the Ferrar Glacier, it will be remembered that the mountains rose on each side of us as we approached the interior, and that when we reached the interior plateau at a height of 8,900 feet we observed *nunataks* to the north standing above our own level. From these observations I think there can be little doubt that the land rises behind the coastal mountains of the Prince Albert Range, and that the interior ice-cap nearly maintains the altitude which it has to the southward.

To the south of the Ferrar Glacier there are a number of detached mountain ranges of great altitude that flank the coast. In the distance at which we first saw them they bore the appearance of islands, but closer approach narrowed the glaciers which lay between them, and revealed an extensive mountain region beyond, behind which must lie an ice-cap of great altitude and extent.

Coming now to our journey over the ice-cap, it will be remembered that we travelled to the westward over a plain which did not vary in altitude more than sixty or seventy feet for 200 miles ; but as one's view on such a plain was very limited, it would be impossible to state definitely that the conditions were the same for many miles north or south of our course. We did not reach the inland plateau until we were fully seventy miles from the coast, and it is therefore extremely improbable that the full height of the ice-cap could be seen anywhere from the sea or from the Barrier surface.

From the facts before us, therefore, we may say with

certainty that the ice-cap is of very great extent, and
that in the latitude of 78° it is comparatively uniform in
altitude ; while, beyond this, the evidences which I have
briefly sketched serve to increase the impression of its
vastness, and to indicate that it maintains an approximately uniform level over the whole continent.   Whether
we accept what our imagination must suggest or pause at
the actual facts which have been discovered, this great
ice-sheet is unique ; it has no parallel in the world,
and its discovery must be looked upon as a notable
geographical fact.

Glaciers.—There are innumerable glaciers on the
coast of Victoria Land, but the great majority merely
discharge local névé fields lying in the coastal valleys ;
very few run back to the inland ice, and these may be
divided into two classes—the living and the dead.   In
the long stretch of coast between Cape Adare and Mount
Longstaff, over 11° of latitude, there appear to be only
four living ice-discharges from the interior.   The first falls
into Lady Newnes Bay, the second into the ice-river
in 75° S. to which I have referred, whilst the Barne and
Shackleton Inlets form channels for the other two.   The
Skelton and Mulock Inlets may also actively discharge
from the inland ice, but this is very doubtful.   From
observations which I have mentioned one must gather
that the movement of the most northerly of these discharges is very slow, but, judging by the movement of
the Barrier, the southern ones are more active.

The Ferrar Glacier is typical of the dead glaciers ; the
ice lies in the valley practically stationary and gradually

wasting away from the summer thawing, so that to all intents and purposes it is a dead limb.   The most conclusive proof of the stagnant condition of the ice in this region was afforded by the north arm of this glacier; the reader will remember that I descended this to find that the ice-stream ended in the tamest manner far from the sea. All these evidences, and many others which space will not allow me to mention, lead up to one great fact—namely, that the glaciation of the Antarctic Regions is receding.

For us in the South the appreciation of this fact and all its consequences served to throw a flood of light on many a knotty point, as I shall presently show, and, indeed, the fact itself was wonderfully impressive when we came to consider what must once have been the condition of Victoria Land.   The Ferrar Glacier probably contains as much ice as any hitherto known in the world; the Barne and Shackleton Glaciers contain a great deal more.   Yet in the first of these we saw that the ice must have been from 3,000 to 4,000 feet above its present level, and we knew that naturally the others must have been enlarged in like proportion.   It is difficult to conceive the vastness of these great ice-streams at the period of maximum glaciation.

The Great Barrier.—If the lofty plateau of Victoria Land is unique and wonderful, surely this great plain on the sea-level is still more marvellous.   It was a surprise to everyone, and not least to ourselves, to find that our long journey to the south was made without a rise of level.   What was the thickness of the ice-sheet to the south, or what lay beneath it, was obviously impossible for us to determine, but on collecting all the indirect evidences which bear on these points, I came to a conclusion which I still hold—that the greater part of it is afloat; and, strange as it is to imagine that the sea should run beneath such a solid sheet for so many hundreds of miles, I have yet to learn any reasonable argument against such an idea. As there are some, however, who do not agree with my conclusion, I will endeavour to give the reasons which guided me in forming it.

In first considering the edge of the Barrier the reader will see that on the chart the height of the cliff is given in feet and the depth of the sea in fathoms; if the proportion of five or even six to one be taken as the depth of the submerged ice, a small calculation will show that there are still some hundreds of fathoms of water between the bottom of the ice and the floor of the sea. And the Barrier edge sixty years ago was in advance of its present position, in places as much as twenty or thirty miles; consequently our soundings lie directly beneath Sir James Ross's Barrier and a long way from its edge. The part that has broken away must therefore have been water-borne, and this at least shows the possibility of the ice-sheet being afloat for an almost indefinite distance to the south. But had there been any doubt about the flotation of the present Barrier edge, it must have been dispelled by the fact that during our stay in the Balloon Inlet, although we had evidence of considerable tidal movement, the ice rose and fell with the ship.

We have so far proved, therefore, that the edge of the Great Barrier ice-sheet is afloat, and since thirty

miles of this floating sheet have been broken away
without altering this condition, there is no reason for
limiting the distance for which it continues.

Passing now to our southern journey, it remains to be
shown that, as I have stated, we travelled practically over
a level plain.   Of this the gradual disappearance and re-
appearance of land masses over a continually level horizon
left little doubt, but a yet clearer indication was the uniformity of the barometric pressures.   The aneroid readings were recorded three or four times a day, and were
frequently checked with the hypsometer.   On my return
from the southern journey I tabulated the readings on
each half-degree of latitude, in comparison with simulta-
neous readings taken in the ship, applying the necessary
corrections.   When an empirical correction for a height
of 250 feet is applied to the Barrier readings, the comparative differences are small, and if anything the Barrier
readings are the greater, showing a fall in level, or, what
is more probable, a rise in the barometric gradient.
The following is extracted from the table in question :

Latitude	Difference between Means of Ship and Barrier Readings corrected, and with allowance of 250 feet for height of Barrier
79°	+ ·045
79° 30'	+ ·06
80°	+ ·04
80° 30'	+ ·085
81°	+ ·06
81° 30'	− ·02
82°	− ·035

The sign shown in the second column indicates the manner in which the difference must be applied to the ship readings to produce equality.

It must be remembered, of course, that this comparison of pressures cannot be an exact method of determining levels in such circumstances. A small difference in pressure may be due to the normal barometric gradient or to local disturbance, as well as to a small difference of level, yet I do not think that anyone studying these figures can come to any conclusion but that we travelled over a level plain, except perhaps for a slight rise where the last two readings were taken, and this is easily explained by our exceptional nearness to the coastline at the time.

As this great ice-sheet moves along the coast of Victoria Land, the thrust of the immense glaciers in the Shackleton and Barne Inlets tends to push it from the land and thus the vast chasms of which I have given some account are formed. For many miles from the entrances of these inlets the ice is waved into long undulations, and as one approaches them the waves become more marked, the confusion increases, and the cracks and crevasses grow numerous. Within ten miles of the coastline at any place there are signs of disturbance, and, as my story showed, such a region is ill adapted for the sledge traveller. But without the region of these disturbances, or some ten or fifteen miles from the land (except immediately off the mouths of the inlets, where the confusion is wider spread), the Barrier moves with tranquillity, no ridge or crevasse or other irregularity is met with, and the surface presents one monotonous, even plain of snow. Although it may be possible, it seems to me highly improbable, that a mass of ice could be travelling over the land in such an even, undisturbed fashion. Where the ice-sheet is pushing past the Minna Bluff and around the north and south ends of the White Island, it is starred into long radial crevasses, running from ten to twenty miles from the land. The rifts are so straight and close so gradually that on crossing them the sides appear to be mathematically ruled straight parallel lines. It is scarcely imaginable that such extraordinary uniformity of fracture should occur in an ice-sheet that is resting on the land, where there must be some irregularity in friction and ice-tension tending to divert the straightness of the rents.

One other evidence of importance remains to be noticed in this connection. In one of the crevasses extending from the north end of White Island Mr. Royds took some serial temperatures. Close to the land he found that the temperature fell with the depth to a mean level of $-9°$, but at a distance of ten miles from the land he got a different result. Here at first the temperature fell, but as the thermometer was lowered its column rose again until, at a depth of nineteen fathoms, it showed zero. Deeper than this he could not go on account of the snow in the crevasse, but I think it must be conceded that the only reasonable cause for such a rise of temperature as was observed is the presence of water beneath the ice.

When all the facts which I have mentioned are considered, I do not see that there can be any reasonable

cause to doubt that the Great Barrier ice-sheet is afloat
at least as far south as we travelled.

Movement and Extent of the Great Barrier.—After
our observations of the stagnant condition of the ice
about our winter quarters and in the Ferrar Glacier, the
report of the Barrier movement came as a surprise.
The reader will remember that its discovery was more
or less accidental, and resulted from the fact that Mr.
Barne, on visiting Depot 'A' in 1903, found that its
bearing was altered, and thirteen and a half months after
its establishment he carefully measured its displacement,
which he found to be 608 yards. The direction in which
it is travelling must be a little to the east of north, and consequently this figure probably represents the whole movement during the period. The direction of movement is
indicated by the vast disturbances encountered off the
eastern slopes of Mount Terror. Here the sheet is
pressing up and shearing past the land-ice, raising
numerous huge parallel pressure ridges. It would almost
seem possible that movement was taking place along
each of these according to the state of the tide. Dr.
Wilson, who had the greatest opportunity of examining
this region, thinks that there must be a submarine land
ridge between Mount Terror and the White Island,
checking the flow of ice in that direction. He also
observed that glaciers on the south side of Erebus and
Terror, where there is an exceptionally heavy snowfall,
are pressing towards the south-west, eventually finding
relief around Cape Armitage. That there was some
pressure from the Barrier around White Island was

shown by the ridges which formed on the eastern side of our peninsula.

I am inclined to place the eastern limit of the floating portion of the Barrier near the Balloon Inlet in longitude 163° W. It is noticeable that the ice-cliff immediately to the east of this has not broken away since Sir James Ross traced it. The disturbed condition of the ice in this vicinity is no doubt due to King Edward's Land, but it is not easy to see why the effect should be precisely what it is.

The full extent of the Barrier ice-sheet must, for the present, be a matter of surmise. At our most southerly point we saw long snow-capes running out beyond Mount Longstaff and meeting the level horizon, while further still the mirage threw up small patches of white, indicative of still more distant capes and mountains. The scene to the south was much what it was to the north, and the weather so bright and clear that we can at least make one statement with certainty. The high mountainous coastline does not turn to the east before reaching the 84th parallel beyond the slight trend it already has in that direction. But at such distances one can only speak of the high land ; whether the level surface of the Barrier continues to skirt those lofty land masses it is impossible to say, but, for my part, I am strongly of opinion that it does.

Speculations on Former Ice Conditions.—Having given the reasons for my belief that the Great Barrier is afloat, it may be interesting to add some ideas which have come to me with regard to its origin, although I make no pretence to being an expert in glacial matters.

It is evident that when the Southern glaciation was at a maximum, when the glacier valleys were filled to over-flowing, and when the great reservoir of the interior stood perhaps 400 or 500 feet above its present level and was pouring vast masses of ice into the Ross Sea, the Great Barrier was a very different formation from what it is at present. There are abundant evidences of its great enlargement ; granite boulders were found on Cape Royds and high on every volcanic island in our neighbourhood ; on the slopes of Terror, Dr. Wilson found morainic terraces 800 feet above the present sur-face of the ice ; Mr. Ferrar showed that nearly the whole of the Cape Armitage Peninsula was once submerged ; and, in fact, on all sides of us and everywhere were signs of the vastly greater extent of the ancient ice-sheet.

It is not until one has grasped the extent of the former glaciation and the comparatively rapid recession of the present that one can hope to explain the many extraordinary ice formations that now remain in the Ross Sea, but armed with this knowledge one is at least able to advance a theory concerning their origin.

My opinion is that at or near the time of maximum glaciation the huge glaciers, no longer able to float in a sea of 400 fathoms, joined hands and spread out over the Ross Sea, completely filling it with an immense sheet of ice. At that time the edge of the sheet and the first place at which it could be water-borne bordered on the ocean depths to the north of Cape Adare. Then followed the receding ice conditions, when the ice-sheet as a whole grew thinner, and at length a time came when it was curiously circumstanced. The Ross Sea is comparatively uniform in depth north and south ; the icesheet pressing out over this level floor would consequently have been more or less uniform in thickness, and finally the wastage would have been more or less uniform over the whole area. As a result of these conditions there came a time when the whole ice-sheet became buoyant, and when it had either to break away with great rapidity or to float whilst remaining fast. I imagine that it floated and broke away gradually, and that the present rapidly diminishing Barrier is the remains of the great ice-sheet.

It is not the only remains, for the whole coast bears signs of the old ice-sheet in curious ice formations that can be accounted for in no other way. Lady Newnes Bay contains a large fragment of it ; the present ice discharges are wholly insufficient to account for such a sheet as fills this bay ; moreover, its surface is not gradually inclined but advances in long and steep undulations, the outer waves cut off by deep hollows from the interior mass. The single sounding taken in this vicinity shows that here, too, the greater part of the icemass is still afloat. In the course of the narrative I referred to the long ice-tongue in latitude 75° S. ; this also must be a remnant of the heavier glaciation. Other typical remnants are to be found in the steep snowslopes and ice-cliffs which fringe many parts of the coast. These slopes, which are very common about our winter quarters, start on a bare hillside and, wedge-shaped in section, gradually increase in thickness till they end in a perpendicular cliff dipping into the sea, consequently they have no present source of supply.

In conclusion it may be said that there are few photographs of the coastal scenery which do not exhibit in some way or another evidence of the vastly greater extension of the ice-sheet in former times.

Former Climate.—A word may be added as to the change of climate which has caused the recession of the ice conditions in the Far South. It has been a surprise to me to find that the idea that a great glacial epoch is the result of a comparatively mild climate is supported by much authority. Both Mr. Ferrar and I arrived at this conclusion independently when in the South. The chief argument in its favour is that it is physically impossible for cold air to contain much moisture, but living in a severe climate it was impossible not to realise that greater severity would have meant more sterile ice conditions. In this connection it is also interesting to note that our greatest snowfall occurred in the summer, and that the Balleny Islands are more heavily glaciated than Victoria Land.

There can be little doubt, therefore, that at the period of maximum glaciation the climate of Victoria Land was milder than it is at present.

Physical Geography of Victoria Land.—Mr. Ferrar has dealt with this subject at such length in his geological summary that it is unnecessary for me to add many remarks concerning it. He has set forth the general results of his labours, and I think it must be admitted that they are of great importance.

It has to be remembered that little or nothing was known of the geology of this land before we set forth, that since our return the formation of a very large part of it has been revealed, and that there is much evidence to show that this part may be taken as typical of the whole.

The simple horizontal structure which Mr. Ferrar describes, and the absence of lateral pressure in the formation of such a huge and extensive range of mountains, appear to have been wholly unexpected, and to have excited the interest of many geologists. The details of Mr. Ferrar's reports and collections have yet to be investigated, but there can be little doubt that, when all is made known, the geology of the Antarctic Continent will have received an immense addition. In this connection, however, we have to record one disappointment; we confidently hoped that Mr. Ferrar's discovery of fossil remains would prove of great importance, but an examination of them since our return has shown that they cannot be identified, and consequently much of the value of the discovery is lost.

Speaking at the Royal Geographical Society, Dr. Smith Woodward said on this subject : 'The carbonaceous matter is really of great importance, because it was discovered 500 miles south of the fossil plants brought back by the Swedish Expedition. . . . All who have seen it are quite agreed that this carbonaceous matter must be due to vegetation, but it shows no structure whatever. . . . It seems impossible to determine whether it is due to land vegetation or to marine vegetation.' It seems, therefore, that the fossils of which we hoped so much are in too carbonised a state to be of use in indicating the age of the great sandstone formation in which they were found.

Although Mr. Ferrar has dealt with the general disposition of the mountain ranges and the more recent volcanic outbursts on the coast of Victoria Land, a word might be added in speculating on the distribution of land beyond the limits of our discoveries. I recall once more that in our most southerly position we saw the high mountainous coastline running in a S.S.E. direction. If such a line be carried for a hundred miles beyond our position, it will be seen to be making directly towards Graham Land, and I cannot but think that it continues to do so. If so, the geographical pole would be situated 200 miles or more from it, and on the high ice-plateau which must continue behind, if we are to allow for the comparatively rapid movement of the Barrier. The alternative theory held by some is that this coast sweeps round and joins King Edward's Land; if so, the turn, as I have pointed out, must be made a very long way south. Unfortunately, our knowlege of King Edward's Land is very limited. Judged by the outline of the hills and the blackness of the rocks, it appeared to be of the same comparatively recent volcanic formation as the land in the vicinity of our winter quarters, and if this is so, there would be little to prove a connection with Victoria Land; but, on the other hand, pieces of granite were brought up with the lead from the shallow water in its vicinity, and this would seem to show that it is continental.   I have already described our view of King Edward's Land, and it will be remembered that we saw nothing of the wild rugged mountain scenery of Victoria Land.

In all such remarks as I have made concerning the extension of Victoria Land to the south, and the limits of the Barrier ice-sheet, there is one factor which must be acknowledged to be extremely confusing. I can think of no reason to account for the comparatively rapid motion of the ice sheet ; it is certain that there must be a supply of ice from some region to the south, and it would seem that in this region there is a heavier precipitation than that which we experienced in the vicinity of the ship, but it is most difficult to reconcile these facts with the general conditions of glaciation which came under our observation.

The cause of the Barrier movement remains therefore a problem of extraordinary interest, and shows that there are still conditions in the extreme South of which we have no knowledge. It would seem not altogether unreasonable to suppose that there may be some connection between this matter and the warm snow-bearing southerly winds which we so constantly experienced.

In considering the northern extension of Victoria Land it would appear probable that the coast runs more or less in a straight line from Cape North to Adélie Land. With reference to our work in this region, I have already shown the probable cause of Ross's error in imagining the Russell Islands to be a group separate from that discovered by Balleny, and I have described our course to the westward. Concerning the latter I may add that whilst it is certain that we must reject Wilkes Land to the eastward of Adélie Land, Wilkes' soundings still remain as a guide to the limit of the continental plateau in this region. Our own uniform soundings of 250 fathoms, together with his, show that there is a considerable extent of shallow sea, limited more or less by the track of Wilkes' ships, approximately, along the Antarctic Circle.

Meteorological Conditions.—The meteorological work of our expedition consists of that laborious record kept by Mr. Royds, which embodied continuous observations for two years in our winter quarters four hundred miles south of any former meteorological stations, as well as such as were taken on our sledging journeys. All these observations have to be corrected and reduced before definite results can be obtained, and therefore their full value cannot be known at present. The reader can hardly have read the narrative of our voyage without gleaning some idea of the climate in which we lived, and of some of the interesting meteorological problems with which we were confronted; so that a few additional remarks concerning them may not be out of place.

In some respects our meteorological station was very fortunately situated, whilst in others it was less satisfactory. From this point of view the proximity of Mount Erebus was a great stroke of luck, as the smoke of that volcano gave us an indication of the direction of the upper air currents, and showed that they blew almost constantly from the west. In this connection it will be remembered also that there were some interesting evidences to be gathered from the surface of the snow on the high level plateau of Victoria Land ; here also, as shown by the *sastrugi*, the wind blows continuously from the west.

As regards the winds at our winter quarters, the commonest direction was S.E., but although one would wish this to be typical of the whole region, I fear there is much evidence to show that this wind was purely local. It was often possible to see very varying weather conditions simultaneously at different places about the ' Discovery.' For instance, at one time a bank of heavy nimbus cloud hung over Cape Bird ; the western ranges were in calm and sunshine ; clouds of drift were being swept from the slopes of Mount Discovery by a southerly wind ; the wind was S.E. at the ship ; whilst off Cape Armitage and a mile or two to the eastward of our peninsula it was again calm. The same confusion was shown by the snow-waves : as a rule, in the vicinity of the ship they pointed to the S.E. ; outside White Island they were confused from W.S.W. to S.S.E. ; south of White Island and to the Bluff they were south ; at the depôt S.W. ; and off the eastern slopes of Terror again south.

All this, together with the observations made on sledge journeys, shows such a confused condition of air-currents that it would be impossible to assert that the prevalent wind in our region was S.E. It is true that at the eastern end of the Barrier we experienced east and S.E. winds, but if this is the general direction over the whole Barrier, it is difficult to see where the body of air goes to, unless it turns to the north on arriving at Victoria Land; it certainly does not go over the mountains.

The prevalent direction of the wind has naturally an important bearing on the general circulation of the atmosphere in the Southern Regions, and it is therefore unfortunate that we should have been subject to local winds. The reduction of barometric pressures will doubtless throw light on the question, however. Another drawback common to all polar expeditions is the impossibility of measuring the snowfall on account of surface drift, &c. There is no form of snow-gauge that can be used with success. One effort was made to ascertain the precipitation in our region, which, although it was not exact, is perhaps worth recording. When the ice about Cape Armitage was a year old it occurred to me that we might get a rough idea of the net annual deposit by measuring the depth of snow at various points on its surface. This was done with difficulty, owing to the *sastrugi* and varying nature of the snow, but I calculated that a rough average of the results would represent between four and five inches of hard packed snow. Rough as it is, this figure is something of a guide, for it means that the surface of the Barrier is annually augmented by about this amount. It may be added that excavations into the surface of the Barrier invariably revealed a succession of crusts at irregular intervals, the amount of snow between being usually in fair agreement with the deposit mentioned.

In speaking of the deposit on the lower level of the

Barrier, a word may be added concerning that on the lofty plateau of Victoria Land. It may be remembered that in many parts of this plain we found the surface covered with a shining crust traversed by innumerable transverse cracks which gave it a scaly appearance, such as may be seen in the mud of a dried pond. I thought at the time that this could be no recent formation, but it was only much later that the possible meaning of it occurred to me—namely, that there was no net deposit of snow on this plateau ; or, in other words, that the climatic conditions were such that the evaporation equalled or exceeded the deposition.

The meteorological condition which puzzled us most was the warm southerly blizzard to which I have repeatedly referred, and it must be admitted that the fact of our highest temperatures coming with a southerly wind is a very extraordinary one. On this, as on other matters, however, it is premature to speculate at present, and I have only made the foregoing remarks to show that there are many interesting and curious problems which it is to be hoped a close study of the' Discovery's ' meteorological records will solve.

Vertebrate Zoology.—This department, with exceptions, lay in Dr. Wilson's hands, and as it is one which must excite a very general interest I have asked him to supply to this book a summary of his work. To this I can add little except to remark that, if the birds and beasts that came under his observation were few in species as compared with those observed by others, it is because our expedition laboured on the limit of such life, and for the first time travelled beyond its limit. It is only reasonable that the expedition which most deeply penetrates the sterile polar area should have least to record in this respect.

Invertebrate Zoology.—The readers of my narrative will have gathered that Mr. Hodgson, our biologist, was a very active member of our community, and I certainly breathed a sigh of relief when I learned that his collections had been safely received at the British Museum. But this is only the commencement of the work which has to be done in this connection, and it will be many months, and possibly years, before the full results of this important department are published.

Physical Work.—The most important branch of this work carried out by our expedition was that connected with magnetism. The magnetic work may be divided into three classes : that done at sea, that done at the shore station, and that done on sledge journeys. The first consists of observations taken around the belt of the Southern Seas and throughout the area of the Ross Sea ; the second, of the continuous records taken with the variometer instruments ; and the third, of the important observations taken by Mr. Bernacchi on the Barriers, others taken by Mr. Armitage to the west, and observations for declination taken on my southern and western journeys. The reduction of all these data requires much patience and skill, and it must be a long while ere the full results are made known ; but it can at least be said that the mass of material obtained will go far to accomplish the main object which was named by the Royal

Society when it appealed to the Government for the despatch of an Antarctic Expedition.

Of other physical work performed by the expedition I have made mention in the course of the narrative, and in this connection the reader will no doubt remember the seismic, the gravity, and the auroral observations, as well as those taken for atmospheric electricity and for tidal movement, the whole of which must show that many valuable records were brought back by the 'Discovery.'

Oceanography.—A considerable number of soundings were taken during our voyage, and in most cases in very interesting places, but it must be confessed that the oceanographical work as a whole was very limited. The reason is obvious, as the greater part of our time was spent either locked in the ice or cruising in shallow seas ; yet, as I look at the vast amount of this work which remains to be done in this area, I cannot but regret that we were unable to effect more.

In the foregoing summary I have been forced to pass rapidly from subject to subject, and yet I hope that in so doing I shall have persuaded the reader that the voyage of the 'Discovery' was not conducted in a spirit of pure adventure, but that we strove to add, and succeeded in adding, something to the sum of human knowledge.

The natural result of such an attack as the beginning of this century has seen on the Antarctic Regions is a period of reaction and quiescence, during which the light thrown on Southern conditions will be considered and discussed and fresh problems will be evolved.   But it is not reasonable to suppose that this period will continue indefinitely; all experience shows that as long as problems remain to be solved, sooner or later their solution will be attempted. With the full knowledge, therefore, that the time will come when others will follow in our footsteps and pass beyond them, I have written these pages for the future as well as for the present.

APPENDIX I

SUMMARY OF THE GEOLOGICAL OBSERVATIONS MADE DURING THE CRUISE OF THE S.S. 'DISCOVERY,' 1901-1904

By H. T. FERRAR, M.A., F.G.S., Geologist to the National Antarctic Expedition

PREVIOUS KNOWLEDGE.

IT is unnecessary to recapitulate the numerous voyages that have been made to the southward of latitude 60° S., therefore we will very briefly touch on the points of interest obtained by the expeditions which have entered our area, in so far as the information obtained bears on this subject.

In the year 1839 Captain Balleny, of the shipping firm of Messrs. Enderby, of London, discovered five islands near the Antarctic Circle in about longitude 163° E. On one of these islands (Buckle Island) an active volcano was observed, and on another specimens of 'scoria and basalt with crystals of olivine' were found.

Sir James Clarke Ross, in the year 1841, when in charge of the Magnetic Survey Expedition in H.M.S. 'Erebus' and H.M.S. 'Terror,' made the discoveries on which the work of this expedition has been built. These discoveries may be summed up very briefly :

(1) An open shallow sea to the south of the Antarctic Circle.

(2) A great range of mountains which rise occasionally to heights of 15,000 feet, and extend in a north-and-south direction for at least 500 miles.

(3) An active volcano (Mount Erebus), over 12,000 feet high, 'emitting flame and smoke in great profusion.'

(4) A wall of ice (the Great Ice Barrier) on an average 150 feet high and about 470 miles long.

Dr. Robert MacCormick, who was in charge of the geological work of the expedition, landed on two islands lying off this coast. The specimens he obtained have been recently described by Mr. G. T. Prior ; they include basalt, palagonite-tuff, phonolite and muscovite-granite from Possession Island, and basalt from Franklin Island.

Dr. MacCormick considered the whole range to be volcanic, but this is obviously not the case, for all the higher peaks are pyramidal in outline and exhibit house-roof structure—a structure which could not be produced by the eruption of rocks from local centres.

The French expedition under Dumont D'Urville, during this international attack on the South Pole, obtained specimens of granite from some low rocky islets lying off the coast of Adélie Land, and it was thought that these strongly suggested the existence of a continental mass of land. The fact that H.M.S. 'Challenger,' in 1874, in an area about 2,000 miles from South Victoria Land, dredged up gneiss and granite, probably dropped from icebergs, was also given as evidence of the existence of a continent, and it was thought that these rocks had been derived directly from that continent.

Many years elapsed before any additional information was obtained. Captain Jansen, in the year 1895, returned from Cape Adare bringing, among other rocks, a granitic pebble, which Dr. Teall tells me ' has been crushed by earth movements, and must at one time have formed part of an extensive tract of land.' In the same year Mr. Borchgrevink obtained schistose and granitic rocks, and these are said to show a strong similarity of the South Victoria Land rocks to those of Adélie Land.

The ' Southern Cross ' collection (Sir George Newnes' expedition, 1898–1899) includes various plutonic and volcanic rocks as well as slates and quartz grits, the latter being apparently the only sedimentary rocks found by them *in situ* in South

Victoria Land. These have been carefully described by Mr. Prior in one of the British Museum publications. The slates and quartz grits are noted as occurring at the head of Robertson Bay. Being cleaved they must have been subjected to earth pressures, and as such pressures were probably long anterior to the stretching tension which dislocated the Beacon Sandstone formation of the Royal Society Range, these rocks would seem to be of a much older date.

SOUTH VICTORIA LAND.

If reference be made to the chart, it will be seen that we have to consider :

(*a*) Islands lying off the coast of South Victoria Land.

(*b*) A magnificent range of mountains, proved by the great journey of Captain Scott to be at least 800 miles long.

(*c*) The rocks composing this range.

(*d*) The ice in all its forms.

THE ISLANDS.

The islands such as the *Balleny Group* and Beaufort Island may be dismissed with the observation that these, like the islands from which specimens have been obtained, were surrounded by cliffs. These cliffs occasionally display irregular coloured bands similar to the bands on Cape Adare and Coulman Island, and as the latter proved to consist of basalt agglomerate, it is highly probable that the same rock is developed in all. The soundings near these islands showed the depth of the sea to be about 270 fathoms, and as the outlines of the Balleny Islands, at any rate, are stepped cones, great denudation must have taken place in the past.

Scott Island, in latitude 67° 24′ 5″ S., longitude 179° 55′ 5″ W., was discovered by Captain Colbeck in December 1902, and the specimens collected by Mr. Morrison are all of the same type of olivine basalt.

The Possession Islands have already been mentioned, but it is very probable that the specimens previously obtained here were not found *in situ*. The rocks collected by Mr. Morrison may be safely taken as representative of this group of islands. Two varieties were procured by him : the one a palagonite-tuff very similar to the tuffs found on Cape Adare and Castle Rock near the 'Discovery's' Winter Quarters, and the other a grey olivine basalt with large porphyritic crystals of olivine.

Coulman Island, like the other islands, is surrounded by very high and almost perpendicular cliffs, which show occasional bright red and yellow patches. These patches prove to consist of basalt-agglomerate at Cape Wadworth, the northern end, and it is probable, therefore, that the coloured bands on Cape Anne consist of the same rock. The 'Southern Cross' obtained a hornblende-basalt, and the 'Discovery's' collection includes a specimen from a basaltic dyke which was exposed at the north end. The rocks of this island appear to lie horizontally as a whole, but an anticline on the west side shows that they have been gently folded over an east-and-west axis.

Franklin Island has been visited three times, the first time by Ross, who describes the north side as 'a line of dark precipitous cliffs between 500 and 600 feet high, exposing several longitudinal broad white bands, two or three being of a red ochre colour.' The specimens he collected are all of basalt of the same type, and in the 'Southern Cross' collection there is a specimen of limbrugite remarkable for the number and large size of the olivine enstutite nodules. Mr. J. D. Morrison, of the 'Morning,' supplied similar specimens with a note to the effect that this rock 'forms a belt about 30 feet thick running horizontally along one side about 300 feet above sea level.' In addition he mentions a pebbly beach similar to that at Cape Adare, and therefore probably due to the same cause.

ROSS ISLAND GROUP.

This group of islands includes practically all the land within fifty miles of the 'Discovery's' Winter Quarters, and is by far the most extensive mass not attached to the mainland. The rocks of which these islands are composed are all volcanic, and point to volcanic activity of the first magnitude, which dates back from the present day, but does not quite bridge over the very long period since the intrusion of the dolerite sheets on the mainland.

Ross Island is practically made up by the material ejected from the four volcanoes, Erebus, Terror, Bird, and Terra Nova. It is roughly triangular in shape, and measures almost exactly fifty miles from north to south and from east to west.

Mount Erebus, in the year 1841, was observed to be emitting flame and smoke in great profusion, but during the years 1902–1903 only steam was seen to be produced. The mountain rises more as a dome than as a cone, and the flowing convex curves give it a very massive and undenuded aspect. It appears to have been built up in three stages, the activity becoming less as each stage was completed. The earliest stage is marked by a girdle of rock encircling the mountain at a height of about 6,000 feet above sea level, which on the north side appears as a huge crag. The second stage ended with the production of a crater at about 11,000 feet above sea level, and the lava streams which issued from it are still preserved. The last stage produced the small cone placed asymmetrically in the upper crater, and from this cone the steam now issues.

Mount Bird, the low dome at the northern foot of Mount Erebus, and Mount Terra Nova, the dome which joins Mount Erebus to Mount Terror, are both undenuded and obviously have craters at their summits, and therefore belong to the same recent eruptions.

Mount Terror, like Mount Erebus, is entirely covered by snow, and as it is more conical than Mount Erebus it covers almost the same area, though it is only a little over 10,000 feet high. The cone is truncated, apparently by a crater half a mile in diameter, and the sides of the cone, where bare of snow, display many small parasitic vents.

The rocks collected from this huge island are chiefly of volcanic origin, but granites, sandstones, and rocks of a hypabyssal nature are found as erratics in certain localities.

The 'Southern Cross' obtained hornblende-basalts from a bare rock-cliff, ten miles or so to the westward of Cape Crozier, and Mr. Morrison brought back a portion of a basaltic bomb from a boulder on the beach at Cape Crozier. Lieutenant

Royds, Dr. Koettlitz, and Dr. Wilson have all added to the collection from this locality by bringing rocks on sledges over the ice under very trying conditions. These rocks, with the exception of the columnar olivine-basalt obtained by Dr. Wilson from the so-called Crozier cliffs, do not differ materially from those collected near the penguin rookery. The latter include granites and sandstones, which are probably erratic, olivine-basalts from recent lava flows, yellow trachytic rocks which occur as bosses on the slopes of Mount Terror, and tuffs from below the lava flows.

From the 'V' cliffs, Hogsback and the Sultan's Head, Mr. T. V. Hodgson has supplied the expedition with vesicular basalts and a great variety of palagonite-tuffs. Hutton Cliffs, near Turtle Back Island, are composed of bedded tuff-rocks, which strike N.E. and S.W. and therefore may be contemporaneous with the tuffs of Sultan's Head. The Turtle Back is composed of fragments of black basalt similar to that of Winter Quarters. Cape Royds, Cape Barne, and the Skuary, three bare areas on the west side of Mount Erebus, besides supplying boulders of granite and other rocks, give us the basalt which contains lenticular crystals of felspar in parallel orientation. Cape Royds consists entirely of this basalt, and it is found also at a height of 1,500 feet on the side of Mount Erebus.

WINTER QUARTERS.

About four square miles of bare rock, entirely of volcanic origin, was the only land within walking distance of the 'Discovery's' Winter Quarters, and therefore did not offer a promising field for discovering the geological history of South Victoria Land. Of this area, Castle Rock, a crag 400 feet above the snow and 1,400 feet above sea level, consists of palagonite-tuff very similar to that at Cape Adare and Possession Island, and is probably the neck of some ancient volcano.

The three heights called *Harbour Heights*, as well as the cone called *Crater Hill*, are scoria cones, but the chief ejecta from them consists of black fine-grained basalt, both compact and vesicular. On one of these masses of black basalt, near the base of Castle Rock, a small quantity of native sulphur was found, and this was the only example of solfataric action observed in the immediate neighbourhood.

At the base of Crater Hill, on the S.E. side, an olivine basalt of high specific gravity was found ; a similar basalt also appears on Cape Armitage, and the rock at both places occurs in almost horizontal sheets.

Observation Hill, about 750 feet high, consists principally of hornblende-trachytes, and these, having been erupted from a local centre, practically form the hill. The rock with parallel structure which is found at the north foot of the hill and in the Gap is an earlier extrusion than the rest, and lies unconformably below them.

Turning now to the other islands, *White Island* is so covered by detritus that it is only near the summit that the rock met with is undoubtedly *in situ*. Here also extrusions of basalt are found, which suggest that this island is of the same general age as Ross Island.

Black Island likewise consists mainly of basalt, and near the north-west extremity vesicular and amygdaloidal flows were encountered. At the south-west end yellow trachytic rocks form a bold headland, but do not cover an area greater than about four square miles.

Brown Island has a well-defined crater at its summit, which is quite undenuded, and from it have issued basalts in various conditions. A great part of the summit consists of a yellow trachytic rock, but owing to lack of time a specimen was only obtained from an off-shoot of this huge boss of rock. The northern end is comparatively low, and the bright red areas around small conical depressions point to the presence of scoria cones similar to those at Winter Quarters.

The *Dailey Islands* are fine small conical masses surrounded by the ice in the middle of McMurdo Sound. Only one of these—the largest—has been visited, and the usual scoriaceous basalts were procured.

The *Dellbridge Islands*, situated near the base of Mount Erebus, have supplied a rather surprising variety of rocks.

Razor Back consists of vesicular basalt which is very much contorted and locally is scoriaceous.

Tent Island has an exposure of about 100 feet of conglomerate on the steep north-west face. The upper part of the island consists of sheet on sheet of basalt, making up a thickness of about 200 feet. These sheets dip at an angle of about 15° to the S.E., and mainly consist of red basalt glass with lenticular crystals of feldspar.

Inaccessible Island was visited by Mr. Hodgson, and the specimens he obtained include tuffs, vesicular basalts, and trachytic rocks. He tells me the rocks are all very confused, but generally dip to the north at an angle of about 40°.

THE VOLCANIC CONES ON THE MAINLAND.

Four or five perfect cones, quite undenuded, stand at intervals along the coast of South Victoria Land, and form a very striking contrast with the comparatively unbroken outline of the mountain ranges that abut on the Ross Sea. There are one or two other cones which need not be considered, such as that on the summit of Cape Jones, but all are isolated and do not form, as was previously supposed, a continuous belt.

Mount Brewster, probably only 4,000 feet high, is situated near Lady Newnes Bay, and is important as it obviously does not belong to the high land which rises to heights of over 10,000 feet on the west of it. This small mountain is an almost perfect dome, and has a slightly flattened summit. It rises rather suddenly from the low foothills at the base of the great Admiralty Range, and the snow-covered curves differ essentially from the comparatively bare precipitous cliffs of that range.

Mount Melbourne is conical, but has a small crater, probably a quarter of a mile in diameter, at its summit. It is situated on the south side of Wood Bay, and rises directly out of the sea on two sides. The mountains to the west of it recede from the coast, so that it stands in icy isolation guarding the entrance to the bay. Basalt was obtained near the mountain by the 'Southern Cross' Expedition, and pumice pebbles, which must have come from its flanks, have since been found on a small floe floating in Wood Bay.

Mount Morning is about 5,000 feet high, and is situated near the foot of the Royal Society Range. It is a low dome which covers a comparatively large area, and lava-streams are still apparent on its sides ; but as no specimens have been collected, nothing further need be said.

Mount Discovery is a most striking mountain of accumulation, as it has the shape of a pear standing on its broader end, and the curves which meet at its summit descend symmetrically on all sides almost to sea level. It appears to be composed of basalt similar to that of the Ross Island Group, and parasitic vents are not conspicuous. The Minna Bluff, a long narrow peninsula projecting from it towards the south-east, is also composed of basalt similar to that from Winter Quarters.

KING EDWARD VII. LAND.

King Edward VII. Land, between the latitudes of 76° and 78° S. and the longitudes of 160° and 150° W., does not show great relief, but a bold headland stands out conspicuously before the main mass. As fragments of plutonic and gneissic rocks were obtained from an iceberg which had grounded near here, it is possible that the main mass is made up partly of rocks of these types.

THE CONTINENTAL RANGE.

South Victoria Land, as far as we know at present, consists of a great range of mountains, stretching in a north-and-south direction for at least 800 miles, and apparently it is the eastern edge of a vast plateau. The only direct evidence of the existence of this plateau was obtained between latitudes 77° and 78° S., where Captain Scott travelled 200 miles westward at a uniform height of 9,000 feet above sea level.

The land as a whole does not show great relief, though Surgeon MacCormick considered the whole range to be volcanic. The Ross Expedition was less fortunate than the ' Discovery ' : the latter was able to steam in close to the land and so see the peaks from many points of view. Thus, just south of Cape Washington a tabular mountain was observed with apparently horizontal bedding planes and almost perpendicular scarps which showed plateau structure, but the earlier explorers were too far from the land to see this.

The great chain of mountain ranges naturally divides itself into sections or links, and these may be conveniently considered separately.

(1) The area between Cape Adare and Cape North, a distance of 100 miles, is more snow-covered than is the land further to the south, and near Cape North the cloak of snow is almost uniform. The coast, which is parallel to the mountains, faces north-east, and the peaks, which are generally pyramidal, have their shoulders truncated sharply at the shore. There are very few deep valleys, but the snow often exhibits prominent terraces, one above another and parallel to the coast, and the whole suggests the existence of some horizontal structure in the rock beneath.

(2) The *Admiralty Range* occupies the 250 miles of coast between Cape Adare and Cape Washington, and forms the highest and perhaps the largest land mass. Here one sees the possibility of a division of the area into two distinct geological districts, for low foothills are almost continuous along the whole length of this part of the coast. Behind the foothills there appears to be a depression, and behind this, again, a wall— possibly a fault-face or escarpment—which rises up to heights of 10,000 feet and which has weathered into a series of fine pyramidal peaks.

(3) The *Prince Albert Range*, an area 200 miles in length and trending due north and south, is the lowest large land mass seen by the Expedition. This range is important, not only because it is practically a new discovery, but because of its extreme uniformity of character. It is remarkable that here the eastern border is always steep and gives the impression that it is only the outlying edge of some great plateau from which streams of ice flow down between nunataks. The structure of the Royal Society Range is perhaps the key to the explanation of this uniformity of landscape.

(4) The *Royal Society Range* has a length of some fifty miles, and is the only part of South Victoria Land which has been examined in detail. In the main, all the structures observed in the Admiralty Range are again seen, but are much more striking. There are foothills of insignificant height, a north-

and-south valley separating the foothills from the main mountain mass, and a mountain mass rising in a uniform cliff behind to a height of 10,000 feet, and with occasional peaks rising to 12,000 or 15,000 feet in altitude. From our Winter Quarters this range could always be seen, though quite fifty miles away ; and even at this great distance, so clear was the atmosphere, the plateau form was always evident, and was rendered still more striking by the broad band of lighter-coloured rock below, which extends from end to end of the range. Thus the form of the range appears to be determined by the horizontality of the rocks which compose it—a fact abundantly proved by the sledge parties who traversed it.

(5) The *four ranges* which determine the 300 miles of almost straight coast to the south of latitude 79° S. appear to be exactly similar to those already considered, and may be dismissed with the mention of the plateau character which is strikingly shown and beautifully illustrated by Dr. Wilson's sketches. These were made during Captain Scott's great journey to the south, when latitude 82° 17′ S. was reached, and are all the more valuable in that they were made by an unprejudiced observer. At the same time, Mr. E. H. Shackleton obtained some valuable photographs, and the next year Mr. Barne reported a horizontal structure in the land at about 80° S. Mr. Mulock has carefully surveyed the land in this high latitude, and the great plateaux separated by the deep, steep-sided channels or inlets are being carefully charted, and this will form a valuable addition to the geology of the area.

THE ROCKS OBTAINED IN SOUTH VICTORIA LAND.

The rocks obtained by the expedition fall naturally into five quite distinct groups. Briefly they may be classed as gneisses, granites, sandstones, dolerites, and recent volcanics, but little is known of the field relations of these types, except the order in which they occur. The important deposit of sandstone provides a convenient stratigraphical datum line with reference to which the other phenomena may be considered, and the above order may be taken as chronological.

The Gneissic Rocks.

As the gneissic rocks occur at sea level at the foot of the highest part of the Royal Society Range, and as they are also found in the interior of the range below a sequence of rocks 12,000 feet thick, they may safely be regarded as forming the ancient platform on which the central part of South Victoria Land is built.

The foothills of the Royal Society Range appear to be mainly composed of metamorphic limestone, which Mr. G. T. Prior tells me probably belongs to the gneissic series. These limestones form rounded hills which rise to heights of over 4,000 feet above sea level and are quite isolated. Dr. Koettlitz and Dr. Wilson both aided me in collecting from these hills, and Mr. Barne procured a specimen of schist from near latitude 80° S.

On both sides of the Blue Glacier the rock shows important structural planes which dip to the east at an angle of 70° while the strike is north and south. The hills end sharply on the west in a very straight and steep face, which is suggestive of a fault. The limestone is almost pure white, and the calcite is in rather well-formed rhombohedral crystals often an eighth of an inch across. When weathered it becomes so crumbly that it was difficult to get a hand specimen from the rounded surfaces that were exposed. Basic dykes cut obliquely across the planes of division, but only at one spot, where one of these dykes is twenty yards thick, was thermal metamorphism evident.

Cape Bernacchi and the low rounded hills to the west of it appear to consist of gneissic rocks which are similar to the gneisses forming the lowest part of the left bank of the Ferrar Glacier. At the point where the ice of this glacier just begins to float in its narrow fjord-like channel there is an exposure of the limestone, which dips to the north-east at an angle of about 70°. The New Harbour Heights, as well as the north-western extremity of the foothills, are composed of hornblende-gneiss. The rock at the latter spot is dark, fine-grained, and very streaky; the foliations dip to the south-west at an angle of 60°—

a fact of some importance when we consider the dip of the rocks of New Harbour Heights, which is to the north-east.

At the foot of Cathedral Rocks, at a distance of forty miles from the coast and over 2,000 feet above sea level, there is an exposure of gneiss some 500 feet high and three miles long. There is a very sharp dividing line between the gneiss and the granite which overlies it, but numerous dykes of both grey and pink granite form a network over the face of the cliff. The cliff of gneiss is covered by the ice on the west side, and is cut off suddenly on the east by a tongue of granite ; and occasionally quite isolated patches and wisps of gneiss may be observed in the middle of a mass of this granite. The gneiss as a whole is dark in colour, being composed of thin laminæ, usually under a quarter of an inch thick, in which light and dark minerals are alternately dominant.

THE GRANITES.

Numerous fragments of granite rocks have been recorded from the Ross Sea area, but up to the time of the departure of the 'Discovery' Expedition nothing is recorded as to the occurrence *in situ* of this type of rock. Granites are very abundant in all the moraines from Cape Adare to Cape Crozier, and therefore must have a very wide distribution.

The first locality where this type of rock was found in place is in latitude 77° S., at the entrance to the so-called Granite Harbour. Here a prominent headland, two miles long and some 500 feet high, proved to be composed entirely of granite, and no other rock in contact with it was examined during the short time spent ashore here. The massif consists of an ordinary grey granite in which occur basic dykes and segregation veins. These segregation veins as a rule consist of a coarse-grained variety of granite with large pink idiomorphic crystals of feldspar. They are usually vertical and about ten yards wide, and shade off almost gradually on each side into the ordinary grey rock. It is noteworthy that the change from grey to pink is not quite gradual, but takes place in stages represented by bands a foot or so across, which is suggestive of a composite dyke. These bands become successively coarser and pinker from the edges towards the centre, and are separated from one another by smooth vertical joints.   Schistose, gneissic, and various hypabyssal rocks, as well as the ordinary dolerites and sandstones, occur as boulders on the narrow beach at the foot of this hill.

Between the Royal Society Range and the foothills several isolated knolls of granite occur, but they are almost completely buried in snow.

At a height of 5,500 feet Mr. Skelton collected a grey granite in which schistose veins had been developed dipping towards the south.   Again, at a height of 4,000 feet, he collected a somewhat coarse-grained pink granite with phenocrysts of feldspar up to a quarter of an inch across.   This exposure has suffered denudation, and it is here that the type of hollowed crystalline rock with the white incrustation occurs.   Mr. Prior kindly analysed parts of this incrustation for me, and tells me it consists mainly of carbonate of lime.

The hill on the east side of Descent Pass rises to a height of 4,900 feet, and consists mainly of granite with abundant large crystals of orthoclase, and here the second type of cavity occurs.   On the north side of this hill, and in the Ferrar Glacier, the same type of granite is found ; but in it occur basic dykes which, by weathering, produce black patches visible on the hillside at a distance of at least eight miles.

Dr. Koettlitz collected granitic and gneissic rocks from an exposure more than 3,000 feet above sea level in the transverse valley at the east foot of the Royal Society Range, while the author obtained quite a normal grey granite from one of the neighbouring isolated hillocks.

The gneiss of Cathedral Rocks is overlain by a mass of granite nearly 4,000 feet thick, which appears to build up this the northern extremity of the Royal Society Range.   Dykes of both grey and pink granite ramify into the gneiss, but as a whole the granite has nearly horizontal upper and lower surfaces, which can be traced round the spurs of the range for a distance of four or five miles up the south arm on the western side.   At the foot of the first of the three shoulders which go to form the Cathedral Rocks, a tongue of granite appears to burst through the gneiss from below. This tongue is mainly grey in colour, but great masses of pink feldspar rock seem to have been caught up in it ; but the masses become scarcer as one proceeds eastwards along the foot of the cliff. The connection of this granite with that of the hill on the east side of Descent Pass has not been established owing to the glaciers which descend from the valleys at the foot of the Camel's Hump.

Granite has been obtained from three spots on the north side of the Ferrar Glacier, or rather on the north side of the East Fork.

The mountain north-east of Cathedral Rocks rises to a fine gable nearly 7,000 feet high, but does not rise much above the mountains to the west, of which it is a part. The gable is about 5,000 feet above the ice, and of this height 4,000 feet appear to be of granite, and a specimen of augen-gneiss taken from the foot is probably a modification of the mass above. The dark rock producing the gable is separated from the granite by a very definite and almost horizontal line which may be traced westwards for over ten miles.

Half-way between this gable and the point where this group of hills terminates on the west, a dolerite has been found to lie directly upon the even surface of the granite. The former appears to have flowed out over the surface of the latter, and the contact plane dips to the west with an inclination of about 2°. The western end of this exposure of grey granite is hidden from view by a rise in the surface of the ice, but on gaining the western extremity of these hills a pink granite is found. This granite appears to be intrusive in the dolerite ; tongues of the former extend upwards into the latter, and the usual vertical columns of dolerite are very much disturbed.

Fifty miles inland, in the Dry Valleys, and at a height of 5,000 feet above sea level, small and large boulders of both grey and pink granite were found. These boulders were resting on the side of Beacon Height West on a surface of sandstone ; and since the hills to the southward rise to great heights, it is possible that granite occurs at a greater elevation than 5,000 feet. On the side of Knob Head Mountain great boulders of granite lie on a surface of dolerite, and as the mountain consists mainly of sandstone, these boulders must have their source further inland.

THE BEACON SANDSTONE FORMATION.

The existence of a fossiliferous sedimentary rock in South Victoria Land has always been considered probable since the 'Challenger' dredged up sandstones, limestones, and shales in a high southern latitude; but, on the whole, it seemed very doubtful whether the 'Discovery' would be able to encounter any of these, as it was thought the coastal belt of the land was composed entirely of volcanic rocks.

Granular sandstone fragments were dredged up by the 'Discovery' near Coulman Island, and the tabular structure of the Prince Albert Range pointed to the possibility of a sandstone rock being developed. Sandstone was also found in Granite Harbour, and when a broad band was observed extending horizontally from end to end of the Royal Society Range, it seemed probable that here a sedimentary rock would be found. Mr. Armitage's pioneer journey through the mountains proved the existence of plateau features as well as horizontal structure, and among the specimens he brought back were a quartz grit and an arkose. Therefore there was a very great possibility of fossiliferous sandstones, shales, or even limestones being developed locally. He reported the sandstone to reach a height of 8,000 feet, and to be accessible at a spot eighty miles inland and at the very edge of the inland ice.

Captain Scott therefore arranged that I should accompany him to the edge of the inland ice, and should do as much geological work as was possible on the return journey. At the second attempt to gain the inland ice, the parties were confined to their tents for a period of six and a half days. At the end of this time, November 11, 1903, I found I had a month in which to examine 600 square miles of new country and get back to the ship by December 12.

Accordingly, as soon as the gale abated, I made straight for Depot Nunatak. Utilising the outward journey as a reconnaissance, I knew that here the capping dolerite would be encountered, and possibly the very top of the Beacon Sandstone.

The latter was not exposed, but in the moraine at the base of the nunatak I found abundant masses of sandstone, the majority of which were locally blackened by what I took to be graphite.

My companions, Kennar (P.O.) and Weller (A.B.), had meanwhile spread out our gear in order to get rid of the moisture that had accumulated in it during the lie-up, and that night hopes ran high as, under the shelter of the nunatak, we exchanged *minus* temperatures and driving snow for bright sunshine and not more than thirty degrees of frost, and we all looked forward to finding something new. The next day, therefore, saw the camp at a spot about ten miles south-west of Finger Mountain, where 300 feet or so of the sandstone could be seen cropping out below the 500 feet of overlying dolerite. Imagine my delight when, taking bag and hammer up to the rock face, I discovered thin, irregular, black seams running through an almost pure sandstone. The seams here were in close proximity to the dolerite, and were therefore much charred ; so, after collecting the best specimens, a move was made diagonally down the valley to the Inland Forts, where 2,000 feet of sandstone was exposed. Here I hoped to find better specimens on the base of the sandstone or the surface on which it rested, but, after carefully examining 1,500 feet, no better specimens were obtained, nor was the old floor to be seen.

The Beacon Sandstone was also examined at the foot of Finger Mountain, in the Dry Valleys at the foot of Beacon Height West, and at the foot of Knob Head Mountain. In character it is marvellously uniform, and the horizontal bedding planes have seldom been tilted by the intrusive sheets of dolerite. Locally the beds have been disrupted, but, as masses have been lifted bodily, no great changes in the character of the rock have been produced.

The relation of the dolerite to the sandstone can perhaps be best studied at Finger Mountain. Here dykes are displayed cutting upwards across the bedding planes of the sandstone, sills forcing their way between the strata, or even pipes which appear to feed the superincumbent sheets.

The Beacon Sandstone as a whole is very uniform in texture but the grains of quartz are not very firmly packed together

Locally it becomes almost a quartz grit, or, again, arkose characters are developed. Current bedding and collections of quartz pebbles appear and disappear quite suddenly in the mass, and these may even form part of the carbonaceous seams. Only at one spot did the rock become calcareous, and the calcite, by cementing the quartz grains together, produced a more durable rock, which therefore projected as a shelf beyond the remainder.

This calcareous band is only about four inches thick, and as it occurs near the top of the sandstone, and as such abundant traces of organic matter occur in the sandstone blocks at the foot of Depot Nunatak, it is highly probable that this vicinity will yield more abundant organic matter than any other. A nunatak higher than Depot Nunatak, and about six miles from the south of it, displays dark bands in what is possibly the Beacon Sandstone, and this spot therefore may be worthy of closer examination in future.

The two following sections will give a general idea of the nature of the great Beacon Sandstone formation :

A. At a spot ten miles south-west of Finger Mountain—

(8) 700 feet   columnar dolerite.
(7) 200 „   almost pure sandstone with occasional pebbles.
(6)   2 „   carbonaceous band with fossils.
(5) 12 „   sandstone with brown bands.
(4) 12 „   hard white sandstone, with a three-inch fibrous strip.
(3) 12 „   black shale.
(2)   6 inches hard calcareous band.
(1)   6 feet   black shale.

B. At the Inland Forts—

(13) 100 feet dolerite cap.
(12) 200 „   white sandstone.
(11) 200 „   sandstone with ferruginous concretions.
(10) 200 „   yellow sandstone.
(9) 100 „   sandstone with rod-like impressions.

(8) 200 feet yellow sandstone with ferruginous concre-
        tions.
(7) 50 „ white sandstone.
(6) 200 „ yellow sandstone.
(5) 100 „ marble-like sandstone.
(4) 50 „ white sandstone.
(3) 10 „ sandstone with stalagmites.
(2) 60 „ almost white sandstone.
(1) 30 „ variegated brown and yellow sandstone.

THE DOLERITES.

The dolerites appear to be confined to the mainland, where
they occur as very extensive sheets, which in the main cap the
Beacon Sandstone. The top of these sheets, which probably
form the highest summits of the Royal Society Range, has not
been attained, and therefore there is no direct evidence that
surface flows have not been produced. As indirect evidence
we have the fact that no scoriaceous rock of any description
has been found in any of the moraines, and therefore it is
probable that no surface flows occur in this district.

It is convenient to commence at the highest point above
sea level, about 8,000 feet, from which doleritic rocks have been
obtained, and work down the great valley to the lowest point
where they occur, at a height of about 4,000 feet above sea
level.

Mr. Armitage, on the first journey through the Royal
Society Range, returned with weathered specimens of dolerite
from Depot Nunatak, and at the same time Mr. Skelton photographed the rock, which rises as a mass of great columns through
the snow. The rock is an outlier, and rears itself up to a height
of 500 feet above the snow, and the columns, which are continuous from top to bottom, are about twelve feet in diameter.
The Nunatak is about sixty miles from the coast, at an elevation of about 8,000 feet, and appears to be part of the great
sheet capping the sandstone five or six miles to the eastward.

This sheet, on the east side of the South-West Arm, is quite
similar in outward form to Depot Nunatak, and rises some
700 feet in an almost sheer cliff. Locally portions of sandstone

have been lifted bodily by the dolerite, and the junction specimens prove that the dolerite is the younger rock. A great pipe
fifty yards in diameter bursts vertically across the bedding
planes of the stratified rock, and appears to feed the sheet,
which extends continuously as far as Finger Mountain.

At the Inland Forts on the north side of the Ferrar Glacier
the hills rise to a very uniform height and are capped by
dolerite. Two or three small pipes rise through the sandstone,
but these could hardly have supplied an appreciable proportion
of the great mass above.

Finger Mountain rises 500 feet above the ice, and is composed of alternate layers of sandstone and dolerite. Near the
ice-cascade the lowest rock visible is part of the Beacon Sandstone formation, and above this is a sheet of columnar dolerite
which unites with another sheet on the west side of the hill.
These two sheets are partially separated by a wedge of sandstone half a mile long, and the wedge is 200 feet thick where it
is cut off by the eastern slope of the hill. The bedding planes
are horizontal, and are made conspicuous by the metamorphic
action of the dolerite. Where the dolerite sheets are in contact
the columns are continuous and vertical, but where the sandstone intervenes the columns of the upper portion have a slight
tilt to the west. Here also numerous dykes and sills prove the
intrusive nature of the dolerite.

These same relations were observed in the Dry Valleys and
on the Terra Cotta Hills, and need not be reiterated.

The summits of both the Beacon Heights, of New Mountain
and of Knob Head appear to consist of dolerite; and in all
four a second sheet, almost identical with the lower sheet in
Finger Mountain, separates 200 feet or so of sandstone from
the main mass which forms the greater bulk of the said
mountains.

At the foot of New Mountain and at the foot of Knob Head
there is another sheet of dolerite. The outcrop at the last spot,
which is 100 yards long and 200 feet high, exhibits columns about
twelve feet in diameter and between twenty and 200 feet in length.
There are occasional horizontal joints, but cup-and-ball structure
is not developed to any great extent. The sandstone appears to

rest upon the surface of this dolerite, but the junction of the two could not be discovered.

We have already seen that the mountains which separate the North from the East Fork are capped by dolerite, and that another sheet of dolerite, apparently arising at the western end, has flowed over a surface of granite. This last feature appears to be again developed in the Cathedral Rocks, for a black columnar rock is separated from the granite by a very definite line. Therefore dolerite probably helps to build the Cathedral Rocks as well as other parts of the Royal Society Range.

In Granite Harbour a dark rock lies unconformably upon the surface of a light-coloured one, and as the lower rock was proved to be granite, and boulders of dolerite were found on it, we may very reasonably assume that here also a sheet of dolerite lies upon an older mass of granite.

A few additional notes on the basaltic rocks of Cape Adare may be included here. It may be remarked that this Cape lies at the foot of the gigantic mountain range and possesses horizontal sheets of basalt, basaltic agglomerate and tuffs, and its rocks may therefore have some connection with the same rocks in Coulman Island and the other islands off the coast. The sheets consist of both olivine and hornblende bearing basalts which are occasionally cut through by vertical dykes.

This structure appears to be characteristic of the steep coastline between Cape Adare and Cape Jones, a distance of 150 miles. This part of the coast is a cliff varying in height from 500 to 1,000 feet, and always shows layers arranged more or less horizontally, making up the whole cliff. Low ·anticlines and synclines with east and west axes, occur at intervals along this piece of coast, and occasionally red bands could be distinguished which appear similar to those on Coulman Island or Cape Adare.

THE ICE.

The Sea-ice.—The term *Sea-ice* is perhaps the most suitable for all ice produced by the freezing of the sea, and it also draws a distinction between this ice and that which has another origin. In high latitudes the sea freezes over during the winter months often in a very uniform sheet. This sheet breaks up during the summer and floats north to form the pack-ice, which is usually encountered by exploring ships near the Antarctic Circle. The pack varies from year to year, and its structure in Arctic regions has been described by Dr. Drygalski and others. The first two inches frozen are composed of plates of ice lying horizontally. These plates are usually under half an inch across and are separated from the greater mass of ice by a half-inch layer of very confused crystals. The major part consists of bundles or sheaves of fibres arranged perpendicularly to the surface of freezing, and this fibrous structure extends to the bottom of any given floe.

The *salinity* of sea-ice seems to depend more upon the rate of freezing than upon the depth or distance from the upper surface. The amount of salt varies greatly, as may be seen if reference be made to our observations on the salinity of the sea-ice. The mean salinity is about 4·3 grammes of sodium chloride per litre of melted ice, but by fractional crystallisation a salinity up to 266·6 grammes per litre may be produced.

Snow accumulates on the surface of the ice, and by pressing it down below sea level weakens it ; and sometimes so much snow accumulates that a drift is formed which has its under surface dissolved by the sea during the ensuing summer. Thus, then, we see that it is possible for water substance to pass from the atmosphere back to the ocean without taking part in the glaciation of the land.

Hummocks are rather exceptional in the sea-ice of McMurdo Sound, but where the Ross ice-sheet moves in towards Winter Quarters Peninsula a great series of hummocks was produced some two miles long. These hummocks in the year 1903 rose to heights of from twelve to twenty feet above sea level, and were sometimes merely bucklings of the ice, or at other times were fractured slabs standing up vertically.

The *thickness* of the sea-ice varies according to circumstances. Where snow accumulates any thickness may be produced, but in an exposed spot, such as 100 yards off Hut Point, the thickness produced by freezing is under 8½ feet in the year. In Arrival Bay, where the land precludes a rapid circulation of the water, as much as ten feet has been produced by freezing alone. The following observations were made at the ice-gauge off Hut Point :

> *March* 1, 1903.—A water-hole, or an area uncovered by floe-ice.
>
> *April* 24, 1903.—Sun below the horizon ; thickness 3 feet.
>
> *August* 23, 1903.—Re-appearance of the sun ; thickness 3 feet 6 inches.
>
> *December* 5, 1903.—Nearly midsummer ; maximum thickness 8 feet 5½ inches.
>
> *January* 5, 1904.—Summer month ; thickness 5 feet 10 inches.
>
> *January* 28, 1904.—Air becoming colder ; a water-hole.

The ice is therefore dissolved from below, and the water-hole observed three years in succession off Cape Armitage is further proof of this action of the sea-water.

The sea-ice in McMurdo Sound gradually creeps north during the winter, but the ice-foot protecting the land prevents the sea-ice acting as an abrading or transporting agent to any great extent.

The *Shore-ice* may be taken to include all ice that fringes the shores of South Victoria Land and remains firmly frozen to them. Three types may be distinguished :

(*a*) The fringe due solely to the spray from the sea which freezes on the land. This is the 'typical ice-foot,' and owing to the small rise and fall of the tide its height never exceeds three feet. The chief function of this fringe is conservative, for it protects the beach from the action of floating ice and eroding breakers.

(*b*) There is a border of glacier-ice around the land of Winter Quarters. This ice has no apparent source. It slopes gently seawards, and ends as a cliff which varies in height from six feet to 300 feet, and the distance between the cliff and the bare land varies from ten yards to a mile. This fringe is even more effective than the ice-foot as a conservative agent, for its surface is inclined at an angle of less than 20°, and seldom allows stones to roll over it on to the sea-ice.

(*c*) The third type of shore-ice is more in the nature of

a " piedmont." The great snow-fan between the hills and the stranded moraines on the west side of McMurdo Sound may be taken as an example. This mass of snow is about ten miles long and five broad, and the whole of it is aground. It has no obvious source, and the surface rises from a few feet at the seaward edge to about 1,000 feet on the sides of the foothills. As it is practically motionless, it must afford a very material protection to the land.

THE LAND ICE.

The Inland Ice. — By the term inland ice we mean the uniform cloak of ice and snow of unknown extent which covers land of continental dimensions. In South Victoria Land this uniform covering has been met with on the west side of the Royal Society Range at a height of nearly 9,000 feet, and has been traversed by Captain Scott and party for a distance of about 200 miles. The inland ice drains eastwards through very deep and steep-sided valleys, and no nunataks have been observed far from the actual edge of the bare land. The Ferrar Glacier lies in one of these valleys, and it is remarkable that the ice from the hinterland which flows into the North Fork does not reach the sea, but ends in an insignificant cliff some distance from it. No gradual passage from granular snow to compact glacier-ice was observed at the edge of the inland ice ; the granular snow as a rule lies directly upon a corrugated surface of massive blue ice.

The inlets, which seem to be characteristic of the South Victorian mountain ranges, appear to be best developed south of latitude 79° S. The inland ice drains through these inlets, and augments the Ross Piedmont, or ice-sheet. The Prince Albert Mountains appear to be a fringe of land buttressing a vast interior ice-field. This ice drains into the Ross Sea through channels the breadth of which appears to be greater than the length, and therefore in form the ice-streams resemble the Greenland glaciers made familiar to us in Dr. Drygalski's work.

Local Ice-caps.—This type of ice-covering may be described as being continental on a small scale. The covering of snow on

Ross Island is a very good example of an Antarctic local ice-cap, and any features exhibited by it may be applied to the mantles of snow upon other isolated land masses.

On Mount Erebus, as on the mainland, there are streams of ice which drain radially and are separated from one another by nunataks. The streams of ice do not follow definite depressions that could be described as valleys, but descend to the sea in an almost uniform cloak. This cloak is interrupted along the margin of the land by hills of lava which have all the characteristics of nunataks. The streams, which thus become individualised, end in cliffs which vary in height between fifty and 200 feet, and occasionally give birth to icebergs.

Piedmonts.—Large areas of ice which lie at the foot of high land and which have no obvious single source may be described as ' piedmonts.'

(*a*) Three types may be distinguished, and the first may be termed a piedmont on land. The slope of snow west of the stranded moraines in McMurdo Bay should probably be included here, but as there is evidence that it is a relic of a once greater glaciation, it has been included with the more permanent developments of ' shore-ice.' Along the foot of the Prince Albert Range there appear to be many such snow-slopes, and together they produce a continuous series of piedmonts which coalesce almost imperceptibly with the great ice-streams flowing between the hills.

(*b*) The second type of piedmont is well represented on the sides of Coulman Island. The flat top of this island sheds its superfluous snow over the bare rock-cliffs, and produces along the base of the cliffs great snow-talus fans. These fans, which are sometimes separate, sometimes continuous, end as a cliff of ice in the sea. The outline of this cliff is an undulating line, and the height usually varies between fifty and 100 feet. This type may be called a ' piedmont aground,' because the ice is resting on the sea-bottom, and the bergs seem to be calved just at that point where the ice becomes water-borne.

(*c*) *Piedmonts afloat* are by far the most important and are represented by three very prominent examples—namely, the sheet of ice in Lady Newnes Bay, the sheet near Cape Gauss, and the great Ross Ice Sheet. All three have, as characteristics, a surface of great extent which may or may not be slightly undulating, a seaward edge forming a cliff between fifty and 200 feet high, and a depth of water at that edge which is without a doubt sufficient to float the ice. (As far as possible I have avoided using the word 'barrier,' as it does not imply area, and in preference employ the term 'sheet' in a restricted sense, as it does imply a plane superficies.) In this summary it is not necessary to marshal the evidence in favour of the view that these ice-sheets are afloat, and we will therefore conclude with the suggestion that the term 'piedmont afloat' is descriptive of this class of ice formation. No foreign matter was observed in the great ice-cliffs of these piedmonts, and no rock debris was met with on its surface either by Mr. Royds and Mr. Bernacchi on their journey south-eastwards, or by Captain Scott and his party on the great journey southwards. Soundings made in an area which was covered by ice only sixty-five years ago proved the sea-floor to be mainly rock-floor with occasional pebbles and diatoms, which show that the soles of these floating sheets do carry rock matter.

The Glaciers.

All Heim's types of glaciers may be recognised in South Victoria Land.

(a) The ice-streams, or the Greenland type of glacier, which have their source in the inland ice, end in the sea; these are present in great number in the Prince Albert Mountains, as well as in the succession of ranges forming the coast between latitudes 79° and 83° S. They also appear to be developed in the Admiralty Range, and there are two examples—the Ferrar Glacier and the Koettlitz Glacier—which lie north and south respectively of the Royal Society Range.

(b) The Norwegian type of glacier consists of streams of ice flowing down well-defined valleys from a large firn field. This is exemplified by the Blue Glacier, which arises in the Royal Society Range and ends in McMurdo Sound in a cliff some seventy or eighty feet high.

(c) Valley glaciers, or those of Alpine type, occur in great profusion in the Royal Society Range. Some of those flow into the Ferrar Glacier and blend with it, while others, such as the three flowing southwards into the North Fork, end some distance above the ice in the main valley.

(d) Cliff-glaciers are best represented on the left bank of the East Fork of the Ferrar Glacier, but others may be seen along the coast of South Victoria Land, notably on Cape Washington. The cliff-glaciers among the Royal Society Mountains often arise in corries and are often only an intermediate stage between a 'corrie' and a 'valley' glacier.

(e) The corrie-glaciers that are found at the foot of the Inland Forts are perhaps the most notable. Four occur here, and they fill up the cirques between the Forts. At present they flow southwards and are building up crescentic moraines around their terminal faces; whereas, at some former time, they drained northwards through cols into another valley-system.

(f) Ice-slabs occur among the foothills of the Royal Society Range, and consist of masses of ice about fifty feet thick, and four to six square miles in area. They appear to have been nourished by the Snow Valley until their supply was cut off by decrease of precipitation, and they now lie as relics among the comparatively ice-free hills.

ICEBERGS.

When the slow rate of movement of the glaciers of South Victoria Land is considered, we are driven to the conclusion that they do not supply an appreciable number of icebergs. Therefore the piedmonts afloat, which have been proved to move at the greatest rate, must supply the majority. If this is the case, then the preponderance of the well-known tabular form is not surprising. It has long been established that bergs travel with the ocean-currents, so that little need be said regarding the transport of rock-material by floating ice beyond stating that the drift is north up the coast of South Victoria Land; therefore any rock-fragment dredged from the sea-bottom in the Ross quadrant must have come from a point further to the south.

THE MORAINES.

The so-called beach at Cape Adare appears to be a collection of old moraines, and even on the summit of the cape at an altitude of 800 feet moraines and ice-scratched stones may be seen.

On Possession Island as well as in Wood Bay similar flat areas covered by moraines are said to occur, and Mr. Morrison's description of the beach on Franklin Island leads one to suppose that here also ice has played its part. These observations are in keeping with those made on Ross Island and elsewhere during our stay in the Antarctic, and the simplest explanation of the occurrence of isolated moraines in this frigid region is that the ice was once developed on a greater scale than at present. Other moraines have been seen near Cape Crozier, above the cliffs on the eastern side of Mount Terror, near Winter Quarters, and on the side of Mount Erebus above Cape Royds. The islands at the south end of McMurdo Sound, and also the ice between them, are literally buried in transported material.

Englacial rock debris is only encountered near the snouts of glaciers, where it is usually found in well-defined layers separated by almost pure ice. The Blue Glacier and the ice-slabs in the foothills of the Royal Society Range afford the best examples, and these are brought into prominence by the fact that thawing usually proceeds at a greater rate where ice and gravel occur together. In the channel at the foot of Knob Head, and also in the Dry Valleys near Finger Mountain, englacial matter may be seen below a layer of ice at least fifty feet thick. At the former locality two streams of ice flowing in opposite directions meet, glacial upthrust takes place, and the boulders which are raised to the surface form an ordinary medial moraine.

Supra-glacial material is very scarce if we take the Tasman Glacier of New Zealand, or the Zmutt Glacier of the Alps, to be normal. The lateral and medial moraines of the Ferrar Glacier consist of long lines of stones which are sometimes three feet in diameter, and are seldom accompanied by finer material. These lines are usually about thirty yards in width, and the larger boulders are generally five or six feet apart.

The stranded moraines both on Cape Royds and on the mainland often have a core of ice, and it is often difficult to make sure what proportion of a given moraine is formed of rock matter. During the summer this ice melts, and the finer material is separated from the boulders and gravel by water action, so that stratified and false-bedded sands and gravels are now being produced in an area which is virtually the centre of a continental ice-sheet.

Among the moraines on the west side of McMurdo Sound, as well as on one of the Dellbridge Islands, and among the moraines on the west side of Discovery Gulf, great deposits of sodium sulphate in well-formed crystals have been found. Among the isolated moraines in the bay between Black and White Islands, large bosses or mounds of the same white salt have been seen ; and at one spot near White Island a mass of perfect crystals was found on the surface of pure ice. In the White-Black Island Bay balanus′ shells and sponge spicules occurred upon the ice in association with this salt. The occurrence of this salt, mingled with shells and ice-scratched stones, is a freak of Nature which is difficult to explain.

Temperatures at fixed depths in the ice fringing the land around Winter Harbour were determined during the year 1903. It will suffice here to note that the highest temperature recorded at a depth of six feet was −9° C., and the lowest −24·4° C. The change throughout the year was very gradual : the minimum reading was made some time after midwinter, and the maximum in January.

Observations of temperature in crevasses at greater depths show that the seasonal variations occur at considerably later date than the corresponding air temperatures, and that the maximum temperature reached by the ice is far below its freezing-point. One observation may be quoted in conclusion : Crevasse near the meeting-point of the ice of the South-West Arm and of the main stream from the inland ice, November 3, 1903, 7 P.M., depth thirty feet.

Temperature of the air, +20° F. (−6·7° C.)
„   „   ice, −21° F. (−29·4° C.)

DENUDATION.

Wind.—The winds of South Victoria Land prove to be as strong and as constant as any oceanic trade-wind. Around Winter Quarters the bare land surfaces are usually covered by a loose cloak of rock debris quite six inches deep. Below this depth the earth is permanently frozen throughout the year, and from this zone rocks with fresh unweathered fractures may be obtained. The wind removes all the finer disintegration products, so that the exposed surfaces are always composed of stones loosely packed together, which protect a mixture of small stones and impalpable powder beneath. These loose stones are often smoothed and pitted in the manner peculiar to wind-worn stones, and some of the harder ones have a superficial glaze on their exposed surfaces.

In the Snow Valley at the foot of the Royal Society Range there are granite boulders which have become hollowed by some agent which may be aided by wind. These hollowed blocks resemble cavities in Corsica and elsewhere, to which reference has already been made.

Water.—In the area covered by our observations the effect of water as an agent of denudation is limited. On the sides of glaciers and among the moraines it serves to separate the gravel from the finer material and to distribute the latter over the surface of the ice. On the north-east side of Brown Island its present-day effects are most marked, for after a summer snowfall in January 1903 thawing took place at such a rate that cascades were produced. These coursed down the hillside in narrow channels and spread mud and sand in deltaic form over the lower slopes.

On the sides of the Ferrar Glacier, the streams that are produced during the summer follow channels between the ice and the rock, and in this way must undercut such cliffs as the Cathedral Rocks.

The presence of the Beacon Sandstone formation proves that water in times past had at any rate an important constructive action, and even since the deposition of the sandstone and the intrusion of the plateau dolerites, water seems to have had a destructive effect upon the original plateaux of the Royal Society Range.

Chemical Action.—Decomposition of rocks by chemical action is more obvious in the dry climate of South Victoria Land than in other areas where rain removes the soluble salts as soon as they are formed. The common occurrence of soluble crystalline salts in the moraines has already been mentioned, and perhaps the fact that many ponds among the moraines are extremely saline to the taste suggests a clue to the peculiar distribution of the soluble matter.

Frost Action.—In high southern latitudes the precipitation of water-substance is very small, and therefore frost-riven rock masses are not very conspicuous. As wind usually removes thin coverings of snow from bare rock surfaces, it is only on the edges of local snow-fields that thawing and freezing can take place with any degree of regularity. Snow is drifted by the wind on to the north side of Castle Rock during the winter, and during the summer great masses of rock are split off and litter the area at its foot. Cathedral Rocks likewise face north, and appear to be more subject to frost-action than the more isolated peaks of the Western Mountains.

The Action of Ice.—The types of surface clearly due to ice action are rather inconspicuous. A few *roches moutonnées* have been observed in Granite Harbour and on the foothills of the Royal Society Range, but owing to the extremely low mean annual temperature the ice appears to be more conservative than erosive in its action.

Transport has taken place on a great scale in the past, but now, owing to the almost stagnant condition of the ice, it has practically ceased. The icebergs, which appear remarkably free from foreign matter, are the chief agents of transport at present, and, as we have seen, they always carry matter from a higher to a lower latitude. So great is the quantity of loose rock material on the surface of the land that one is tempted to speculate on the effect that would be produced if a slight increase of the ice were to bodily remove this covering and distribute it over the clayey floor of the Ross Sea.

In conclusion, it is my pleasant duty to briefly express my thanks to Captain R. F. Scott, R.N., C.V.O., D.Sc., &c., and the officers of the ' Discovery,' who, by their interest in my work, and their ever-ready help, were a very material assistance to me. The photographs taken by Lieutenant-Engineer R. W. Skelton, R.N., are invaluable, and by them I was able to decide before leaving the ship what localities would repay close examination. The kindly interest Captain Scott took in my work and the arrangements he made for me were more than I could possibly have expected. To Mr. W. G. Fearnsides, M.A., F.G.S., Fellow of Sidney Sussex College, and to Mr. Bernard Smith, B.A., of Sidney Sussex College, my thanks are due for many valuable suggestions. Lastly, I am indebted to Mr. R. H. Rastall, B.A., F.G.S., of Christ's College, for reading the manuscript and suggesting many improvements in the text.

APPENDIX II

ON THE WHALES, SEALS, AND BIRDS OF ROSS SEA AND SOUTH VICTORIA LAND

By EDWARD A. WILSON, M.B., F.Z.S., Zoologist on the
National Antarctic Expedition

THERE are no land mammals, properly so called, within the Antarctic Circle. There are no South Polar bears ; there are no Antarctic foxes ; there no large mammals of any sort or kind save whales, which live entirely in the water, and seals, which spend more than half their time there.

Geology has not disclosed to us any lost Antarctic mammalian fauna, although it has suggested to us the possibility that at one time there was a climate, and perhaps a vegetation, that might have suited it. There are deep and difficult questions upon which it appears right to hold whatever theory best suits our immediate requirements, as to the various connections and communications, whether of land or ice, which have or have not existed between all or any of the Southern Hemisphere land masses and the Antarctic continent. There is every probability that in some bygone age the Antarctic land mass acted as a bridge between some of the Southern continents, but whatever it may have done of service in the distribution of types for them, it has apparently done little or nothing for itself. Separated now by some hundreds of miles of very stormy ocean from the nearest habitable lands, with currents of wind and water all setting in precisely the wrong direction, it maintains an almost perfect barrenness.

The Antarctic continent now boasts of a vegetation which includes a few low forms of moss and lichen, and a terrestrial fauna which consists of one minute and primitive form of wingless insect. Of the whales and seals and birds, the last-named alone have any pretension at all to a terrestrial habit of life, in that they use the moraines and rocky cliffs of the continental shores as nesting sites. But they are all pelagic sea-birds.

Yet in this exceedingly unpromising land of barren rock and ice there are forms of life which are to be met with nowhere else, and in this very fact lies the interest that attaches to a study of the Antarctic fauna.

To begin with the mammals, there are whales and seals ; and of these a somewhat surprising number of different species. In Ross Sea alone we met no fewer than seven different whales and dolphins. In Ross Sea also we found five different kinds of seal, and as many as twelve different species of bird. Of these at least half are known to make use of the coasts of South Victoria Land for nesting.

Of the whales, the most prominent of all are the Killers, or Orca whales, which scour the seas and the pack-ice in hundreds to the terror of seals and penguins. The Killer is a powerful piebald whale of some fifteen feet in length. It hunts in packs of a dozen, or a score, or sometimes many scores. No sooner does the ice break up than the Killers appear in the newly formed leads of water, and the penguins show well that they appreciate the fact by their unwillingness to be driven off the floes. From the middle of September to the end of March these whales were in McMurdo Strait, and the scars that they leave on the seals, more particularly on the Crab-eating seal of the pack-ice, afford abundant testimony to their vicious habits. Not one in five of the pack-ice seals is free from the marks of the Killer's teeth, and even the Sea Leopard, which is the most powerful seal of the Antarctic, has been found with fearful lacerations. Only the Weddell seal is more or less secure, because it avoids the open sea. Living, as it does, quite close in shore, breeding in bights and bays on fast ice some ten or twenty miles from the open water, it thus avoids the attacks of the Killer to a large extent.

Two other dolphins are commonly to be seen on the out-

skirts of the Ross Sea pack-ice. Of these one is known as the
Dusky dolphin, a very handsomely marked animal, with dark
brown back and whitish under-parts.

The other is an allied species that has hitherto been undescribed. We were not able to procure one, though many attempts
were made with the harpoon, but as all these dolphins, the
Killer included, are easily seen as they play in herds around the
ship, the fact that the back and belly are dark brown, and the
sides have two white patches like an hour-glass, sufficiently
distinguishes the animal from any other that is known. It is
not well to name a beast that has not been captured, but for
convenience sake amongst ourselves we called it the ' Hour-glass
dolphin.' It never was seen to associate with the Dusky form,
though both occurred in herds about the same latitude and
longitude, and both were much the same in size—from eight to
ten feet long—and of a similar colouration.

We saw also a very large number of Rorquals in Ross Sea,
but not a single Right whale. When Sir James Ross reported
large numbers of the latter in the seas of South Victoria Land,
considerable hopes of a new and valuable whaling ground were
raised, and a number of whaling ships left Dundee for the Antarctic. But their hopes were not realised, for no Right whale
was either seen or taken where Ross had seen so many.

The real reason for this has been an open question ever
since ; and the explanations given vary between a lack of faith
in Sir James Ross's power to identify the Right whale on the
one hand, and, on the other, a belief that the animal which
had been hunted almost to extermination in more northern
waters had disappeared in consequence from the Antarctic ; or,
thirdly, perhaps, that it had changed its summer feeding-grounds
to seas still less accessible than these.

Whichever is the true explanation, the fact remains that
no one has since seen a Right whale in Ross Sea. It still
occurs in the more northern waters, round Chatham and Camp-
bell Islands, and in the Southern oceans generally, but apparently
it avoids the ice.

The Rorqual, on the other hand, is abundant. Hardly a day
passed, in cruising along the coasts of South Victoria Land, but

one or two, and sometimes a much larger number, were seen. Near the Balleny Islands they were for some days particularly in evidence, and the broad, blue slate-coloured back, with its small dorsal fin, was almost constantly in sight, while the spout was to be seen on all hands, a high jet of condensed vapour rising vertically for twelve or fifteen feet into the cold grey air. The Rorqual, or Blue whale, as it is called, has a habit of appearing at the surface to blow without showing the dorsal fin at all. This has led to the belief that Sir James Ross mistook it for the Right whale. But as one watches the Rorqual, one sees that before each deeper sounding the dorsal fin comes plainly into view, and it is hardly to be believed that experienced whalers whom Ross had with him on the 'Erebus' could have made such a mistake as this. The spout of the Rorqual, moreover, is characteristically high, single, and upright, whereas the spout of the Right, or Whalebone whale, is definitely shorter and divided into two to form a double spout.

There are still two other forms of Finner whales which must be mentioned : the one, a round-backed, black, and solitary whale of from twenty to thirty feet, with a very small hook-like dorsal fin ; and the other, in direct contrast to this, a gregarious whale having a dorsal fin of quite enormous length and prominence. This latter, which was apparently noticed in Ross Sea by MacCormick as well as Ross, has not been named. No example has yet been taken. It is a square-headed whale of some twenty feet in length, black above, but white, so far as we could see, beneath the throat. The dorsal fin, which comes well out of the water, must have been between two and three feet in height, long, curved, and pointed, somewhat like a sabre. There was no possibility of mistaking it for the only other high-finned form, the Killer, for the ochre-coloured saddle of the Killer and the buff patch on the head are recognisable even at a distance. The shape of the head, too, is more pointed in the Killer, and its movements far more active and restless than those of the High-finned black whale.

Beaked whales were also to be seen in schools from time to time, and we had the good fortune in McMurdo Strait to see one 'breeching.' The whole school of whales, about ten in number, was blowing and splashing in the bay, when suddenly we saw one of them leap clean out of the water and fall back with a resounding splash.

It would be unwise to attempt to give specific names as yet to these various whales, but if, as may some day happen, their study should be more systematically taken up, it may be of use to know that there are at least these seven different species that I have mentioned to be found within the limited area of Ross Sea alone, and that two, at any rate, are new, and at present undescribed.

Leaving now the whales, we come to a group of animals, which are very typical of the polar regions. There are five species of Antarctic seals, of which three are only to be found within the Circle. These are the Crab-eating or White seal (*Lobodon carcinophagus*), the Ross seal (*Ommatophoca rossi*), and the Weddell seal (*Leptonychotes weddelli*). Of the other two, the Sea Leopard (*Stenorhynchus leptonyx*) and the Sea Elephant (*Macrorhinus leoninus*), the former is constantly to be found in the pack-ice, though it wanders more or less freely to the shores of all the Southern ocean continents and islands.

But the Sea Elephant has not the same right to be included in the Antarctic list as the others, since his occurrence there is almost certainly accidental, just as the occasional occurrence of the Weddell seal in Kerguelen Island and the river Santa Cruz must also be considered as purely accidental. The Crab-eater also has been reported twice from Australia, both accidental occurrences of a typical Antarctic species in temperate regions, and to be explained by the fact that large masses of ice drift up into more northern waters from the south, no doubt very often with seals upon them. It is less easy to account for the appearance of the Sea Elephant so far south as latitude 77°50′, in McMurdo Strait, for the animal must have traversed some hundreds of miles of open sea against the prevailing winds and ocean currents.

That seals do travel long distances by sea is obvious, and a fact well known to sealers, but it is curious to find one so far from its usual home as this. The headquarters of the Sea

Elephant are the Macquarie, Kerguelen, and other islands of the Southern oceans, as well as the coast of California.

The one Sea Elephant which fell to our lot in the Antarctic was a young male of eleven feet in length and a girth of no less than eight feet under the fore flippers. He was the only example seen, and was discovered as he lay asleep on a sandy beach at Cape Royds. The stomach itself was empty of food, as also were the intestines, which were contracted into firm, hard cords, and contained only a few threadworms ; yet the seal was heavily blubbered, having upwards of two inches of fat under the skin all over. The Sea Elephant, as we had the opportunity of seeing also on the Macquarie Islands, uses his fore flippers much more as do the Eared seals than the Earless, both for support and for progression. The colour of the beast is a uniform dirty yellowish grey, somewhat darker along the back than underneath, and without either spots or streaks ; the head is enormous. The lion-like breadth of the flattened muzzle, the wide gape of the mouth showing a huge pink cavern, with massive canines, the immensity of the neck and shoulders raised high on the fore flippers, the very large brown eyes, and the protruding nostrils, all combine to give a most characteristic appearance to this seal which distinguishes it at once from all the others.

The nostrils are extensile sacs which give the appearance of a short proboscis to the animal when much excited, and the openings, when at rest, instead of facing upwards, as in the other Antarctic seals, look straight ahead from an enormous width of muzzle. It has a peculiar habit of throwing up the head and tail simultaneously, while it gives vent to a hoarse and wide-mouthed roar which is intended to dismay the onlooker as the seal himself makes clumsy efforts to retire.

The animal, as is now well known, is becoming very scarce ; it was a few years ago within the danger limits of extinction, thanks to the thoughtless methods of the sealers who worked on the Southern ocean islands. There is now, however, a close time which protects the animals to some extent, and although it is now almost impossible to find the older full-grown males there are still in certain favoured spots a large number of young males and females.

The Sea Leopard is, after the Sea Elephant, the least strictly polar of the Antarctic seals. It is to be met with, however, fairly constantly in the pack-ice, but always solitary. It runs to twelve feet in length, and may have a girth beneath the flippers of six feet. Its head is large in proportion to its body, and holds a most formidable array of teeth. It is very long and snake-like, and most admirably adapted to move rapidly under water, where its diet, as we verified by examining the contents of the stomach, includes not only fish and Emperor penguins, but, when occasion offers, the young of the other more harmless kinds of seal.

It is, as a rule, dark grey, with blacker back, and rich black and silver splashes on the flanks and shoulders. There is, in some cases, a tendency to a tawny colour in the under-parts and flippers, but the most sure way of determining the species, as it is of every other species, is to examine the teeth. In this animal the canines and the incisors, particularly the outer incisors of the upper jaw, are very large, recurved, and powerful. The post canines, five on each side above and below, are powerful three-lobed tridents, admirably made for catching and holding fish and tearing flesh to pieces. This seal is a carnivore of the most aggressive type, and probably in the Antarctic has but one enemy to fear, and that enemy is the still more aggressive carnivorous dolphin, the Orca or Killer whale.

The Crab-eater, the common White seal of the Antarctic pack-ice, is the most variable in appearance of all the Southern seals. In the summer months it is possible to find a group of chocolate-brown seals with a very beautiful silver sheen and handsome dappling on the sides of the neck and flanks and shoulders. The flippers may be a rich dark brown with blacker shades, and nothing on the whole could be less appropriate than to call the animal white. Again, one may find an individual with a chestnut dappling on a creamy-coloured coat, with a long line of chocolate colour down the centre of the back. This animal would be moulting, and by casting off the coat which has been bleached to a creamy white, would become converted into the dark and handsome silvery-coated seal described above. But in an old seal the coat may have become bleached to such an extent as to have lost all trace of the characteristic dappling on the flanks and shoulders. In this condition it is as nearly white as possible. It is not so large as either of the seals that I have yet described, nor is it nearly so large as the Weddell seal, which will be mentioned later on. The Crab-eater runs to about eight feet in length, and is one of the most active seals in all its movements. It lives almost entirely upon a shrimp-like crustacean which it collects in large numbers with mud and gravel by grouting along the bottom of shallow seas or along the submerged foot of an iceberg. The use of the extraordinary development of the lobes of the post canine teeth in this seal was suggested by Captain Barrett Hamilton, in an article on the seals of the 'Southern Cross' collection. These lobes, as he pointed out, form a sieve when the jaws are closed, through which the water can be ejected from the mouth, while the mud and crustaceans are retained and swallowed. There is probably some object to be served in the swallowing of mud and gravel with the food, as it is a habit common to many of the seals, and the most probable object to be gained by so doing is the trituration of the shells and bones of the fish and crustaceans which form their staple diet.

The Crab-eater, or White seal, is to be found in little groups of from three to four or six, lying out in the sun on the floes of the Ross Sea pack; and in this tendency to collect in companies it differs markedly from the next one to be mentioned, the Ross seal, which has, without exception, always been found alone.

The Ross seal is the smallest of all, and is not often found of a greater length than seven or eight feet. It is a blackish or brownish grey above, and lighter below, with the chin and throat in some quite pale, in others black, and a number of paler streaks pass obliquely backwards along the sides of the neck to the hinder third of the body.

This seal has the most astonishing power of withdrawing its head within the blubber-laden skin of the neck till its face is almost lost. Its vocal powers have been well described by M. Racovitzi, of the 'Belgica.' As the Weddell seal, so far as our own observations go, has vocal accomplishments of even a higher order than the Ross, I will reserve my description of them till we come to deal with the species later on.

Until the return of the recent Argentine Expedition no young Ross seal had ever been discovered. The precise age of the one brought home by that expedition has not yet transpired. It is likely, however, that the skull may throw fresh light upon an interesting question in this connection—namely, the relationship which apparently exists, and has been before this suggested by Captain Barrett Hamilton, between the *Ommatophoca* and the more Northern forms *Cystophora* and *Macrorhinus*.

The teeth of Ross's seal are still a puzzling problem. It is obvious that the post canines are in process of disappearing, for in those cases in which they have not already gone they are as often as not quite loose and ready to drop out. The canines and incisors alone have been properly developed into needle-pointed recurved hooks for dealing with such slippery prey as jelly-fish and squids, which apparently form their food.

There is now only one more form of seal to be described, and to ourselves it was the most important of all, for it provided us with a fresh meat diet in abundance during the greater part of our sojourn in the ice. The Weddell seal is the most sluggish of all, and is to be found only along the coastline. It herds together in a manner which must be considered thoroughly gregarious. In the breeding season, which occupies October and November, there are colonies at the head of bights and bays in the fast and unbroken ice, which number in some cases many hundreds of seals, scattered often over a very vast area, along a crack which runs perhaps for miles across the strait or bay.

The Weddell seal avoids the pack-ice of the open sea, and so avoids the attentions of the Killer whale, and can procure its food, which consists of fish, without either fear or molestation.

The wisdom of this course is obvious, and accounts for the absence in this seal of the scars and rents which disfigure so many of the Crab-eaters.

In McMurdo Sound we had an abundance of Weddell seals around us throughout the summer months, and as they spent most of their time in sleeping on the ice outside their blow-holes, there was no difficulty whatever in supplying the ship's company with meat.

But in the winter months there was often a scarcity, as the seals preferred to remain in the water below the ice, breathing and sleeping at their blow-holes, and along the coastal tide-cracks, instead of coming up to lie in the bitter wind and lower temperatures that were constant during the darkness of the winter. At this time it was found feasible by certain of the crew to harpoon them as they came up to breathe, and land them on the ice with a line; and the contents of the stomach on these occasions proved especially interesting, as they included whole fish just swallowed of a kind which we were unable in any other way to obtain.

The Weddell seal is perhaps the most handsome of all that I have mentioned. Measuring upwards of nine to ten feet, and having a girth of from six to seven, this enormous beast has a coat richly marked with black and grey and silvery white; the upper parts are the darkest, but below these shades are blended in a most striking manner.

In character the seal is wholly devoid of fear until actually and intentionally annoyed or frightened. Lying on the ice by its open breathing hole, as often on its back as on its belly, it will merely wake to glance at the strange intruder and then often go to sleep again. At times it exhibits a certain amount of nervousness and rolls over the better to gaze at the disturber of its peace, blinking and blowing through its nostrils the while in an unwonted endeavour to realise the unusual condition of things before it. Sometimes it is induced to lope away, with suspicious glances over its back from time to time, to see whether anyone is following. If this actually happens, it may get really scared, and losing all its dignity at once, may hurriedly flop itself along with a breathless, quivering, blubber-burdened haste, which shows how seldom the necessity for speed arises except in its aquatic life.

The young of the Weddell seal, the only species whose breeding habits we were able to observe, were born during the last week of October and the beginning of November. They lay on the ice at the mouth of the blow-holes, which the parents kept open for the purpose of procuring food. The old seals showed very little fear, and would generally allow us to handle their young without much tendency to interfere.

The young were born in a thick and woolly coat of dull ochre grey and black, showing something of the markings which would appear later on in the adult. This woolly coat began to drop off at the end of fourteen days, and by the end of a month the moult was finished. The young seal, attired now in a very handsome coat of glossy black and silver hair, could for the first time enter the water and take a share in finding its own food. Still, for a variable time, these young were suckled on the ice, but sooner or later they would be separated from their parents, and from that time onward would lead an independent life. The Weddell seal takes at least two years to arrive at full maturity, and the size of the animal appears to increase considerably for many years, if one may judge by the immensity of some of the oldest breeding bulls and cows, compared with what were evidently younger ones.

The teeth of the Weddell are less strikingly adapted to a special food than are those of the Crab-eater or the Ross ; but the incisors are again recurved and hook-like, to assist the canines in procuring fish. The bigger teeth in an old seal are often broken and worn down almost to the gums by the habit of using them to enlarge the blow-holes in the ice. On several occasions this habit was actually watched in progress, and the action was somewhat like that of a centre-bit, the central fixed point being the sharp teeth of the lower jaw, while the upper jaw was revolved upon it.

The bulls have desperate fights with one another for the possession of the females, and their coats are cut to pieces by December. From head to tail they are at this time covered with ugly sores, and are to be found in secluded corners amongst the hummocks of ice-pressure ridges, often apparently feeling far from well, and unwilling to fight again.

Old seals at the point of death retire to the most secluded spots. It was therefore not altogether unaccountable to find the remains of dead seals many miles from the actual coast, and

high up on the biggest glaciers.   Almost all the sledging
expeditions which made their way to the west up the glaciers of
the Royal Society's range of mountains found these dead seals ;
and they included not Weddells only, but Crab-eaters, of which
we saw only very few in McMurdo Sound during the whole two
years that we were quartered there.   Not one, but several, were
found by Armitage at a height of 2,000 feet, and between twenty
and thirty miles from the actual coast.

I have already mentioned the Weddell seal as a rival of the
Ross in its powers of producing vocal music.   It was a constant
source of amusement to us to stir up an old bull Weddell and
make him sing ; he would begin sometimes with a long and
musical moan at a high pitch, which gradually got lower and
sounded much like the ice-moans that are common on an extensive sheet of ice.   This was followed by a series of grunts and
gurgles, and a string of plaintive piping notes, which ended up
exactly on the call-note of a bullfinch.   Then came a long, shrill
whistle, and a snort to finish, as though he had for too long held
his breath.

All this was leisurely, and interrupted with the sleepy blinking that characterised his half-awakened consciousness of something strange and unusual in the look of the observer standing
near him ; one could not but wonder how long the impression
of such a novelty would last upon the memory of a seal, for
while one watched and wondered he would fall asleep again,
and be just as puzzled if he was awakened two minutes later.

We were well situated to observe the Weddells, as they were
with us throughout the year, but of the others we saw much less
for the reasons given above.   There is no probability that any
new form remains to be discovered, and the breeding habits of
the others will become known only to such as have the luck of
wintering in the pack-ice as did the ' Belgica.'   And it is my
belief that the pack-ice around Cape North and the Balleny
Islands is one of the strongholds of the Ross.

There is no doubt that so far as birds were concerned our
position in 78° S. latitude was too far south.

Although in the pack-ice and during our cruise along the
coast of South Victoria Land we saw twelve different species of

bird, this number, except for an occasional straggler, was reduced to three in our winter quarters. At the mouth of McMurdo Sound we saw occasionally a few Giant petrels, Snow petrels, and Wilson's Stormy petrels, but where the ship was wintered, ten or twenty miles farther to the south, they were very rarely seen. In the pack-ice and in the Ross Sea we saw the Southern Fulmar petrel (*Priocella glacialoides*) and the Antarctic petrel (*Thalassœca antarctica*), but not in McMurdo Sound.

On the outskirts of the pack we saw besides a few small whisps of Tern, a Sooty albatross or two, a Black-browed albatross or two, and a few of the blue-grey Whale-birds; but all these left us as we entered the denser pack, and were not seen again till our return more than two years later.

From the first day till the last on which we encountered ice, we saw no other birds but those that I have mentioned; and except for a few hours on shore at Cape Adare, where we found the little Wilson's Stormy petrel nesting, we had no opportunity of investigating the nesting habits of any of them, except of the three that were with us in McMurdo Sound.

Nevertheless, what could be written of the three birds that we had there would alone suffice to fill a volume, and we consider ourselves exceedingly fortunate in that the Emperor penguin was one of them; for no one had previously seen its breeding grounds, nor had anyone been enabled to throw any material light upon its habits since the time that the bird was first discovered.

The second of our trio was the other most typical Antarctic penguin, the Adélie Land penguin (*Pygoscelis adéliæ*), which bred at Cape Crozier, within our reach, and had there one of the largest rookeries of the species that is known. We had also on Cape Royds, at the mouth of McMurdo Sound, another small rookery, or breeding colony, and we were thus well placed for making further observations on this bird. And of the third, the McCormick's skua (*Megalestris maccormicki*) we saw no end, and were able to investigate a very large number of its nesting sites.

Now, of all the birds that I have mentioned, the Emperor

penguin's history is by far the most interesting and important. I will therefore deal first with the others, and write somewhat more fully of the Emperor below.

The nesting places of a large number of the petrels, even in temperate climes, are still unknown, and in our hasty visit to South Trinidad we were able to procure the eggs and young of two petrels, neither of which had been obtained before. It is therefore not surprising to find that the eggs and young of the Antarctic petrel (*Thalassæca antarctica*) are still unknown ; nor have any of the recent expeditions succeeded in finding them. Yet the bird is plentiful not only in the pack-ice but throughout Ross Sea, and particularly in very large numbers first about the Possession Islands, and then in a very local area about King Edward's Land, at the extreme eastern end of Ross's Great Ice Barrier, where a search for the nesting grounds might quite possibly be well repaid.

It is, further, a fact not widely understood that this bird leaves the Antarctic Seas during the winter months, and is then to be found in large numbers in the South Pacific Ocean, away from ice and out of sight of icebergs.

The blue-grey Southern Fulmar petrel (*Priocella glacialoides*), a bird of wider range, is to be seen during the winter months in large numbers about the Magellan Straits. In the summer it is constantly met with in the pack, but, so far as is known, does not breed within the Circle. We saw it more abundantly around the Balleny Isles than elsewhere, and its absence was particularly noticeable south of Cape Adare—so much so that along the coast of South Victoria Land and in McMurdo Sound it was never seen.

The Wilson's Stormy petrel (*Oceanites oceanicus*) is to be found in Ross Sea throughout the summer months, but very rarely came so far south as McMurdo Sound. We discovered its burrow on Cape Adare, and after excavating it sufficiently to admit an arm, we found a nest of penguins' feathers on hard blue ice, with two adult birds, a male and a female, a fresh egg, an addled egg, and a flattened dead bird under all.

This little petrel is a great wanderer in the Northern Hemisphere as well as in the South, and we ourselves twice saw it apparently exploring the Great Ice Barrier in latitude 78° some twenty miles from the nearest open water, where alone it could find its food, which consists of minute crustaceans.

The Snow petrel (*Pagodroma nivea*) is perhaps the most beautiful of all the Southern petrels. In size about as big as a turtle dove, it is pure white all over, with black eyes and bill and feet. It hovers about the ship often in considerable flocks, and was our most constant companion so long as we had ice in sight during the summer months of cruising. It was a rare visitor to our winter quarters, and, so far as we could discover, did not breed in McMurdo Sound. Its eggs were taken by McCormick on the Cockburn Islands, and since then by members of the 'Southern Cross' expedition on Cape Adare. It drops down most daintily to pick up little shrimp-like crustaceans from the ice-floes as they are stranded by the breaking surf.

There is a question of much interest in the reason for the individual variation in the size of this bird, which varies between wide limits, apparently without anything corresponding to it in its geographical distribution.

The largest of all the petrels is the Giant (*Ossifraga gigantea*), which is also one of the most variable of species. It is very commonly white in the Antarctic, although the normal colouration in more temperate regions is a dark greyish brown or black. The reason for this is still unknown, but it seems probable that, apart from all question of avoiding enemies or procuring food, there is an inherent tendency in polar species to take on the Arctic dress. One wonders in the same connection what point there can be in the pure white dress of the Snowy petrel.

The Giant petrel is a great scavenger, and lives principally on carrion refuse even in the South, finding an abundance about the penguin rookeries. It is a very large and ungainly bird, with a composite yellow bill, which looks as though it had many ways of opening. It is often to be seen squatted on the ice-floes, gorged by a full meal of blubber from a dead seal. On finding itself pursued it will deliberately disgorge before it attempts to fly, knowing from experience that even a lengthy run will not enable it to rise and fly away except on an empty stomach. It has never as yet been known to breed on South Victoria Land, and in our winter quarters it was only a rare summer visitor.

Before dealing with the penguins, it remains for me to say something about the one gull which was our constant companion throughout the summer in McMurdo Sound. McCormick's skua (*Megalestris maccormicki*) is a large brown gull with a white patch on each wing. Often as the bird advances in age the moult appears to be deferred, and the feathers become bleached and weathered to a very marked degree—so much so that the head and breast become almost white instead of brown. McCormick's skua is closely allied to the sub-Antarctic species, but is nevertheless distinct. It is smaller than *Megalestris antarcticus*, and has a well-marked golden collar, which is very distinctive in adults but is absent in the young. The bird breeds all along the coasts of South Victoria Land and on all the islands, in company with the Adélie penguins, on whose eggs and chicks it preys. On the gravelly ground it lays two eggs, which are brown or greenish, with spots and blotches of a darker brown and purple grey. The chicks are grey, with pale blue bills and feet and legs, and it is a very noteworthy fact that although two chicks are always hatched, not more than one is ever reared. This is due no doubt to the fact that its neighbours do not discriminate between the eggs and chickens of their own and other species of bird, and find a young skua gull as good to eat as a young Adélie penguin.

The excessive mortality amongst the penguin chickens is due without a doubt to the skua gulls, which were again and again seen to attack and destroy them ; their eggshells, too, lay about in hundreds, yet the penguins allow the skuas to nest and remain unmolested in their very midst.

The skuas were much annoyed if one appeared within sight of their nests ; and while the sitting bird loudly and vehemently protested against such an unwarrantable intrusion, her mate would make frequent dashes at the intruder's head—never, however, touching him with the claws or bill, but frequently striking with the wings. The chickens were able to run as soon as hatched, and pecked their food for themselves from bits that were disgorged and left in front of them by their parents.

The birds were by no mean shy, though easily frightened. They would at times fly up and take a piece of blubber from the hand, and often would attempt to remove a coat or belt or knife-sheath which had been carelessly thrown down while the owner might be occupied in dealing with a seal.

The skuas in our winter quarters lived on anything they could find ; but under ordinary conditions, and when penguins' eggs and chickens are not in season, they catch fish for themselves at sea or chase the petrels that have fed themselves till they disgorge. The skuas used to arrive in McMurdo Sound from the north at the beginning of November. In a month the first eggs were laid, and these were hatched at the beginning of January. About the end of March the exodus was in full swing, and we saw no more of them till the following year.

The Adélie penguins, as I have said, are wont to collect in enormous numbers at certain spots on the Antarctic coasts to breed. Arriving at Cape Crozier during the latter half of October, they spent about a fortnight in collecting pebbles for their nests. They then laid two round white eggs, which were incubated in turns by the male and female for upwards of thirty-two days, when two little sooty-black chickens would appear, the one as a rule rapidly growing to double the size of the other.

The process of feeding during the early stage is managed alternately by each of the parents, who take it in turns to protect the nestlings and go to the sea for shrimps. But the time comes when the chickens are not to be satisfied by the efforts of one bird, and their hunger becomes so urgent that both parents have to go and hunt.

The chickens are now large and independent, and so a new general method develops for the good of all. The young black woolly chickens collect in groups of from twenty to thirty each, and these groups are herded and protected from the skuas by three or four adults who station themselves on the outskirts of the group.

The adults from time to time return with a load of shrimps, and immediately set to work to find their infants. Amongst the first group of infants they pass, however, are three or four too hungry to be patient--so hungry, in fact, that they mistake this bird for their parent, and give him chase. Up and down, and dodging here and there, they run every bit as fast as he, and, heeding not his growls as he stops now and then to swear and punish them, they eventually tire him out and literally force him to feed them because of their importunity. Edging close up to him, the most pressing of the infants squeaks out his dreadful hunger, till at last the old bird can stand it no longer, and allows the little infant's head to disappear inside his own and find its food there.

In this race for life that is thus constantly going on, the weakest rapidly go to the wall. A chick that cannot run down the old bird and its rivals in the race goes supperless. Needless to point out, the next race is still less likely to be successful, and the chicken is soon marked down by a roving skua, who quickly brings an end to its unsuccessful life.

Nothing is more amusing in some ways than to watch the busy life of thousands of these quaint little individuals, and few things more pathetic than the sad side of it all.

Towards the end of January the chickens have shed their down, and now appear in a glossy coat of blue-grey feathers with white breasts and throat. This stage, which lasts a year, is never seen in the breeding rookeries, but is found quite commonly in the pack-ice in January ; and before the fact was recognised that it was only an immature stage of the Adélie penguin, it was burdened with a specific title which has since, of course, been dropped.

By the end of February the old birds have left the rookeries, and only the young remain. These soon learn to take the water, and before long follow their parents in migration to the north, where they spend the winter with them in the looser pack.

It would require a cinematograph to do justice to the peculiarities of the penguin, but certain of their quaintest attitudes are shown in the accompanying illustrations. When annoyed in any way the cock bird ranges up in front of his wife, his eyes flashing anger, his feathers erect in a ruffle round his head, and his language unfit for publication. He stands there for a minute or two breathing out threatenings and slaughter till his rage overpowers him, and putting his head down he makes a dash at one's legs and hails blows upon them with his flippers like bullets from a machine gun.

His ecstatic attitude, too, in making love is beyond all praise; though not a sound escapes him, one can imagine the most seductive music as he slowly waves his flippers to and fro and gazes upwards in a perfect rhapsody. The next moment he will be chasing his nearest neighbour with the most unwarrantable desire to do him damage for having removed one of the dirty little pebbles in the nest he was supposed to be protecting.

There is no end to his drollery, but perhaps enough has been said to lead the reader to understand the rest from what appears in the accompanying photograph.

One would like to follow the bird in his aquatic life—if such a thing were possible. It is tantalising to see him darting about in the water like a fish, shooting zig-zag under the ice-floes to leap up on to the ice a hundred yards away with a Jack-in-the-box appearance merely to wag his tail and 'squawk' to a distant neighbour.

In again he plunges, and, keeping his direction perfectly, comes up exactly where he wished. One wonders how he does so, but half his life is spent in an element into which we cannot follow. We see them, too, in the open sea, shooting out of the water like a school of little dolphins, swimming with strong sharp strokes of their fin-like wings as fast as fish and using their feet and tails for steering; each one follows his leader, and pops up on the ice-floe like a rabbit. Smart, comical, confiding little beasts, the most excellent company imaginable in such a desolate region as the Antarctic, they are like anything in the world but birds.

It is strange to think that at one time they probably used their wings for flight. They are some of the most primitive of birds, but at one time their wings were fully feathered. Even now as one sees them drop to sleep with the bill tucked in behind the wing, exactly as one sees it in a barn-door fowl, one feels convinced that here is a relic of the past, for the wing which is now a comfortless fin was once a bunch of feathers into which with some comfort the bird could snuggle down.

And lastly, the Emperor penguin (*Aptenodytes forsteri*), in all probability the most primitive of all the penguins, by far the largest not only in inches but in weight and width, has also this trait of bygone times. He, too, sleeps upright with the tip of his long curved bill tucked in behind his flipper. Exactly as in a dog which turns round and round before settling down to sleep upon a bare board floor, the habit has outlived the conditions that called it into being, so, too, this habit of the penguin has outlived the comfortable feathering of its wings.

It will be seen on looking at the map of the Antarctic Region that the Great Ice Barrier, which runs four hundred miles east and west as a continuous cliff of ice, comes to an abrupt termination where it impinges on Ross Island at Cape Crozier. Between the rocky cliffs which rise perpendicularly five hundred feet out of the sea, and the ice-cliffs which are here broken and irregular in height, varying from twenty to fifty or sixty feet, lies a bay with about a mile of frontage, sheltered from the southerly winds and open to the north for every ray of sunshine in the spring. A more perfect spot than this for shelter could hardly be discovered, and so circumscribed is it in the corner between land and barrier ice-cliff, that the sea-ice which is formed here in March or April remains intact throughout the winter months, a fixture till the general break-up occurs in the following summer.

In Ross Sea the ice that forms at the commencement of winter, in March, April, or even May, is unstable, and is liable to be broken up by every blizzard from the South, and the ice then drifts to the north to swell the belt of pack in 67° or 68° S. latitude.

But in this small bight the ice is formed to stay; and here the Emperor penguins congregate during the early winter months in anticipation of their approaching duties of incubation.

No doubt in other sheltered bays the ice remains intact as well as here, and where King Edward's Land abuts on the eastern extremity of the Great Ice Barrier, we entered a bay with the 'Discovery' and found ourselves not far from what appeared to be an enormous rookery of Emperor penguins. There were Emperors all round us—in the water and out of the water, shooting up on to the ice-floes, and standing in knots on the edges of the fast ice. Moreover, through the telescope in the crow's-nest could be seen, about five miles distant, groups of hundreds of the birds all huddled together in enormous colonies. It was imperative, as we could see, that we should run no risk of being frozen in prematurely in a place so utterly unsuitable for wintering as this, so we were forced to leave without investigating further; but although at the time we thought the birds were collected there for nesting, we now are almost certain, in the light of what we discovered later on that they were simply moulting birds, waiting patiently for their feathers to drop off, where for three weeks they could sit safely without being forced to take to the water.

Not many birds undertake to lay their eggs in the darkness of a polar winter, nor do many birds appear to think that sea-ice is the most attractive ground to 'sit' on. And when, in addition to this, we find the Emperor penguin hatching out its chicks in the coldest month of the whole Antarctic year, when the mean temperature for the month is eighteen degrees below zero, Fahrenheit, and the minimum may fall to *minus* sixty-eight, I think we may rightly consider the bird to be eccentric.

The Emperor penguin stands nearly four feet high, and weighs upwards of eighty to ninety pounds. He is an exceedingly handsome bird, with a rich black head, a bluish-grey back and wings, a lemon yellow breast with a satin-like gloss on the feathers, and a brilliant patch of orange on the neck and lower bill. His movements are slow and stately, and the dignity of his appearance is much increased by the upright carriage of his head and bill. When a group of these birds is met with in the middle of the desert ice, where all around is grey and cold and white and silent, the richness of their colouring strikes one very forcibly. Their voice is loud and trumpet-like, and rings out in the pack-ice with a note of defiance that makes one feel that man is the real intruder. They have no fear, but an abundance of inquisitiveness, and a party such as I have mentioned will

walk up to one with dignity, and stand in a ring all round, with
an occasional remark from one to the other, discussing, no
doubt, the nature of this new and upright neighbour.   That the
new beast is a friendly one they appear to have no doubt, and
one can only regret that from time to time necessity compelled
us to disillusion them.

In October of 1902 Royds made a sledge journey to Cape
Crozier to establish a record there for the relief ship, and it was
during this visit that Skelton, who was with him, discovered the
Emperor penguins' rookery.   The number of birds using it he
put down at about four hundred, and the number of living
chicks at thirty, with about eighty dead ones.   Everywhere they
searched for eggs, but without success, and nothing but some
scraps of eggshell, evidently swallowed by the birds, was found.

When this party returned to the ship with several chicks
and the news that there was a rookery at Cape Crozier, I
was myself on the point of starting in another direction, so
Royds kindly offered to make another journey, and get further
particulars and examples of the chicks.   He was in this more
lucky than one could have hoped, for he brought back, amongst
other things, the first authentic egg, which Blissett, a lance-
corporal in the R.M.L.I., had found lying frozen in the snow.
He also found that, arriving on November 8, the young penguins had all left the rookery—a most unexpected discovery,
as it was impossible that they could have shed their down, and
so it was impossible that they could have taken to the water to
support themselves on the fish and shrimps and cuttlefish that
form their food.   The only conclusion, therefore, was that they
had drifted up on the ice-floes to the north.

This for the time being brought an end to our observations ;
but the following spring two journeys more were made to Cape
Crozier, for the purpose of filling in the gaps in our knowledge
of the bird's life-history.

The first was undertaken on September 7, about a fortnight
after the sun's return.   The days were short and the nights
were long, and the cold and discomfort were intense.   We
reached the rookery in a week and reconnoitred for the morrow,
when we made our way over the gigantic pressure ridges, and

at last got into the bay where the Emperors were collected. Here, to our surprise, we saw first a number of deserted eggs lying on the ice—some cracked, some crushed, some perfect, some half-incubated, some half-addled, but all frozen as hard as rock.

Just where the birds had been quietly sitting on their eggs we could see that there had been a sudden fall of ice from the face of the Barrier Cliff. Without breaking through, this fall had crumpled and split the sea-ice in all directions, and had so scared the sitting birds that those which had escaped sudden death by burial in the mass had fled precipitately, and left their eggs behind them. In some cases we could see that the birds had returned when it was too late, and had then resumed the incubation of their eggs, though the frost had killed them.

Proceeding next to where the birds were congregated, we found that even so early in the spring as it then was every egg was hatched, and only chickens were to be found under the old birds. There could not have been fewer than a thousand birds and about one hundred and fifty chicks.

The method employed by the Emperor penguin for carrying the egg and chick upon his feet is shared also by the King penguin of the sub-Antarctic area, as we saw in our visit to their rookeries in the Macquarie Islands. The King penguin we saw as he sat in mud and puddles, with his single egg upon his feet, and now we saw the Emperor penguin doing precisely the same thing with his single chicken to keep it off the ice ; and we are agreed that the term 'pouch,' which has been used in this connection, is one which not only does not describe the matter, but is anatomically wrong and misleading. The single egg, or the chick, sits resting on the *dorsum* of the foot, wedged in between the legs and the lower abdomen ; and over it falls a fold of heavily feathered skin, which is very loose, and can completely cover up and hide the egg or chick from view. When the chick is hungry or inquisitive it pokes out from under the maternal (or paternal) lappet a piebald downy head of black and white, emitting its shrill and persistent pipe until the mother (or the father) fills it up.

The feeding is managed as with cormorants and many other

birds, the little one finding regurgitated food when it thrusts its head inside the parent's mouth.

I think the chickens hate their parents, and when one watches the proceedings in a rookery it strikes one as not surprising. In the first place there is about one chick to ten or twelve adults, and each adult has an overpowering desire to 'sit' on something. Both males and females want to nurse, and the result is that when a chicken finds himself alone there is a rush on the part of a dozen unemployed to seize him. Naturally he runs away, and dodges here and there till a six-stone Emperor falls on him, and then begins a regular football 'scrimmage,' in which each tries to hustle the other off, and the end is too often disastrous to the chick. Sometimes he falls into a crack in the ice and stays there to be frozen while the parents squabble at the top; sometimes, rather than be nursed I have seen him crawl in under an ice-ledge and remain there, where the old ones could not reach him. I think it is not an exaggeration to say that of the 77 per cent. that die no less than half are killed by kindness.

This excessive desire to 'sit' on something leads often to the most pathetic sights. One may see quite frequently an old bird go up to one of the numerous dead chickens lying about upon the ice, and try to coax it to sit upon its feet, helping the lifeless little thing with its beak, in evident distress at the total lack of response to its attention. One may see quite frequently the head and neck of a chicken trailing limp and lifeless from under the feather lappet of a broody bird ; and most, if not all, the chicks that are lying dead upon the ice bear marks of having first been torn in life during the quarrels of the adults for their possession, and then of having been nursed persistently after death.

Some of the chickens, of course, survive and leave the rookery, and, thanks to a spell of real Antarctic weather, which for eight days out of eleven confined us to our sleeping-bags, we were enabled to guess how this is managed.

During an interminable blizzard we laid out guiding-posts with our ski, ski-poles, ice-axes, and a length of Alpine rope, which made it possible for us every alternate day to visit the edge of the cliffs that overlooked the rookery ; and here we saw how these birds have come to make use of inanimate nature to serve their ends. They wanted to migrate. They saw that the sea-ice was breaking up and drifting to the north, and they knew that their chicks were as yet in down, and not fit to enter water. So day by day as we watched them we saw parties of a hundred birds or more making their way in single file out from the sheltered bay to the edge of the open water. And here they stood and waited deliberately till the floe broke off and carried them northward to the pack.

The pack-ice, I have now no doubt, is the great Antarctic nursery for the young of the Southern seals and penguins. Here they live in comparative safety. One finds here young Emperor penguins and the young of the Adélie penguins, and one finds them apparently nowhere else when once they have left their breeding-grounds.

Food is abundant, and they are safe from the surf and swell of the heaviest storms ; shelter they can find easily under a berg or hummock, and here the young Emperor proceeds to moult his down.

His first feather plumage appears in January, when he is five months old ; the silver-grey down is changed for a blue-grey coat with a white front ; there is as yet no colour to relieve it. But a year later a second moult occurs, and then the orange patch appears on the neck, and the head and throat turn black. In the third year the full rich plumage of the adult is reached, and this, by a yearly moult in January, he retains until the end.

Of the enemies that the Emperor must avoid I have already said enough. Being strictly an inhabitant of sea and ice, he has no enemies on land, but in the water he has to avoid the Sea Leopard and the Killer whale. His food consists of fish and cuttlefish, and his stomach invariably contains pebbles, which assist him to grind up the bones.

It was with much disappointment that we found ourselves unable to rear the chicks. The heroic self-sacrifice of Cross, who gave up his sleeping-jacket at night, when the temperature was ' sixty below ' and more, to keep his charges warm, deserved a better issue; but it was soon seen to be a forlorn hope, and eventually they died from the result of unnatural feeding. Had we even succeeded in bringing them to the age when they put on their feathers, I fear that the journey home through the tropics would have proved too much for them, as we had no means of making a cool place for them on the ship.

In conclusion I may be allowed perhaps to say what a good right-hand I was given in Cross, who not only learned to make good skins for our bird collection, but who, in the matter of making Emperor's skins, improved upon his teacher. Always willing and thoroughly capable, it was to a large extent thanks to him that I was enabled at times to save much of what would otherwise have been lost, when, as on our visit to the Macquarie Islands, we had far more in hand than one man could possibly have managed.

Of Skelton's help I should also like to say much, for not only was he a keen collector, who gave his time and all he caught ungrudgingly for the general collections, but his notes and observations were at all times excellent, and his photographs of the Emperor penguin rookery unique.

But while it is fair to make a special point of acknowledging the help I had from Skelton and from Cross, it is also right to say that from everyone, without exception, I received abundant help at all times.

INDEX

THE END

OTHER
COOPER SQUARE PRESS
TITLES OF INTEREST

THE *KARLUK'S* LAST VOYAGE
An Epic of Death and Survival
In the Arctic, 1913–1916
Captain Robert A. Bartlett
New introduction by Edward E. Leslie
378 pp., 23 b/w photos, 3 maps
0-8154-1124-3
$18.95

THE GREAT WHITE SOUTH
Traveling with Robert F. Scott's
Doomed South Pole Expedition
Herbert G. Ponting
New introduction by Roland Huntford
440 pp., 175 b/w illustrations,
3 b/w maps & diagrams
0-8154-1161-8
$18.95

CARRYING THE FIRE
An Astronaut's Journeys
Michael Collins
Foreword by Charles Lindbergh
512 pp., 32 pp. of b/w photos
0-8154-1028-6
$19.95

MY ATTAINMENT OF THE POLE
Frederick A. Cook
New introduction by Robert M. Bryce
680 pp., 45 b/w photos
0-8154-1137-5
$22.95

THE NORTH POLE
Robert E. Peary
Foreword by Theodore Roosevelt
New introduction by Robert M. Bryce
480 pp., 109 b/w illustrations, 1 map
0-8154-1138-3
$22.95

THE SOUTH POLE
An Account of the Norwegan Antarctic
Expedition in the *Fram*, 1910–1912
Captain Roald Amundsen
Foreword by Fridtjof Nansen
New introduction by Roland Huntford
960 pp., 155 b/w illustrations
0-8154-1127-8
$29.95

A NEGRO EXPLORER AT THE NORTH POLE
Matthew A. Henson
Preface by Booker T. Washington
Foreword by Robert E. Peary
New introduction by Robert M. Bryce
248 pp., 15 b/w photos
0-8154-1125-1
$15.95

ANTARCTICA
Firsthand Accounts of Exploration and
Endurance
Edited by Charles Neider
468 pp.
0-8154-1023-9
$18.95

THE DESERT AND THE SOWN
The Syrian Adventures of the
Female Lawrence of Arabia
Gertrude Bell
New introduction by
Rosemary O'Brien
368 pp., 162 b/w photos
0-8154-1135-9
$19.95

EDGE OF THE JUNGLE
William Beebe
New introduction by Robert Finch
320 pp., 1 b/w photo
0-8154-1160-X
$17.95

STANLEY
The Making of an African Explorer
Frank McLynn
424 pp., 19 b/w illustrations
0-8154-1167-7
$18.95

EDGE OF THE WORLD:
ROSS ISLAND ANTARCTICA
A Personal and Historical Narrative of
Exploration, Adventure, Tragedy, and Survival
Charles Neider
With a new introduction
536 pp., 45 b/w photos, 15 maps
0-8154-1154-5
$19.95